CLAY SCULPTING WITH THE SHIFLETT BROTHERS

CLAY SCULPTING WITH THE SHIFLETT BROTHERS

ONE TREE PLANTED
FOR EVERY BOOK SOLD

OUR PLEDGE

From 2020, 3dtotal Publishing has pledged to plant one tree for every book sold by partnering with and donating the appropriate amounts to re-foresting charities. This is one of the first steps in our ambition to become a carbon-neutral company with carbon-neutral publications, giving our customers the knowledge that by buying from 3dtotal Publishing, we are working together to balance the environmental damage caused by the publishing, shipping, and retail industries.

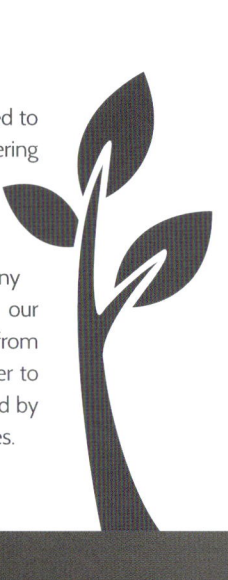

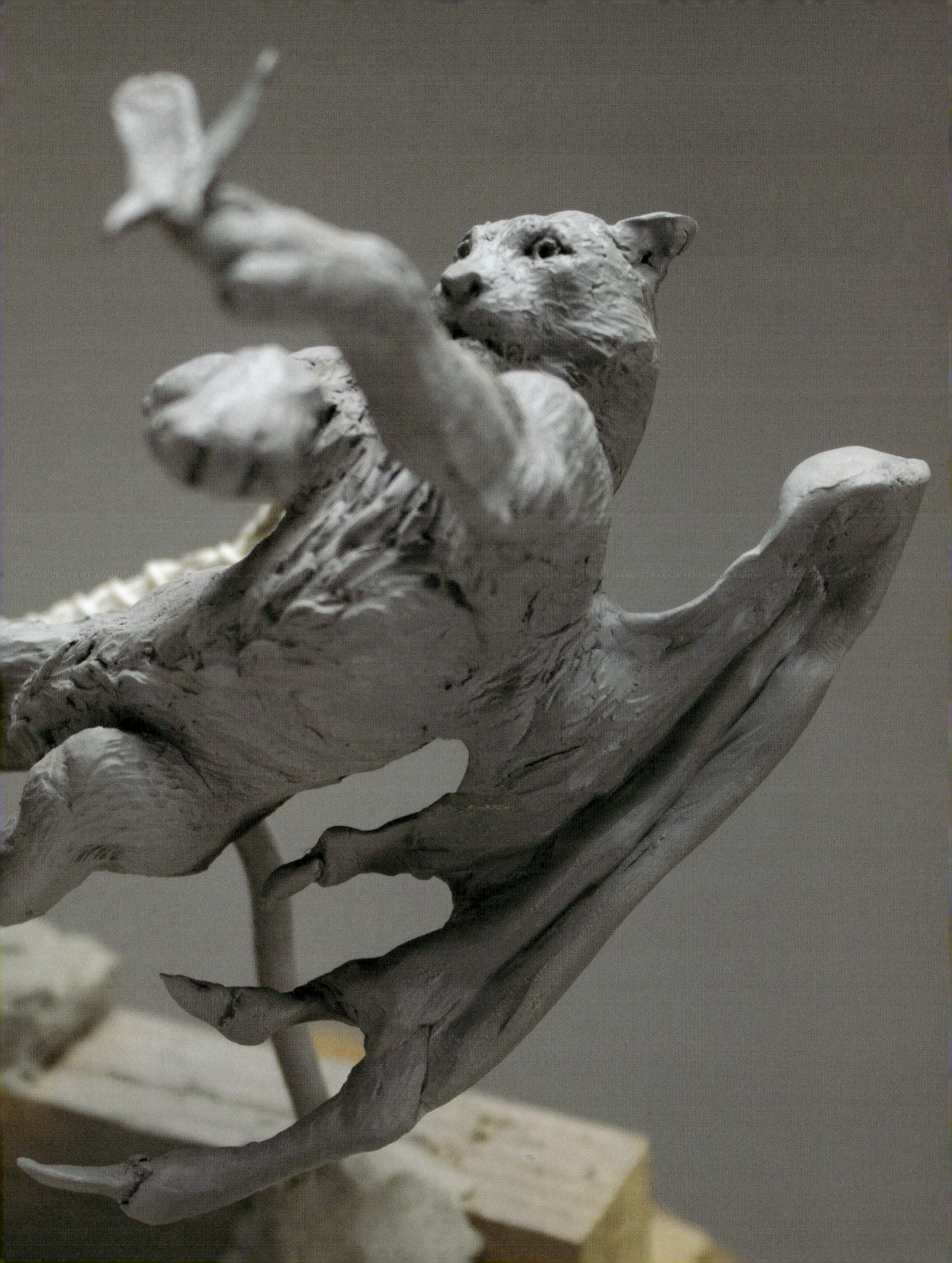

3dtotal Publishing

Correspondence: publishing@3dtotal.com
Website: www.3dtotal.com

First published in the United Kingdom, 2022, by 3dtotal Publishing.

Address: 3dtotal.com Ltd, 29 Foregate Street, Worcester, WR1 1DS, United Kingdom.

Soft cover ISBN: 978-1-912843-47-3
Printing & binding: Gutenberg Press Ltd (Malta) www.gutenberg.com.mt

Visit www.3dtotalpublishing.com for a complete list of available book titles.

Managing Director: Tom Greenway
Studio Manager: Simon Morse
Lead Editor: Jenny Fox-Proverbs
Editor: Sophie Symes
Lead Designer: Fiona Tarbet
Designer: Joseph Cartwright

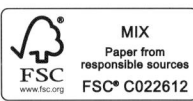

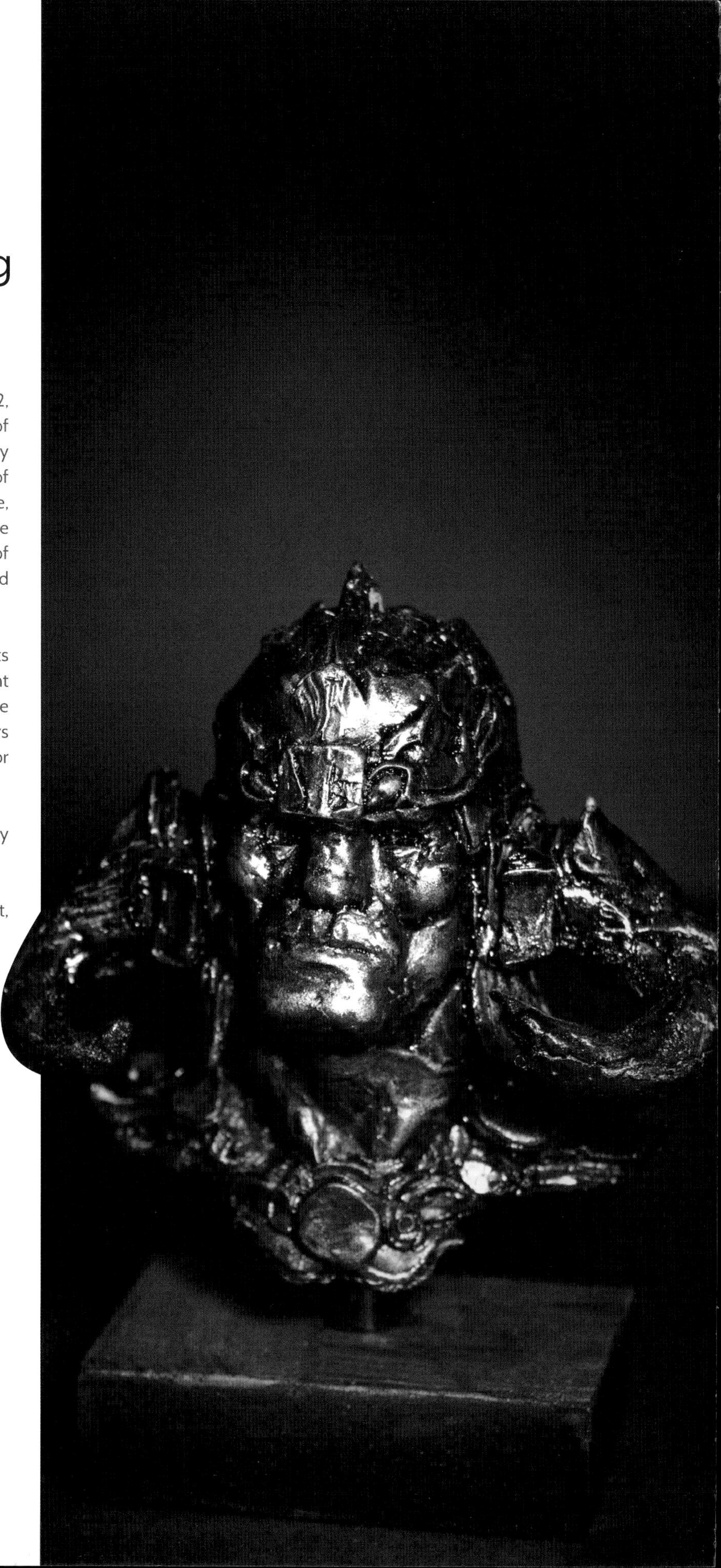

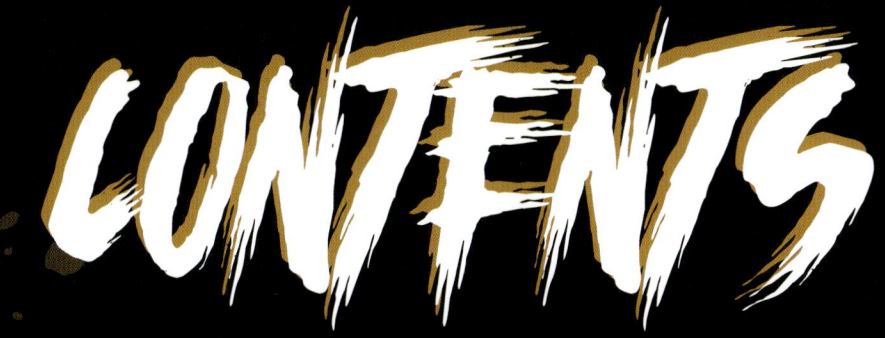

CONTENTS

ABOUT THE SHIFLETT BROTHERS

Based in Dallas, Texas, The Shiflett Brothers have been at the forefront of clay sculpting for many years. Their fantastical works sit in video-game design firms, special-effects houses, and art departments across several creative industries, as well as the personal collections of film directors Peter Jackson and Robert Rodriguez, and Weta Workshop founder Sir Richard Taylor.

The brothers' original designs have featured in international books and magazines, including six volumes of the annual book *Spectrum: The Best in Contemporary Fantastic Art*, and have won them many awards and accolades from some of the best-known artists and studios from across the world. They were also honored to sit on the jury for *Spectrum 18* and astounded to receive the Gold Award in Dimensional Work for *Spectrum 21*.

With a wealth of knowledge to share, Brandon and Jarrod have taught a masterclass on Sculpting for the Comic Book Industry at The Gnomon Workshop in Hollywood, California, and created an instructional sculpting DVD with Gnomon, entitled *Fantasy Sculpting: The Dragon of Argos*. They have also created informative demonstration articles for *ImagineFX*, *Heavy Metal*, and *Amazing Figure Modeler* magazines. To complement their educational work, the Shifletts host the Shiflett Brothers Sculpting Forum, which boasts over 40,000 members and features sculpting contests, advice, and livestreams of work by industry superstars. From their work on iconic Marvel superheroes to their concept pieces produced under the banner of Shiflett Brothers Originals, Brandon and Jarrod continue to love what they do: celebrating science fiction, fantasy, and comic books through sculpture.

A selection of Shiflett Brothers sculpts photographed by Chad Michael Ward.

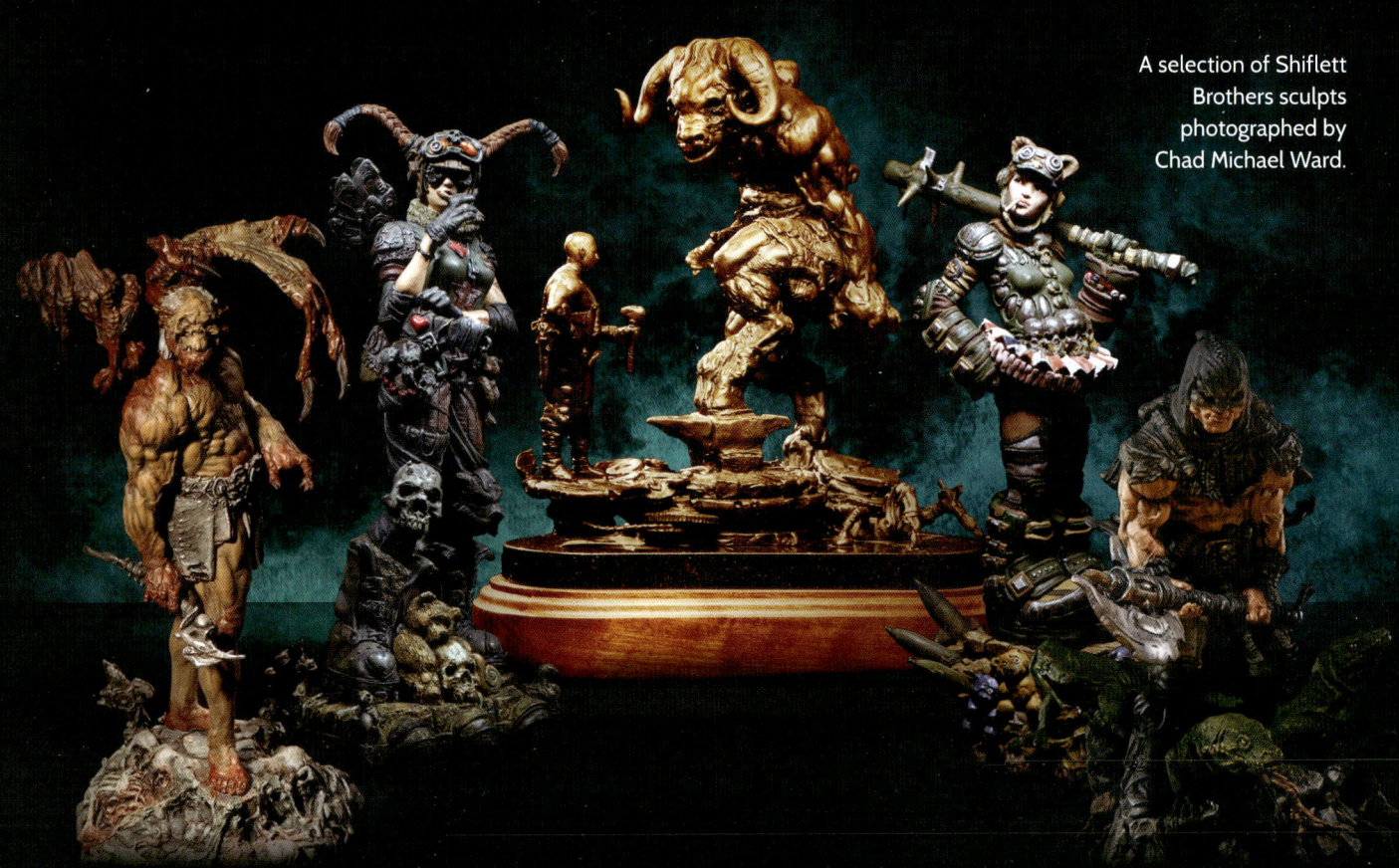

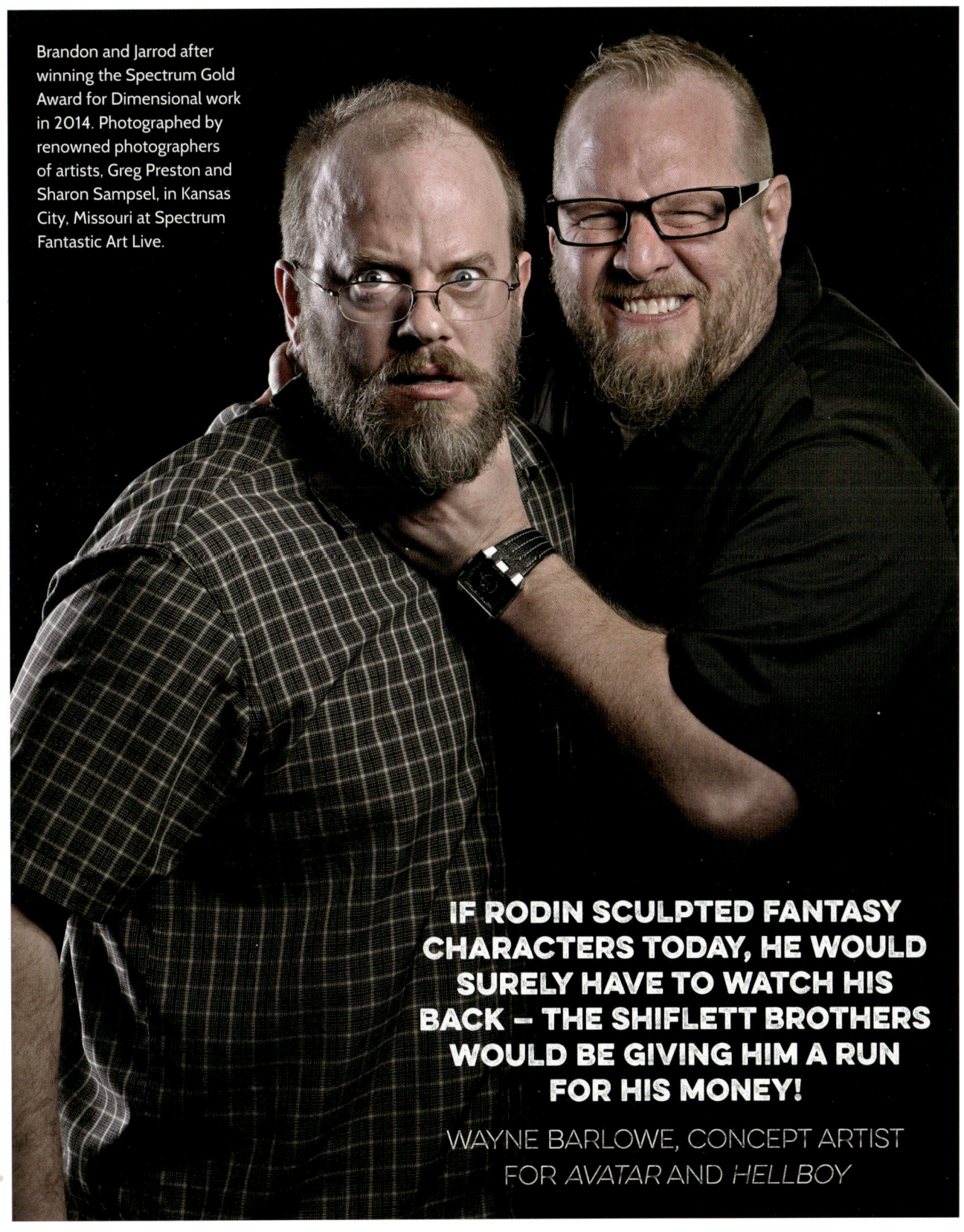

Brandon and Jarrod after winning the Spectrum Gold Award for Dimensional work in 2014. Photographed by renowned photographers of artists, Greg Preston and Sharon Sampsel, in Kansas City, Missouri at Spectrum Fantastic Art Live.

IF RODIN SCULPTED FANTASY CHARACTERS TODAY, HE WOULD SURELY HAVE TO WATCH HIS BACK – THE SHIFLETT BROTHERS WOULD BE GIVING HIM A RUN FOR HIS MONEY!

WAYNE BARLOWE, CONCEPT ARTIST FOR *AVATAR* AND *HELLBOY*

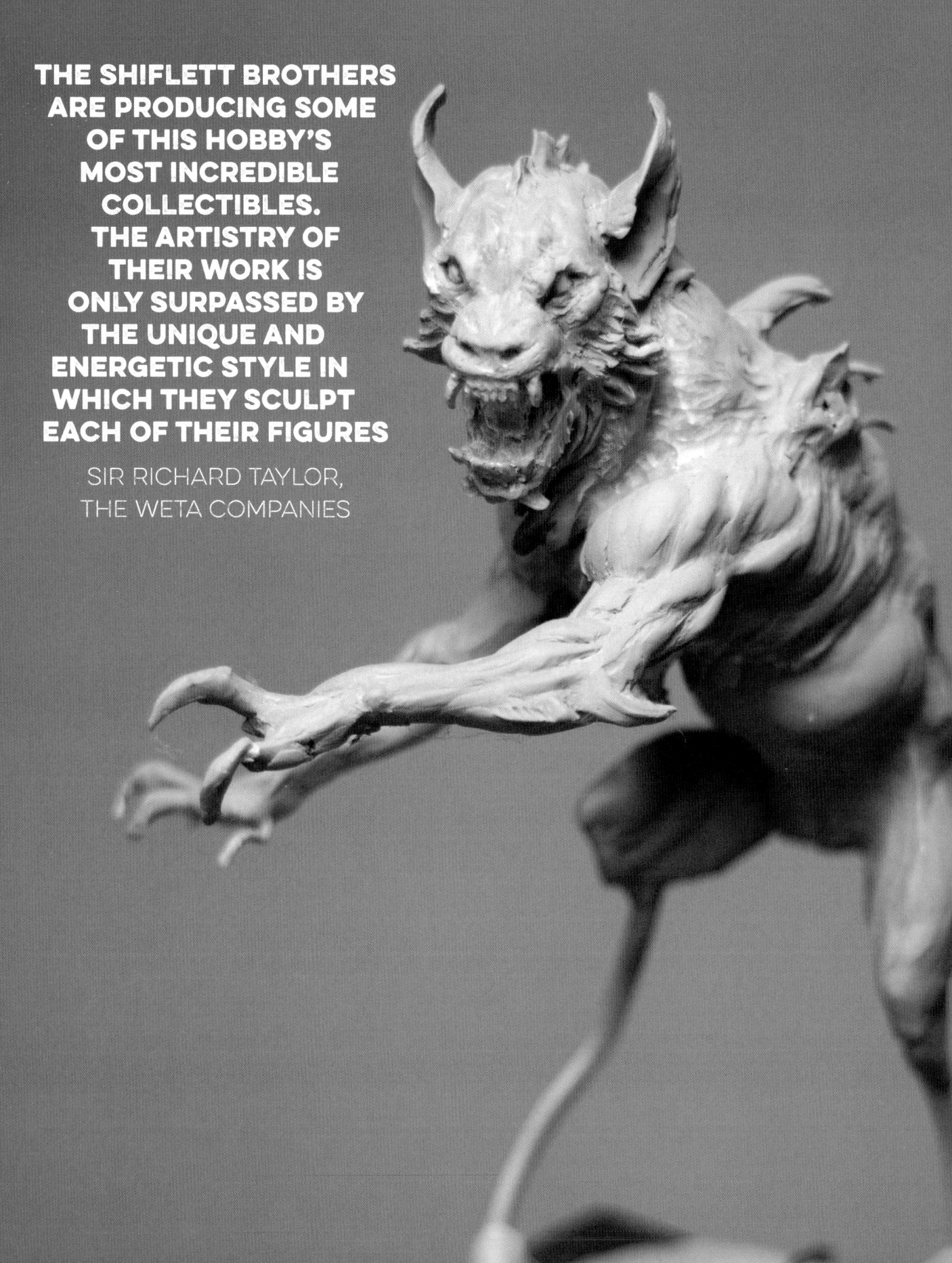

THE SHIFLETT BROTHERS ARE PRODUCING SOME OF THIS HOBBY'S MOST INCREDIBLE COLLECTIBLES. THE ARTISTRY OF THEIR WORK IS ONLY SURPASSED BY THE UNIQUE AND ENERGETIC STYLE IN WHICH THEY SCULPT EACH OF THEIR FIGURES

SIR RICHARD TAYLOR,
THE WETA COMPANIES

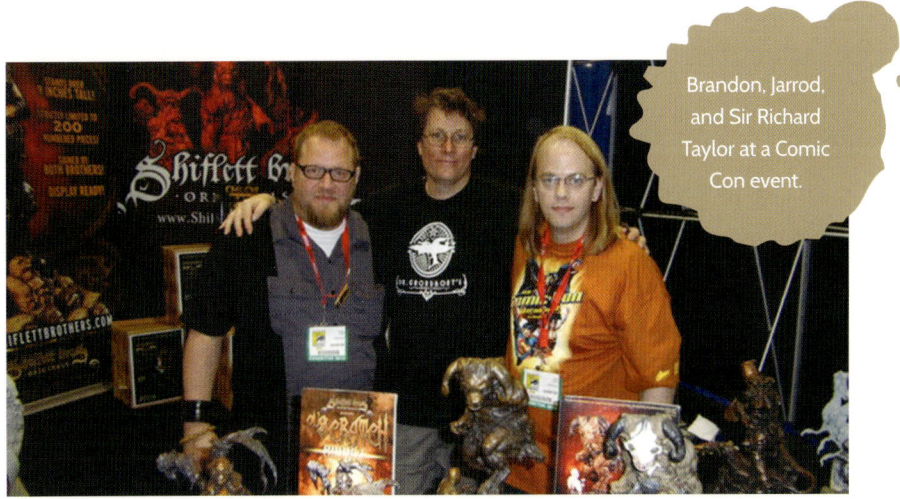

FOREWORD

I have always had a great love of figurative sculpture. My favorite period is the era known as "New Sculpture," starting in Britain in the 1800s and continuing into the twentieth century. Great sculpting luminaries such as Alfred Gilbert, Hamo Thornycroft, Gilbert Ledward, Charles Sargeant Jagger, and my absolute favorite — the great Gilbert Bayes, continually inspire me.

Sadly, for a passionate yet humble collector such as myself, the ability to collect the art of these great masters remains mostly out of reach. Thankfully, what has been accessible to me and has continued to fulfill my somewhat obsessive interest, is the collecting of garage kits and resin figure models over the past thirty years. Some of my most beloved collectables are from the very authors of this book. I think of these resin and vinyl models as beautiful and accessible sculpture for discerning collectors, just like me!

My wife Tania and I also run a sculpting studio as part of our workshop, and our extraordinary team of sculptors have produced many thousands of artworks over the past three decades, for an incredible variety of clients, projects, IPs, and private commissions. Today, working both in physical materials (such as clay and plasticine), and digital software (such as Blender or ZBrush), our sculptors choose the technique that best suits their talents and the project's requirements.

To breathe life into the material of choice, whether that be pixels or atoms, takes a complex and subtle combination of skills that add up to a rare and wonderful talent possessed by a great sculptor. Pose, poise, weight, balance, expression, surface treatment, attitude, energy, dynamism, character, and many other factors are all carefully considered and ultimately give a sculpture the sense of spirit and soul that we all seek to create. I guess to imbue one's work with such qualities is to reach the pinnacle of one's artistic talents.

Regardless of how sculpture may evolve in the coming years as we continue to see a phenomenal uptake and perfecting of digital sculpting, in my view there will always be a significant place for that satisfying connection to physical sculpting. There is a fundamental and foundational knowledge gained through the physical sculpting of real-world materials (complemented with the study of anatomy and figurative sculpture). I therefore implore those reading this book (if you are yet to discover the joys of working in physical materials) to keep a lump of plasticine and some sculpting tools next to your Wacom. Enjoy getting lost in the wonders of this real-world, tactile medium and experience clay under your fingernails from time to time. Couple this with the learning gained from the masters of sculpture from our past — and the inspiration found in the pages of a book such as this one — and the art of physical sculpture will undoubtedly stay alive and well in this ever more digitally focused world.

SIR RICHARD TAYLOR
Effects Designer & Supervisor, the Weta Companies

ABOUT THIS BOOK

To take a guided tour behind the scenes with a creative expert is both rare and sought-after. So, when the tour is led by clay-sculpting royalty the Shiflett Brothers, you know something special is about to take place. This book is the story of Brandon and Jarrod Shiflett, showing us not only what they do and how they do it, but also why.

From the moment they first picked up a ball of clay (spoiler alert: they were naturals!), to taking home the Grand Prize at Comic-Con, working with other industry legends, and establishing Shiflett Brothers Originals, their journey has been inspirational. Their thoughtful storytelling combined with legendary influences and a truly 360-degree approach to each sculpt reveals a depth of understanding only possible after years of dedication to the craft. Generously, they share their philosophy with us, enabling us to see their creations in a different light.

As with all great art, narrative has a role to play, and the Shifletts walk us through how they achieve their own brand of storytelling. They explain their approaches to pose, gesture, and facial expression, as well as other design considerations, such as the "triangle of focus" and the dynamism of multi-character scenes.

Of course, the authenticity of every detail is just as important as any out-of-this-world touches. The believability of the anatomy, proportion, and pose of a sculpture is vital to engage the viewer, and pushing these features to elevate visual impact is something the brothers have experimented with throughout their careers to wondrous effect. Through considered posing and clever composition, the viewer can appreciate a sculpture to the fullest, as their gaze is led around the subject, taking in all of its best and most critical features.

Furfur the Demon resin kit, originally sculpted in Super Sculpey, produced circa 2015.

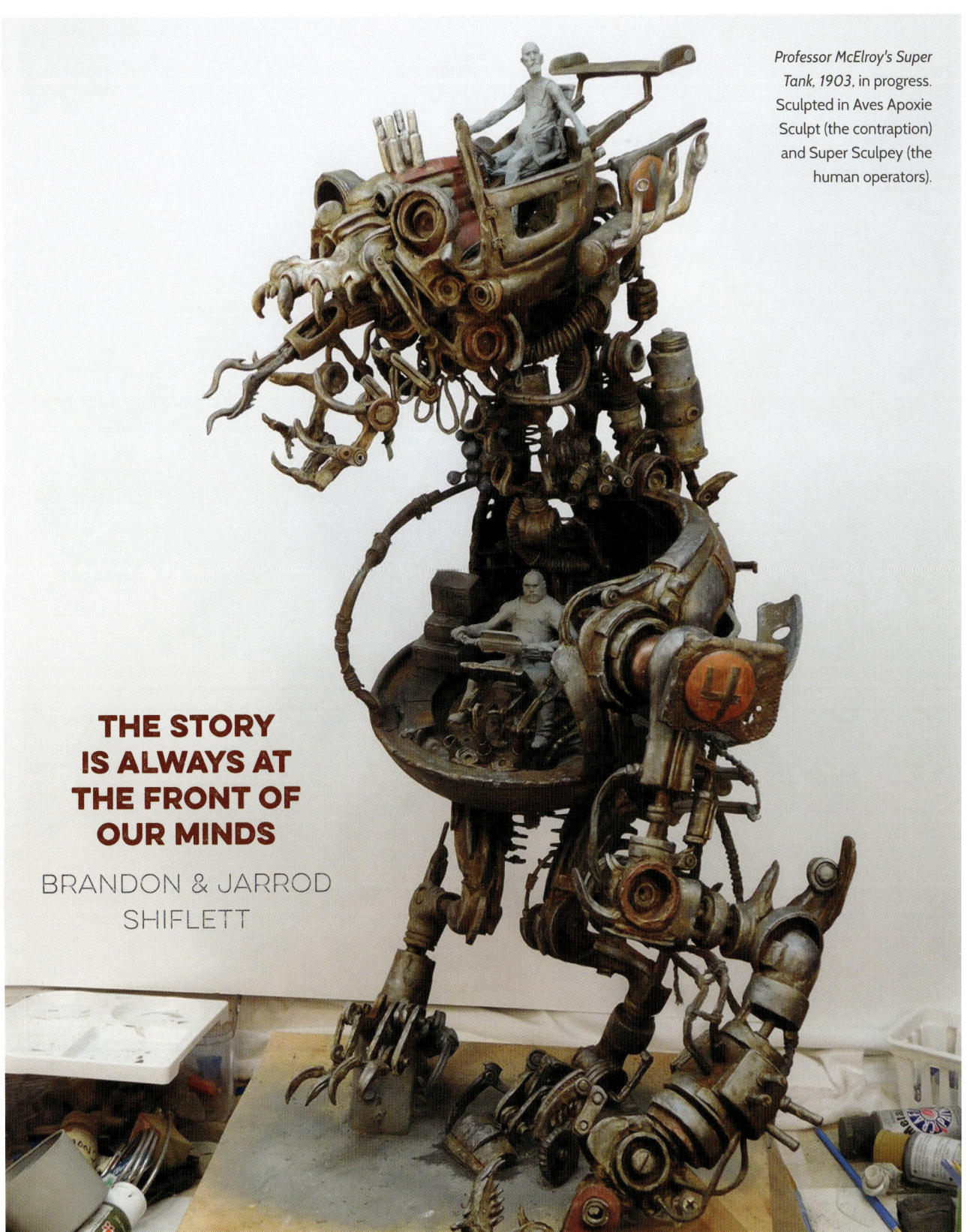

Professor McElroy's *Super Tank, 1903*, in progress. Sculpted in Aves Apoxie Sculpt (the contraption) and Super Sculpey (the human operators).

THE STORY IS ALWAYS AT THE FRONT OF OUR MINDS

BRANDON & JARROD SHIFLETT

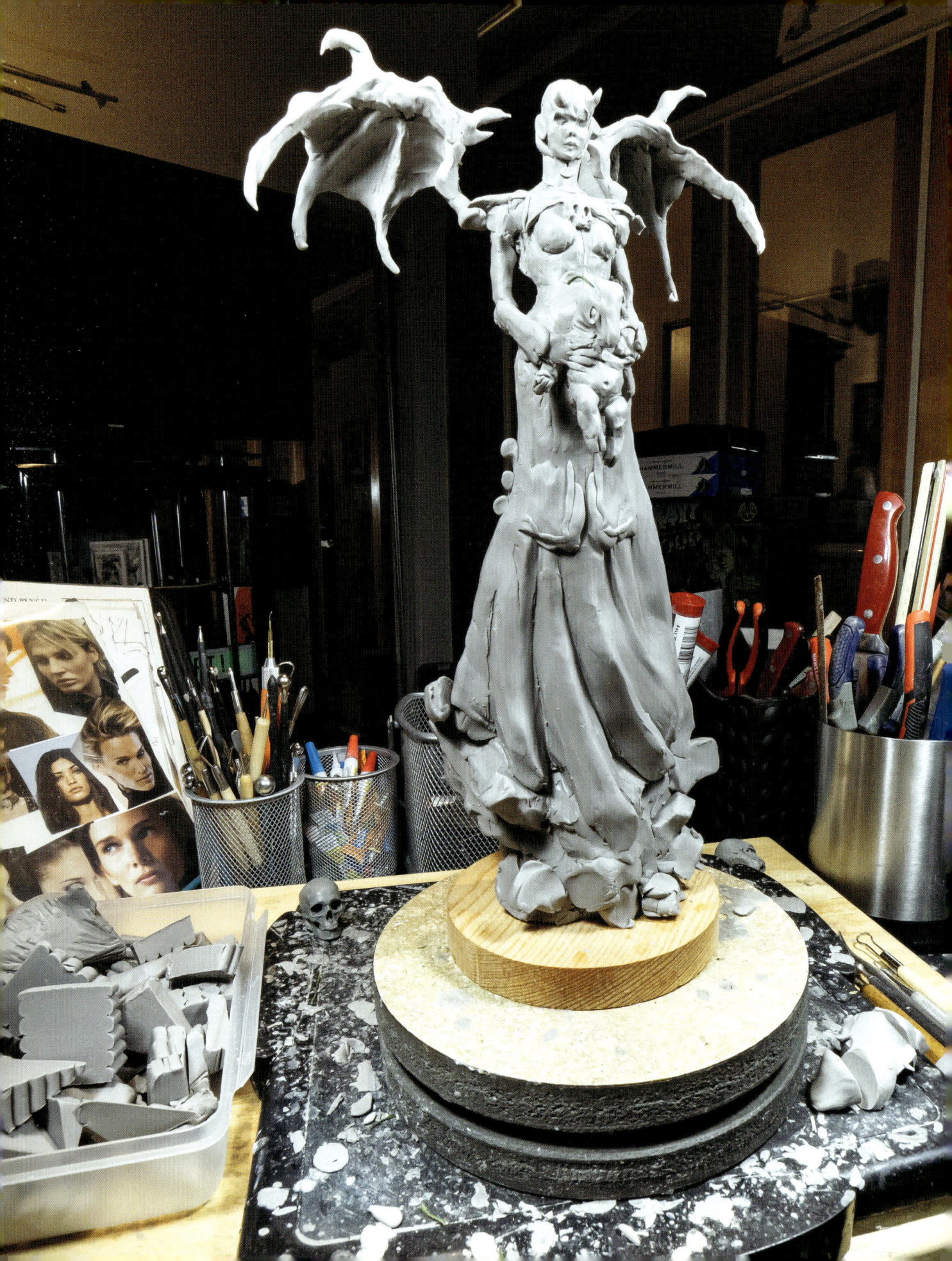

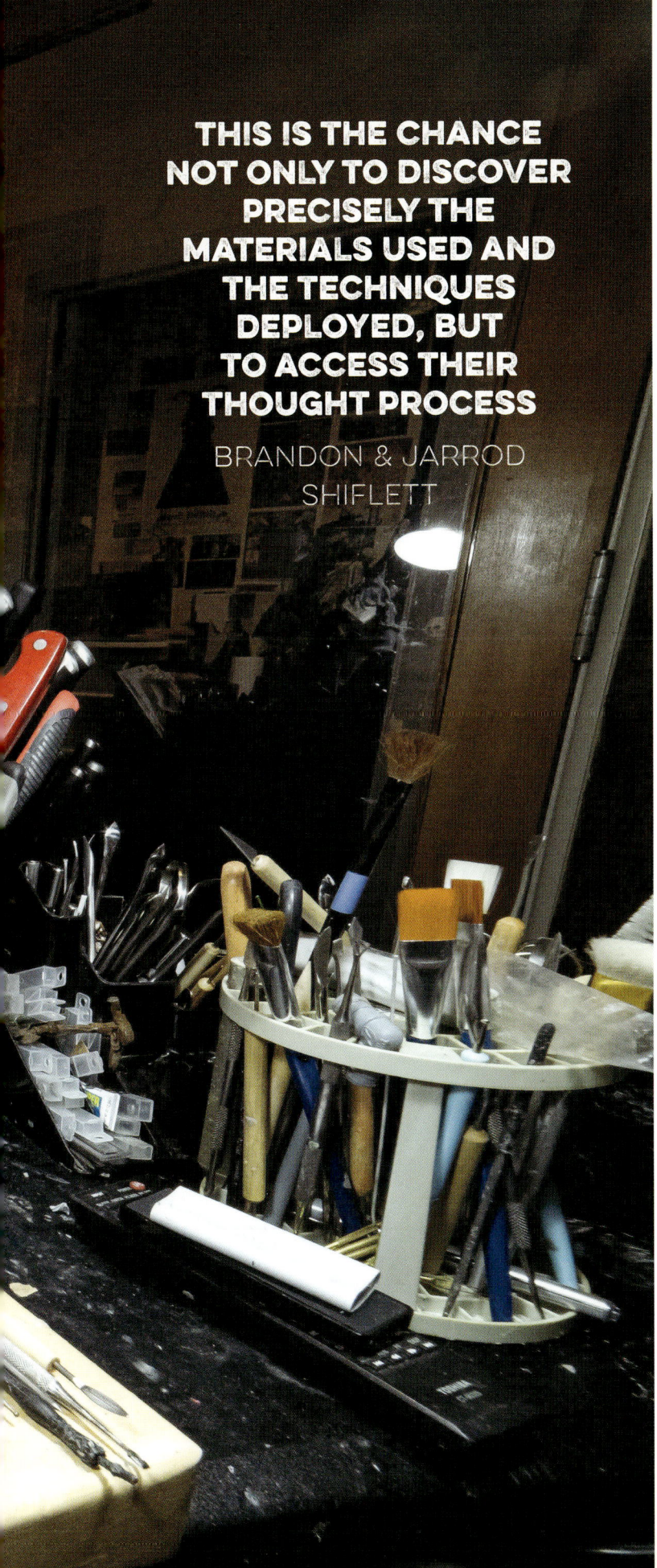

THIS IS THE CHANCE NOT ONLY TO DISCOVER PRECISELY THE MATERIALS USED AND THE TECHNIQUES DEPLOYED, BUT TO ACCESS THEIR THOUGHT PROCESS

BRANDON & JARROD SHIFLETT

Next, the brothers show us their workshop, where the tools of their trade are at once fascinating yet truly functional, and you begin to understand how they achieve the level of precision and detail they're so famous for. But it's when we delve into their loose, "sculptural sketching" methods that we begin to get a unique insight into their processes. From adopting an organic sculpting style for their "living, breathing" creations, to taking inspiration from two other great sculptors, there is much to learn from their process.

The Shiflett Brothers have provided a unique window into their process, walking us step-by-step through three of their own creations. This is the chance not only to discover precisely the materials used and the techniques deployed, but to access their thought process, with their organic approach to design shown in action. These processes are packed with creative insight, professional tips, and practical techniques to try at home. They've chosen subjects that feature in some of their most popular work to demonstrate how they deal with everything from human anatomy to dragon scales and mechanical beings.

Brandon and Jarrod have many friends across the industry, so they have invited three of them along to share their own creative process. Star sculptors Aris Kolokontes, Simon Lee, and Forest Rogers open the door to their respective studios to allow us a look inside. For any sculptor exploring their own style, trying out new techniques, or simply on the lookout for inspiration to feed their sculpting soul, this mix of personalities in one place is an extraordinary gift.

To help you maintain your momentum, the Shifletts have advice and tips gleaned over many years, not only for troubleshooting snags you may come across as you create, but for staying motivated — every artist feels that dip occasionally, but the brothers are here to help you out.

No matter what your skill level, preferred sculpting medium, or favorite subject matter, this book is one to soak up from cover to cover, then return to time and time again.

This is the story of the Shiflett Brothers, from the raw materials to final form.

Workspace photography by Matt Mrozek, mmrozekphoto.wixsite.com/photo

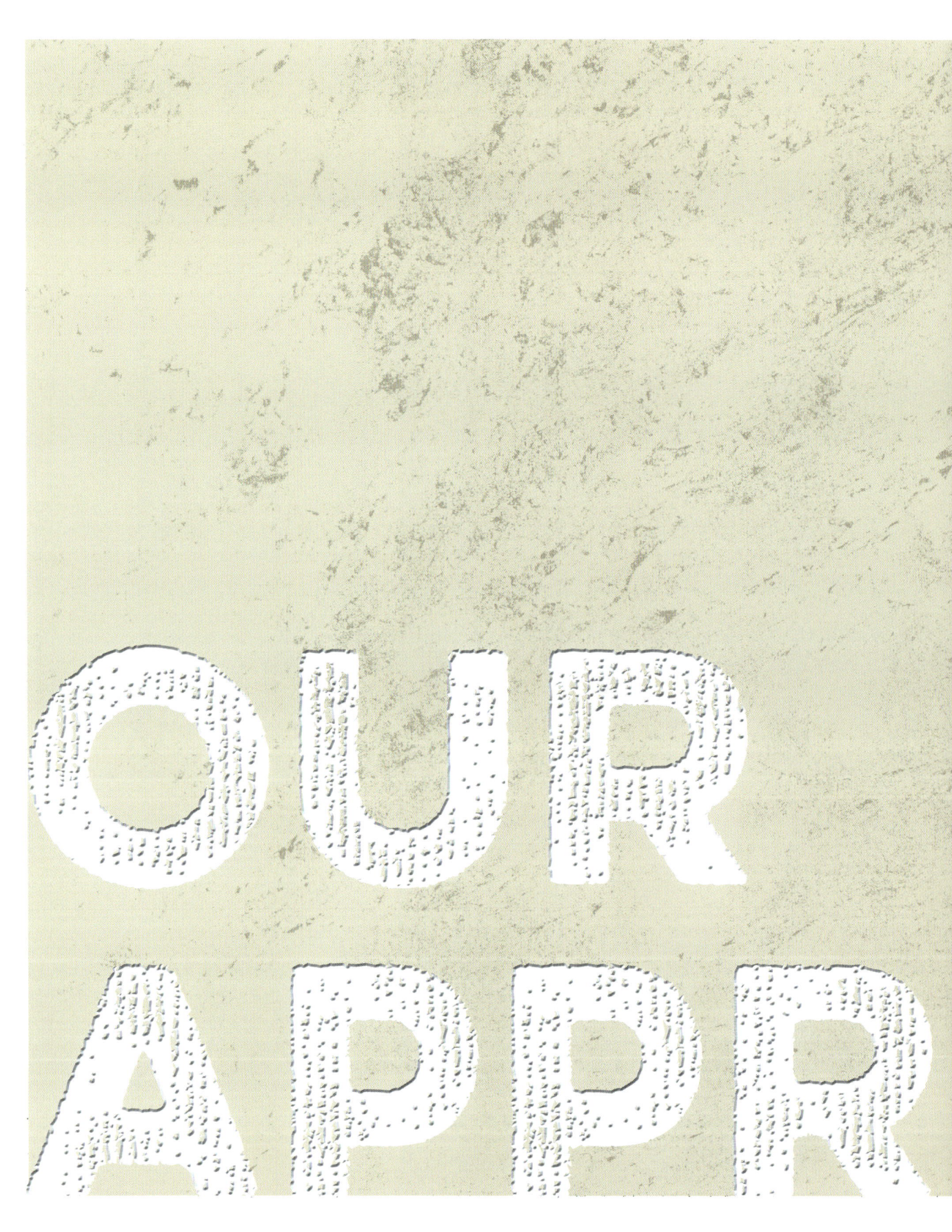

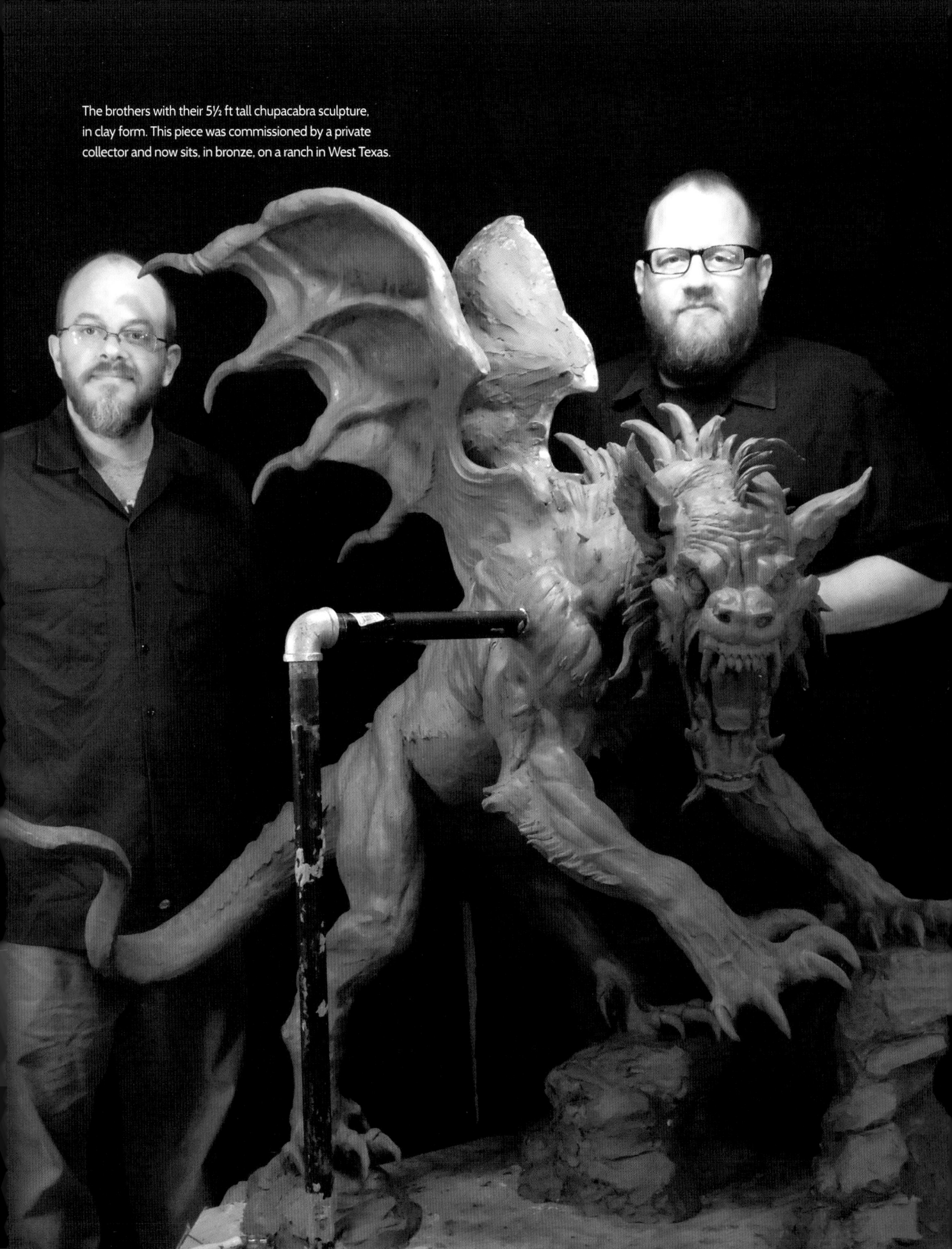

The brothers with their 5½ ft tall chupacabra sculpture, in clay form. This piece was commissioned by a private collector and now sits, in bronze, on a ranch in West Texas.

OUR JOURNEY INTO CLAY

At the very beginning of the 1990s, before the internet was a permanent part of our lives, and long before the advent of sculpting programs such as ZBrush, we were two obsessive comic-book fans — Brandon at twenty years old and Jarrod at sixteen. That may seem very young, and it is young as far as life goes, but it's much older than most of our peers were the first time they ever picked up clay.

We had always been artistic, but we'd never actually tried sculpture before then. Indeed, our most fervent dream as youngsters was to grow up to be comic-book artists. What could be a cooler way to make a living than drawing the adventures of our favorite super-powered characters? We worshiped the guys who drew the comics we read in the same way that the neighborhood kids revered rock stars or pro-athletes. We studied the craft and, when we were lucky enough to see them in person at Texas-based comic-book conventions, would turn into fan-boys upon meeting and speaking with our favorite artists. So, it shouldn't surprise anyone to learn that we were mildly devastated to realize we weren't nearly good enough at drawing to work professionally in that industry. A sad day for those young Shiflett boys! But that didn't diminish our love of comics one bit. We soon discovered, almost by accident while playing with clay, that we had a proclivity for envisioning objects in three dimensions. And once we began sculpting, the thought of dimensional sculptures with their form and dynamism became much more interesting to us than illustration ever was.

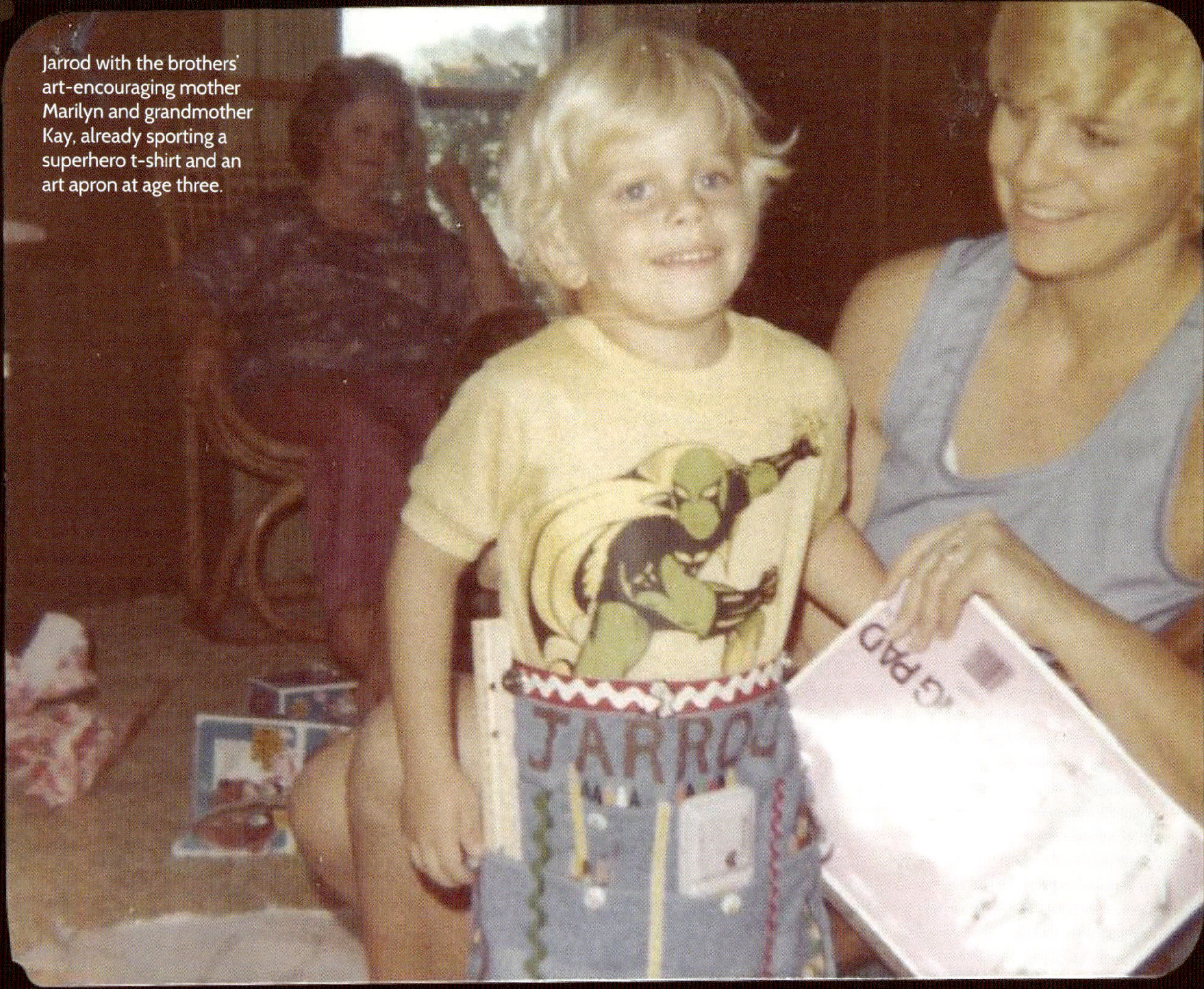

Jarrod with the brothers' art-encouraging mother Marilyn and grandmother Kay, already sporting a superhero t-shirt and an art apron at age three.

Whereas most of our peers in the industry discovered sculpting through a love of movies, we found sculpture through a love of comic books. Of course we adored all of the same science-fiction, fantasy, and monster movies those other guys did, but it was our goal, starting out, to see our favorite comic-book characters represented in 3D, in clay, as we imagined them to be. And so, we started to experiment. We made nearly every mistake imaginable: using the wrong wire for our armatures (household coat hangers are too hard to cut through!); using the wrong clay; putting a Sculpey sculpture into a kiln (it's too hot!). Through trial and error, we finally seemed to figure out how to do what we wanted to do, so we locked ourselves into our house for a year and a half, never showing anyone else the sculptures we were working on, and we attempted to get better. And we did (at least a little bit!).

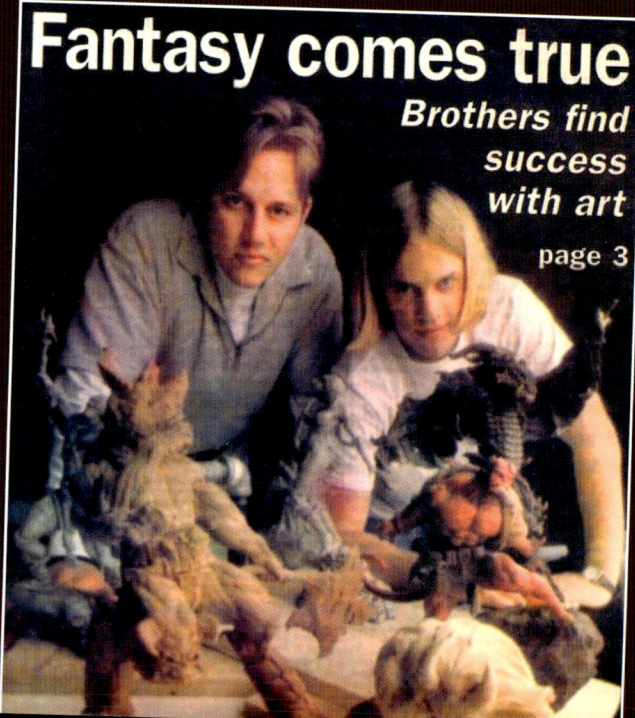

Fantasy comes true

Brothers find success with art

page 3

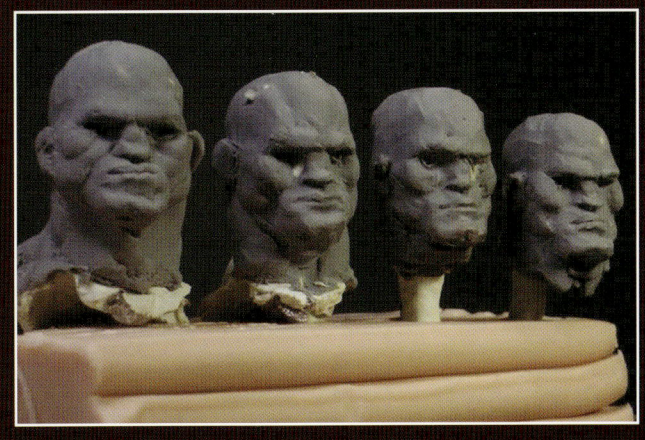

IT WAS OUR GOAL, STARTING OUT, TO SEE OUR FAVORITE COMIC-BOOK CHARACTERS REPRESENTED IN 3D, IN CLAY, AS WE IMAGINED THEM TO BE

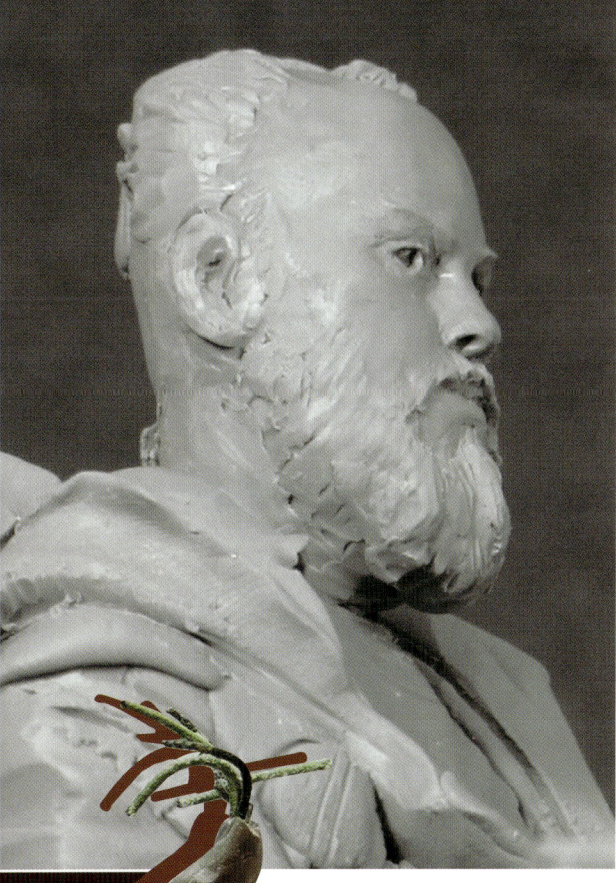

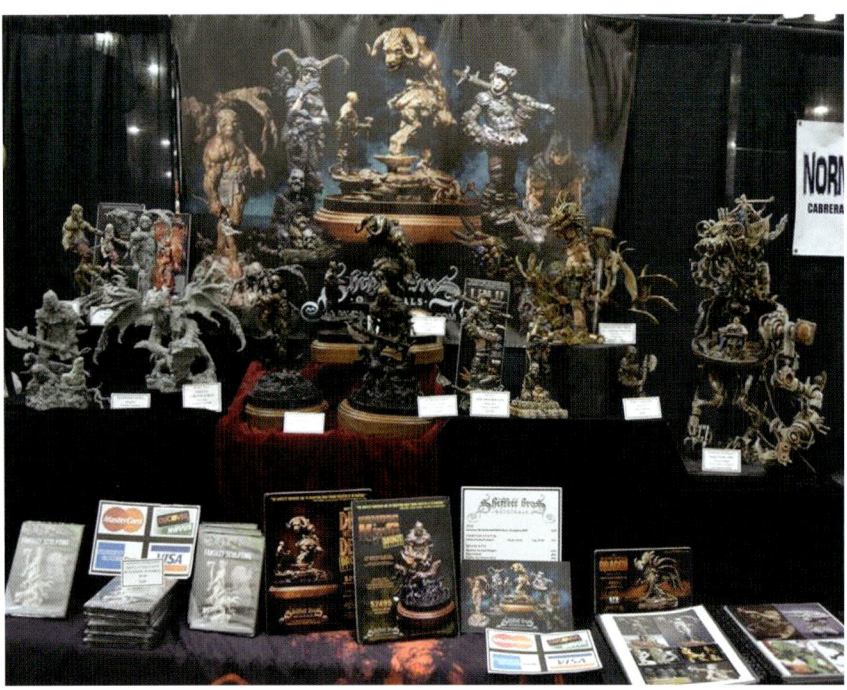

Left: The brothers' display of original work, resin kits, and bronzes at Monsterpalooza in Los Angeles, 2015.

Opposite page, top: Brandon and Jarrod on stage at the San Diego Comic-Con after one of their "Shiflett Brothers and Friends" sculpting panels.

Opposite page, bottom: The Shiflett Brothers standing behind their work at the San Diego Comic-Con, circa 2001.

WE IMMEDIATELY UNDERSTOOD THAT THERE WAS A PLACE FOR US TO EXIST IN THIS BUILDING, IN THIS FIELD, AND IN THIS INDUSTRY

In the early 1990s, we made the trek from Texas to San Diego Comic Convention (Comic-Con) — the largest comic-book convention in the United States and a near-mythical event for us that we'd only ever read about in the backs of comics. It was our Valhalla; where we would meet our people and assemble with our chosen tribe. When our taxi arrived at the San Diego Convention Center that first time, we stepped out onto the curb and standing before us was none other than Marvel legend, Stan Lee, just as we always thought it would happen.

Once we entered the official show floor, we were shocked — there were virtually no sculptures or statues in sight. Nothing three-dimensional stood in the booths or on display. All we could see was flat art: comic books, pages of 2D art, even flat table displays. The collectible comic-book statue boom was yet to happen. Resin kits existed, but as most were unlicensed versions of fans' favorite movie and comic characters, not many could be displayed (after all, the room was full of the companies who were the license holders for these characters). Action figures were present, but relatively simple and uninspired compared to what we see in the incredible world of action figures today. We immediately understood that there was a place for us to exist in this building, in this field, and in this industry.

Putting our work out there for people to judge wasn't easy for us. It wasn't in our nature to show off or seek a lot of attention. We had to keep reminding each other that it was unrealistic to expect strangers to knock on our door and ask, "Excuse me, do you have any cool comic-book inspired sculptures inside?" Instead, we had to take our sculptures out into the wild and present them to the people most likely to care about our subject matter — which were, at that time, the working professionals and fans in attendance at Comic-Con. Over the next few years, we met all manner of video-game developers, budding statue companies, action-figure businesses, and independent comic publishers, all on the show floor looking for sculptors. Super-cool, three-dimensional representations of your independent comic-book character standing on the table next to you at a convention became invaluable. Directors and producers of video games and genre films needed sculptures for pitches. And importantly, licensors began to understand the value of something like a Marvel or DC Comics license to create statues. No-one had predicted the huge demand for statues of popular characters such as Incredible Hulk, yet it seems so obvious now!

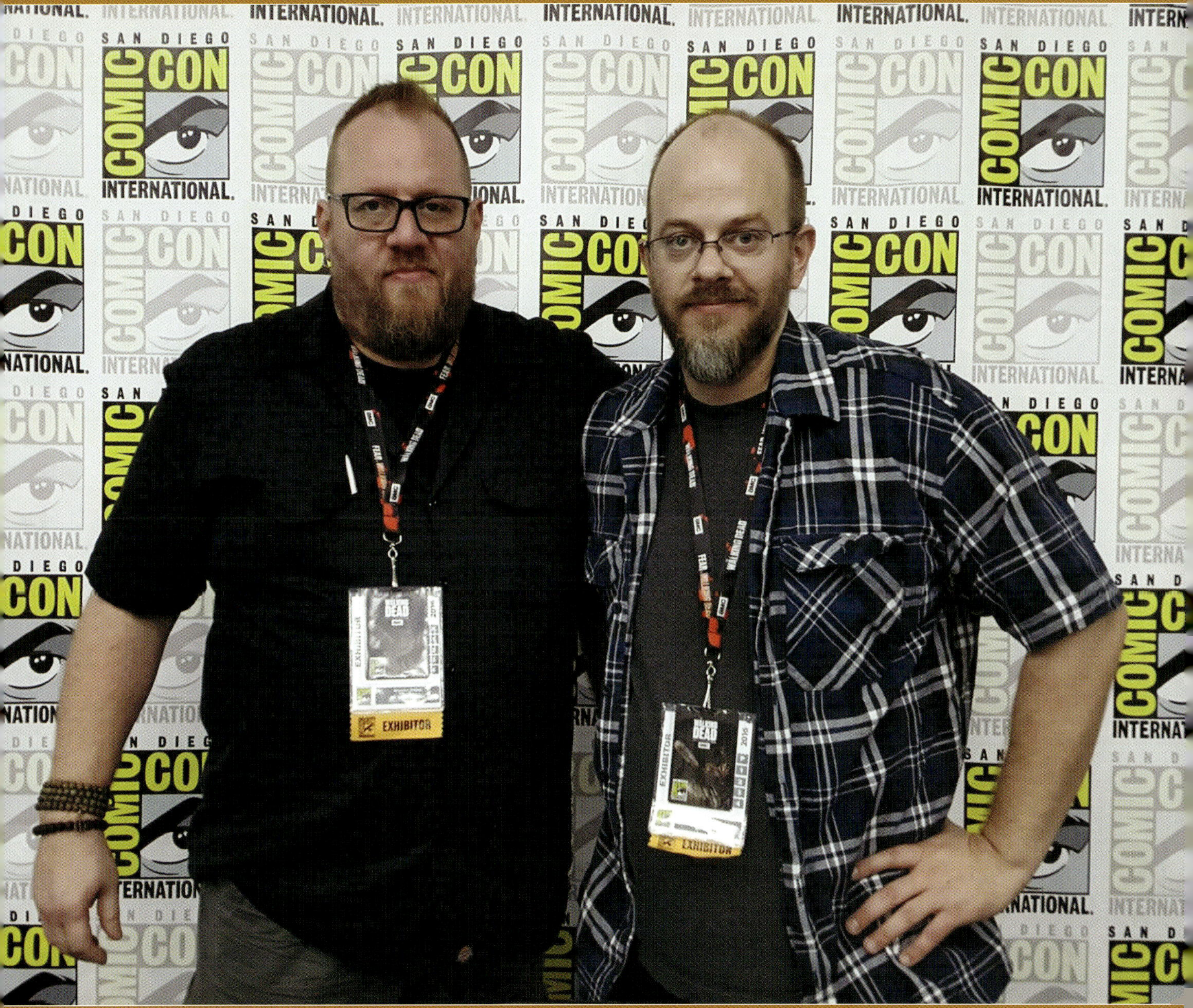

We soon realized that everyone in a position to hire sculptors like us was in that building in San Diego for those specific five days every year. Not only did we put our pieces out on display, but also (against our natures), we'd sometimes see an artist or art director we respected and would set off running after them, portfolio pages fluttering in the wind! Again, before the internet and the ease of reaching out and making contact with people online, we simply had to get our work in front of people's eyes in any way that we could. And that is exactly what we did.

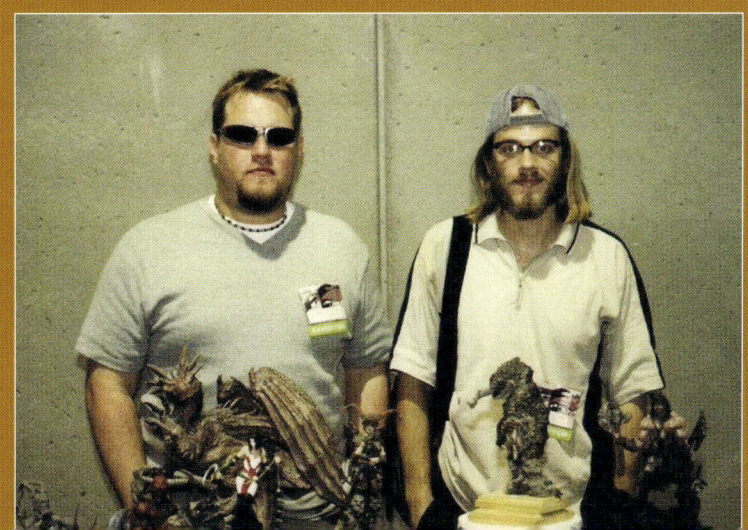

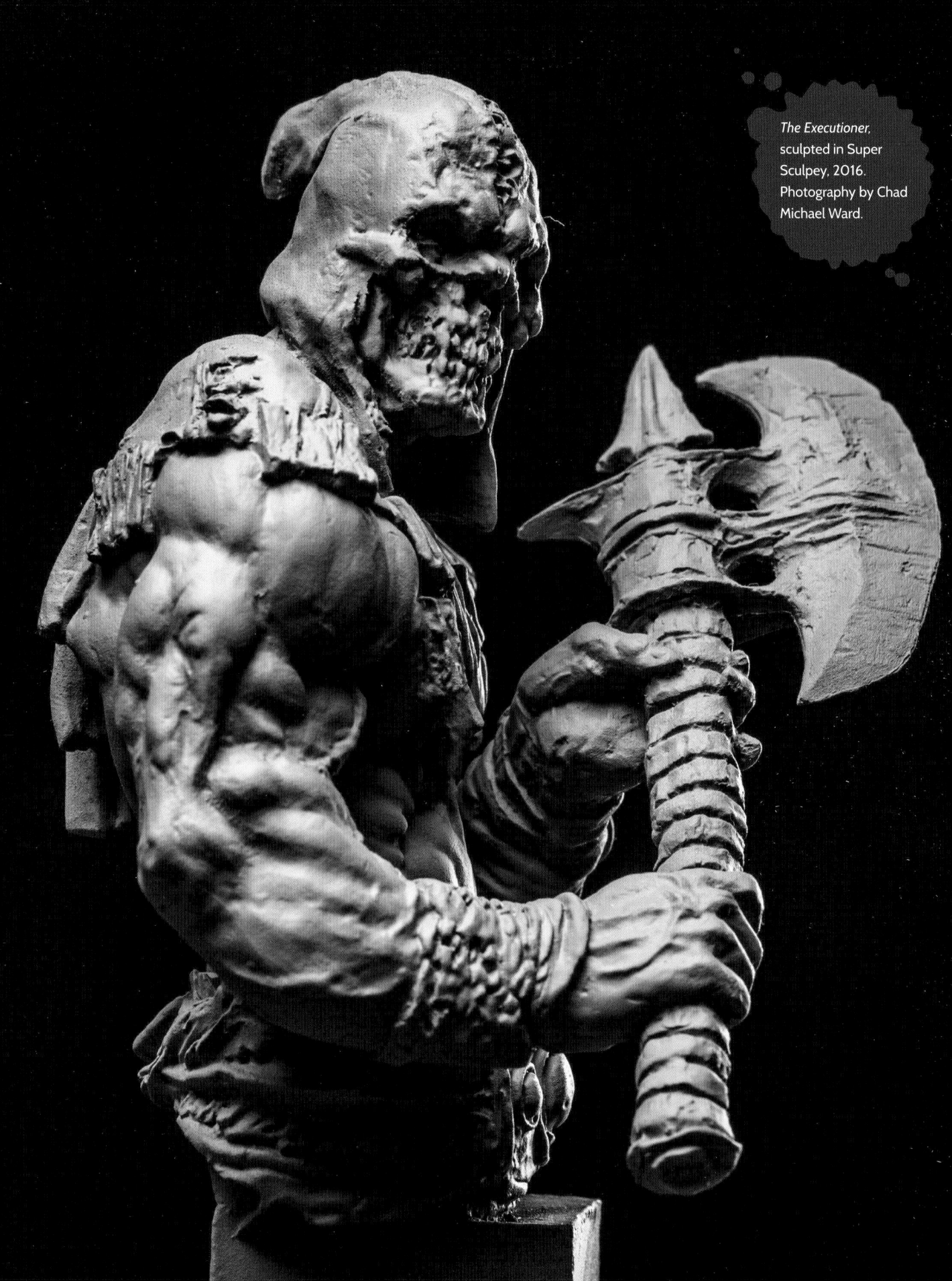

FINDING SUCCESS AND FACING OPPOSITION

The first year we attended Comic-Con, we entered the Comic-Con Art Show and were shocked when we took home the Grand Prize. The art show directors and judges must have been surprised too, because not having foreseen the winners being dimensional sculptural work, they only had an easel to hang the winning piece on. Since none of our sculptures could stand on the easel intended for paintings and drawings, the show runners simply stapled our business cards to it. One of the judges was iconic *Mad* magazine contributor Sergio Aragones — we were huge fans. He told us, much to our amazement and delight, that he had voted for us to win. In the following years, we moved into the convention's Artists' Alley, which at the time consisted almost entirely of comic-book artists and illustrators. We were the only sculptors for as far as the eye could see. In our later years at the San Diego Comic-Con, we moved to a fully fledged booth (a very desirable corner booth!). We showed our work at the San Diego Comic-Con for twenty-six years. For at least the first twenty years of our careers we were able to claim that every job we had ever received came from that single annual show.

To our surprise and great joy, we were discovered relatively quickly, and felt extremely lucky with who saw our work. We were, of course, very grateful for people's positive responses. We were hired to work on the video game *Oddworld: Abe's Oddysee* by its visionary creator, Lorne Lanning. We worked on five or six video games early in our careers and we really loved the experience. The people we had the chance to work with were super-creative, uber-talented artists doing something new and exciting. We sculpted big clay characters for games which were then scanned by a computer and animated. Very cool stuff, but at the end of the day, when we wanted to show family members what we had been working on, it was difficult to hold up a game cartridge or disk and explain it to them. We wanted to hold tangible, physical sculptures rather than something that seemed ephemeral, and this led us farther down the path toward the collectible statue industry.

At the same time as our video-game work began, Glenn Danzig, owner of comic-book publishing company Verotik Comics, asked us to sculpt three of Verotik's central characters. The sculptures were to be produced as resin kits. We were tremendously impressed, not only that a rock star was contacting two boys from Beaumont, Texas, but that he brought two of our all-time favorite artists along for the ride: Simon Bisley and Frank Frazetta, both of whom were working with Verotik at the time. The three kits that we sculpted, Dalkiel, Satanika, and Jaguar God, were all based on artwork by Bisley, or a combination of Bisley and Frazetta. The kits were received enthusiastically by fans. We were thrilled with this result and felt as though as our careers as professional sculptors in the collectible industry were up and running.

TO OUR SURPRISE AND GREAT JOY, WE WERE DISCOVERED RELATIVELY QUICKLY, AND FELT EXTREMELY LUCKY

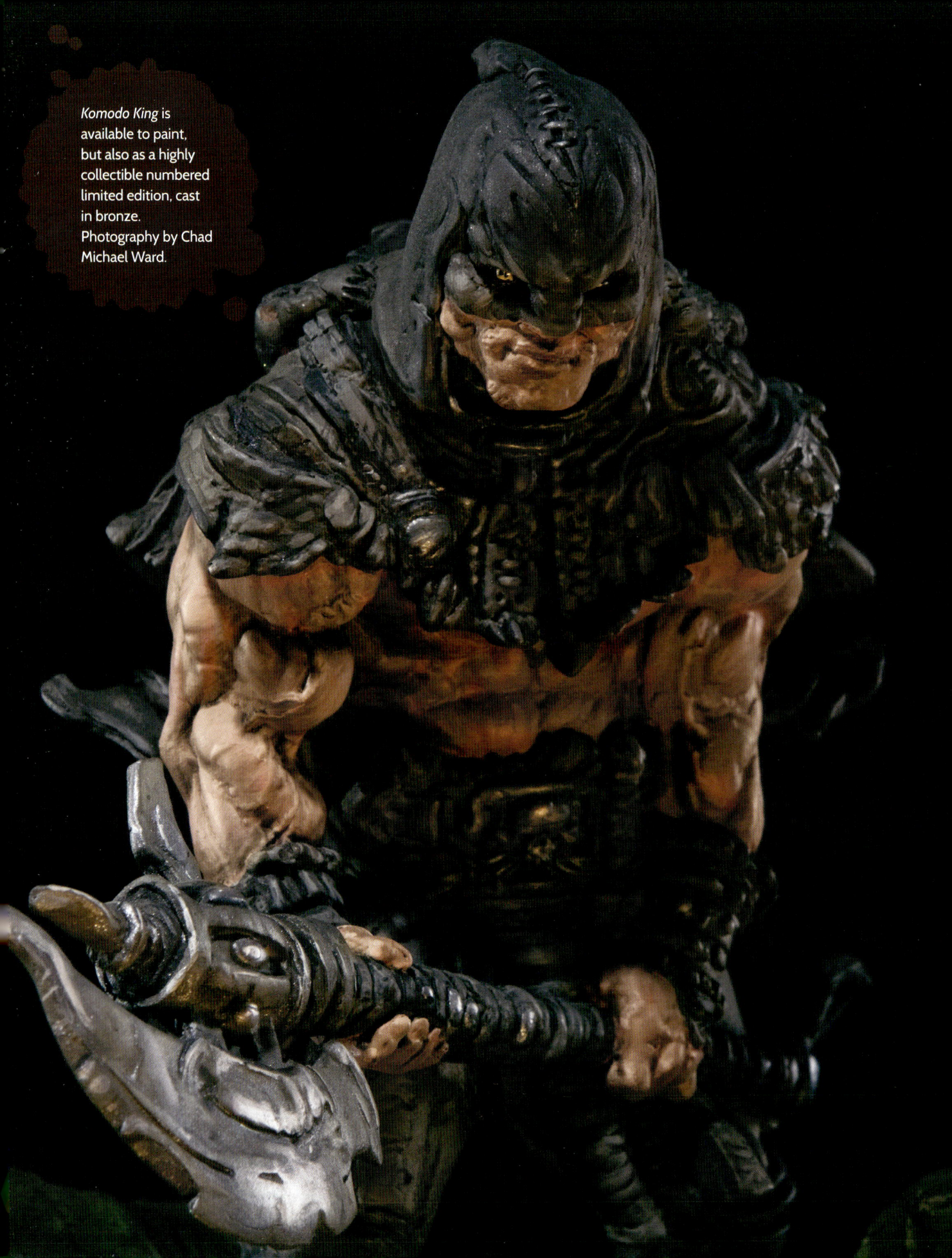

Komodo King is available to paint, but also as a highly collectible numbered limited edition, cast in bronze. Photography by Chad Michael Ward.

Much of our early fan-following was a result of our work on licensed Marvel Statues, created for and with the great sculptor Randy Bowen of Bowen Designs. Working on iconic comic-book characters such as The Incredible Hulk, Wolverine, Sabretooth, Juggernaut, and Thanos, was a huge thrill for us. Randy would often reach out to us when he had a job involving characters and, not entirely coincidentally, Marvel characters were some of our favorites, so it was a perfect match. We had held these characters in our hearts throughout our childhoods (and, in fact, still very much do!) and playing a part in bringing them to life in physical form was truly a dream come true. However, our passion didn't guarantee complete approval from the statue collectors of the time! Many followers of our careers in recent years might be surprised to learn that our early sculptures were often criticized, sometimes savagely, by certain collectors in both the collectible market and on the internet.

Our natural sculpting style and aesthetic, which was (and still is) loose and raw, didn't work with everyone's idea of what comic-book and movie statues should look like. So, who did love it? Answer: other artists. And that's what saved us in the end: big-name, famous artists vouching for our creations by proclaiming publicly that they were supporters of our work and how we were producing it. This included, among others, Sir Richard Taylor, the co-founder of the Weta Workshop in New Zealand, John Howe, legendary illustrator and designer of the Lord of the Rings film trilogy, and famed creature designer Wayne Barlowe. And to this day, we could not be more grateful to them.

The work on Marvel properties was a high point for us both personally and professionally, but even though these big Marvel characters meant almost everything to us, we felt strongly that we should sculpt our own characters as well. Using resin, polystone, and bronze, we began to produce a line of our own character concept pieces, dioramas, and statues. These were all our own creations, and so Shiflett Brothers Originals was born. We were aware of the possibly apocryphal story of how Martin Scorsese would make a movie for the studio, which then allowed him to make a movie for himself as a passion project, if you will. And while we're no Martin Scorsese, we tried to apply this general approach to our sculpting careers. Whether or not that happened to work, we were determined to carve out time between jobs to sculpt our original ideas, and we've been doing that very thing for twenty-five years!

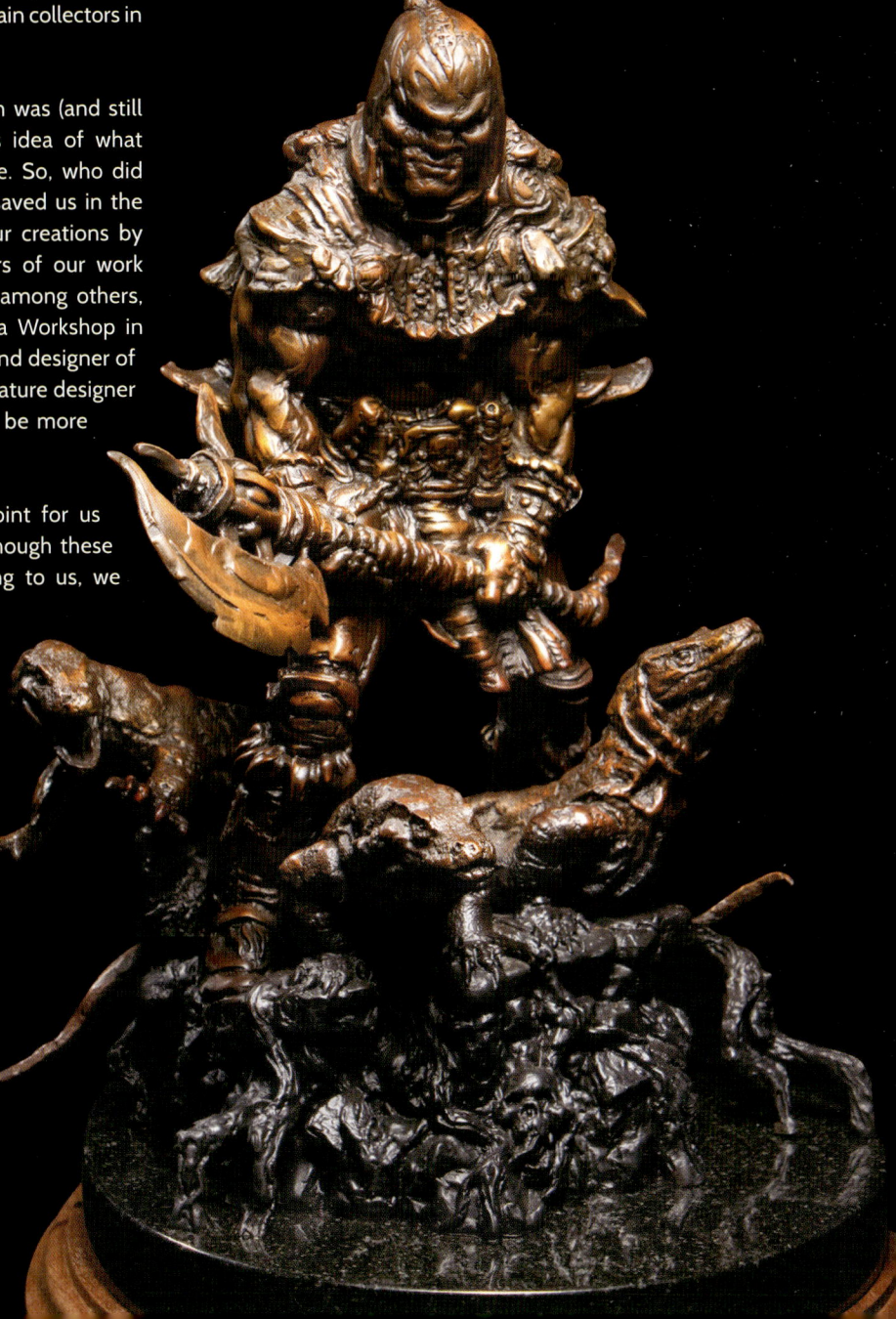

WE WERE DETERMINED TO CARVE OUT TIME BETWEEN JOBS TO SCULPT OUR ORIGINAL IDEAS

OUR PLANS FOR OUR FUTURE WORK ARE BIGGER AND GRANDER THAN THEY'VE EVER BEEN BEFORE

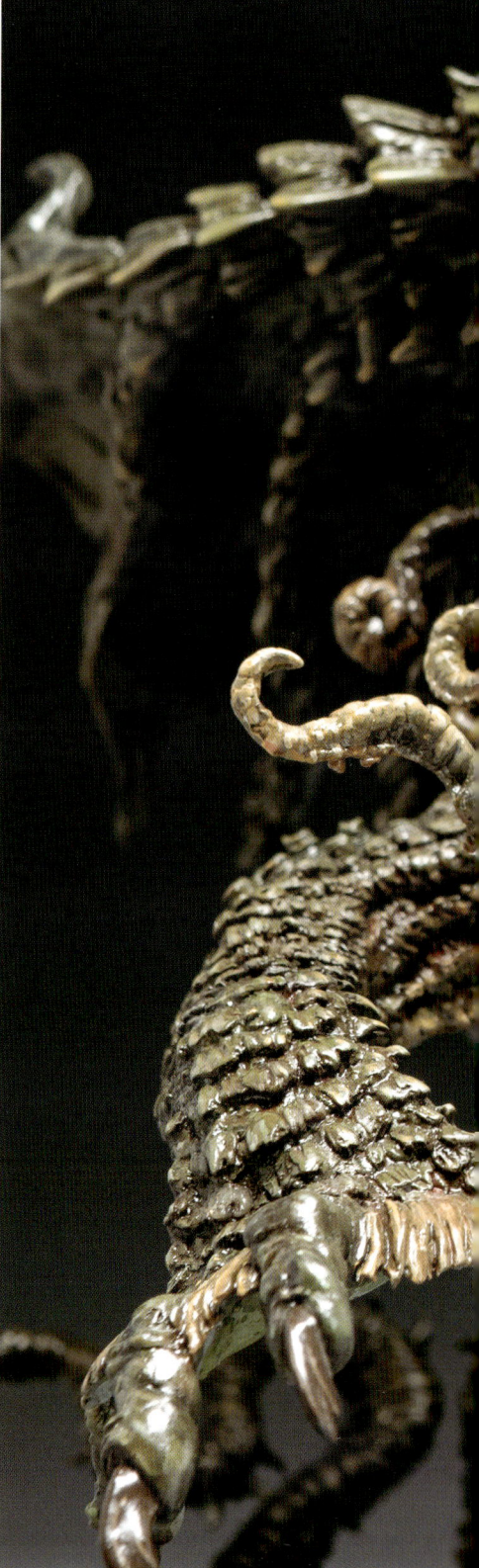

CAREER HIGHLIGHTS

Along the way, we've very much enjoyed the perks that our dream careers have brought us. A highlight was hosting the Shiflett Brothers and Friends Sculpting Panel at the San Diego Comic-Con for over a decade, in which we held a workshop-like talk, to discuss the sculpting industry alongside some of the greatest sculptors of the field, including Simon Lee, Paul Komoda, Clayburn Moore, and Anthony J. Kosar. We've taught masterclasses and produced instructional videos for the Gnomon Workshop in Hollywood, and written numerous tutorial articles for publications. We also had the wonderful opportunity to sit on the jury for the revered annual art book *Spectrum: The Best in Contemporary Fantastic Art* alongside legendary painters Boris Vallejo, Julie Bell, and Greg Manchess. Then, in 2014 we were humbled to win the Gold Award for Dimensional Work in that year's edition of *Spectrum*. We received the award at a magical ceremony in Kansas City with many of the most famous fantasy artists in the world (and our parents!) in attendance.

Our sculpting journey to this point has been action-packed and very eventful. Yet somehow, even now, we have the feeling that we are only just getting started. We often joke that we're "planning world domination, one small fantasy sculpture at a time," but it is actually true to say that our plans for our future work are bigger and grander than they've ever been before.

The brothers' interpretation of H.P. Lovecraft's iconic cosmic entity Cthulhu. This is a one-of-a-kind piece, made from clay and hand-painted by Jarrod for its appearance on the cover of *Amazing Figure Modeler* magazine.

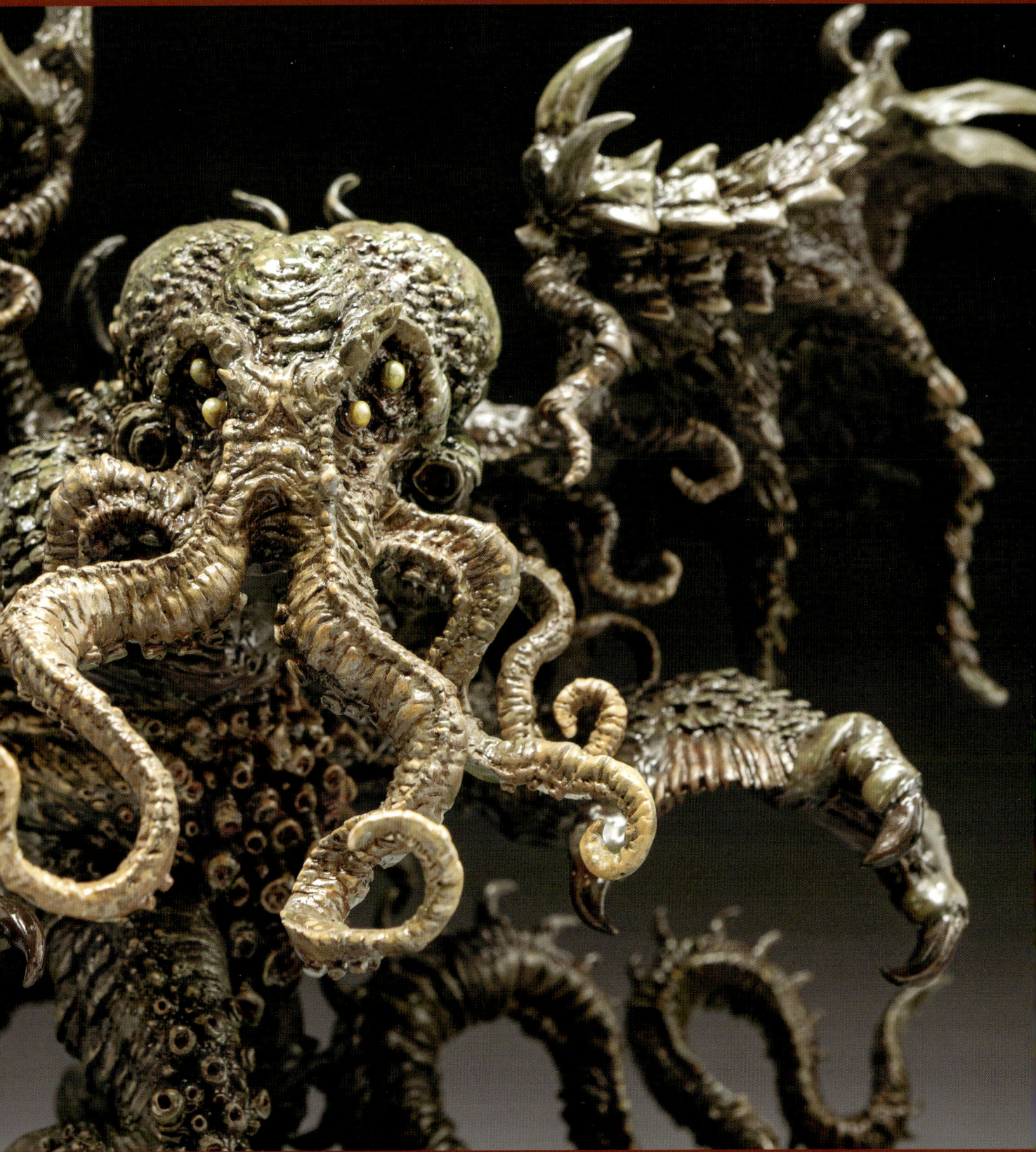

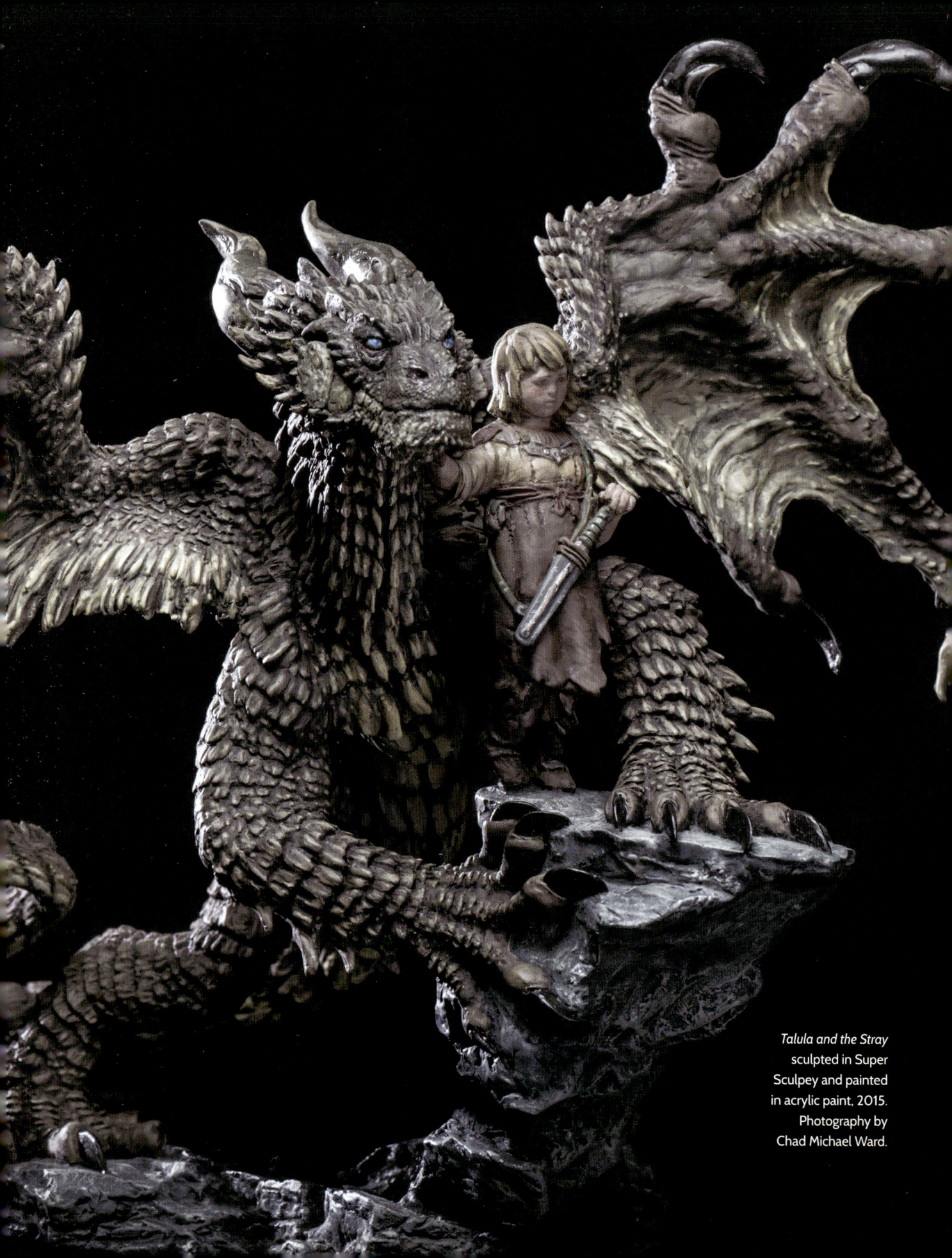

Talula and the Stray sculpted in Super Sculpey and painted in acrylic paint, 2015. Photography by Chad Michael Ward.

OUR SCULPTING PHILOSOPHY

We always aspire to be storytellers in clay, asking each other, "Does this sculpture tell an interesting story?" A single figure can still tell a potent tale. Where has this character been? Where are they going, and why? What were they doing before the moment captured in the sculpture, and what will they be doing in the moments after?

A pair of characters feature in many of our pieces, and often those sculptures center around a creature and a human. There is so much subtext that we aim to impart: what is the relationship between these two? Are they friendly or are they enemies? Is there tension or a perceptible ease between them? Sometimes, we create diorama-type sculptures with three or more characters. Another fun aspect of multiple characters, is the ability to play with scale. A giant monster next to a very small human raises its own interesting storytelling questions, and it goes without saying that we love giant monsters!

One of our favorite ways to present multi-character sculpture is to leave some of these relationships ambiguous. Ambiguity can be a wonderful tool in art because the viewer has the opportunity to contemplate the piece and judge it for themselves. This makes the experience unique to each individual. One of our more popular sculptures features a dragon and a little girl. We call it *Talula and the Stray*. But we've never told anyone which character is Talula and which is the Stray, even though we are asked... a lot!

Whether the final sculpture features a single character or a group, humans or beasts, unexpected proportions, or requires a complex casting, the story is always at the front of our minds throughout the entire process. There are several techniques we use to infuse the sculpt with intrigue, narrative, and energy. But above all, it's about the story.

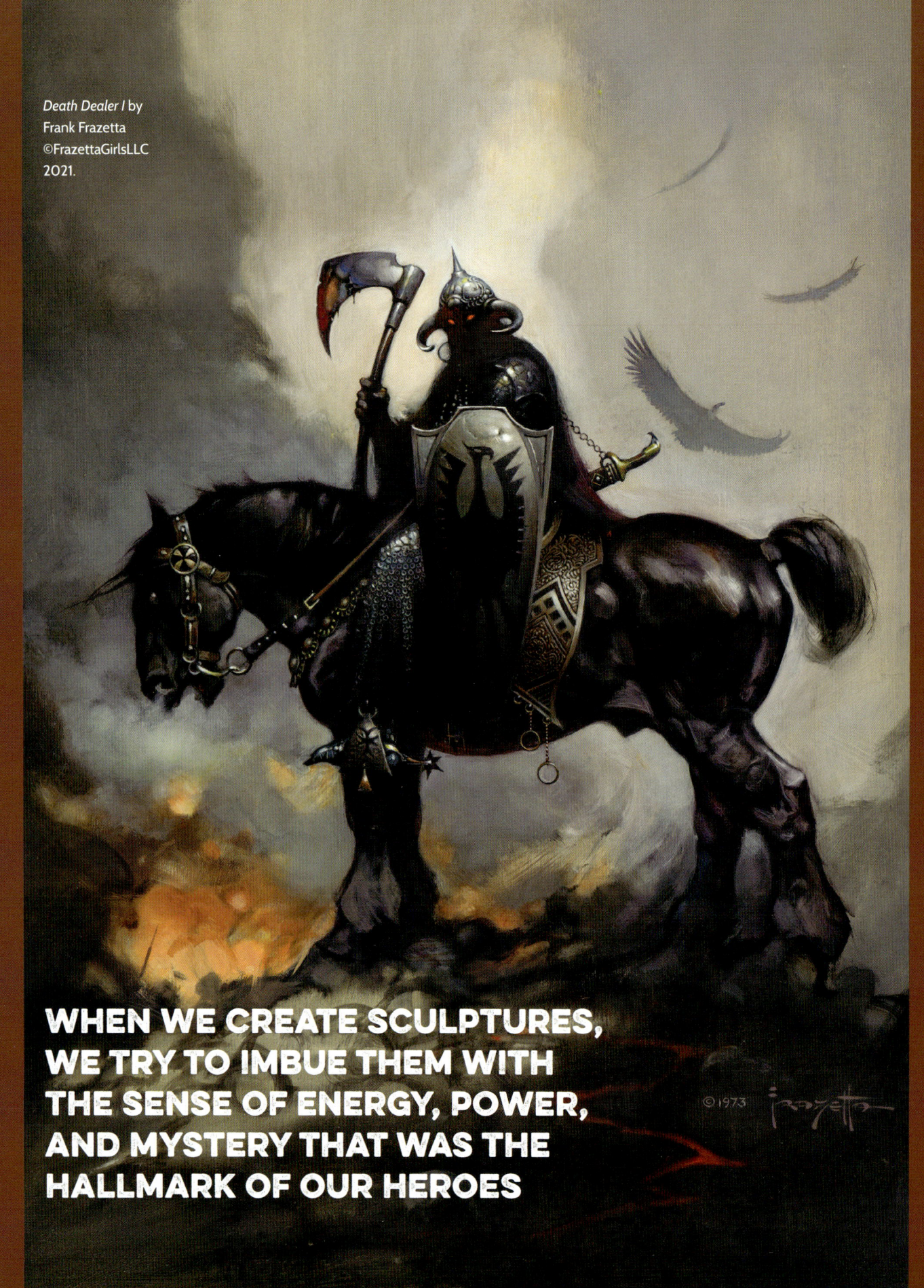

Death Dealer I by
Frank Frazetta
©FrazettaGirlsLLC
2021.

©1973

**WHEN WE CREATE SCULPTURES,
WE TRY TO IMBUE THEM WITH
THE SENSE OF ENERGY, POWER,
AND MYSTERY THAT WAS THE
HALLMARK OF OUR HEROES**

ICONIC INFLUENCES

Many of our artistic philosophies spring forth from our obsessive observation of the art created by our favorite 1970s and 1980s comic-book and fantasy artists. The two most prominent of these figures are the iconic fantasy painter Frank Frazetta, and the legendary French comic-book artist Moebius. When we create sculptures, we try to imbue them with the sense of energy, power, and mystery that was the hallmark of our heroes from yesteryear.

From Frazetta's work, we gained an appreciation for a more free-flowing, raw style. The rise of digital art has done a lot of great things, but it has also made some art too precise, too exact, at least to our eyes. Yes, we use references and try to get lengths and measurements essentially accurate, but we also like to create instinctively and work by eye much of the time. For instance, we notice that many people use a symmetry tool on digitally drawn, painted, and sculpted faces. But in fact, real-world human faces aren't perfectly symmetrical. They have irregularities and incongruities, and to us, those idiosyncrasies are exactly where faces become interesting.

Moebius' work left us with a love of the "sense of wonder" with which he could imbue his drawings and paintings. Many of his original illustrations seemed mysterious to us. They beckoned us deep into his world, inviting us to follow him further into the pages to find out more. We were most inspired when we came across a Moebius drawing (and there are a few) that left us wondering if it represented the long-forgotten past, or the distant future.

Much of what we know and believe about posing our characters comes from our lifelong love of the book *How to Draw Comics the Marvel Way* by Stan Lee and

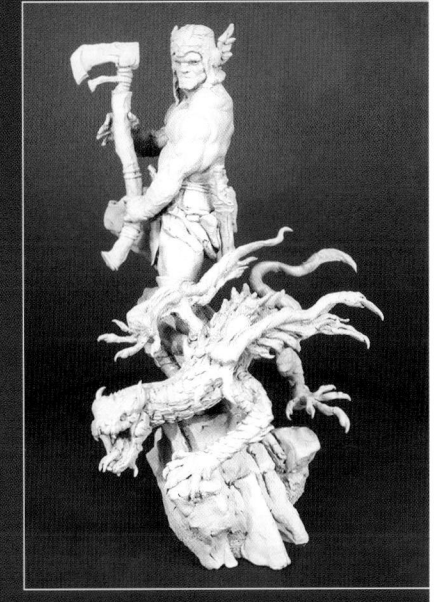

Above: *The Dragon of Argos*, a piece the brothers sculpted in 2009 for an instructional sculpting video produced by the Gnomon Workshop in Hollywood.

Below: A viking warrior sculpture created by the Shiflett Brothers in 2013.

John Buscema. We've had many copies over the years, some beaten-up and dogeared, but all of them very well-read. Lee and Buscema tell us that if one were to see twenty freeze-frame shots of a character throwing a punch, so that you see the action from beginning to end, the most impactful two poses would be the first one, with the character's fist cocked all the way back, and the last one, where the fist makes contact. All of the images in the middle of the action are weaker and less forceful, and therefore less attention-grabbing and effective. This principle applies to drawing comics and we find that it works for sculpture too. When creating a true action pose, we advise sculptors to go for it! Make the pose as extreme and exaggerated as possible, within the limits of anatomy and good sense. Crank the shoulder back a bit farther, place the leg a bit more forward. Posing for us is one of the most enjoyable aspects of what we do, and it should be for new sculptors, too.

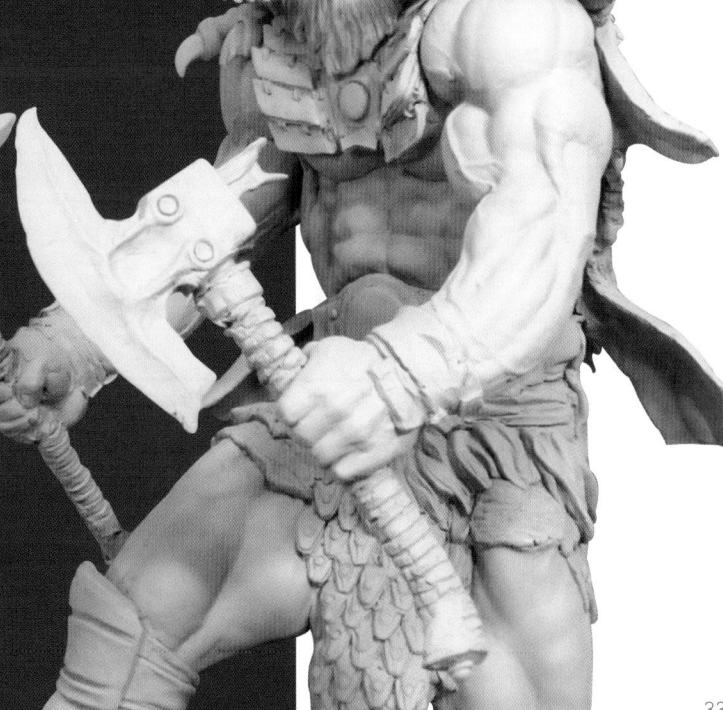

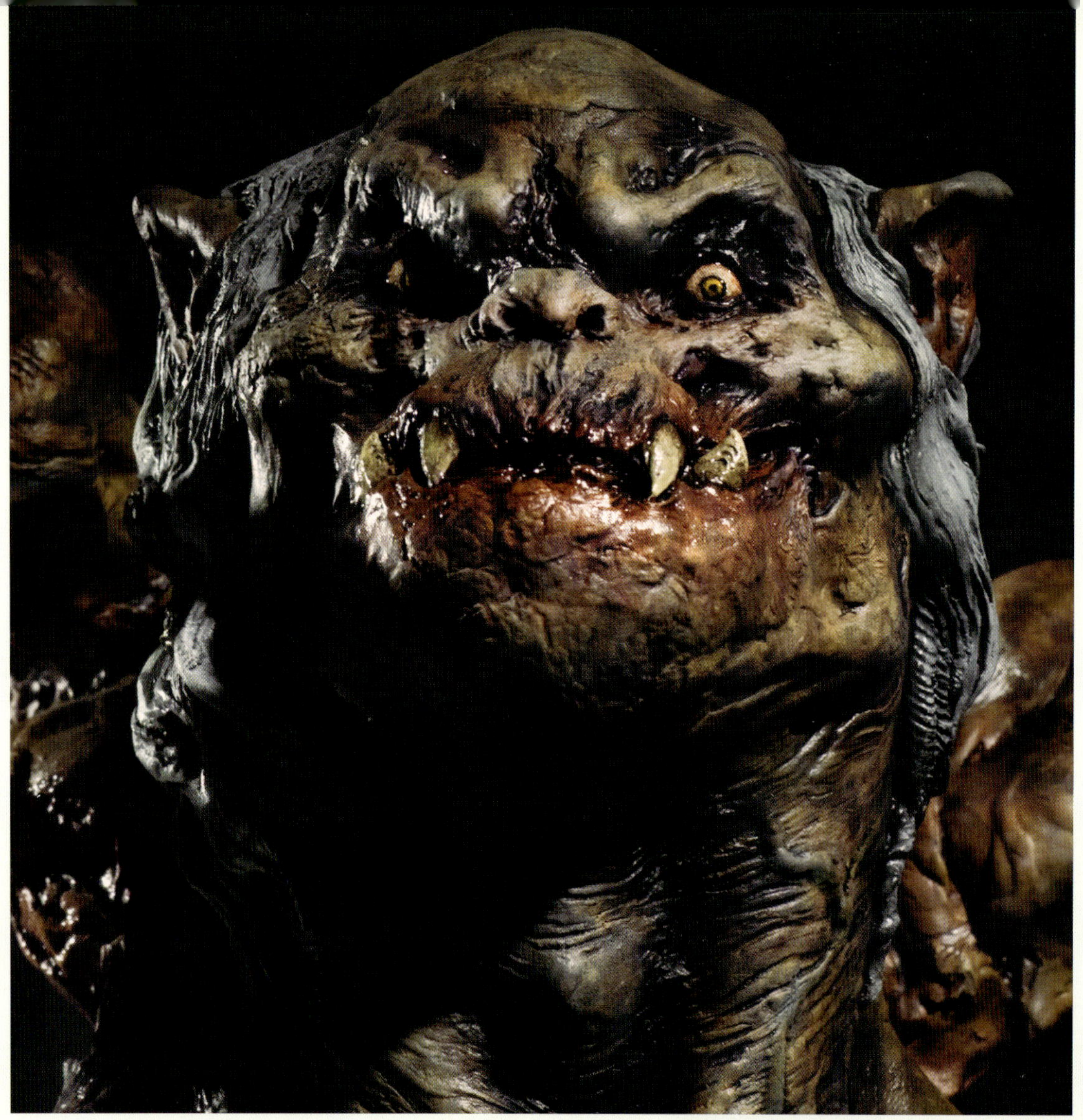

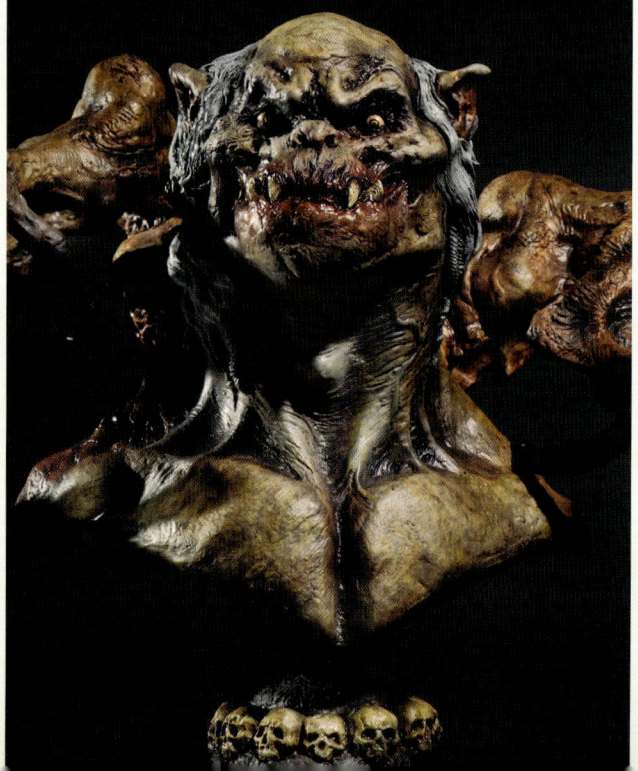

This page: A bust of the Shiflett Brothers' character *Ol' Scratch*, sculpted by their friend Simon "Spiderzero" Lee, and photographed by Chad Michael Ward.

THE MONEY SHOT

Some of our ideas about sculpting are slightly outside the mainstream. The great Hollywood special-effects sculptor Henry Alvarez, whose work includes John Carpenter's cult classic The Thing, once told us in his studio that "a sculpture is something you walk around," meaning that the piece needs to look good from every angle. And while we agree with that sentiment and take it very seriously, we also believe that there is a certain angle, which we like to call "the money shot," that is of great importance. As most people are only ever going to see photos of our sculptures in books and magazines, or on the internet, and may never see the real thing in person, that angle is an important focal point and design consideration in our work. It's not the only angle we want the piece to be seen from, but we would describe it as the first angle from which we'd like each of our pieces to be seen... even though this isn't always controllable!

CASTING

We feel that our rough and relatively unfinished style works best in bronze. And many artist friends, whose opinions we respect, have told us the same thing. We really love the permanence of the metal combined with the raw organic shapes that often crop up in our work. And for us, a key component of the look we love is the patina work that the artists at our foundry (Deep in the Heart Art Foundry) apply to our pieces. We've told them that we like our bronzes to look very dark and very old, almost as if they have been dug up, like artifacts from the past... and they always come through for us, creating the exact feel we ask for.

We do know which pieces will work well in bronze and which might not. And we will, every once in a while, start a piece with the specific intention of having it cast in bronze. Designs that we feel are more appropriate for metal often have a lot of anatomy and possibly a little drapery, and these pieces usually fall into the fantasy (often dark fantasy in our case) and horror genres. We try to avoid using bronze for our more science-fiction-tinged work, as it just doesn't feel right to us.

Another philosophy that we've held onto for many years is not allowing the mold-making process to constrain us. The more complex the sculpture, the more complex the molding and casting job that we create. Many sculptors are concerned with how a piece will need to be molded and how much more work or cost will be involved. We simply try to sculpt the shapes and design aspects we want and worry about the rest later. But to make one thing clear: we don't do our own mold-making and casting! So, the brunt of the problems created by this philosophy is borne by our amazing mold-maker Steve West of Cellar Cast. Almost anything can be molded given the time, money, and effort. Of course, we do pay attention to undercuts and the like, but in our opinion, it's better to have a part of the sculpture that is integral to the design than to remove it due to casting concerns.

Left: *Deal with the Devil,* bronze edition, with a black granite over dark walnut base. The original piece was sculpted in Super Sculpey and the metalwork was done by Deep in the Heart Art Foundry in Bastrop, Texas. Final photography by Chad Michael Ward.

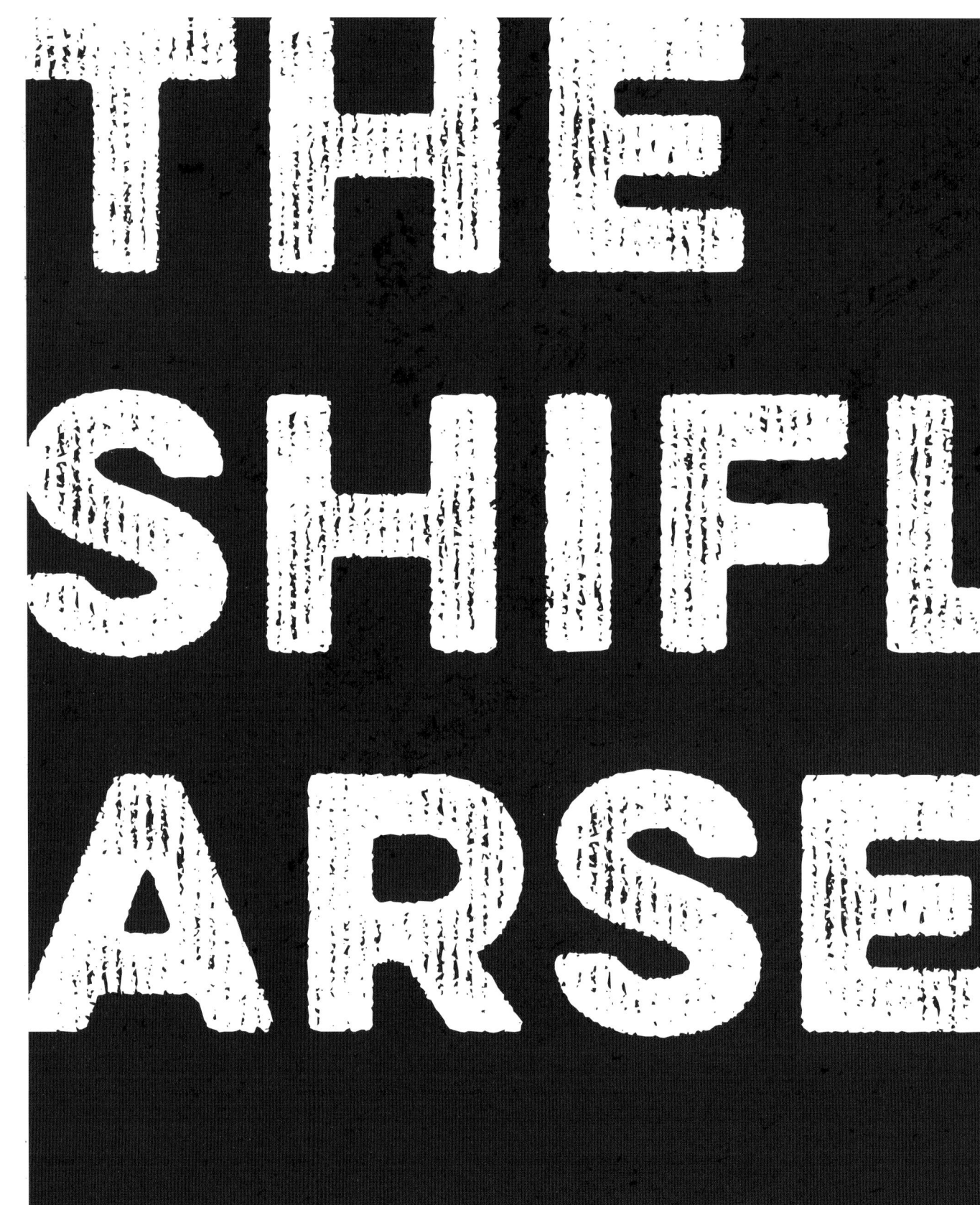

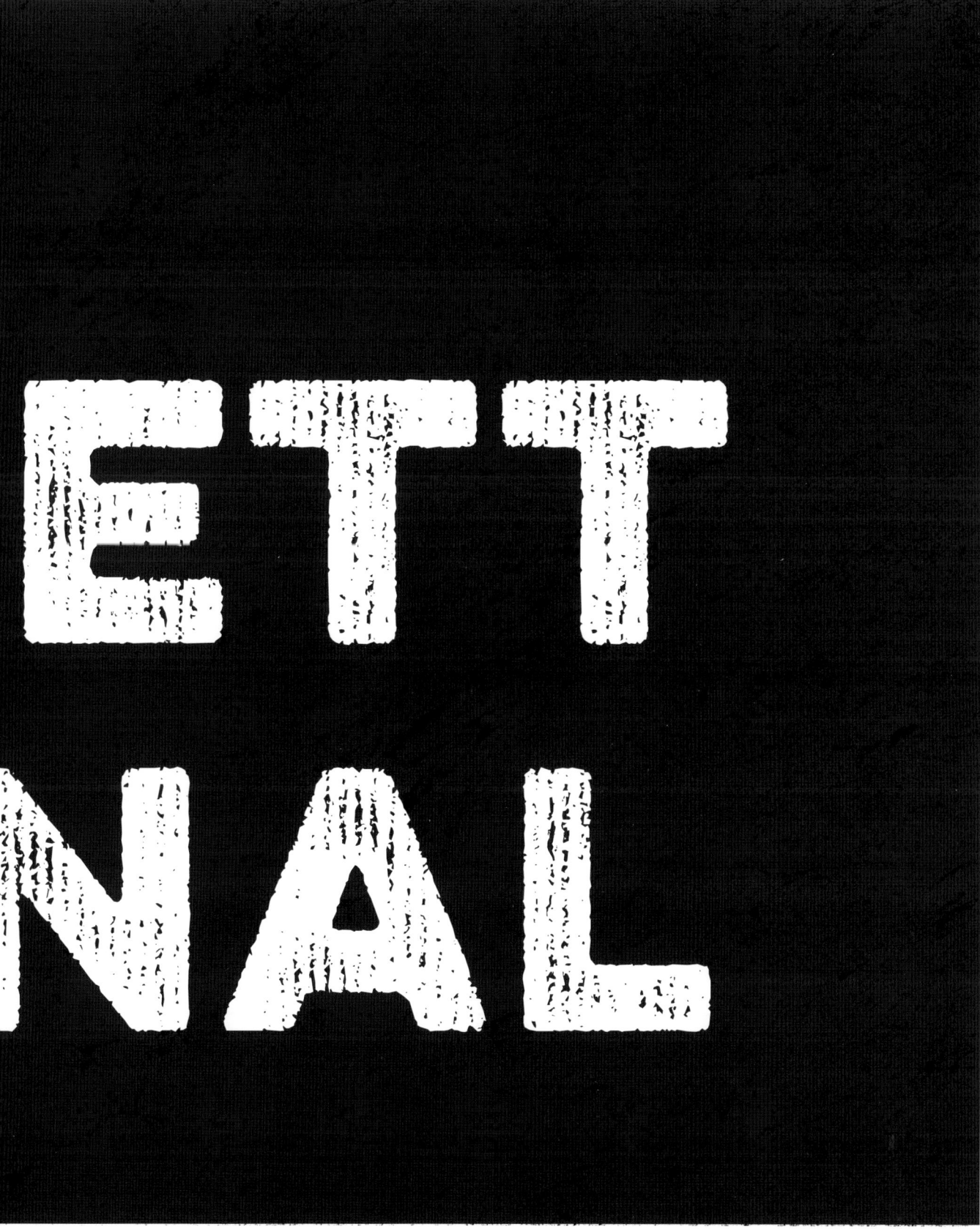

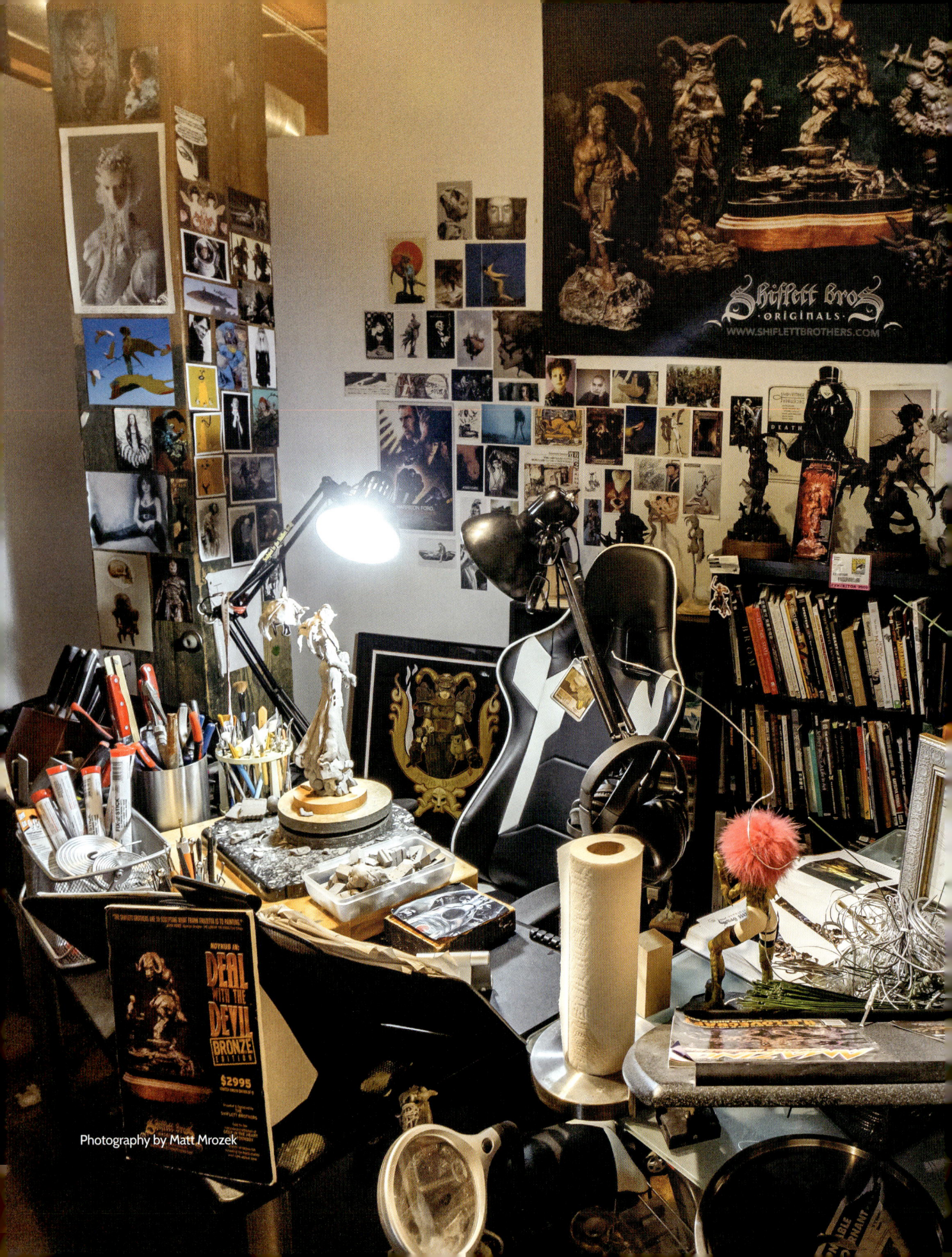

Photography by Matt Mrozek

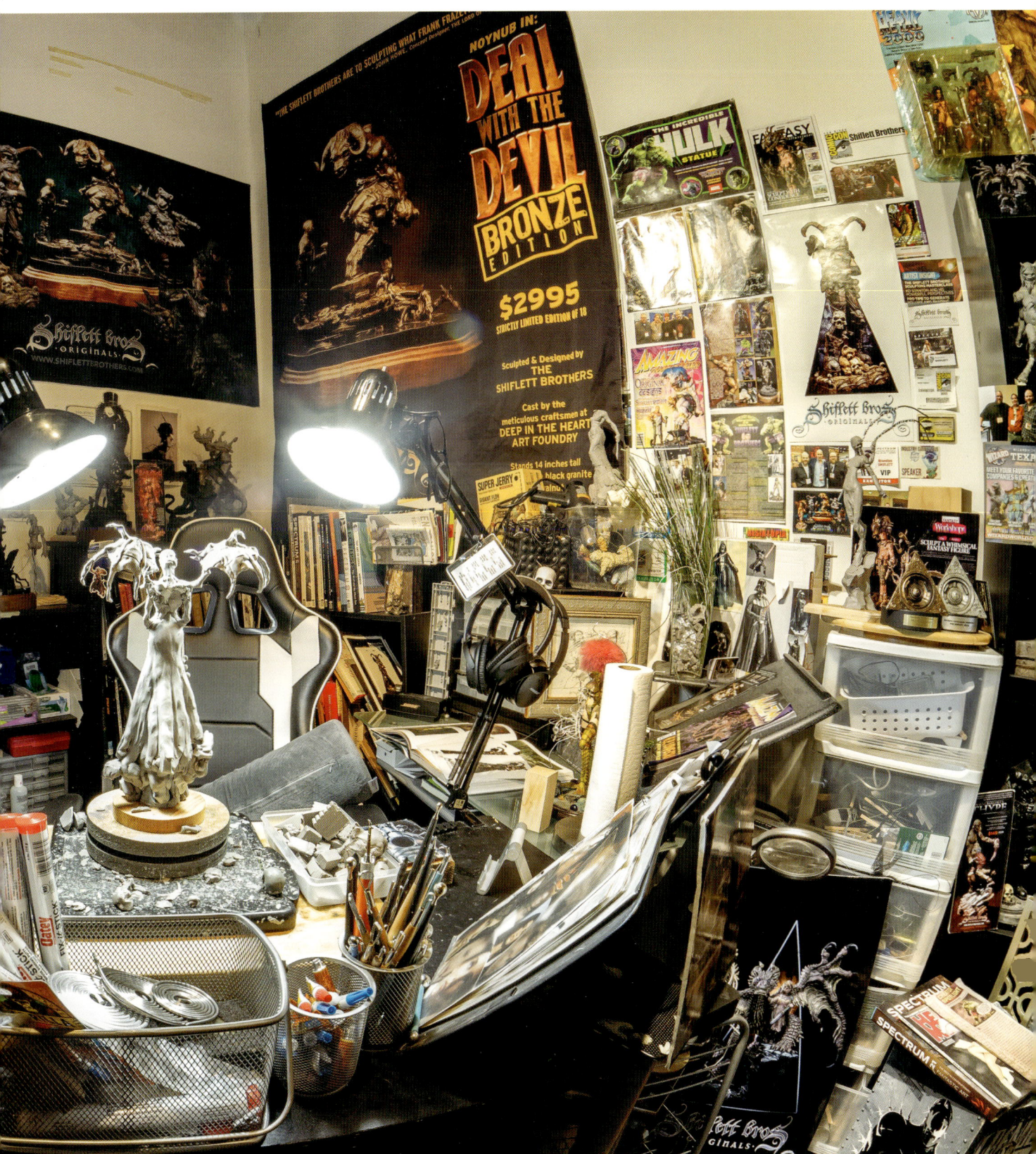

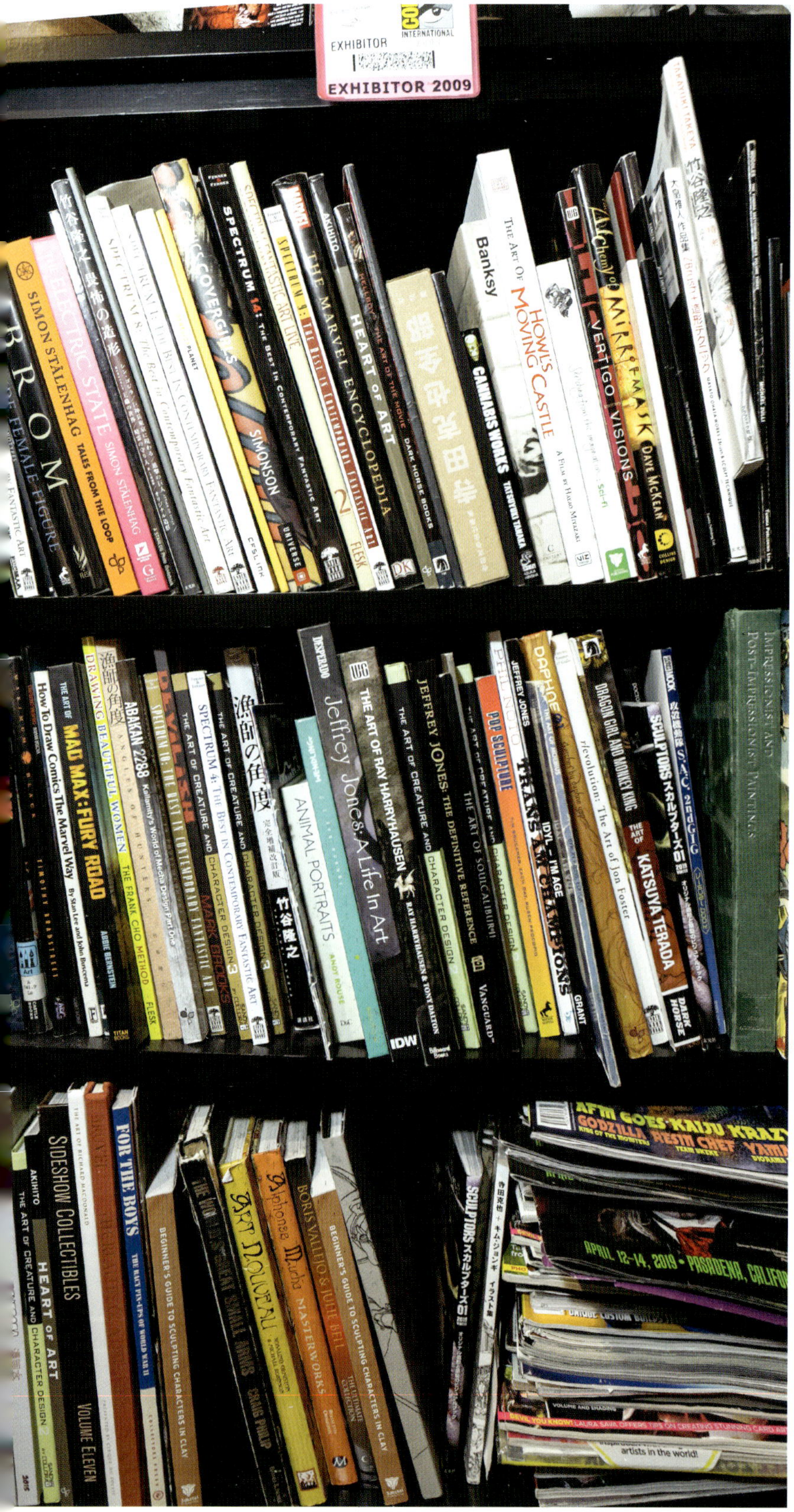

Left: For inspirational purposes, we try to keep ourselves surrounded with an array of art books and sketchbooks by other artists that we admire. Having page upon page of incredible art at hand, both 2D and 3D, to peruse can really pull us out of the creative doldrums and can cure even the most stymying case of "Sculptor's Block."

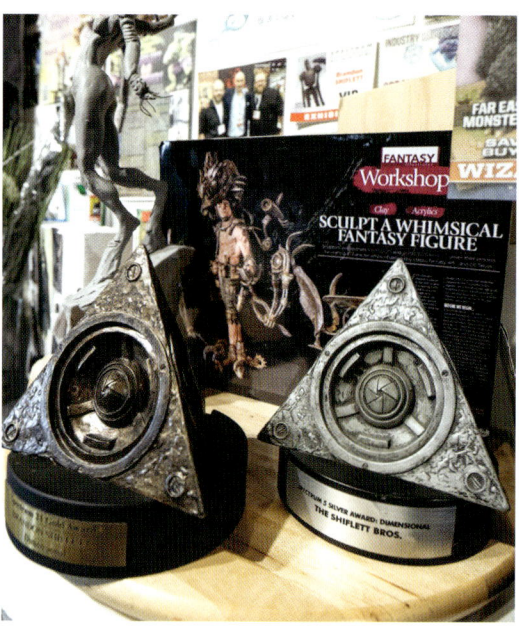

Above: Brandon and Jarrod have won both a Spectrum Gold and a Spectrum Silver Award for Dimensional Work. The Silver came for their work on the collectible statue of Draco from *Dragonheart* produced by Moore Creations in 1997, and they won the Gold Award in 2014 for their original piece *Professor McElroy's Vertical Man-Tank, 1902*.

BEING ABLE TO LOOK UP AND SEE OUR PAST ACCOMPLISHMENTS PROVIDES A MUCH-NEEDED REMINDER THAT PEOPLE ENJOY OUR WORK

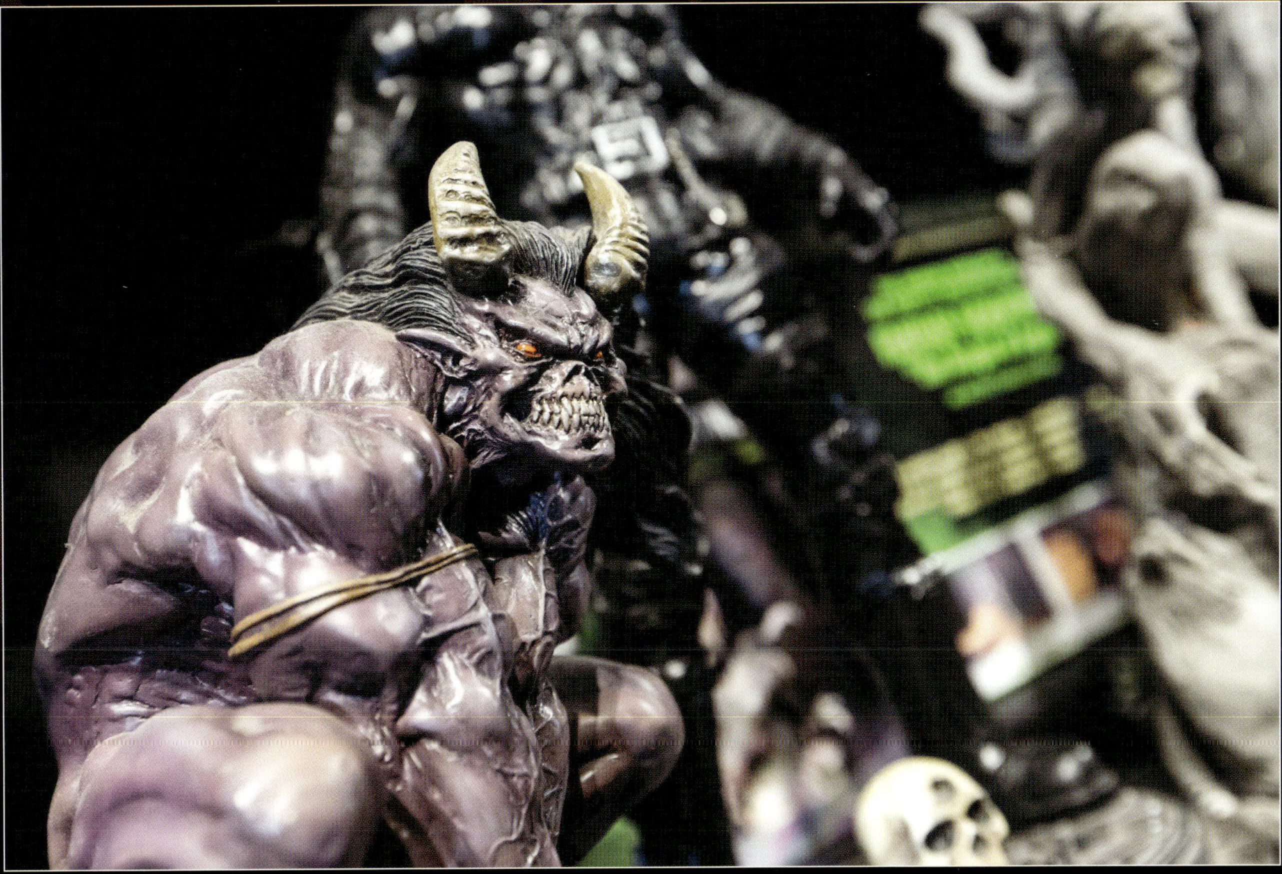

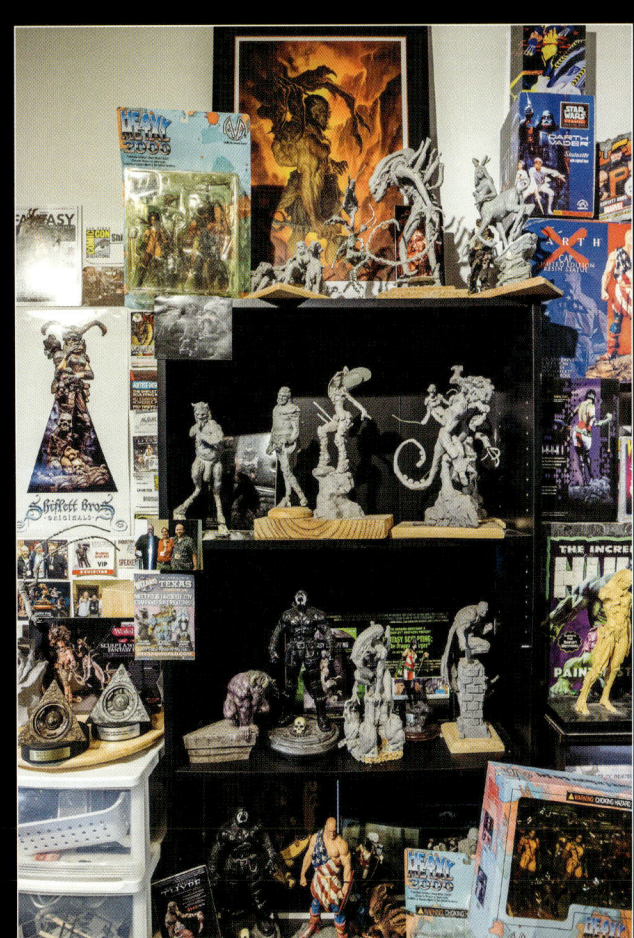

On one wall of our workspace we have photos of art and artists that inspire us and on another wall we have photos of our own achievements and awards. This isn't because we are self-aggrandizing, but it's rather because self-doubt and insecurity in one's own work is liable to creep in during the long lonely days of sculpting on a project. Being able to look up and see our past accomplishments provides a much-needed reminder that people enjoy our work, and gives us motivation to keep moving forward.

When we're in need of photo references, although everything is easily searchable on the internet, sometimes we still use physical paper photos cut out and taped to a larger piece of paper or cardboard. We then try to place this physical reference behind our sculpture and directly in our line of sight so that just a glance away from our piece puts the reference in our field of vision.

During the making process we spend a long time sitting in our chairs sculpting, so the space needs to be really cozy and comfortable for both of us. Any sculptor creating this kind of workspace should focus on making it comfortable and inviting for themselves, to encourage the best (and the most!) work possible.

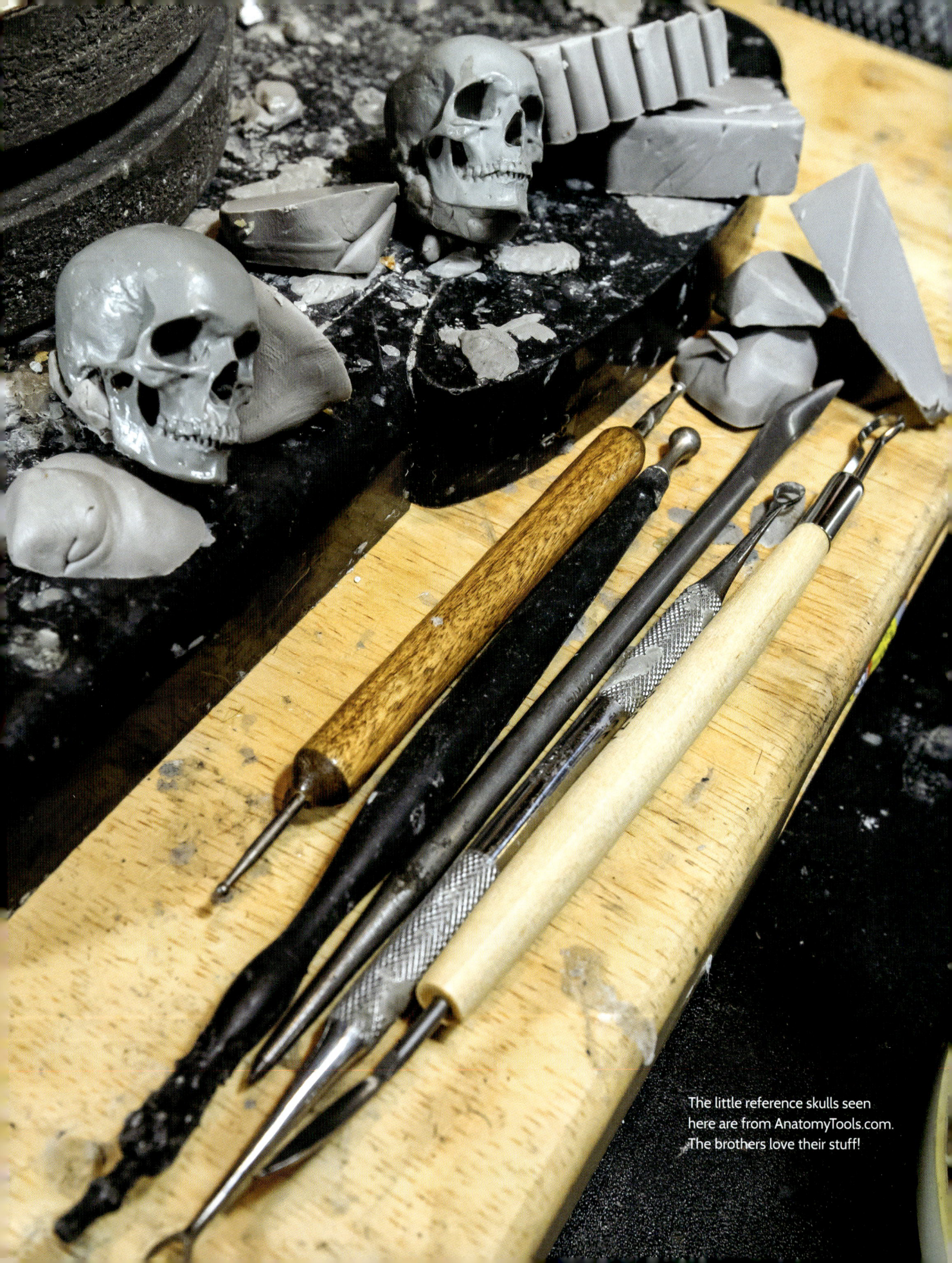

The little reference skulls seen here are from AnatomyTools.com. The brothers love their stuff!

TOOLS OF THE TRADE

Due to its dimensionality, we believe that form is key in sculpting, meaning that the shape and composition are always the most important aspects. Every sculpture we create begins with big chunks of clay to block out the form. All of the initial "large-shape" work is done with the very first tools we use on any sculpture — our own hands. We work using just our fingers, not only building the armature, but working with the clay as well. Fingers are perfect for this kind of manipulation and we tend to use them for as long as possible before picking up our actual tools. Even then, we want to use the tools as extensions of our fingers. No tool or material offers a magic wand, but practice and experimentation will help to build the skills you need to become a better sculptor.

In order to achieve an effective form and finish, you need to use the right tools and materials for the job. We use the following items to bring our otherworldly concepts to life.

WE USE MANY, MANY DIFFERENT MATERIALS

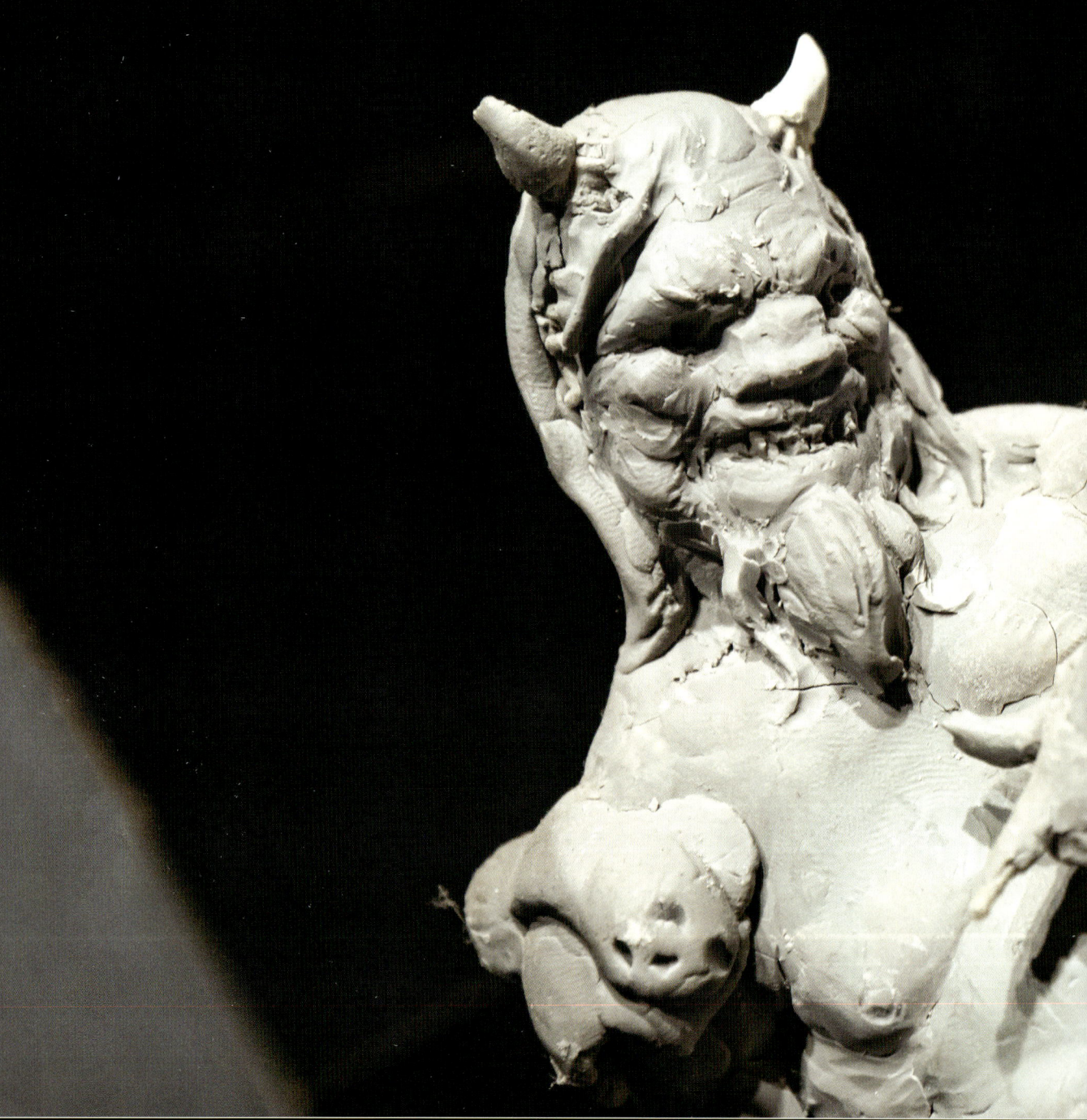

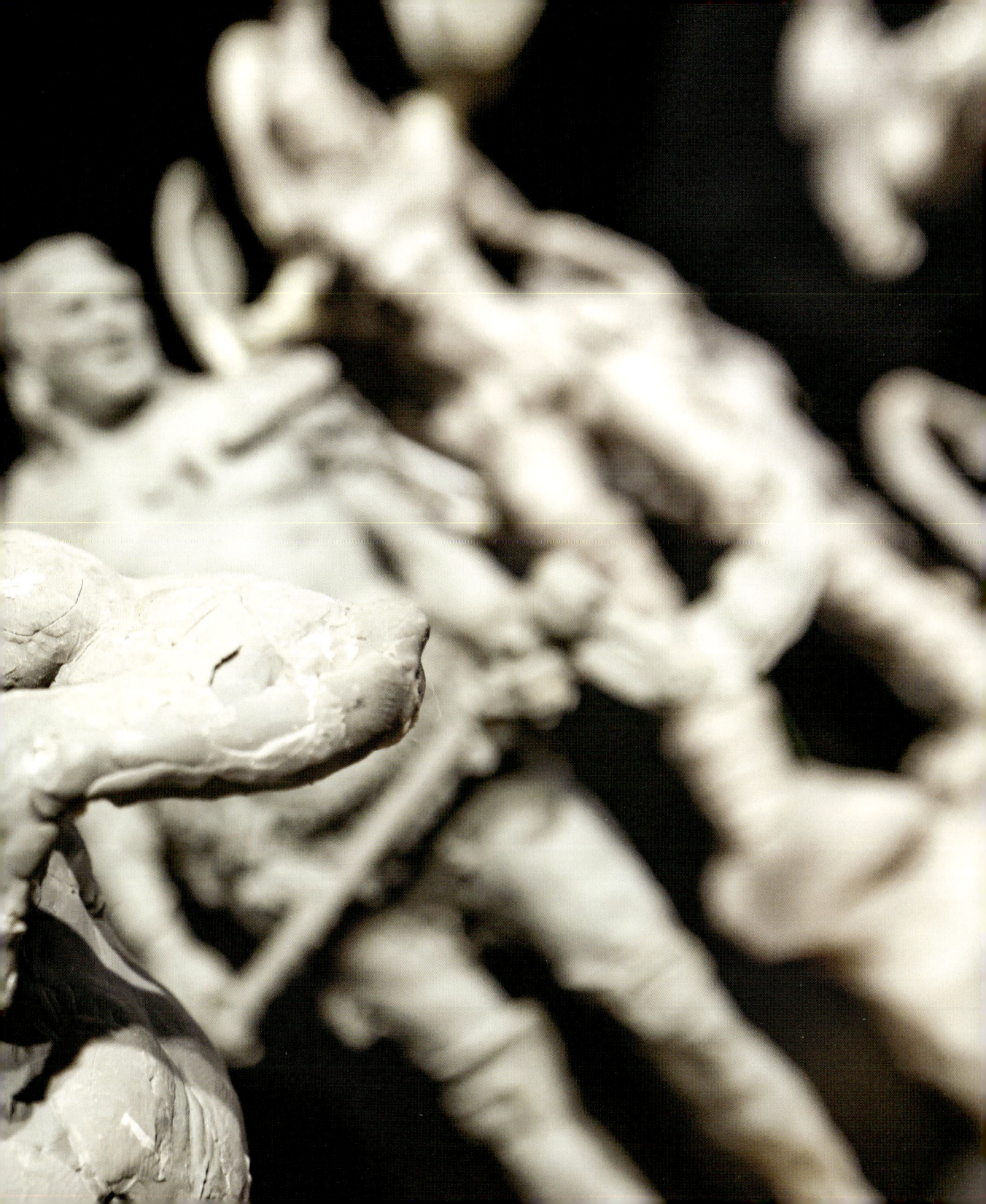

ARMATURE AND STRUCTURE

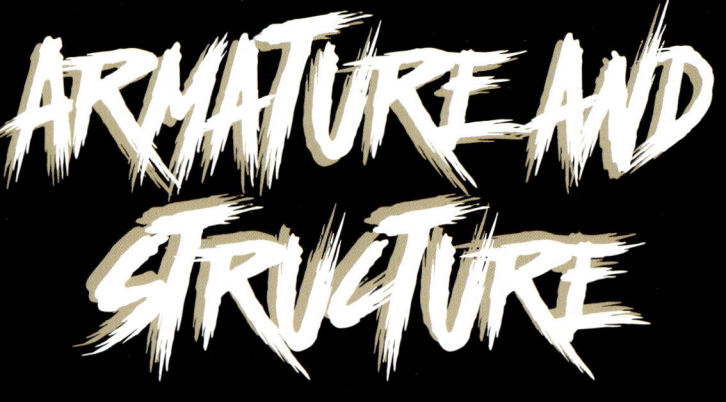

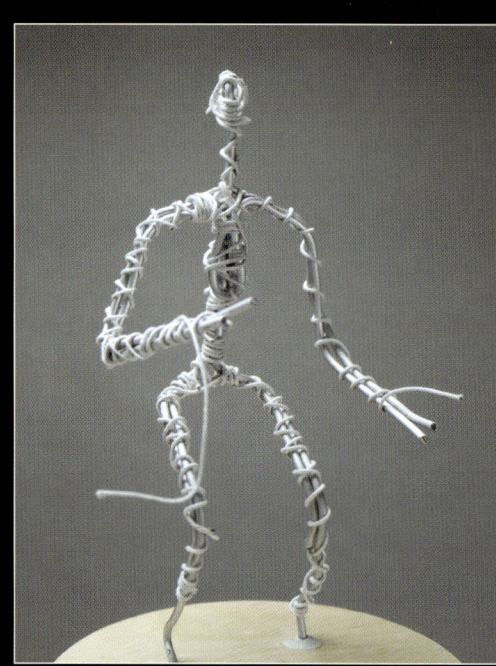

ALUMINUM ALLOY WIRE

This is the main structural component of the armatures we build. It is available in different "gauges" — the higher the gauge number, the thinner the wire. We do use thicker wire for bigger pieces, such as the 12-gauge (2 mm) wire shown. However, our favorite size is 3/16-gauge (8 mm) — it's strong enough to hold its position with clay weighing it down, yet still malleable enough to bend as needed.

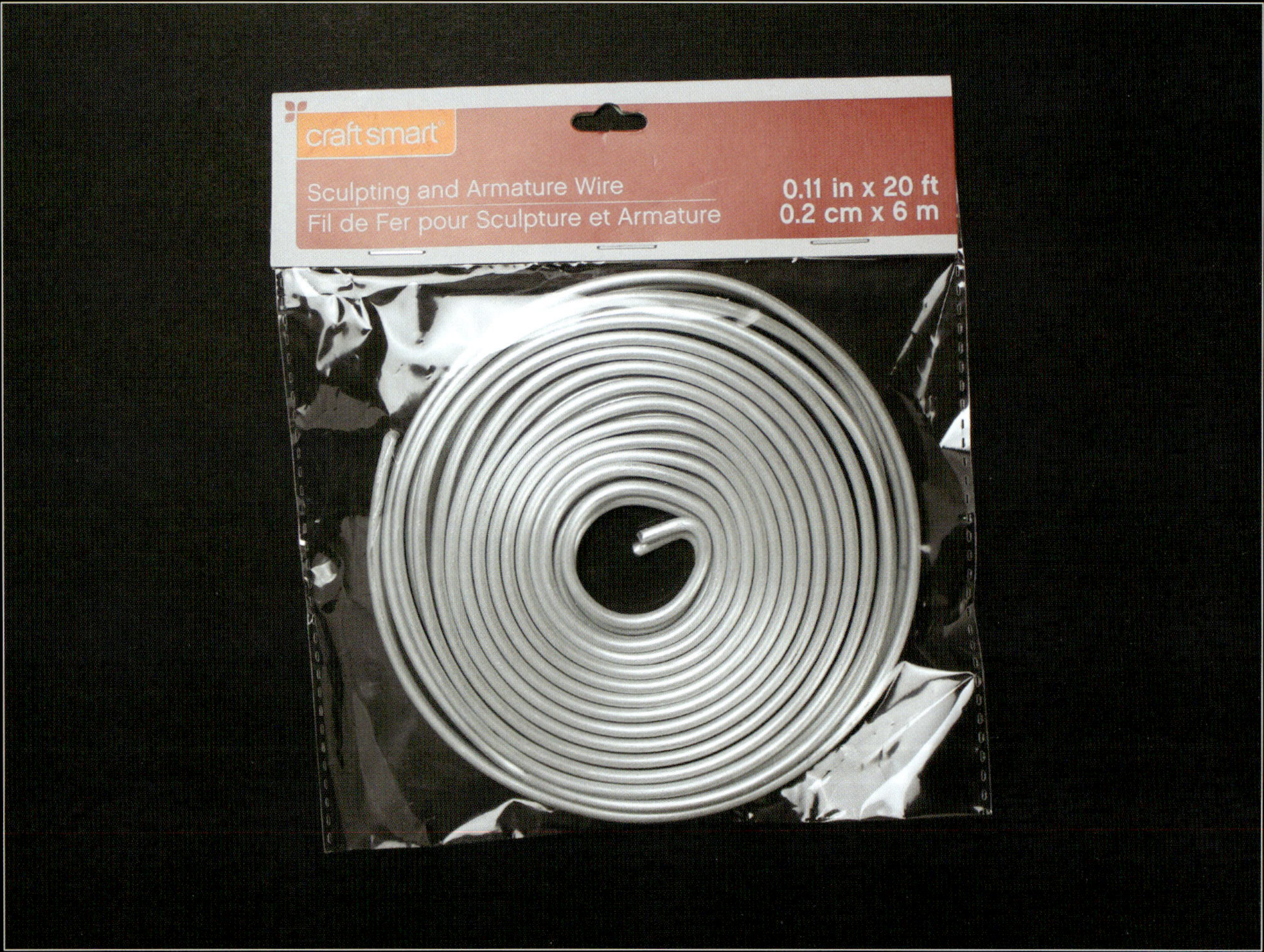

craft smart

Sculpting and Armature Wire
Fil de Fer pour Sculpture et Armature

0.11 in x 20 ft
0.2 cm x 6 m

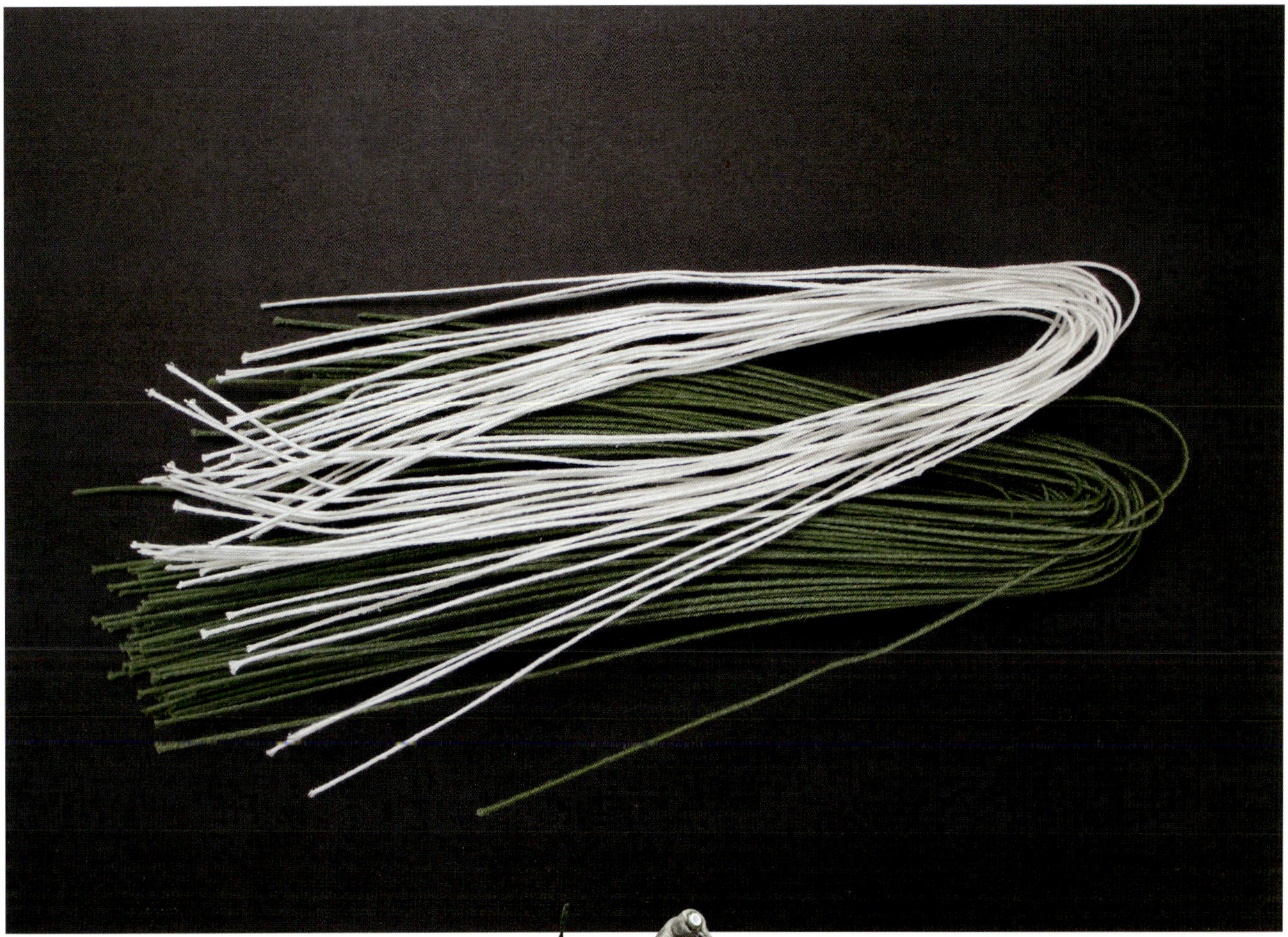

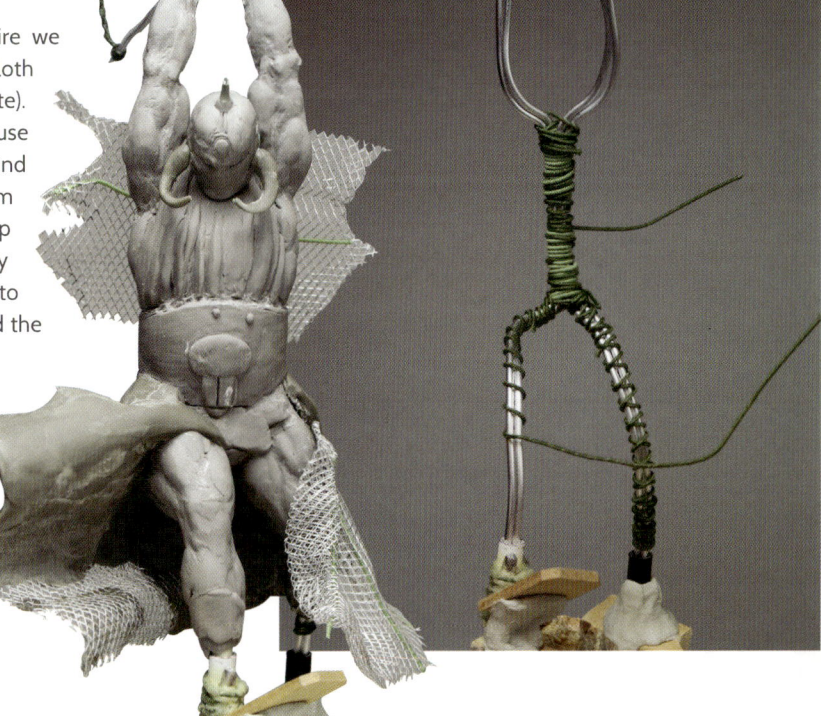

FLORAL WIRE

Predominantly used in floristry, the floral wire we use is a thin aluminum wire wrapped in a cloth cover (commonly available in green and white). It is also measured according to its gauge. We use it in a variety of ways, such as to wrap and bind the main pieces of armature wire (the aluminum alloy wire) together. We also twist floral wire up and down the length of the armature, especially along the arms and legs, in a crisscross pattern to give the clay traction when it is molded around the slick aluminum wire.

INTRICATE ARMATURE

Very thin floral wire is also great to use by itself as armature for fingers, horns, and all kinds of small features sticking out or "flying" from a sculpture.

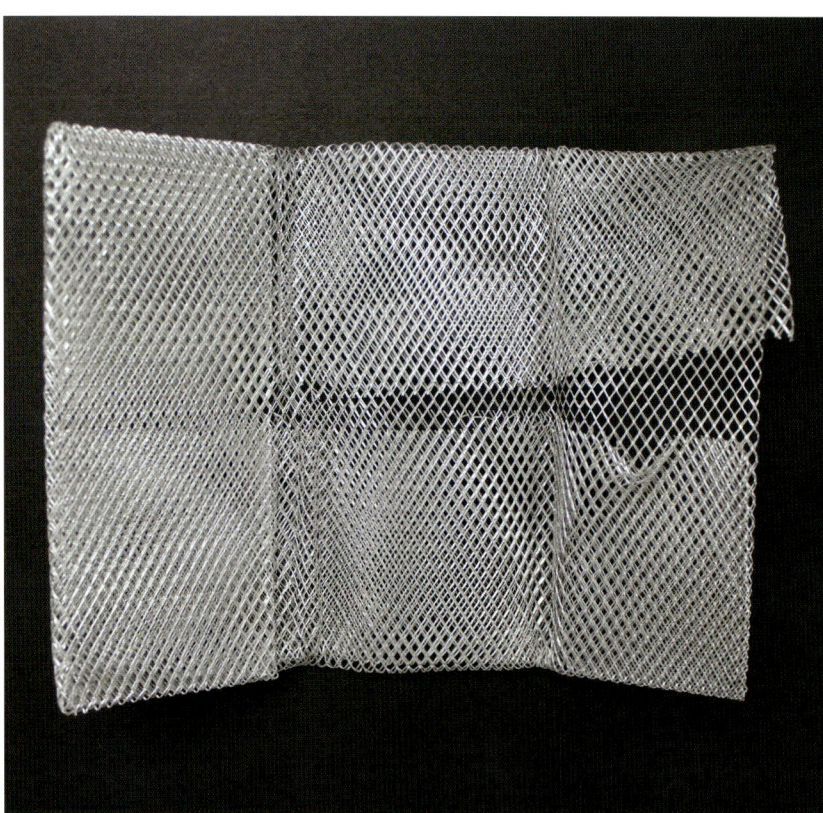

WIRE MESH

Wire armature mesh is a useful material for creating features such as thin wings, where the structure needs to be strong and rigid, but also thin and lightweight. It can be easily cut, and bends to almost any shape. It doesn't rust, so can be combined with wet materials such as papier-mâché, but is also oven-safe for use with Super Sculpey and other polymer clays. The more familiar we become with this stuff, the more we grow to love it!

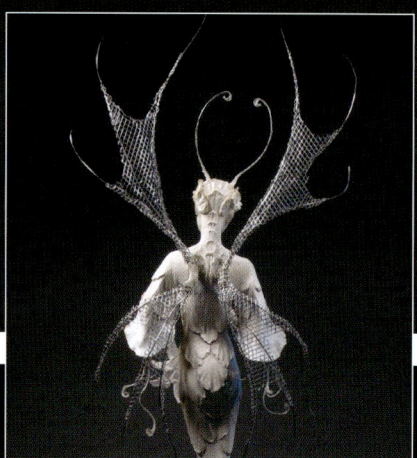

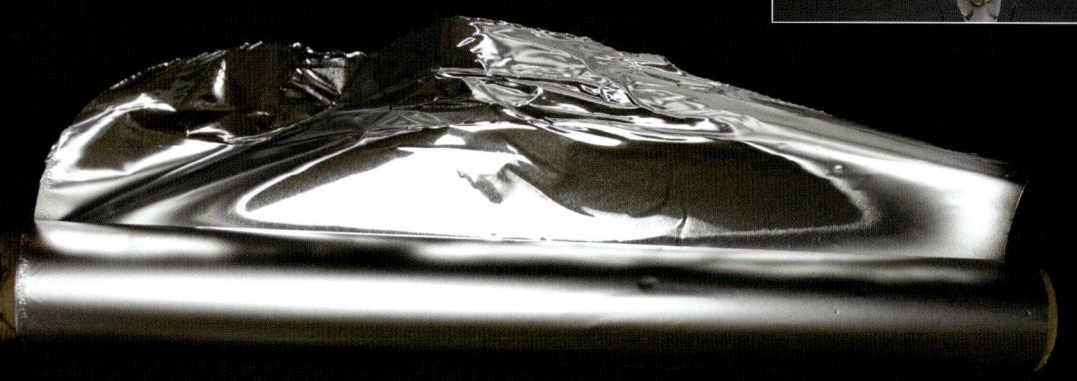

ALUMINUM FOIL

To add bulk to a sculpture without adding a lot of weight, we use aluminum foil. Readily available, it is an inexpensive way to build armature that is malleable and offers more organic forms. We use it to add bulk to the bodies of our muscular characters as well as to the scenery around them.

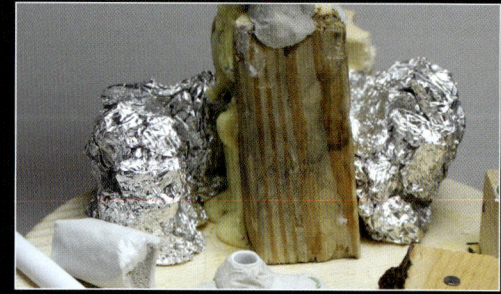

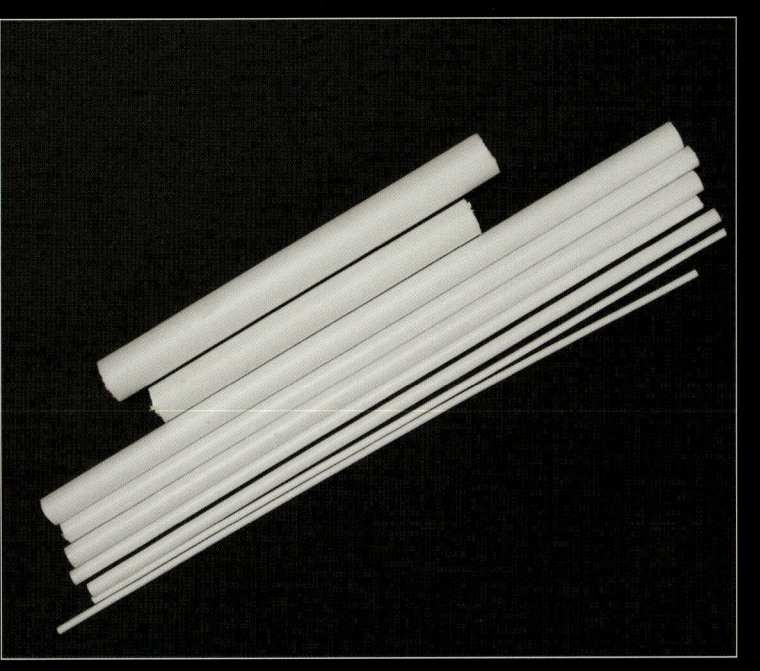

PLASTIC TUBING

Available in a range of different sizes, plastic tubing works perfectly for building our male/female connector rigs. This rig either anchors together two parts of the sculpt, or fixes the sculpt to the base. To ensure the rigs fit snugly for stability and strength, we always get two sizes. The first size of tube should be just slightly bigger than the second. Most of these are made of styrene and are easy to cut and manipulate.

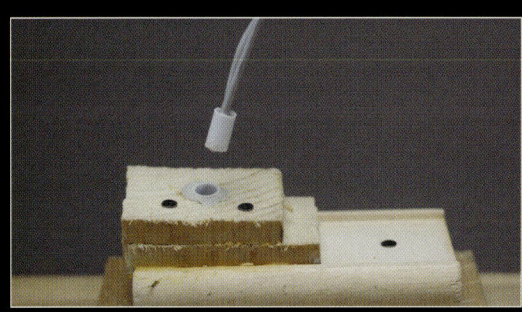

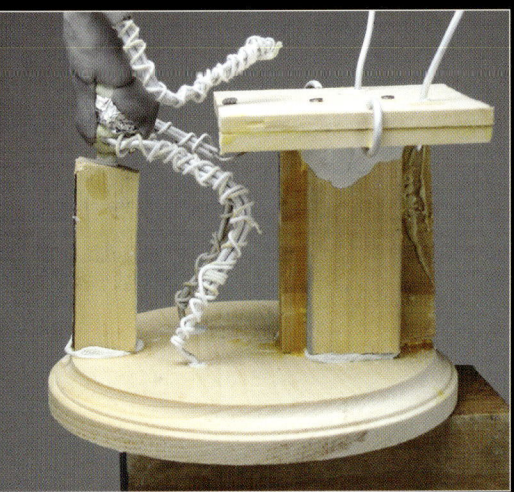

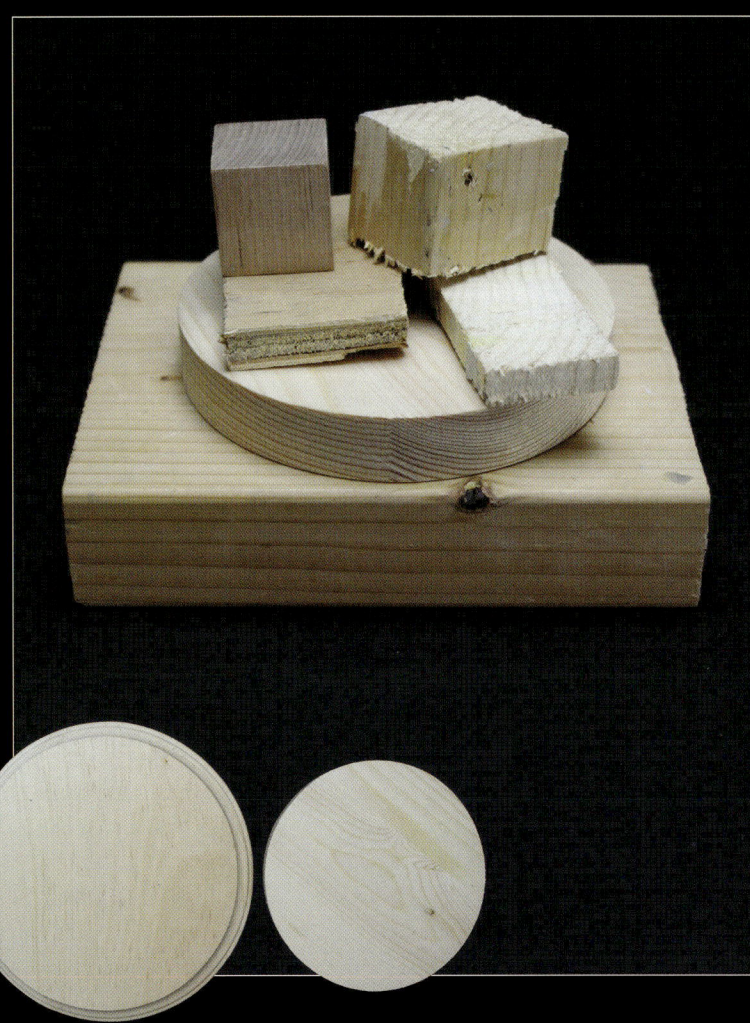

WOODEN BASES AND OFFCUTS

We often start a sculpture on a wooden base. Wooden bases can be found in a range of different shapes and sizes to suit the project. Sometimes we begin a sculpture on a circular base, for extra support and balance. We might then remove the sculpture from the base later in the process, but sometimes the wooden base is actually incorporated into the bottom of the sculpture, covered over completely with clay.

CLAY AND PUTTY

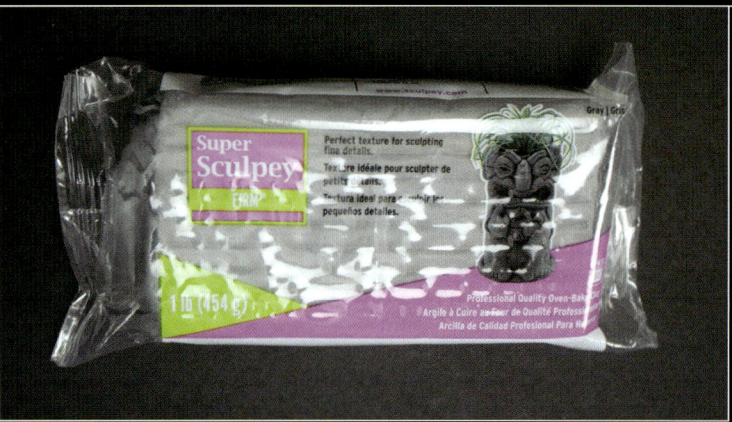

SUPER SCULPEY

This versatile ceramic-like polymer clay is available in different colors and levels of firmness and malleability. Once shaped, this clay oven-bakes to a shatter and chip resistant finish. We employ this clay for a variety of uses and different projects.

AVES APOXIE SCULPT

This wonderful clay is an epoxy resin compound, which means it is a two-part compound that needs to be mixed together to begin hardening. Once mixed, the hardening period takes two to three hours, during which time we place the clay onto the sculpt and manipulate it. By using this product, we can get a much finer level of detail than with plumber's putty. We use Aves Apoxie Sculpt when we need a piece to be very strong and durable.

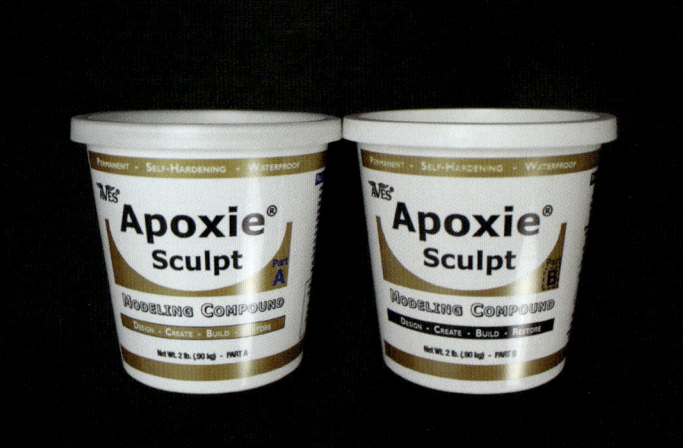

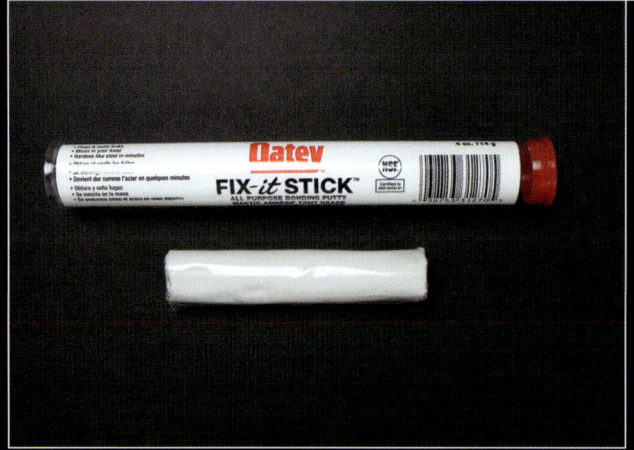

PLUMBER'S PUTTY

Another epoxy clay that begins to harden when two parts are combined. We use a lot of plumber's putty to build our sculptures. Although it can be sculpted, it doesn't hold detail or provide as neat a finish as Aves Apoxie Sculpt. However, we do like to use it on strategic areas of the armature to strengthen points of the skeleton that we believe will be stressed by the weight of the clay. The advantage of plumber's putty (or disadvantage, depending on your point of view) is that it hardens very quickly once mixed together, which means that it is unworkable and rigid in two to three minutes. As a result, you need to have a good idea of what to do with it once mixed!

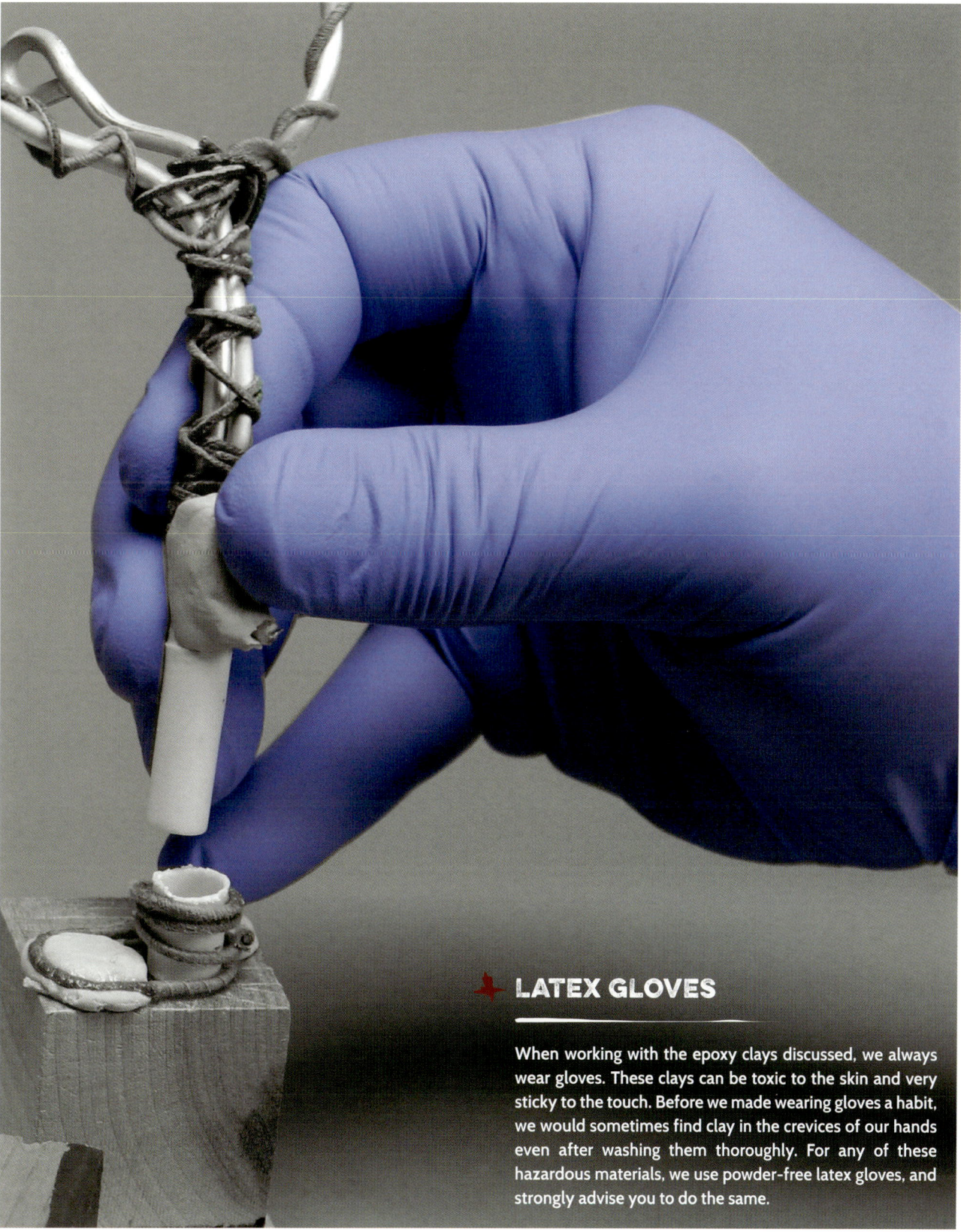

✦ LATEX GLOVES

When working with the epoxy clays discussed, we always wear gloves. These clays can be toxic to the skin and very sticky to the touch. Before we made wearing gloves a habit, we would sometimes find clay in the crevices of our hands even after washing them thoroughly. For any of these hazardous materials, we use powder-free latex gloves, and strongly advise you to do the same.

GLUE AND SEALANT

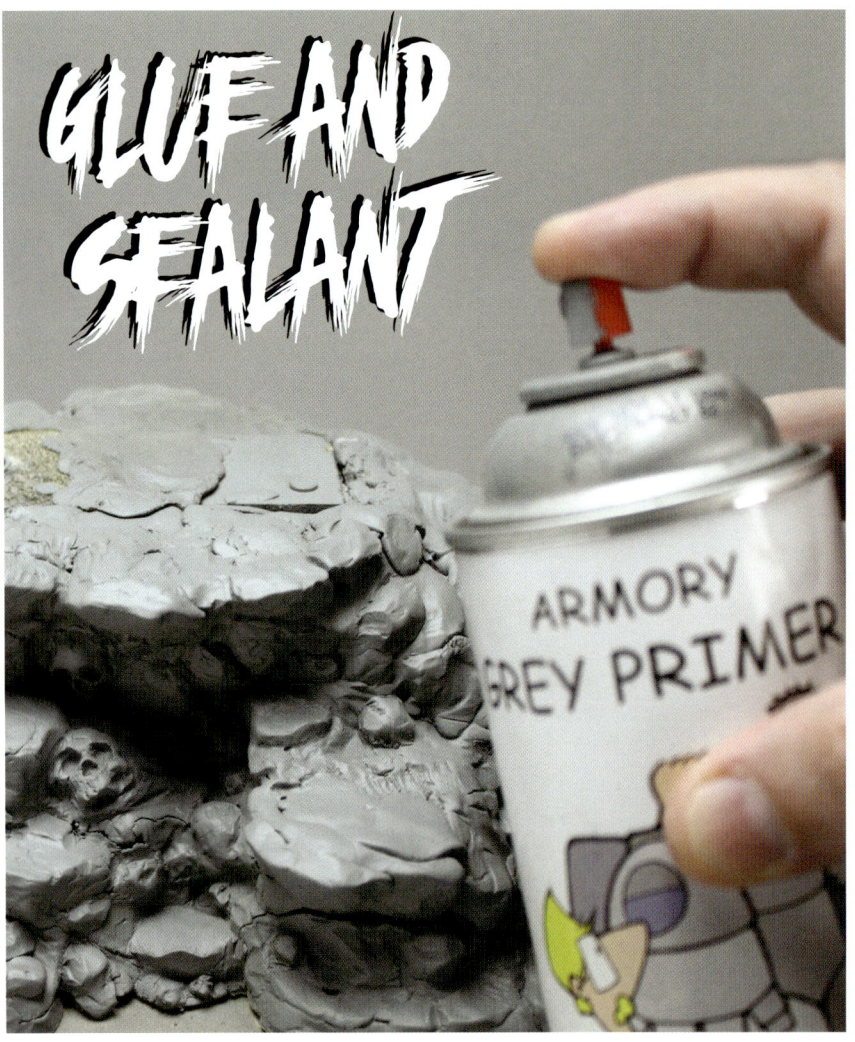

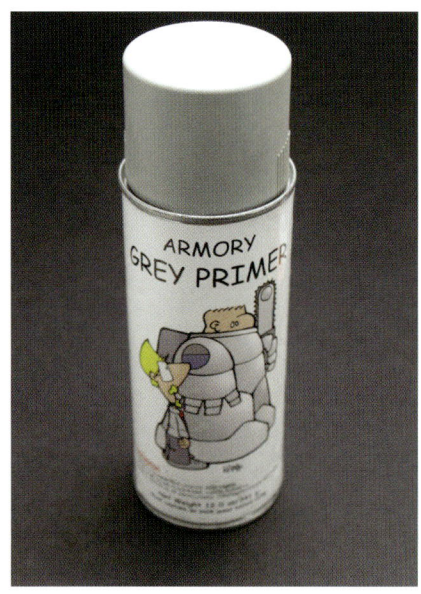

PRIMER SPRAY PAINT

After the sculpting phase of our process, once the piece is baked and sanded, we use a spray paint primer to create a consistent grey color on the surface of the sculpture and unify the sculpted elements. This helps us to see clearly what we call the "true surface," allowing us to see the piece as a whole again, and it can inform us if small repairs to nicks, tool marks, or other imperfections need to be made.

SUPER GLUE

We couldn't complete a sculpture without multiple tubes of our trusty super glue! We always use it with floral wire, including when we glue the floral wire to the main aluminum armature wire to bind the entire skeletal framework in place. We also drench the areas where we have crisscrossed the floral wire around the armature for added rigidity.

Additionally, super glue can be used to attach fingers, horns, and other protuberances to the base armature. After the piece is baked, we repair micro-cracks and small breaks with super glue (see page 214 for a demonstration). We also apply it when "keying" a piece — cutting the sculpt into smaller pieces for molding. Male/female tube parts can also be set in place with super glue.

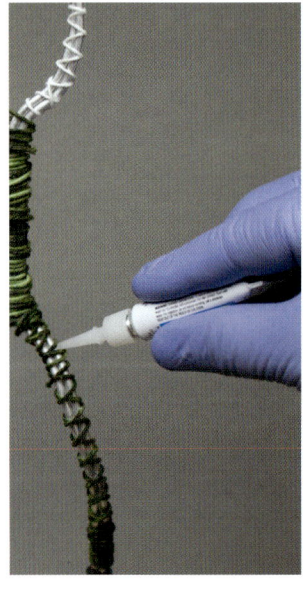

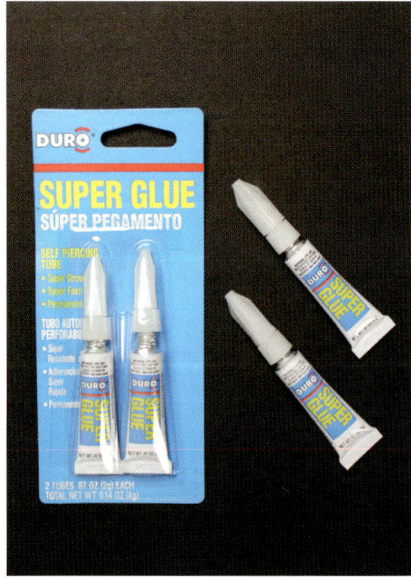

MOD PODGE

This all-in-one glue and sealant dries clear, which comes in handy toward the end of our process. We apply it strategically to baked sculptures to disguise imperfections. Mod Podge is self-leveling, so it will find its own level, thus creating a more uniform surface.

APPLY IT STRATEGICALLY TO BAKED SCULPTURES TO DISGUISE IMPERFECTIONS

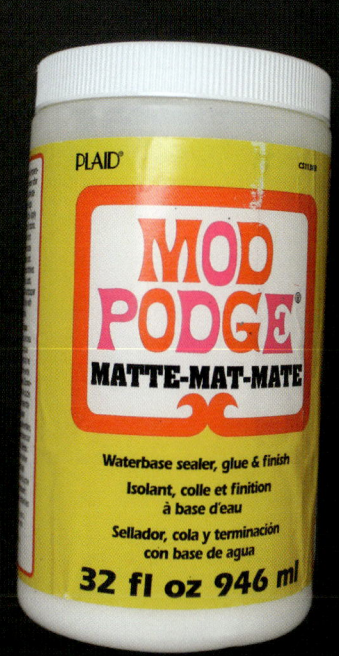

SOLVENTS

Toward the end of the sculpting process, a rubbing alcohol can be worked into the surfaces of the piece to smooth and refine the forms. 91% isopropyl alcohol is suitable for most polymer clays and, when applied with brushes, can be used to clean away imperfections such as fingerprints, tool marks, or leftover crumbs of clay.

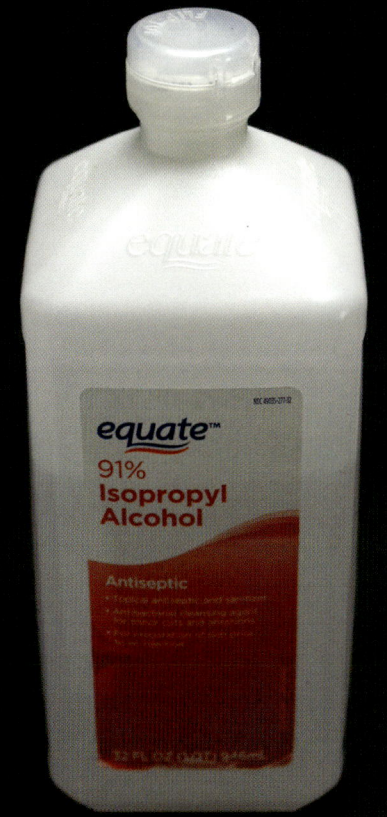

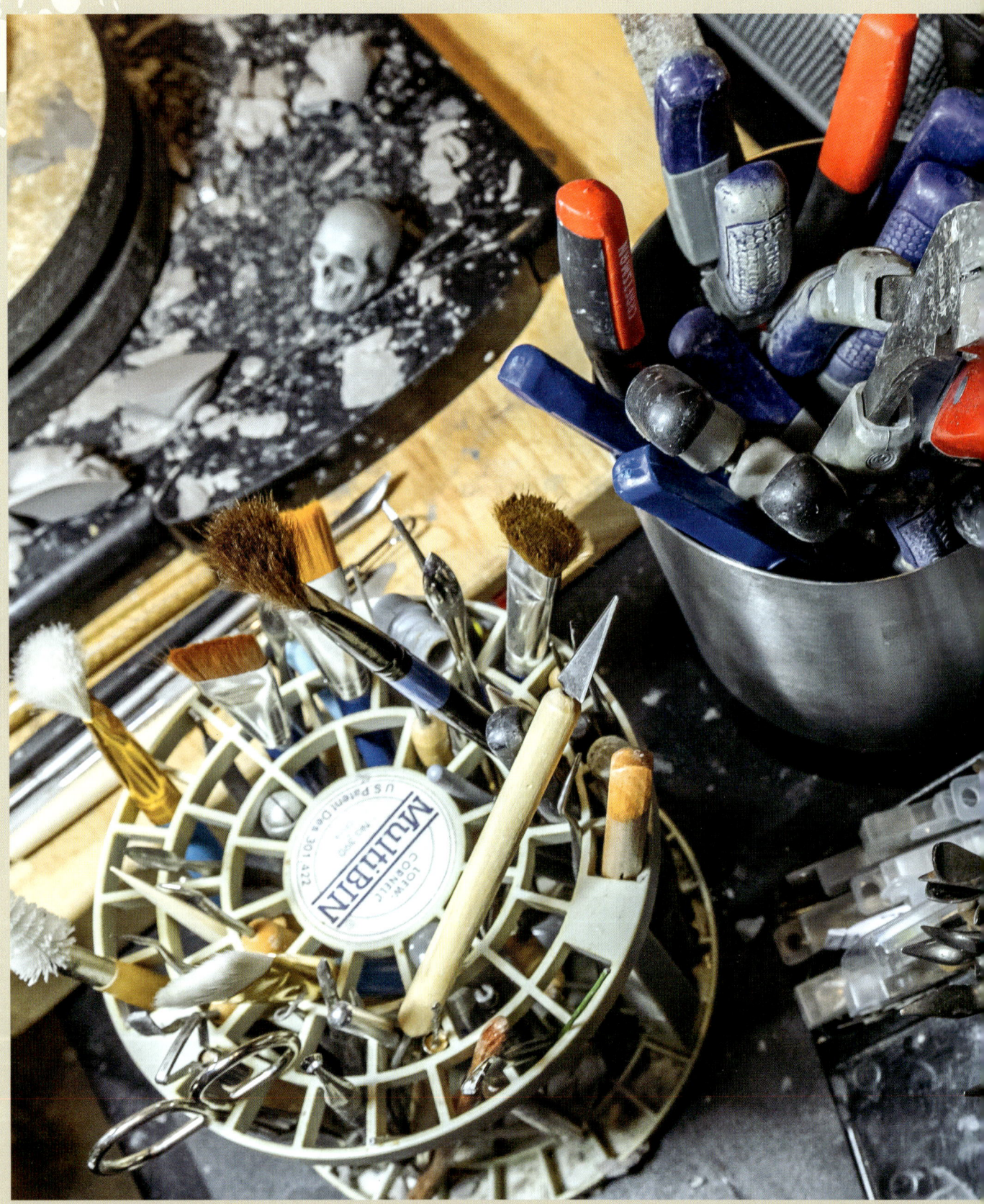

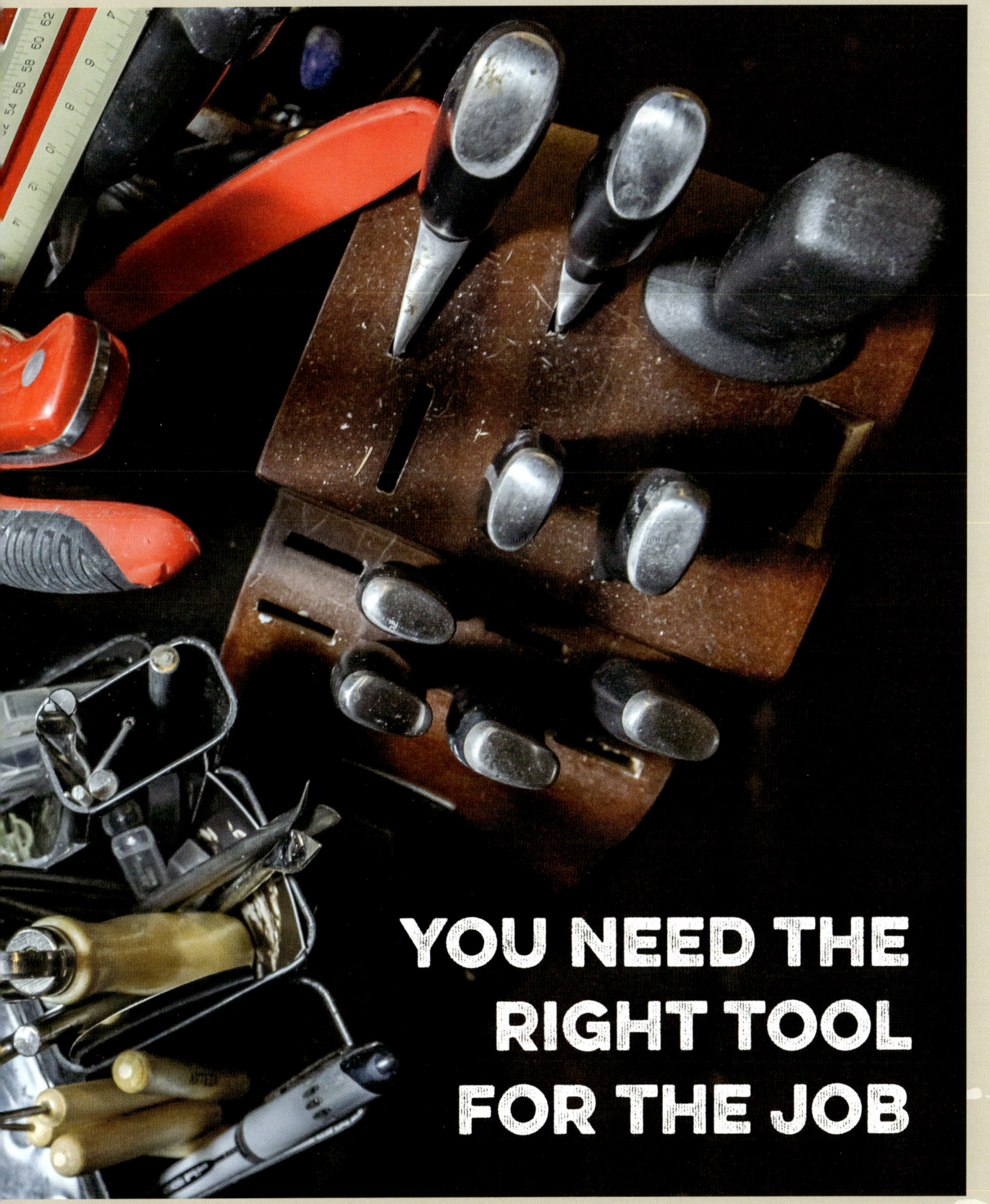

YOU NEED THE RIGHT TOOL FOR THE JOB

LOOP TOOLS

We use loop tools to create indentations and concave shapes of all kinds in the sculpting material. We use the tools to essentially pull away material to create the negative space around the sculpture. We don't use this technique as much as some sculptors do. Those sculptors are known as "rakers," whereas we are "pushers," or additive sculptors, because we work by taking away very little material once it is placed onto the sculpture.

WE ARE "PUSHERS," OR ADDITIVE SCULPTORS, BECAUSE WE WORK BY TAKING AWAY VERY LITTLE MATERIAL

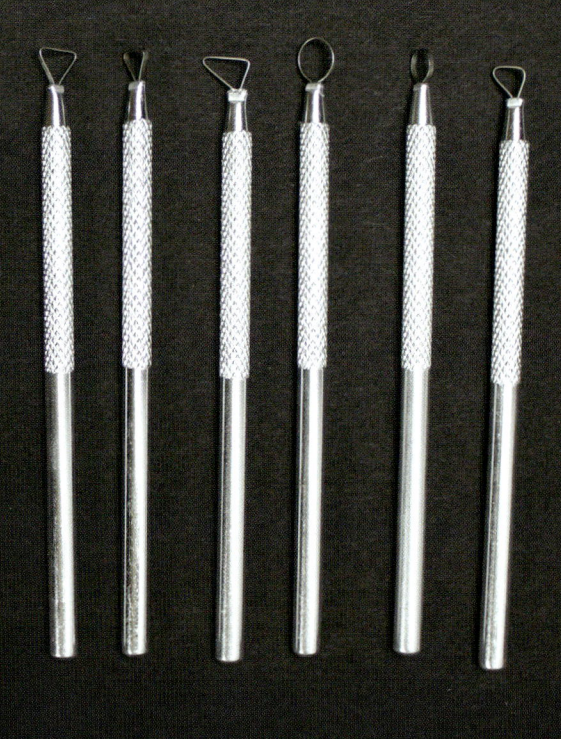

BALL TOOLS

These tools have balls on either end and are perfect for creating small, concave impressions in the clay, for instance, eye sockets for a character's eyes. They also help in keeping the indentations symmetrical when needed. This is especially useful when working on hard-to-reach areas. As mentioned previously, we are more of the "additive" types of sculptors, so we don't use the ball tools as much as some, but we do use them enough that we have dozens of them lying around our studio!

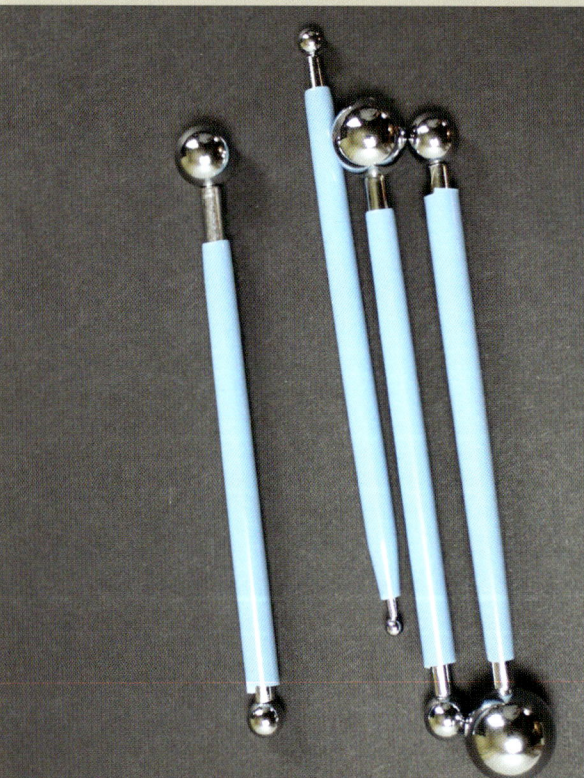

HOBBY KNIFE OR X-ACTO KNIFE

It would be difficult to overstate how much we use hobby knives during our process. From cutting our clay into smaller bits to carving out chunks of baked clay at the end of the process, these blades are constantly in our hands. We've cut our hands a few more times than we'd like to admit, but still, when you see a finished piece, it's definitely worth it!

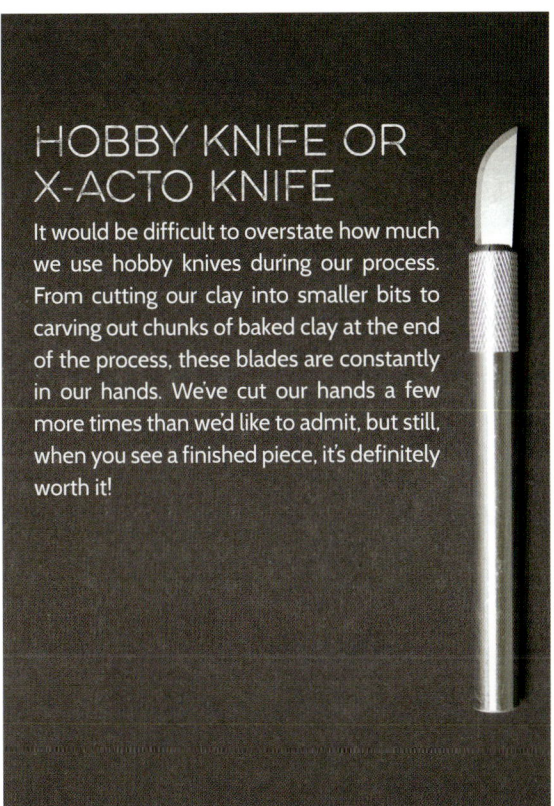

DREMEL ROTARY TOOL AND ACCESSORIES

We aren't alone when recommending that you invest in a rotary tool; so many of our friends and peers in the business swear by them too! A Dremel tool can make the life of a sculptor so much easier. With the addition of a variety of different bits, these tools can do it all: cutting into baked or hardened clay, grinding, chiseling, sanding, and more. They are definitely worth the investment.

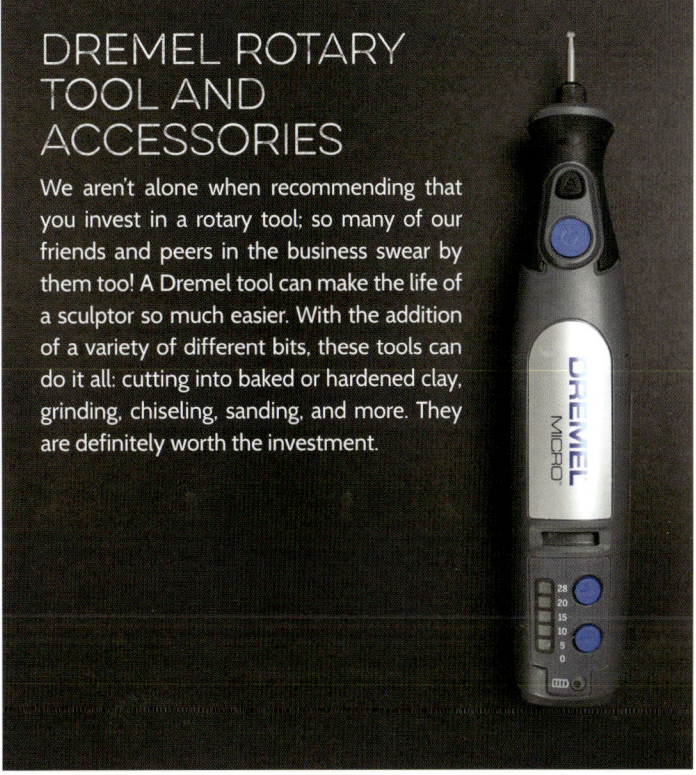

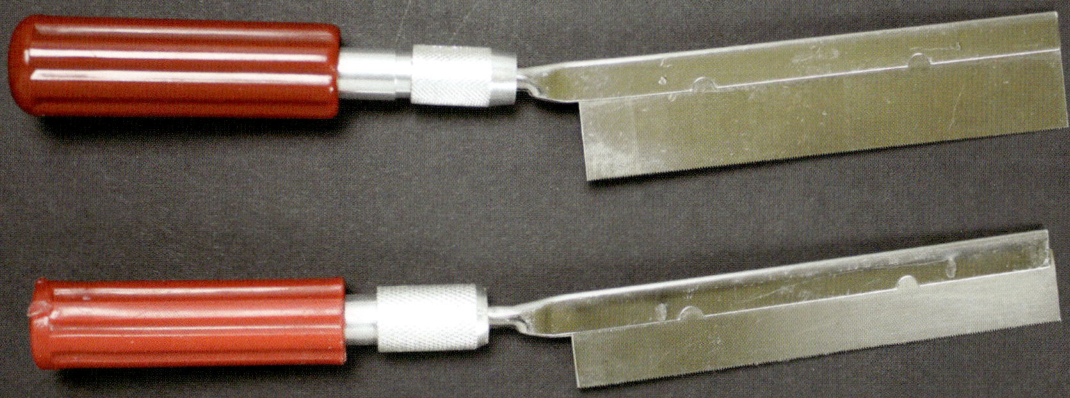

X-ACTO SAW

Small X-Acto saws are great for cutting into all manner of materials, including wood, baked clay, and even some soft metal wires.

SMALL HAND SAW

This small handheld saw is great for cutting specific lengths of plastic tubing, which we use to create our male/female connections to allow parts of our sculptures to be removable.

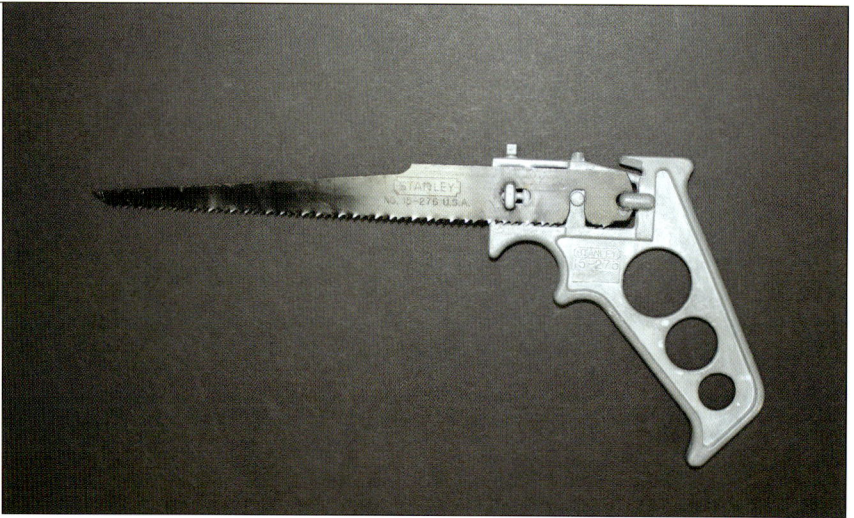

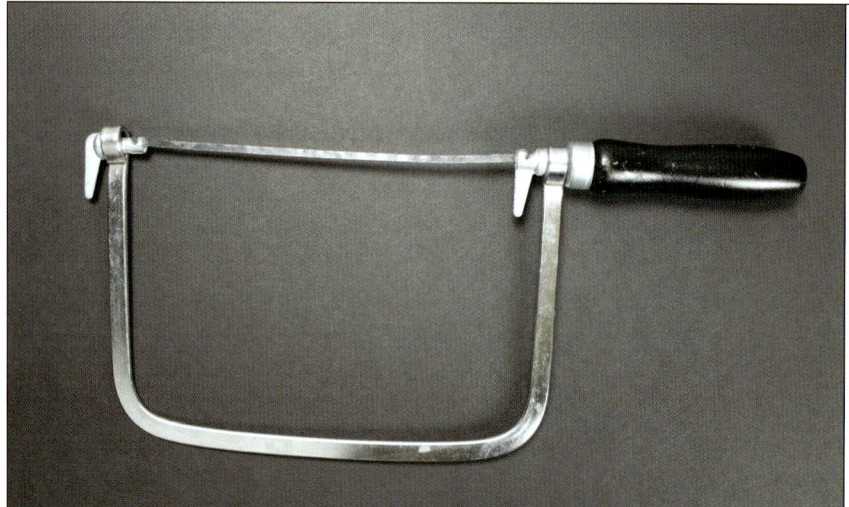

JEWELER'S SAW

We use this fine-bladed saw when cutting away from the baked sculpture. If we decide an arm needs to come off for any reason, we can simply cut through the baked clay, only really destroying a little bit more than the width of the blade. It can also cut neatly through the soft aluminum alloy armature in the middle of the sculpture.

HEAT GUN

Our trusty heat gun is very useful when we need to bake and set a sculpture. While sculpting, we often find that we want to bake just a small part of a sculpture to preserve it while leaving the rest of the sculpt soft and workable. See page 218 for more details on this process. Remember it is always better to do too little with a heat gun, because doing too much can be disastrous for the sculpture. Blackening and bubbling in polymer clay can and does happen very quickly, so it's best to work slowly and steadily.

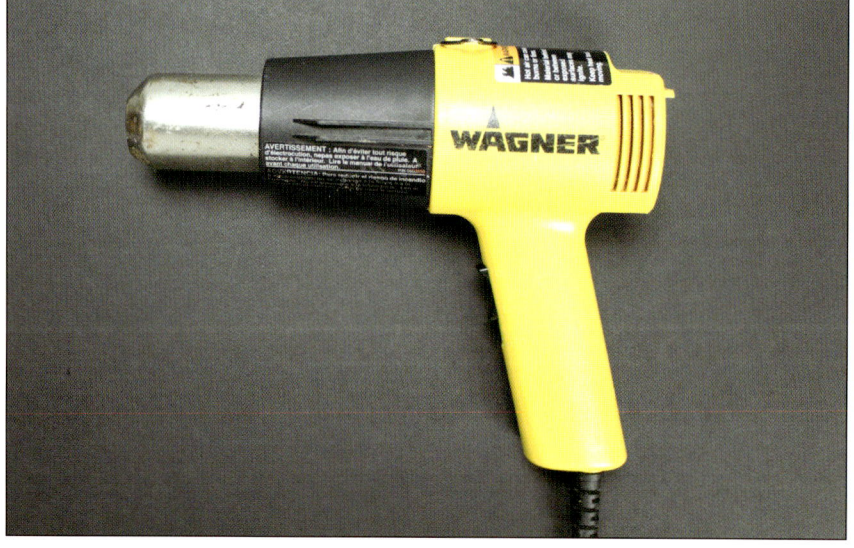

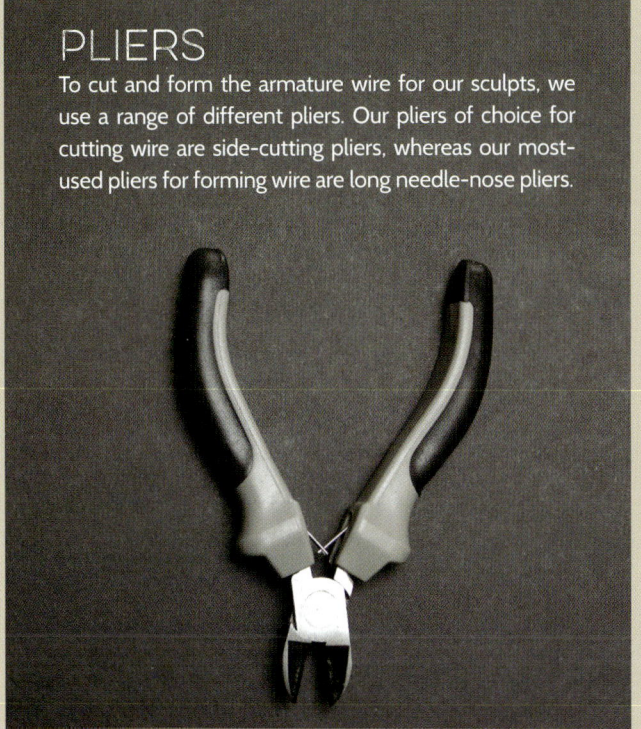

PLIERS

To cut and form the armature wire for our sculpts, we use a range of different pliers. Our pliers of choice for cutting wire are side-cutting pliers, whereas our most-used pliers for forming wire are long needle-nose pliers.

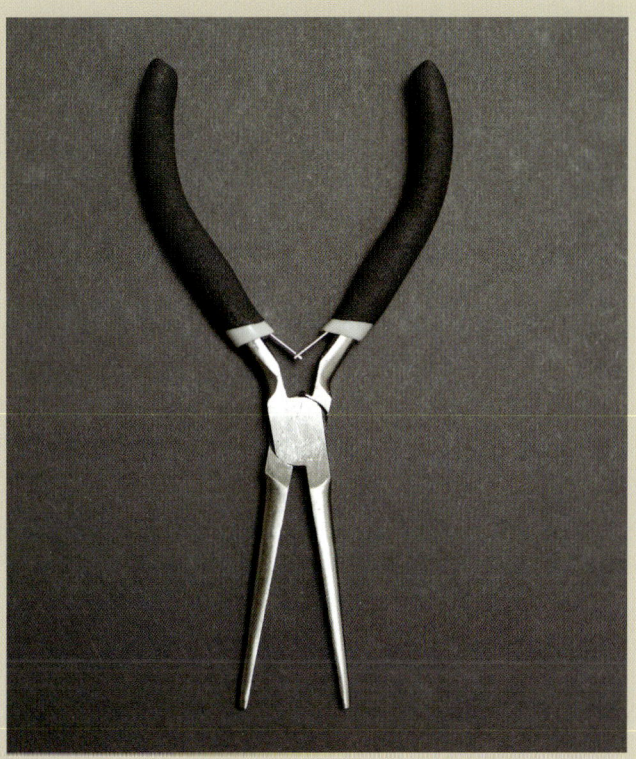

ALWAYS WORK THROUGH THE SANDING GRADES FROM COARSE TO FINE

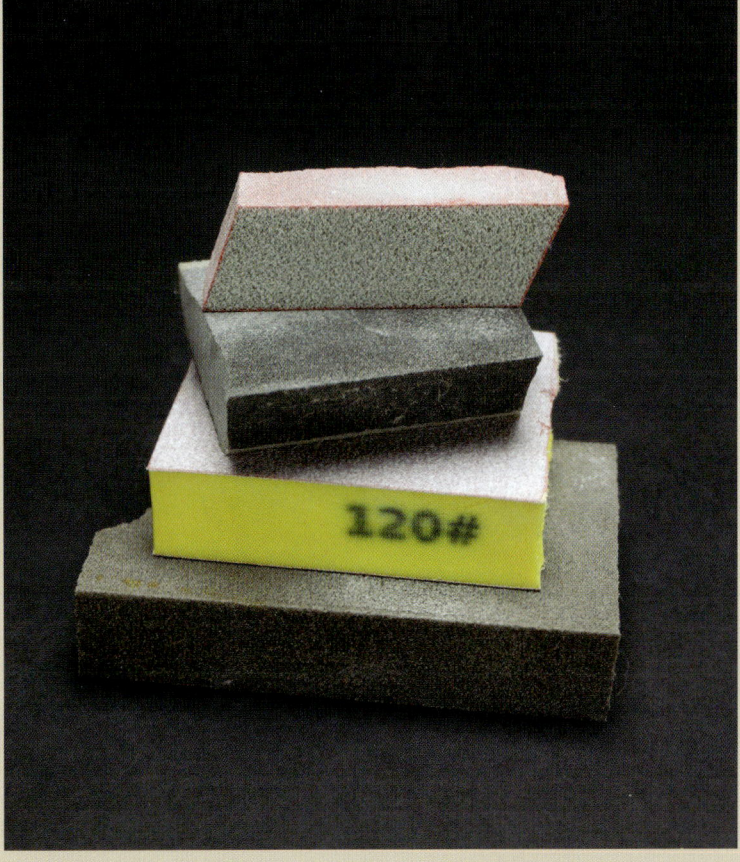

120#

SANDING SPONGES

Our sanding process was drastically improved when we discovered the existence of this type of sanding sponge. You can find these at any hardware store, in different grades of grit, and they are incredibly useful for getting into the hard-to-reach areas of your piece. We often cut these sponges up into smaller shapes with varying interesting angles and then attach the pieces to wooden sticks to create a range of bespoke sanding tools. Remember to always work through the sanding grades from coarse to fine. We often dip these sponges in water and then use them to sand, a process called "wet-sanding" that reduces the scratches in the clay caused by the sandpaper's surface.

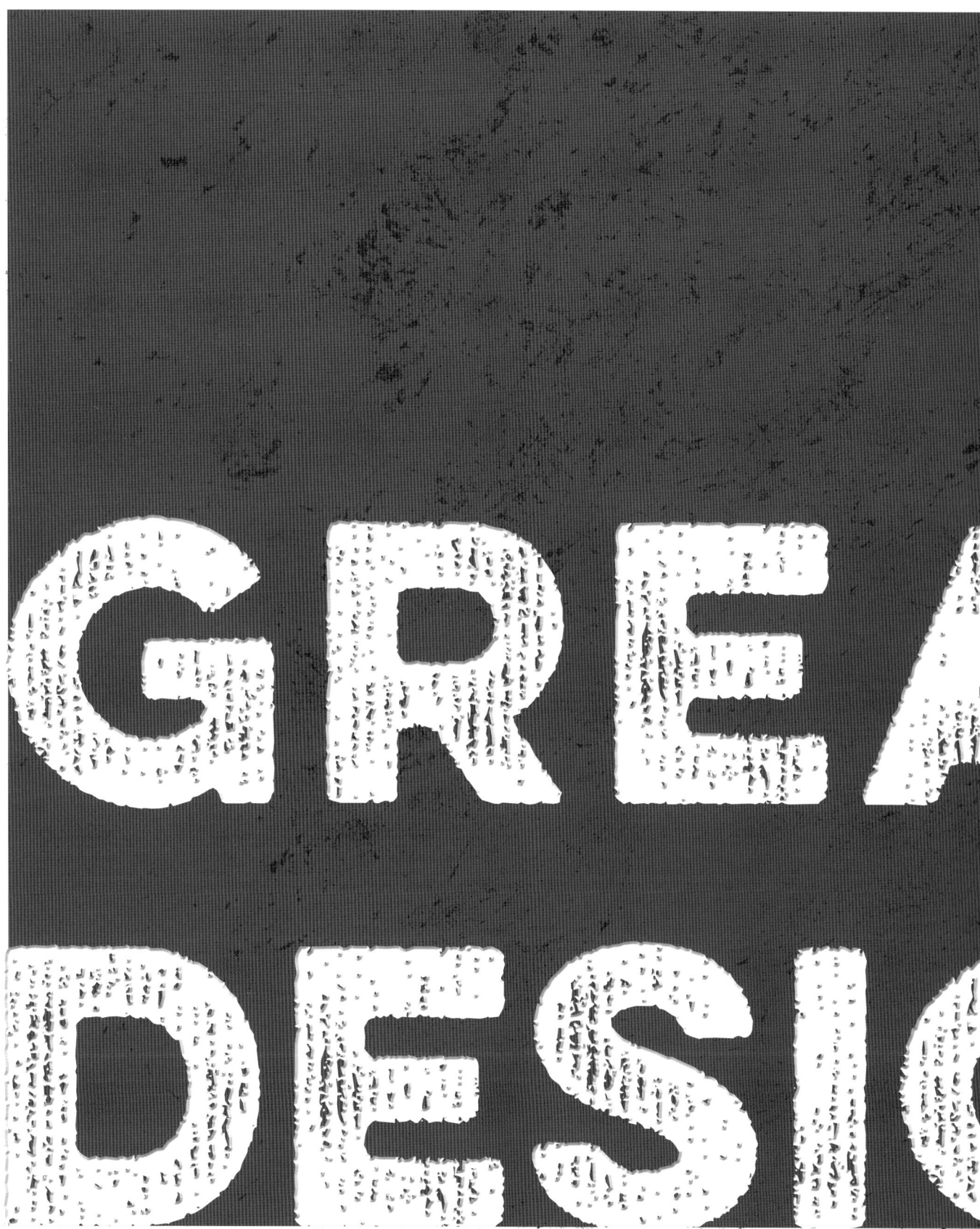

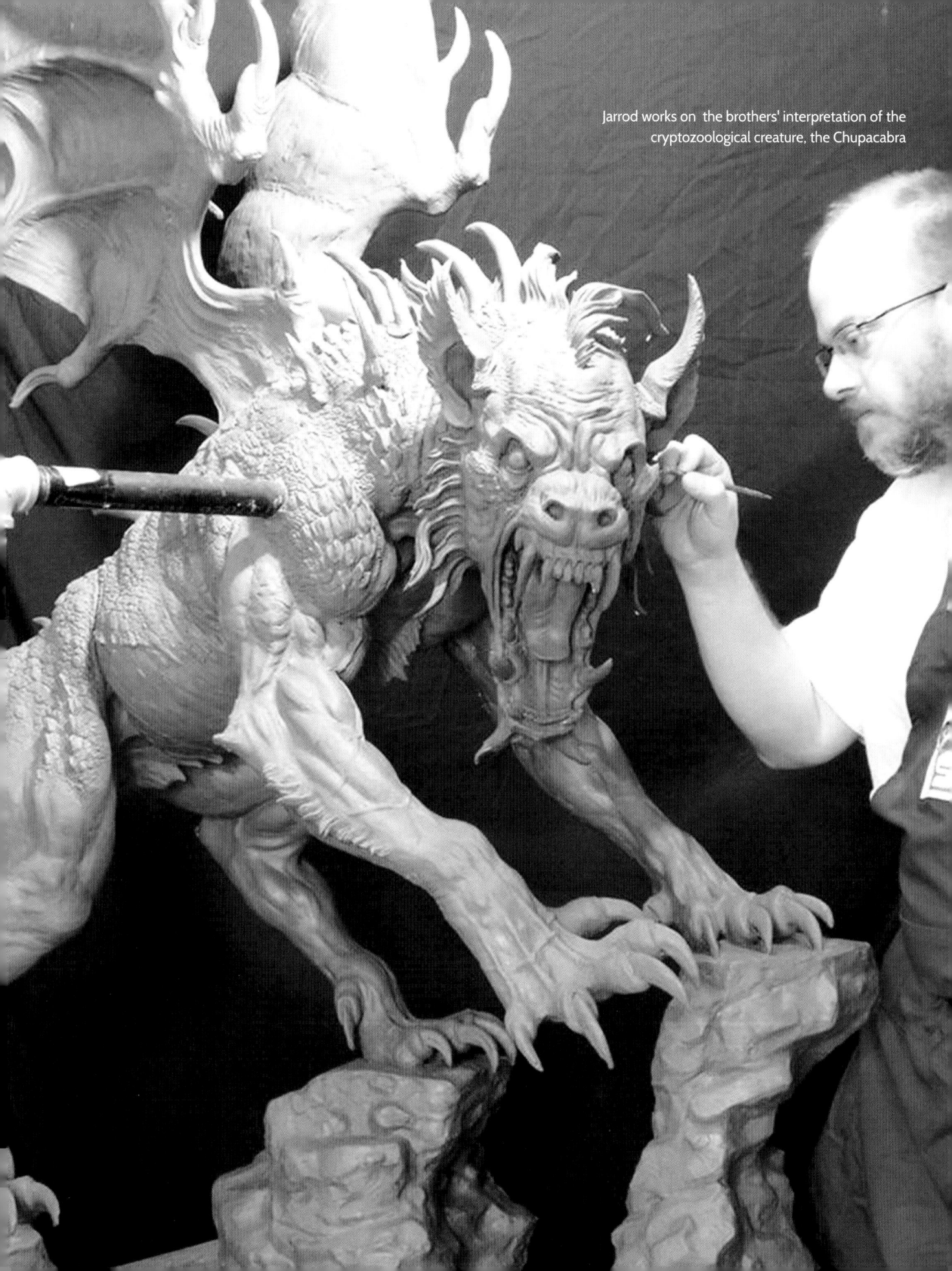

Jarrod works on the brothers' interpretation of the cryptozoological creature, the Chupacabra

SCULPTURAL SKETCHING

Precision and exactitude are hallmarks of the industry we work in, the collectible statue field, but we have never felt comfortable working with those goals in mind. We encourage sculptors at every level to "loosen up." Although sculpting extraordinarily cleanly is not our strong suit as artists, it is also a conscious choice. When sculpting for ourselves, we always turn in the direction of rougher, looser shapes because we find the less finished look can imbue a kind of raw, organic energy and power into a sculpture. We believe these qualities are sometimes lacking in other, very refined sculptures on the market — and never has that been truer than with the advent of digital sculpting. It is both our natural inclination and our personal aesthetic to keep our work rougher and looser. This idea of "keeping it loose" while sculpting can be creatively freeing. When sculpting personal work, don't worry so much about the strictures and constraints of the professional sculpting world, and think instead of the basic shapes and forms needed to achieve the story you are trying to tell.

THE SUPPORT OF OTHER ARTISTS HAS INSPIRED IN US A DETERMINATION TO CONTINUE WORKING IN A STYLE THAT FEELS RIGHT FOR US

The reason that our looser, rougher sculptures work is that form is everything. If the basic form in the clay is wrong, then nothing about the piece can be right, no matter the level of amazing detail added afterward, or how clean your eventual finish on the piece turns out to be. Solid forms, composition, balance, and silhouette are absolute musts in a sculpture. Yes, detail is important, but that comes later. First, perfect the form and the sculpture's sense of balance and weight, while making sure that the pose and composition work from every angle, and not just the key "money shot" (discover more about this on page 34).

When we add detail, we often target spots on the sculpture — areas where detail would be beneficial and areas where little or no detail is required. We do this in an attempt to guide the viewer's eye to where we want it to linger, where we think the important parts of the piece are. We are storytelling in clay, after all. So, if we believe the key to the story is the sword in the character's hand and the look on his face, then those areas may get more of our attention. Other areas, where we believe attention is not as crucial, we choose to leave relatively vague or barren of interest. The idea of detailing a piece uniformly all over is a bit foreign to us. We also believe that a roughly hewn piece can create in the observer a sense that the sculptor just got up and walked away from the piece. The sculpture is an ongoing concern — a living, breathing work of art. Not all collectors have always enjoyed our more organic style, but we've been very fortunate that the people who love it the most seem to be other artists. The support of other artists has inspired in us a determination to continue working in a style that feels right for us.

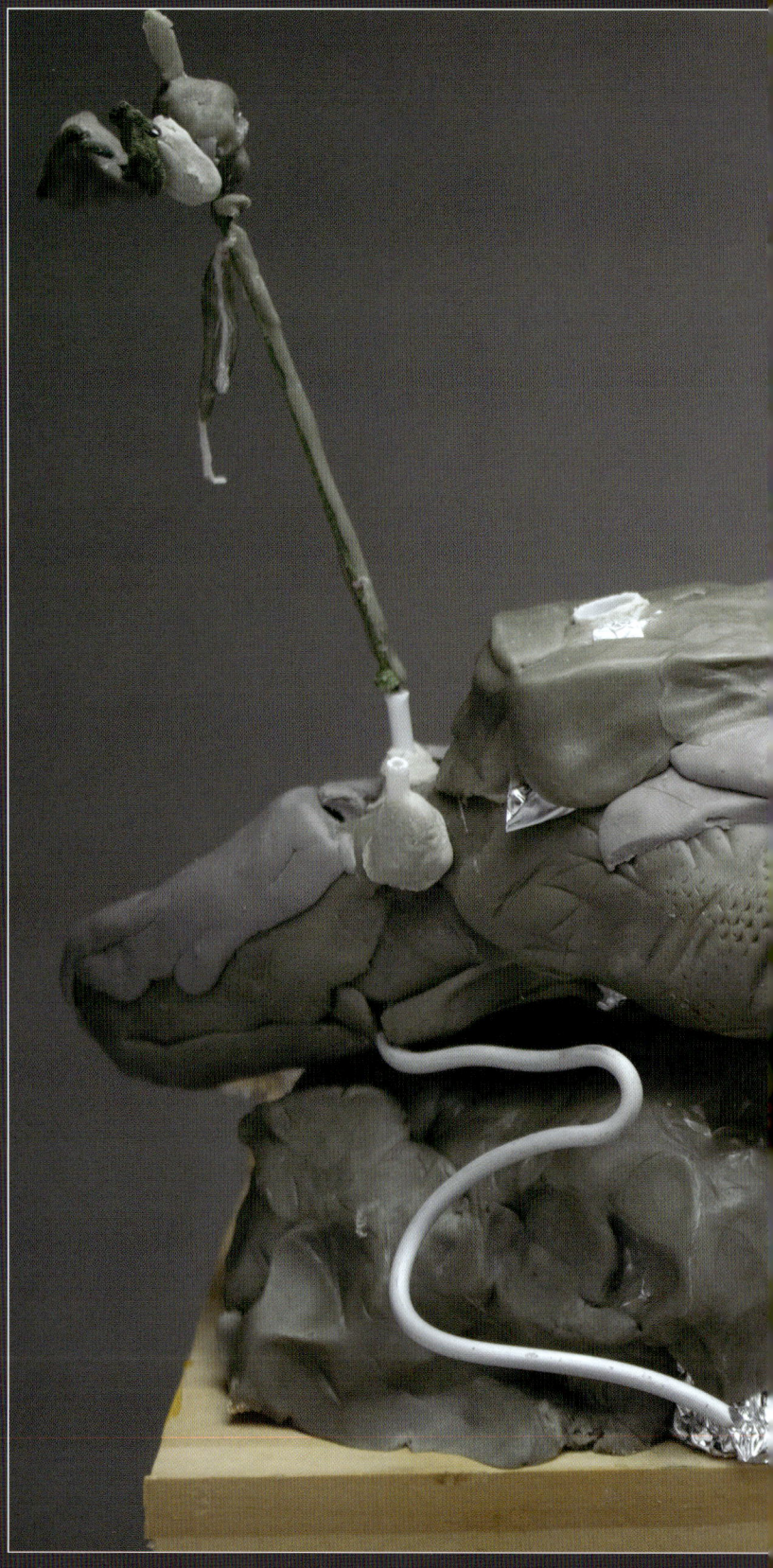

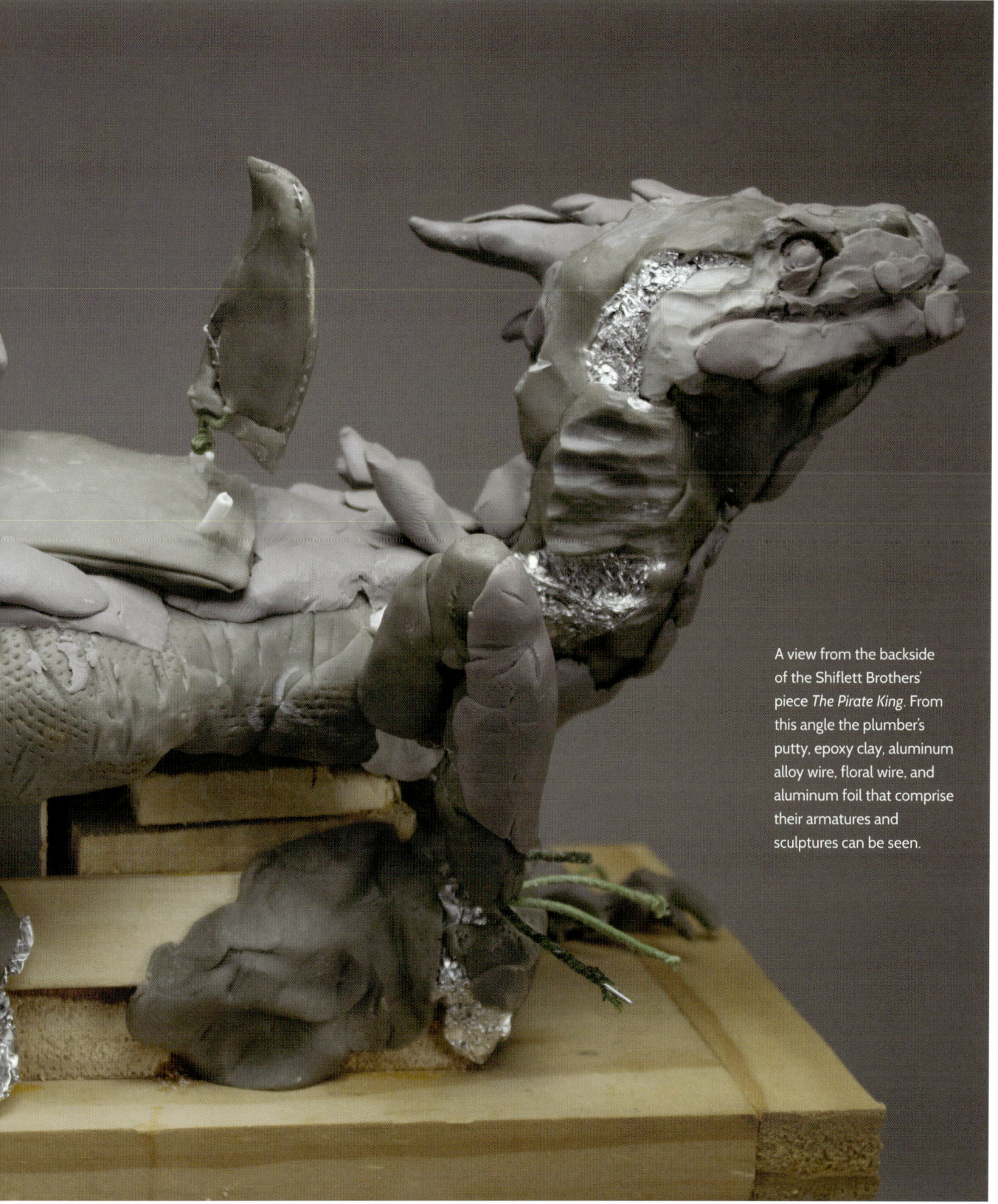

A view from the backside of the Shiflett Brothers' piece *The Pirate King*. From this angle the plumber's putty, epoxy clay, aluminum alloy wire, floral wire, and aluminum foil that comprise their armatures and sculptures can be seen.

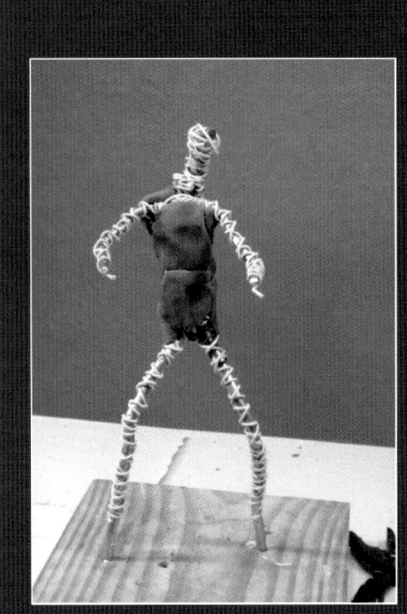

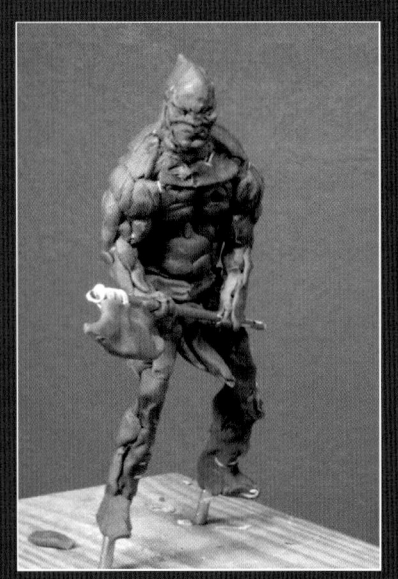

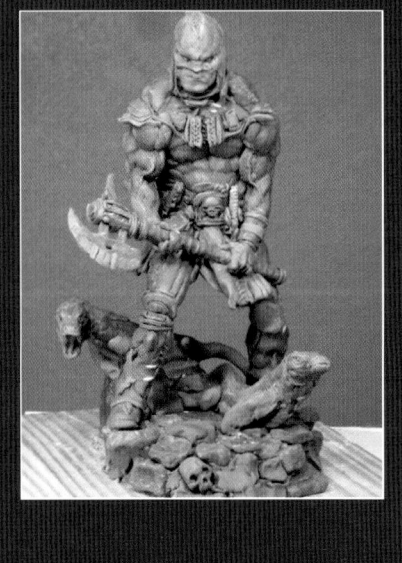

All of this isn't to say that we don't enjoy very finely finished sculptures — we most certainly do! One specific example being that one of our favorite sculptors on the planet is the great Japanese collectibles sculptor Takayuki Takeya, who finishes his work immaculately.

Our sculptural style isn't about what we enjoy looking at, as it is what we enjoy doing and seeing in our own personal work. In the same vein, sometimes we start three or four small sculptures at one time, then determine which roughed-out piece has the most potential. We then take that piece forward to a more finished place. For us, this method can keep us from putting the weight of the world mentally and emotionally on one single sculpture. Not all of the sculptures we begin are successful, and when we have more than one piece in production, it's less of a big deal when one piece doesn't work out. Sketching out multiple possibilities for your next piece can be another freeing practice. Try not to committ to one idea and instead just allow the best sculptural sketch to present itself.

This philosophy that we have of "sculptural sketching" can also be seen at work in our process, in that we don't do any drawings or much pre-planning at all before we dive into a sculpture. In a perfect world, we'd like our minds to be completely open to changes or new ideas that might occur to us along the way. If we decide to change the gender of a character, for instance, or add gigantic horns, insane, stylized bat wings, more limbs, or even decide to convert the armature and basic form from human to creature or monster, then we want to make those changes as easy as possible to implement. Again, sculpting in this manner, believing that anything your mind can imagine can be actualized in the piece sitting in front of you at any moment, can be a liberating way of working. We don't always know what we are making even as we begin a sculpture!

This page: Progress images of the brothers' original piece *Komodo King* takes shape. The fine wire armature is bulked out with clay and detailed as a fully formed barbarian among Komodo dragon companions.

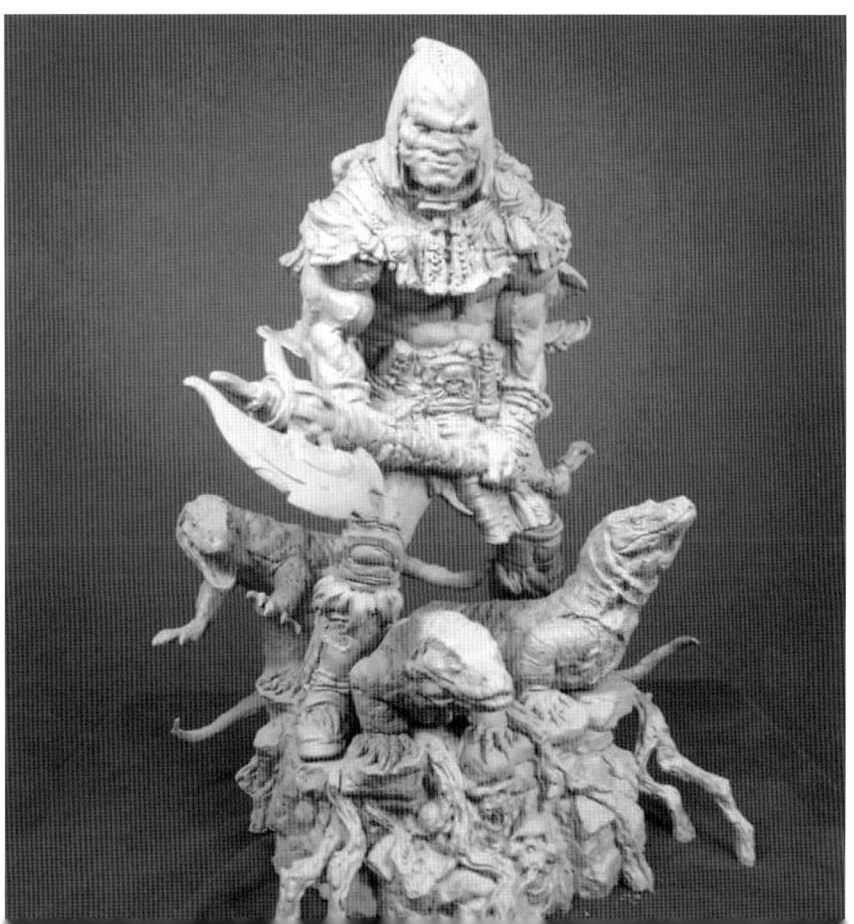

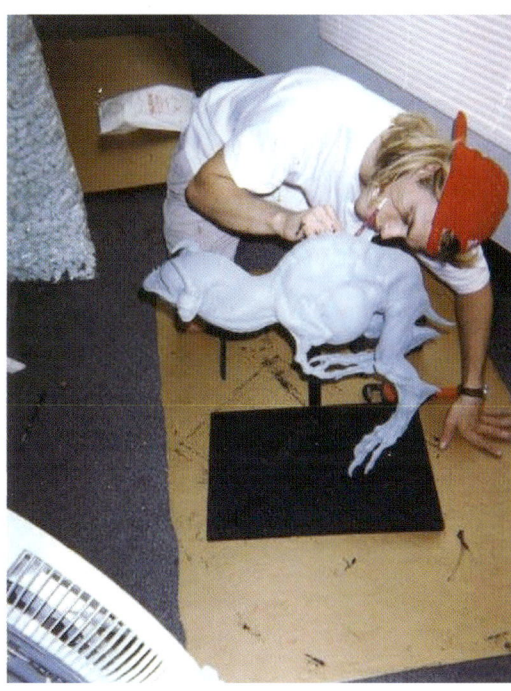

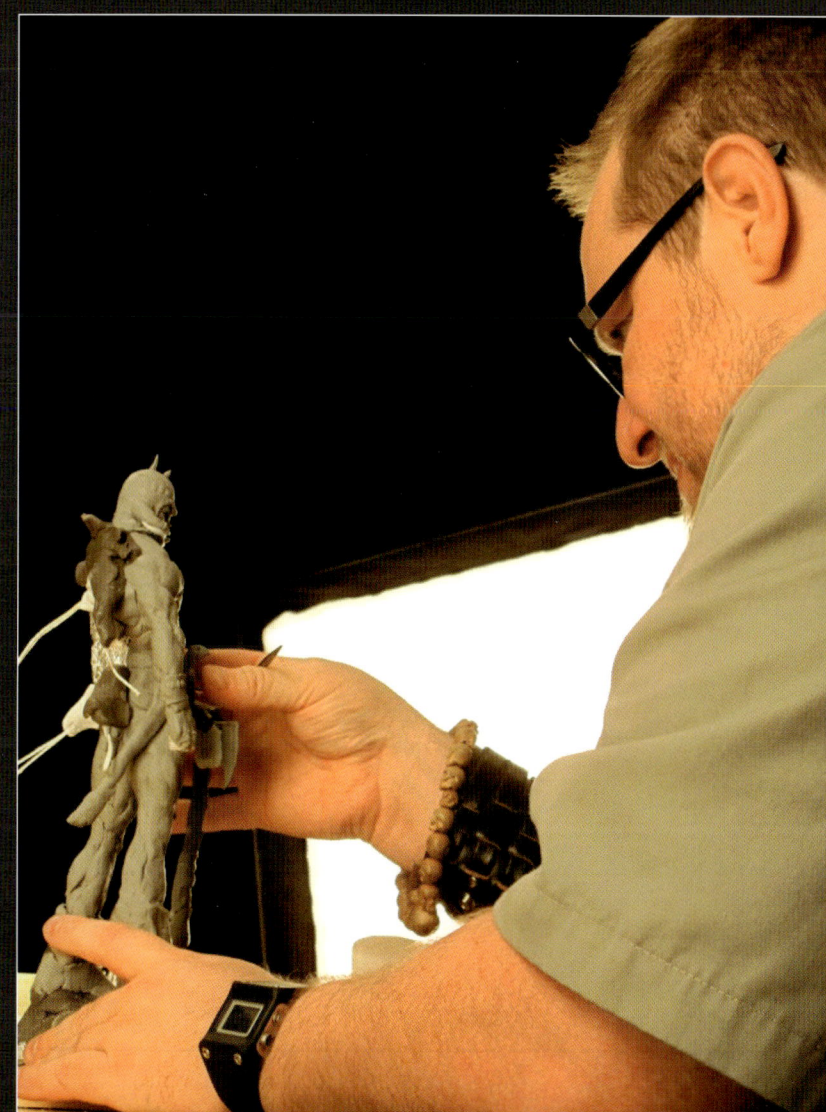

A young Jarrod works on Elum, a character from the ground-breaking video game *Oddworld: Abe's Oddysee* in the mid-1990s. Copyright Oddworld Inhabitants Inc and Lorne Lanning.

INSPIRATIONAL SCULPTORS

When we think of the sculptors who had the greatest influence on our style and approach, two immediately spring to mind:

Frederic Remington

The great Old West artist and sculptor worked extremely loosely and impressionistically. Growing up in Texas, we saw many of his bronze horses and cowboys in homes and businesses during our formative years. While his subject matter wasn't necessarily suited to our taste, his style certainly was, and his sculptures had an effect on us. His intent was not to present a finely finished and tight sculpture, but rather to convey the emotion and dynamism of each particular scene.

Auguste Rodin

We are also huge admirers of the French genius whose textured surfaces can seem rough and unfinished, but were actually painstakingly worked on and thought through. Rodin also created sculptural fragments, which he considered finished pieces. Sometimes lacking arms or head, and these raw pieces focusing on anatomy and an energetic sculpting style greatly affected our sense of what was cool, sculpturally speaking.

Brandon preparing a work-in-progress sculpt for photography.

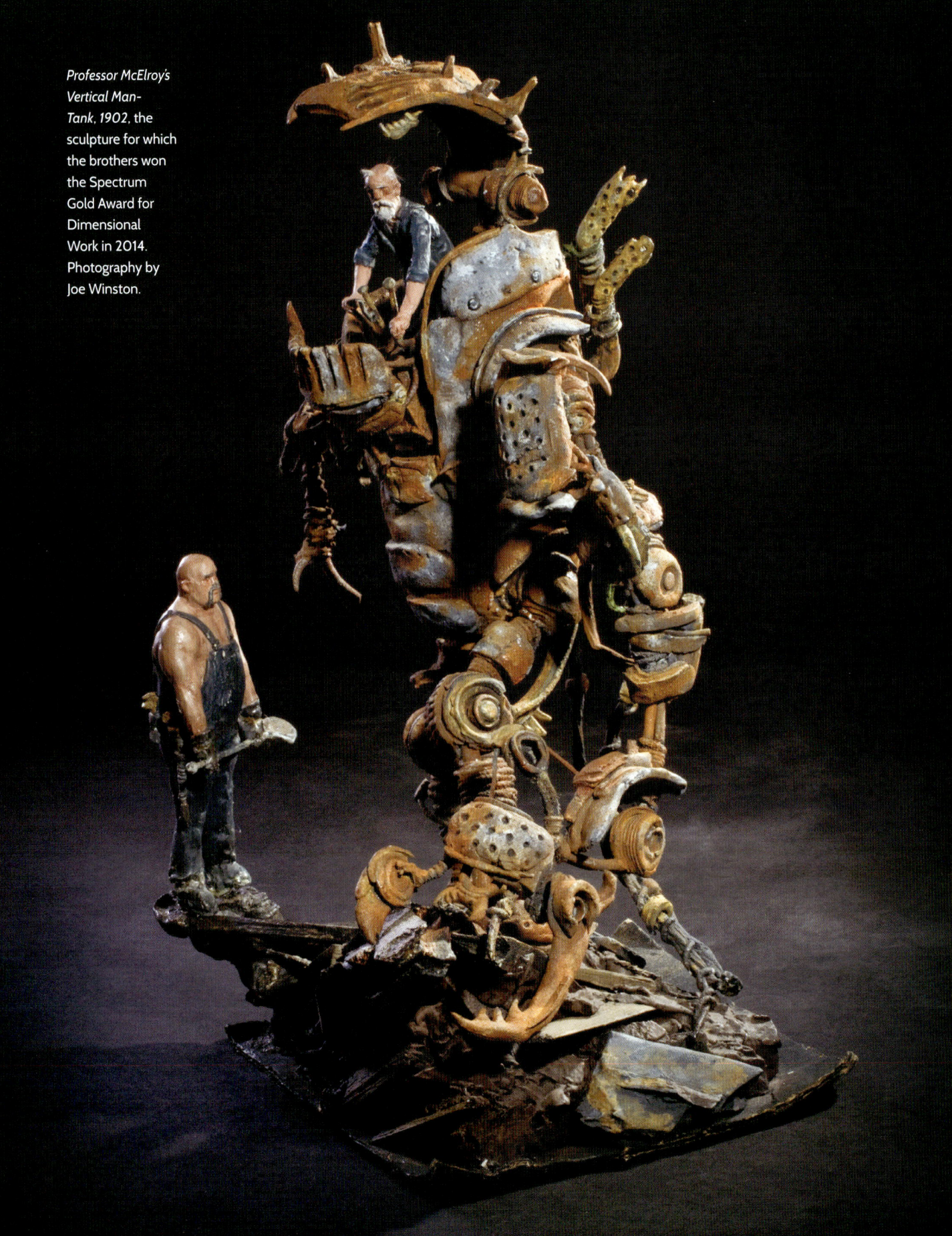

Professor McElroy's Vertical Man-Tank, 1902, the sculpture for which the brothers won the Spectrum Gold Award for Dimensional Work in 2014. Photography by Joe Winston.

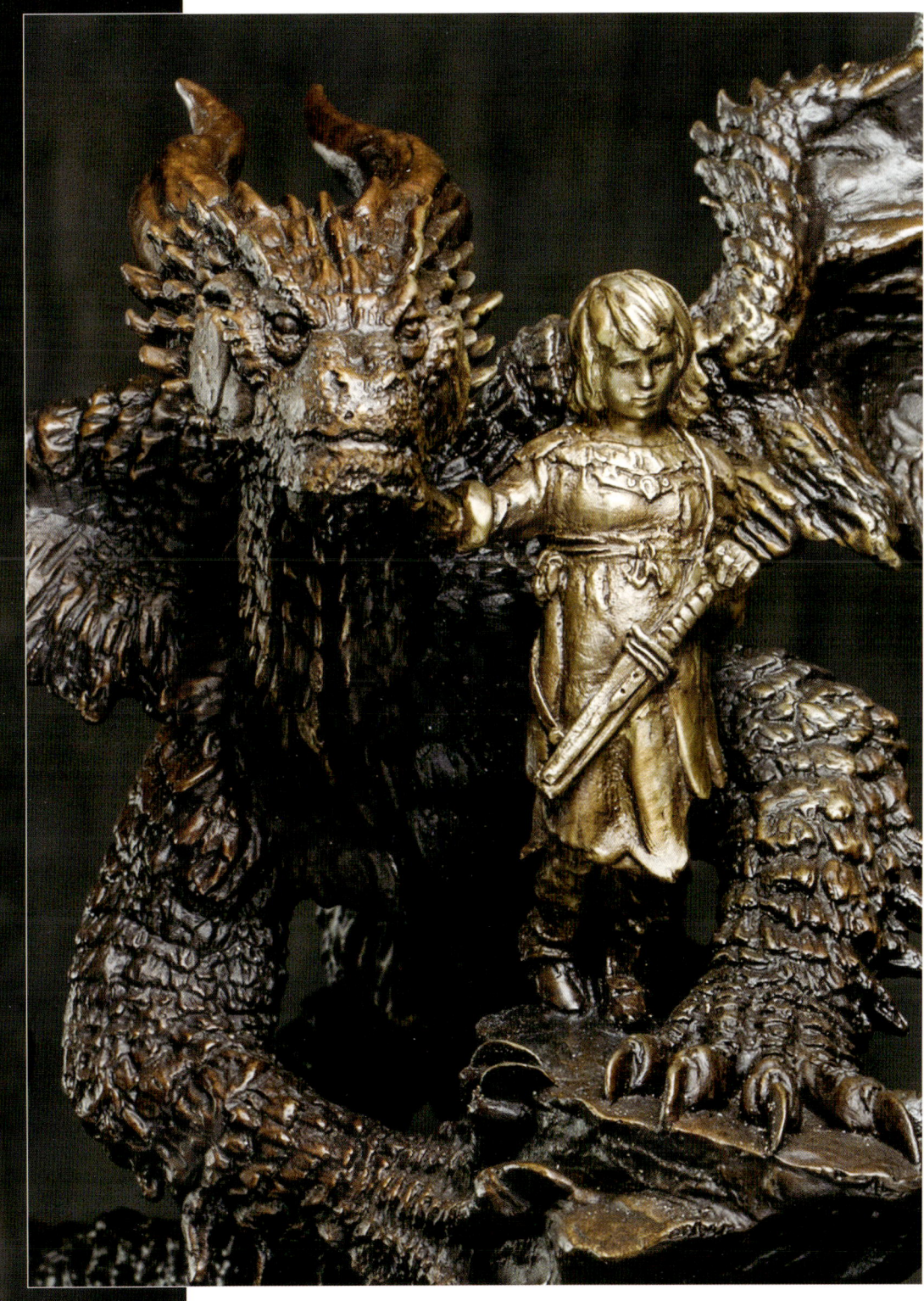

Talula and the Stray, bronze edition, 2018. Originally sculpted in Super Sculpey, the metalwork and fabulous patina, highlighting the little girl in gold, was done by Clint Howard and his fine artists and craftsmen at Deep in the Heart Art Foundry in Texas. Photography by Chad Michael Ward.

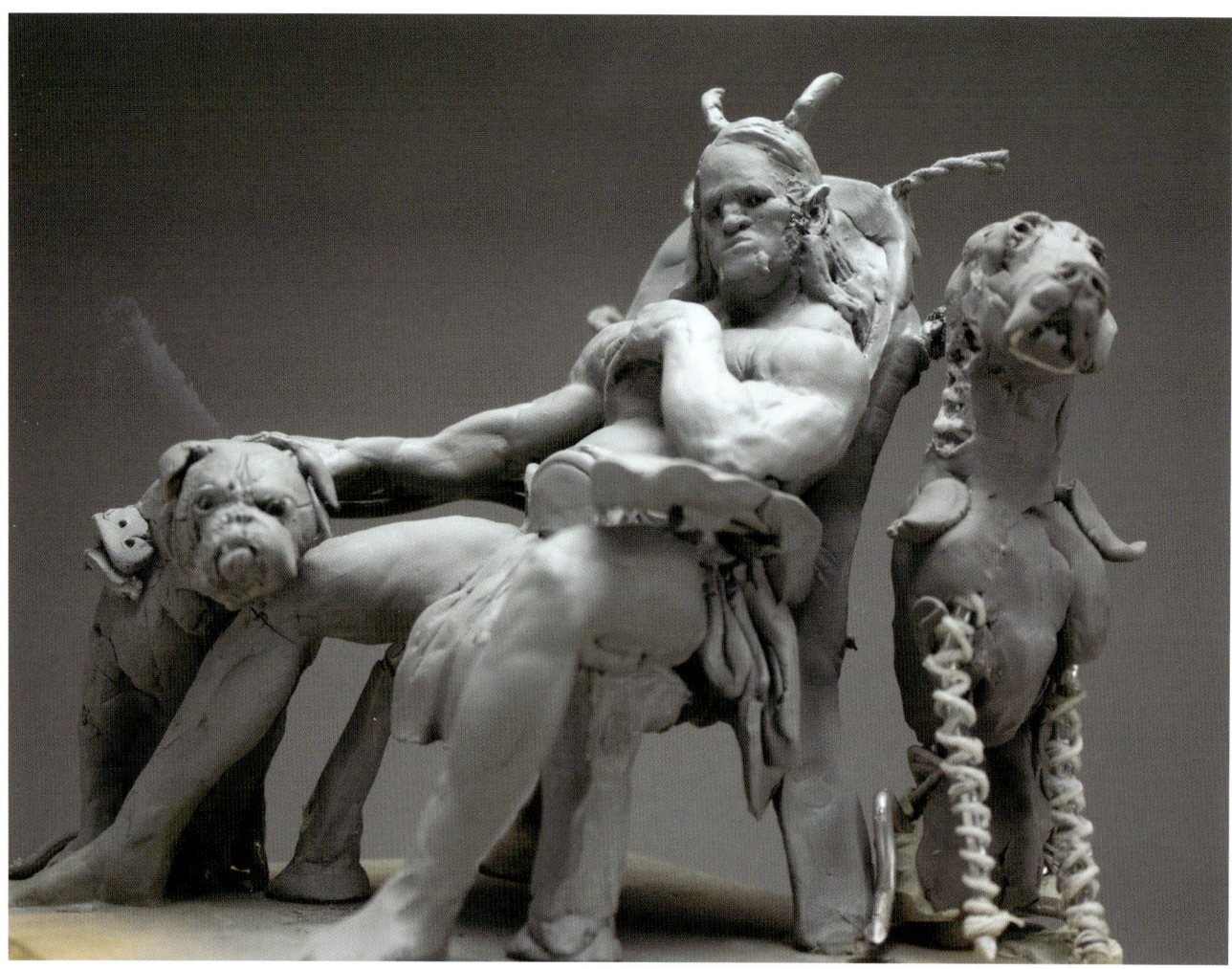

EXPRESSION

One of the most effective ways to infuse personality and narrative into a piece is through the face of the main character. Using their facial expressions, we try to convey the character's inner feelings, creating a snapshot of their current state of mind. Anger is an emotion that we use often in our action work — there's nothing like a charging barbarian or lurking monster with an angry expression. We sculpt this by lowering the middle of the brow and adding extra weight to it. Creating heavy wrinkles in the forehead and sculpting the mouth turned down, or open with bared teeth, results in an expression of fury. We often sculpt the eyes wider to give the character an enraged look. Again, these techniques also work for animals and creatures, especially the more anthropomorphic, semi-human creatures that we like to create!

But we believe that a look even more intimidating than rage can sometimes be an absolutely calm face. This denotes a person or creature in complete control, who isn't worried about anything, which can actually be quite scary if you are on the receiving end of their gaze! For this look, we sculpt more level eyes and might even make them a little heavy-lidded. Of course, sometimes we need a more complex facial expression to convey bemusement or confusion. For any of these expressions, simple or complex, we source photos of faces in the specific expressions that we need and use those photos as our reference. Sometimes we might use a human photo reference when sculpting a creature to give a sense of believability to the expression.

Above: A work-in-progress self-portrait by Jarrod of himself reclining with devil horns and cyborg dogs. Crafted in Super Sculpey.

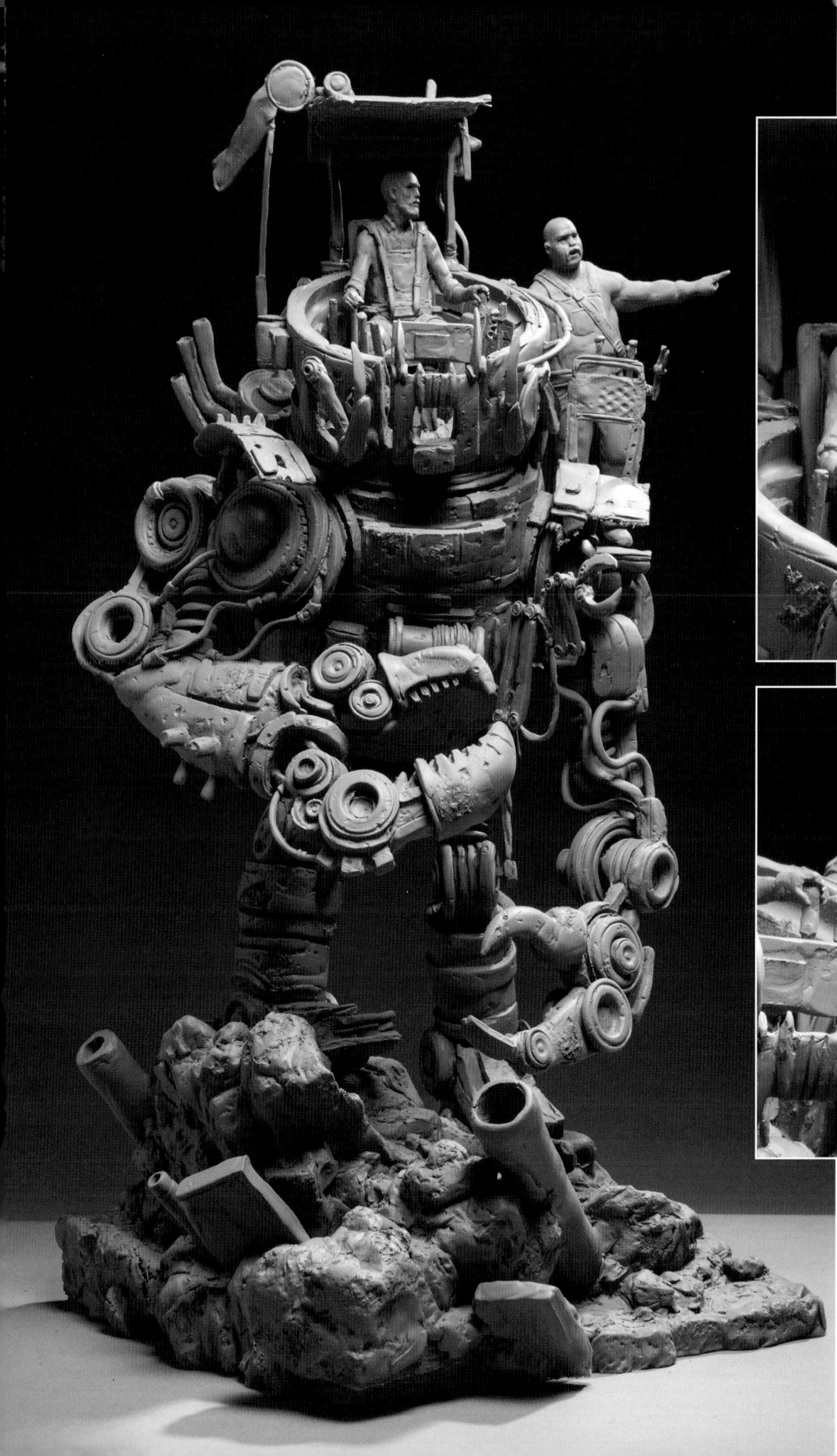

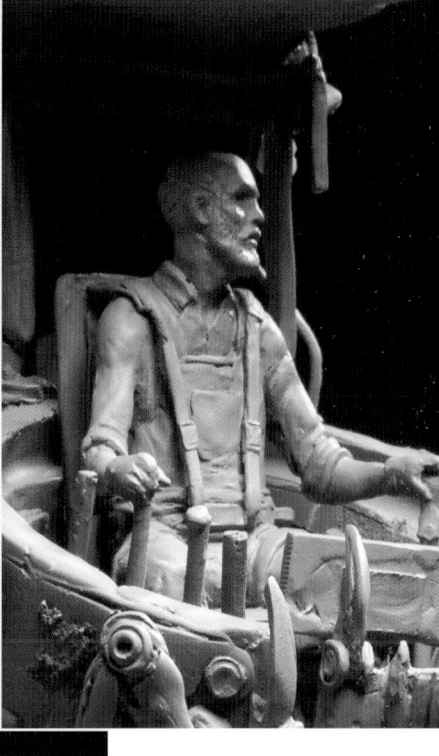

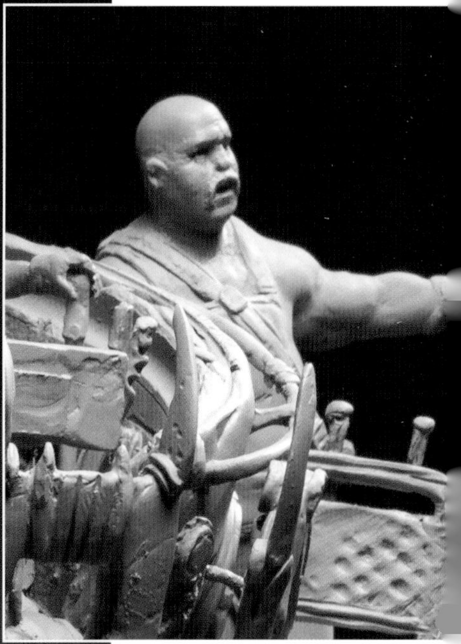

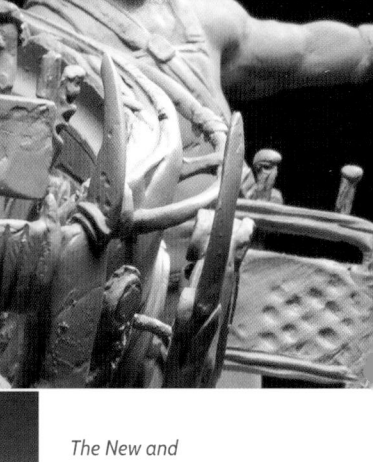

The New and Improved Vertical Man, made in Super Sculpey and photographed by Matt Mrozek.

GESTURE

Another of our favorite ways to create personality and bring a concept to life is through gesture. Like facial expression, gesture can relay emotions such as calmness, anger, agitation, decisiveness, confusion, and so on. We sometimes use slumped shoulders, for instance on the rider in our *Imagining the Pirate King* tutorial (see page 133), to convey a character that is very relaxed and calm. That same dragon-riding character might be said to have the composed facial features that we previously suggested to be an intimidating look.

To use gesture to portray an angry human, we might push the neck forward so that it emerges lower down toward the shoulders, more like an animal. You can see this gesture used in a lot of the comic-book art featuring our favorite X-Men character, Wolverine. We also like to tilt the chin in toward the neck and slightly lower the face to force the head into a position in which the character looks out from under their brow. In our minds, this gesture can show superiority, readiness, and an air of confidence.

Another gestural trick we utilize is to place the character's foot up on a rock as if they are stepping up to a higher position. This pose may be a little overused in the comic book statue world, but it not only conveys dynamism, but also portrays a sense of purpose, and a physical representation that the character is moving forward toward a goal. In a similar way, a twisted midsection, seeing the character turned in a different direction than its hips and legs are oriented, not only adds dynamism, but is a great way to communicate a sense of revelation, as if the character has just discovered a friend or an enemy.

Death from Above, sculpted in Super Sculpey. As well as raising the leg, the head and torso have been lowered and the hands tucked close in to the hips, creating tension and a more dynamic gesture. The piece seen here was scanned into a digital file and sculpted further with a program by the great Argentinian sculptor Martin Canale, creating a traditional/digital collaboration.

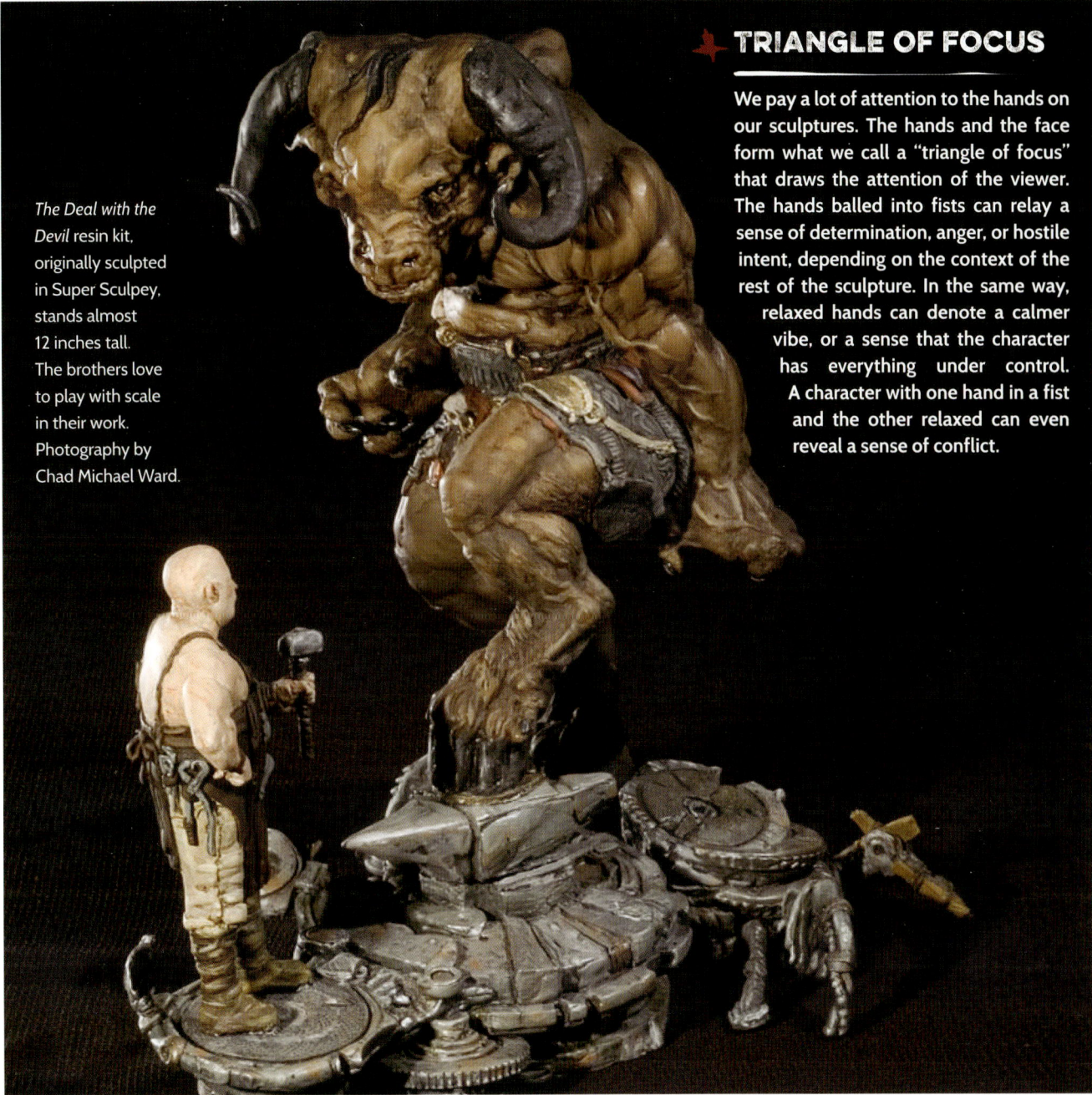

The Deal with the Devil resin kit, originally sculpted in Super Sculpey, stands almost 12 inches tall. The brothers love to play with scale in their work. Photography by Chad Michael Ward.

TRIANGLE OF FOCUS

We pay a lot of attention to the hands on our sculptures. The hands and the face form what we call a "triangle of focus" that draws the attention of the viewer. The hands balled into fists can relay a sense of determination, anger, or hostile intent, depending on the context of the rest of the sculpture. In the same way, relaxed hands can denote a calmer vibe, or a sense that the character has everything under control. A character with one hand in a fist and the other relaxed can even reveal a sense of conflict.

MAKING A SCENE

Some of our sculptures involve more than one character and can even evolve into small dioramas. The potential interactions between humans, or between humans and creatures, can be endless. We have so much fun creating these pieces! These multi-character pieces also allow us to tell stories almost at a glance. The relative size of two or three different characters in a sculpture can immediately set a narrative in motion. We use scale in this way a lot — a minotaur is interesting, but what about a giant minotaur with a human? Is the human in danger, or are they friends with the beast? Is the situation one of calm, or is it filled with tension? Sometimes the most interesting conclusion one can draw is that the characters are involved in a kind of uneasy truce or alliance.

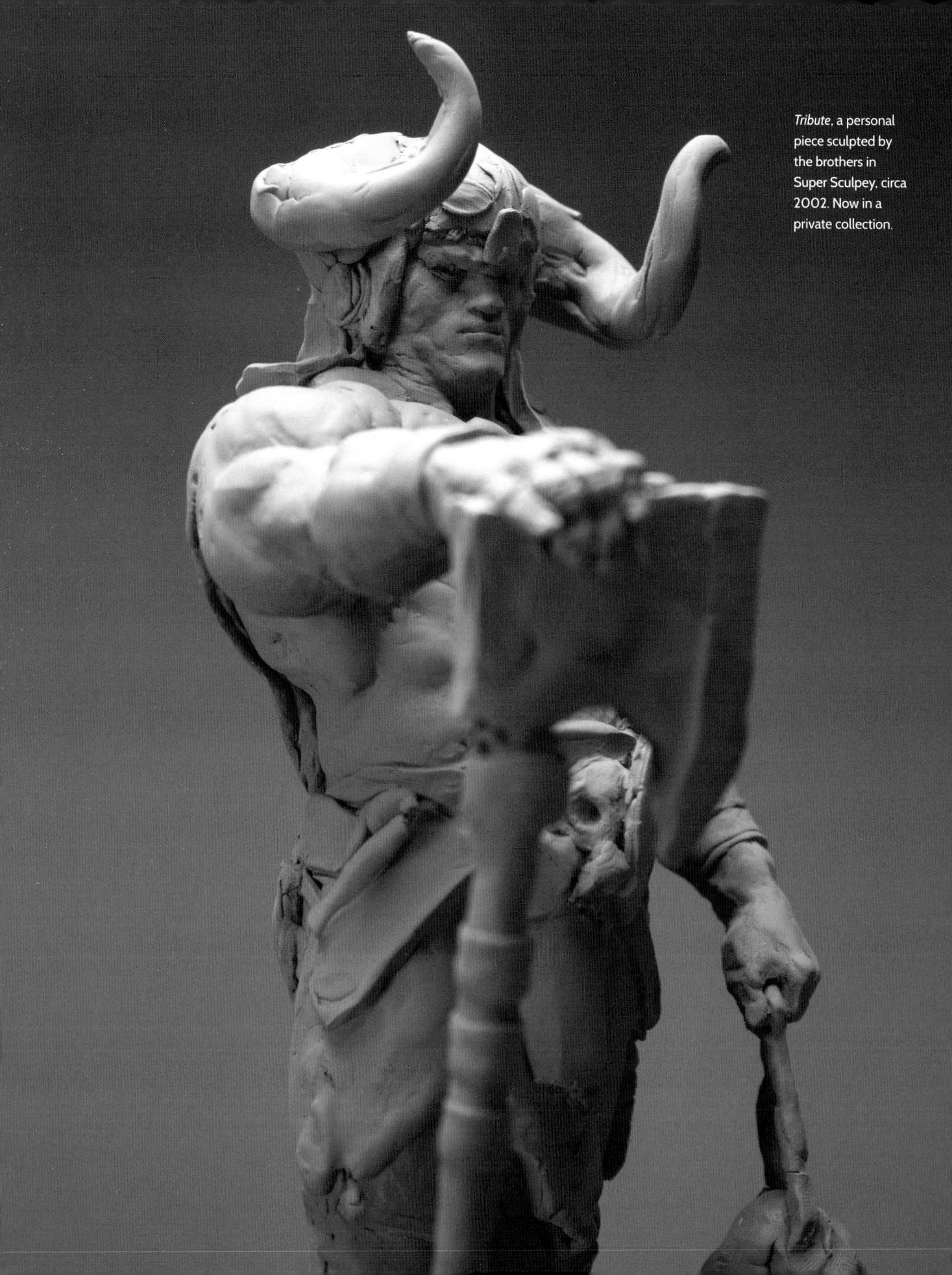

Tribute, a personal piece sculpted by the brothers in Super Sculpey, circa 2002. Now in a private collection.

ANATOMY, PROPORTION, AND POSE

Some sculptors do a lot of planning and preparation before beginning a piece, but not us. We rarely, if ever, do any drawing, sketching, or designing at all before we dive in, preferring instead to start bending the wire for the armature and work instinctively. This gives us a freedom, allowing us to move in the direction that we think looks the best at any particular moment. This freedom stokes our creativity and builds a sense that nothing is outside the realm of possibility. However, as previously mentioned, when starting a piece, our key consideration is the narrative that needs to be conveyed to the viewer.

We always work hard to make sure the narrative is told, even if it is a single character and the message simply explains who the character is and the life they live. In the creation of an effective story, believability is key. The ability to make a design believable comes from understanding real-world concepts, including anatomy, proportion, and pose.

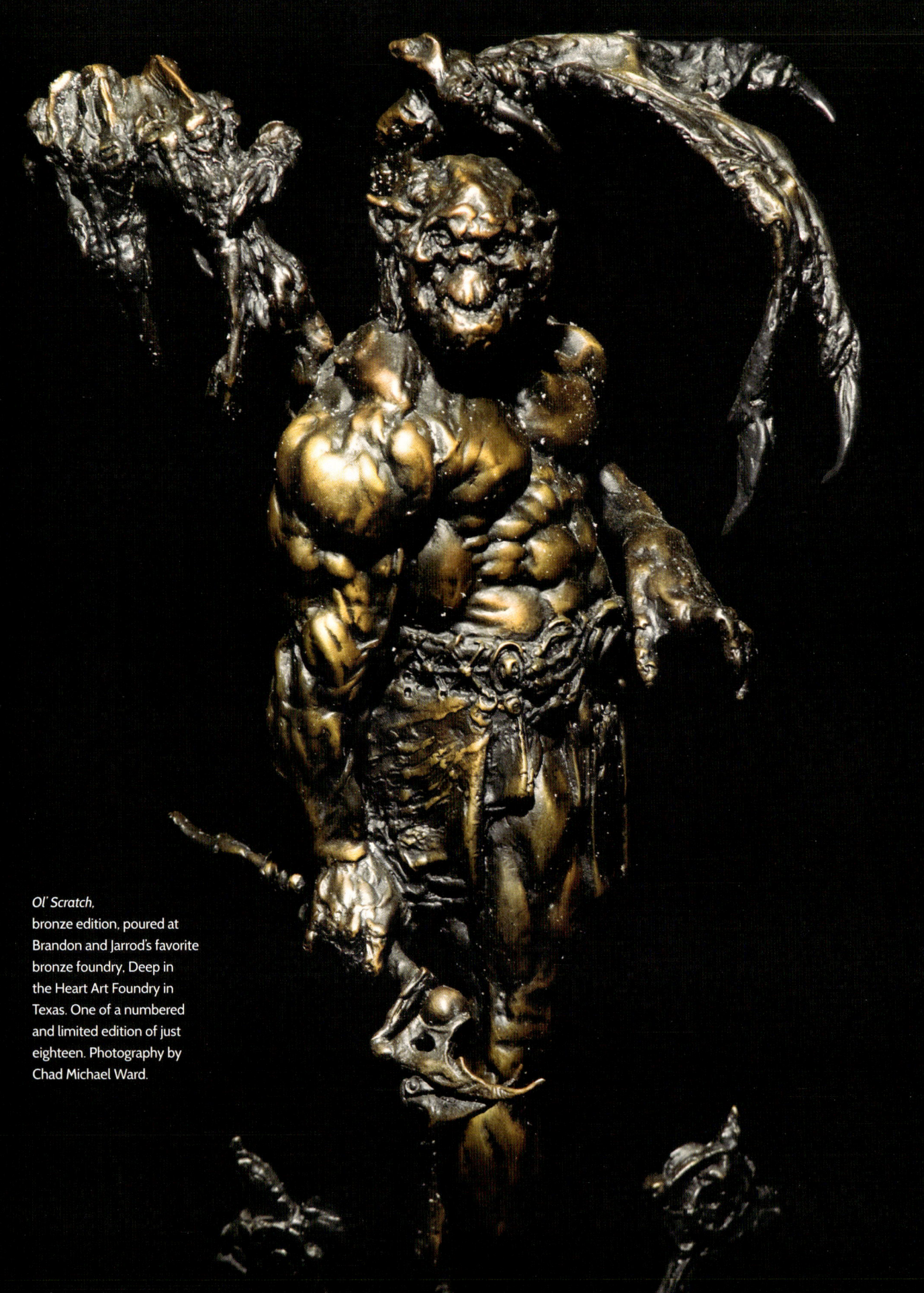

Ol' Scratch,
bronze edition, poured at
Brandon and Jarrod's favorite
bronze foundry, Deep in
the Heart Art Foundry in
Texas. One of a numbered
and limited edition of just
eighteen. Photography by
Chad Michael Ward.

STYLIZED PROPORTIONS

One of the very first aspects we think about when beginning a new sculpture is the proportions of the key figure. If the figure is human, then we already know a few rules about their size. An average human is between six-and-half and seven heads tall, while an idealized human would stand at around eight heads tall. A heroic figure, however, is closer to eight-and-half to eight-and-three-quarters heads tall. Most of the additional height is focused on a bigger, bulkier chest and longer legs. We find that the majority of the character work we create includes heroic proportions, even on our villains! This makes the figure seem more epic and awe-inspiring. We aren't hyper-realistic sculptors. Hyper-realism, and realism in general, is a fine direction to follow, and there are artists who do it incredibly well, but that isn't our style. As sculptors, we are more interested in the fantastic, which sometimes calls for slightly exaggerated forms. We built our aesthetic on the world of comic books, and enjoy the work of many artists who sculpt very stylized figures whose proportions aren't based in reality at all.

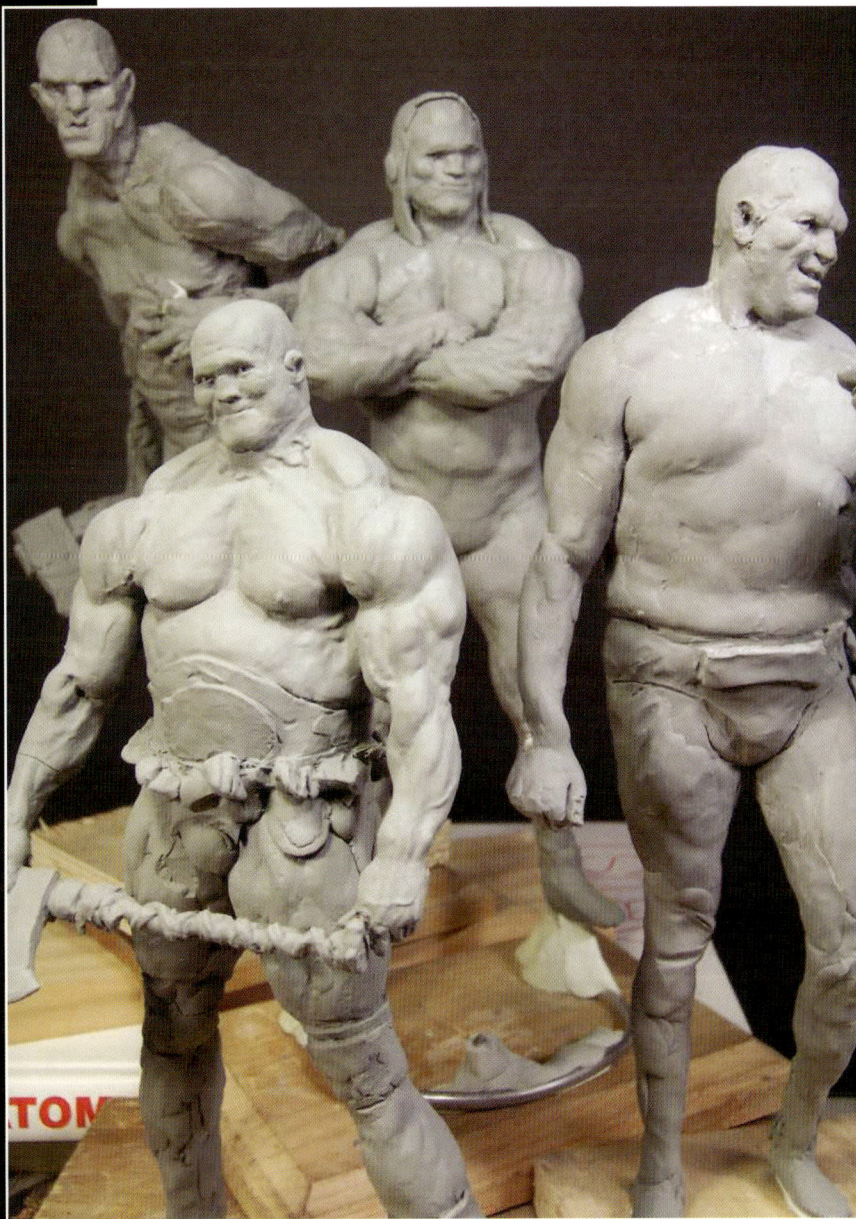

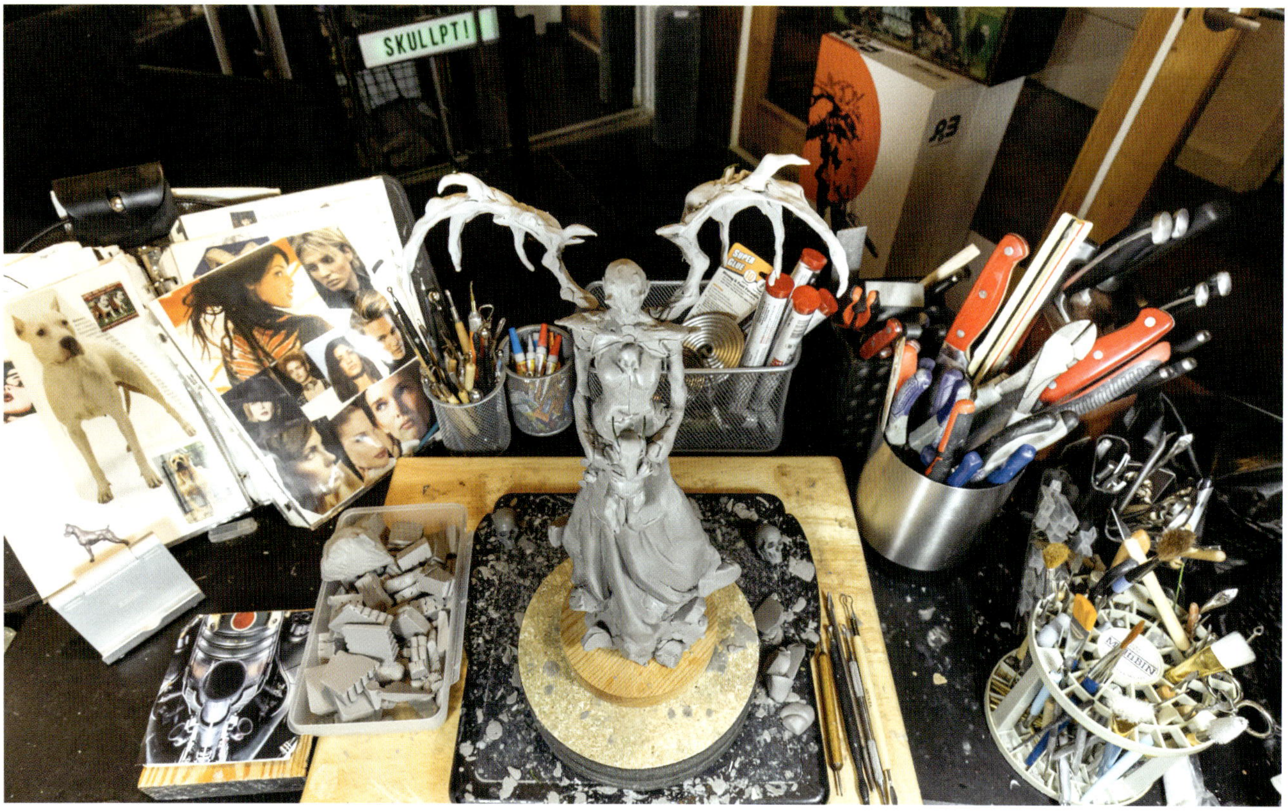

ANATOMY REFERENCES

When we were younger, we wondered if using reference material was a form of cheating. We wondered if we should be making everything up and sculpting from our memories. We know now that this was foolish, and we want to dispel the idea where it exists in any young sculptors that we meet. We use lots of reference material when sculpting and much of it is specifically anatomical reference. Inventing human anatomy is not an option for us as we always try to stay true to what the body actually does, even if we're exaggerating the forms.

Understanding what muscles do under the skin is critical. It's important that we gather photographic reference of muscles, limbs, and torsos doing the exact things that we need them to be doing in a sculpture. You might think you have the chest musculature memorized, but do you understand what that musculature does when it moves, such as when the arms are lifted above the head, for example? Looking for specific references and gaining in-depth anatomy knowledge is key to creating realistic human figures. We usually create a giant mood board of reference images, displaying not only all of the anatomy shots we need, but also drapery and clothing reference photos, rock references if the base is rocky, and so on. But, as turning our heads away from our piece becomes distracting over long sittings, as our eyes are constantly being pulled away from the clay, we place this reference board directly behind our sculpture. Putting the reference board in our line of sight means that all it takes is a quick glance to see the photos.

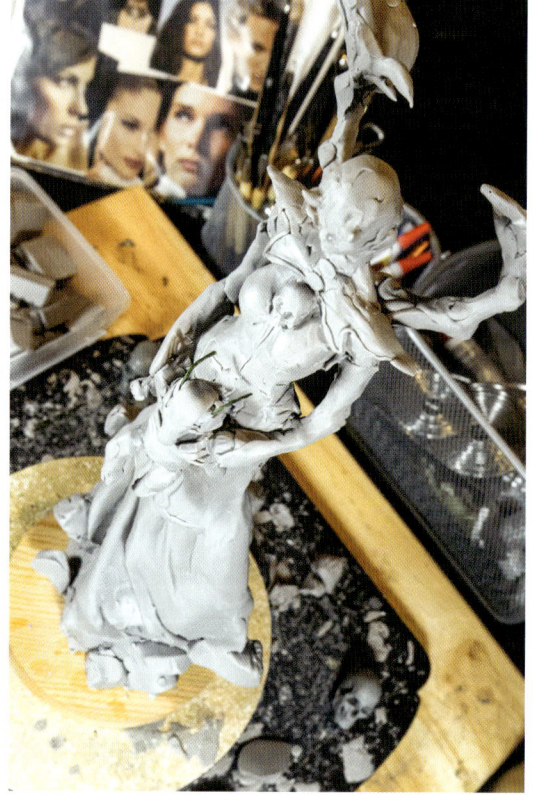

Workspace photography by Matt Mrozek.

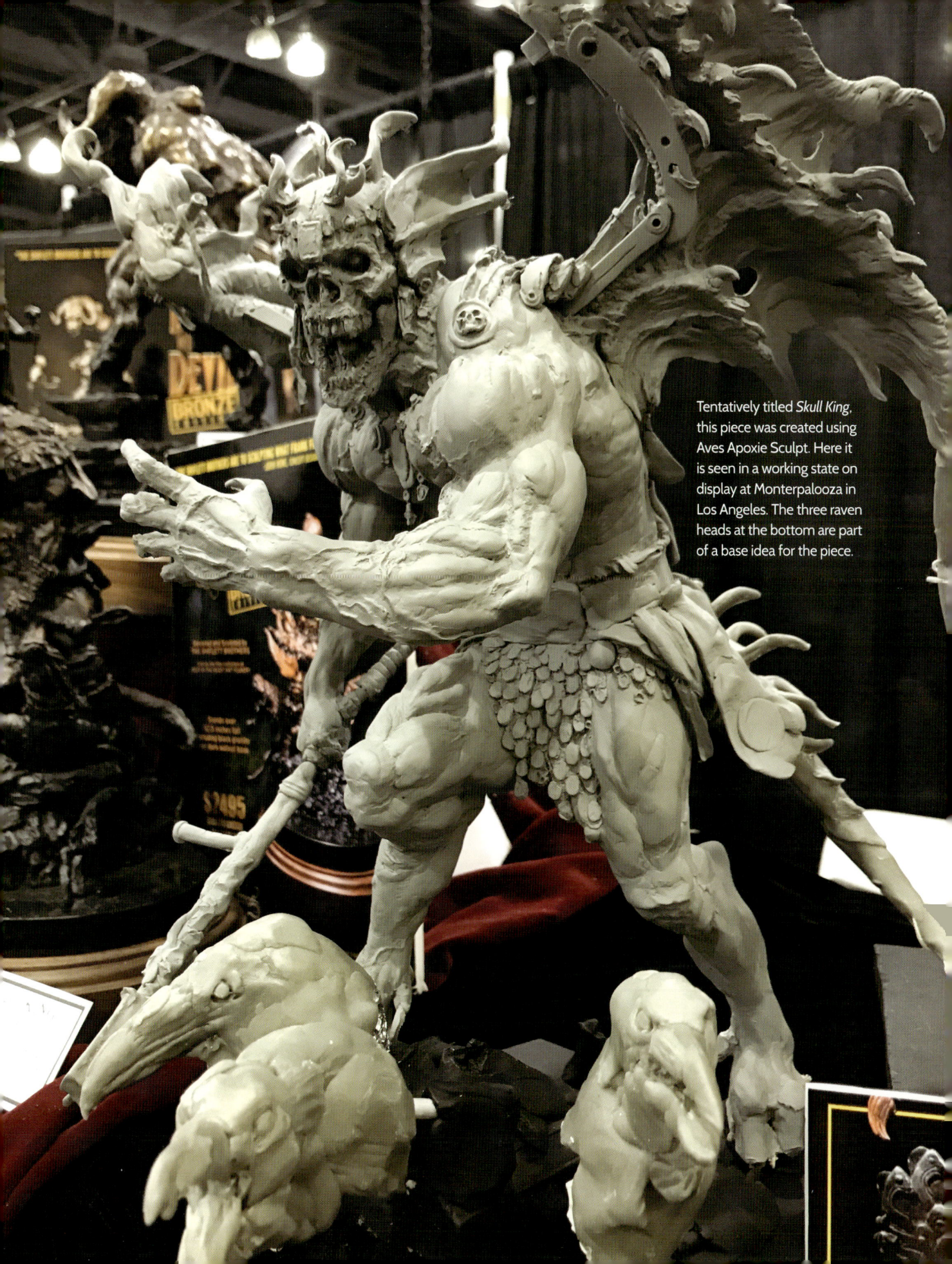

Tentatively titled *Skull King*, this piece was created using Aves Apoxie Sculpt. Here it is seen in a working state on display at Monterpalooza in Los Angeles. The three raven heads at the bottom are part of a base idea for the piece.

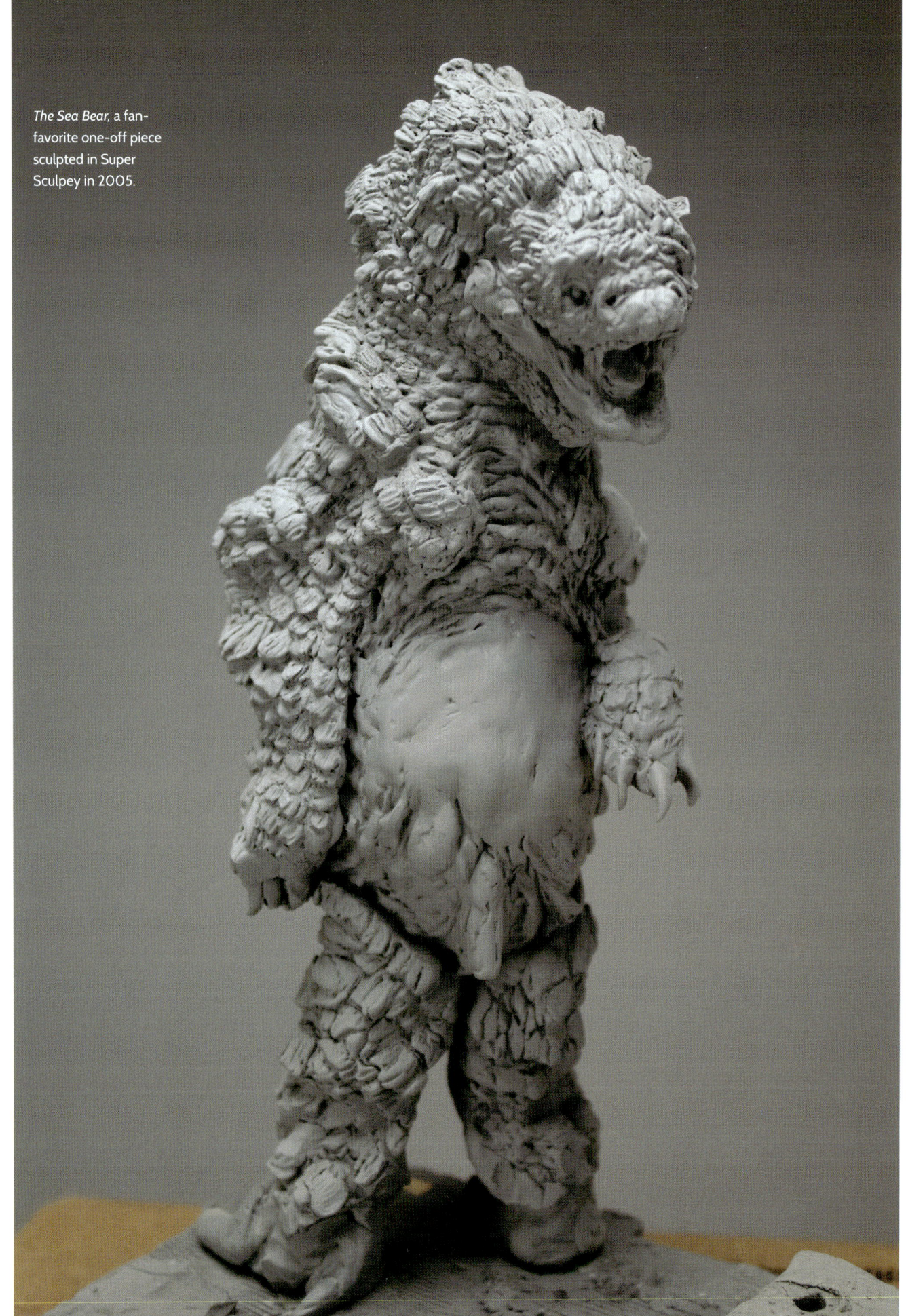

The Sea Bear, a fan-favorite one-off piece sculpted in Super Sculpey in 2005.

Many of our sculptures are of archetypal heroes, barbarians, and men of great size, so the focus of our anatomy reference is often on bodybuilders. We grew up using Arnold Schwarzenegger's *The New Encyclopedia of Modern Bodybuilding* as a vital reference library, and it is still very useful to us today. One reason we use it is because we prefer the sleeker (but still huge!) muscle men of the 1970s and 1980s to today's overly bulky and sometimes comically humongous bodybuilding physiques. For both men's and women's anatomy, we try to avoid reference photos that have been airbrushed or overly touched up. The little dents, creases, and imperfections that magazines and websites always eliminate are often the exact bits of information a sculptor needs to create realism.

When designing and sculpting fantastical or imaginary creatures and monsters, we also encourage sculptors to use references. If the world that the creatures inhabit is our world or similar, with the same rules of physics, then some of the forms and mechanics of these imaginary monsters' bodies will have similarities to actual animals that live here on Earth. For example, when adding a knee-like structure on a mythical animal, it could perhaps bend backward or be re-worked in an interesting way. Knowledge of how a real-world knee functions on an animal such as a horse or a dog (or anything that is of a similar size and shape to the creature) will be helpful. A creature can be ninety-five percent imaginary, but when a viewer recognizes a joint structure or a skin fold, it can ground that creature in our reality. It instantly makes it seem more believable and more plausible. A long-time master of this art is the legendary concept designer and painter Wayne Barlowe, an artist we have looked up to our entire lives.

WHEN A VIEWER RECOGNIZES A JOINT STRUCTURE OR A SKIN FOLD, IT CAN GROUND THAT CREATURE IN OUR REALITY

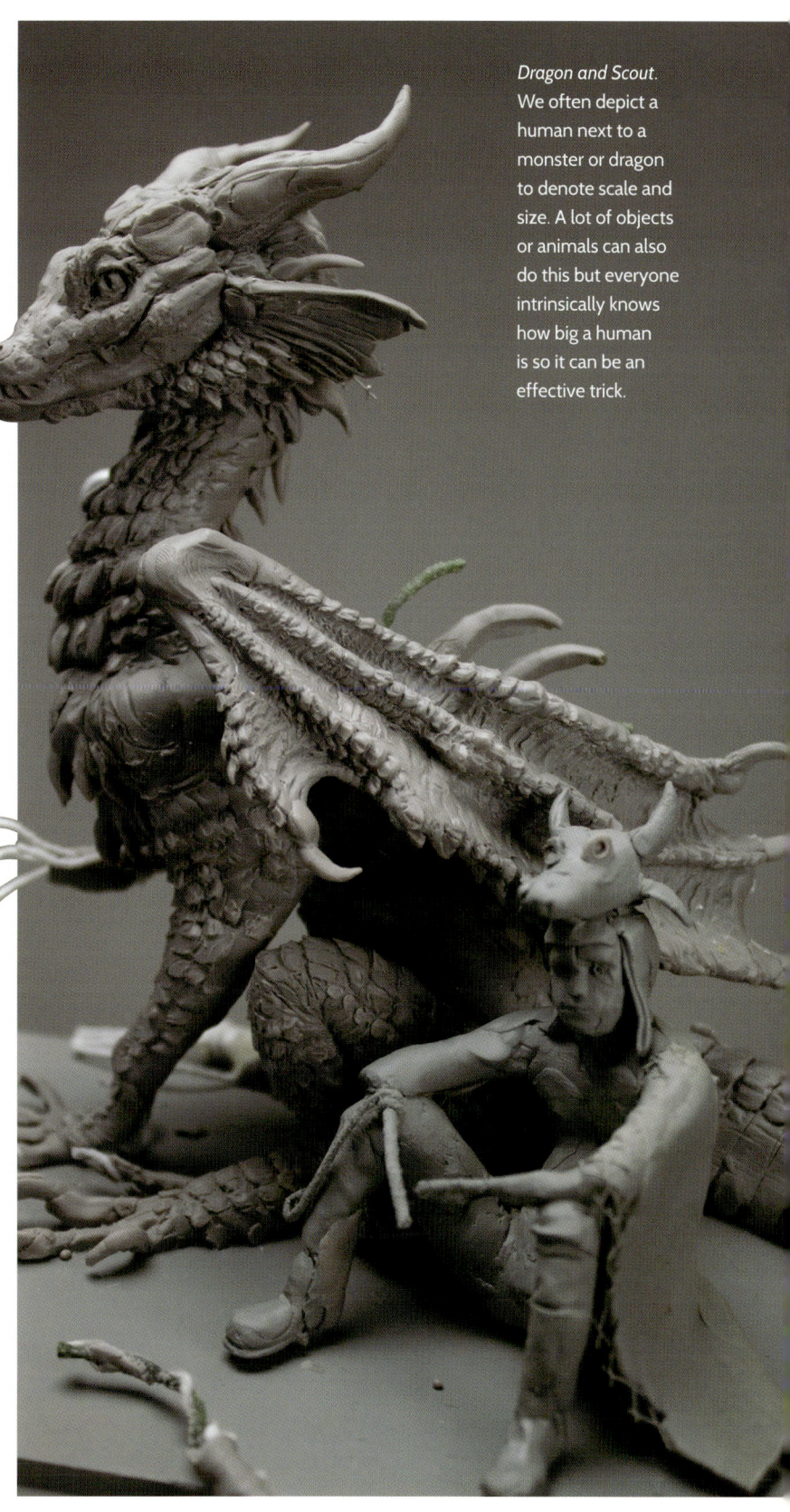

Dragon and Scout. We often depict a human next to a monster or dragon to denote scale and size. A lot of objects or animals can also do this but everyone intrinsically knows how big a human is so it can be an effective trick.

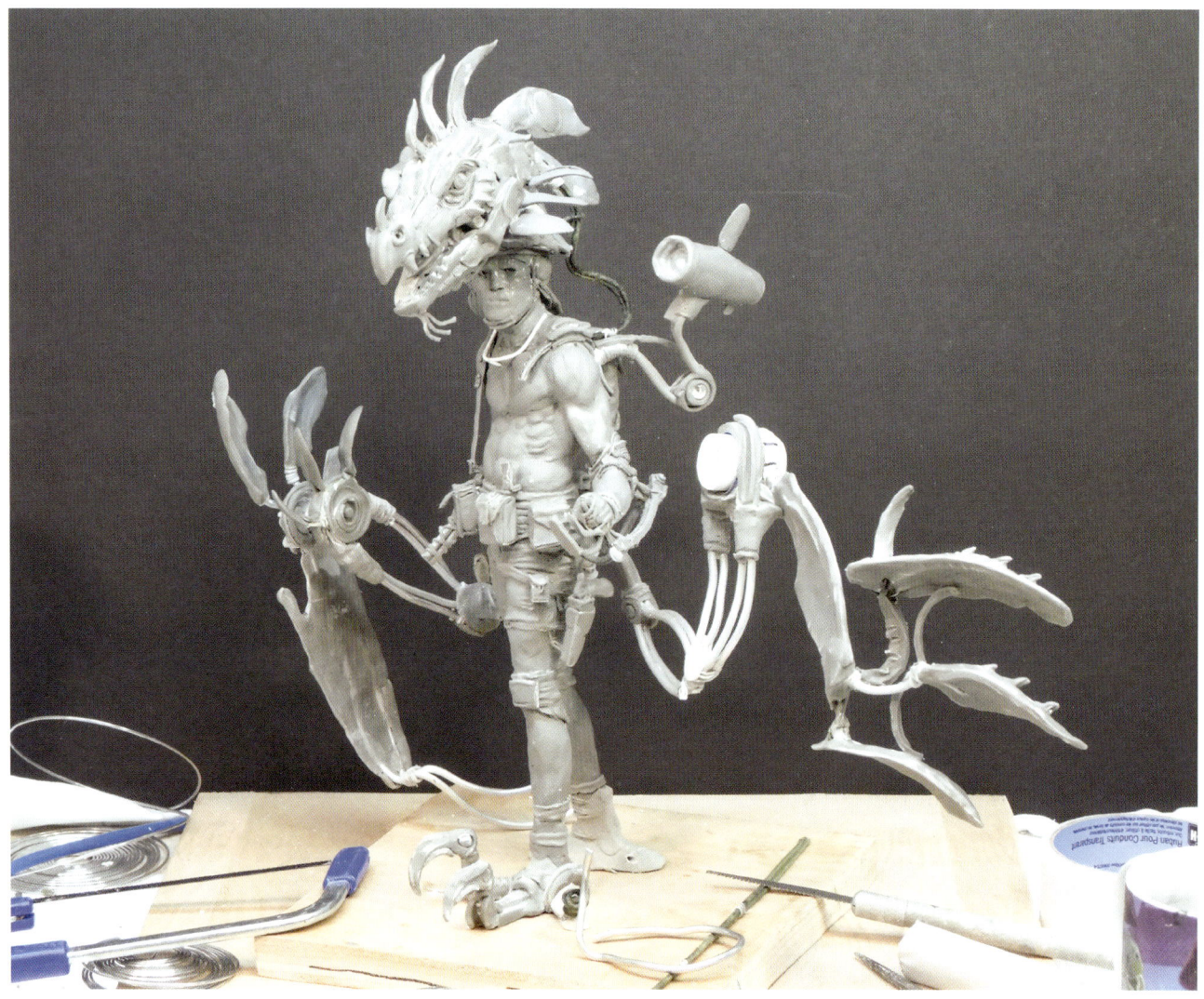

DYNAMIC POSING

We try to create dynamism in all of our sculptures. For some sculptures, we design kinetic action poses, but sculpting with dynamism in mind doesn't just refer to action poses. There is a type of coiled, subtle dynamism that one can see in some Renaissance sculpture, such as Michelangelo's *David*. This masterwork employs "contrapposto" (counterpoise), which is an Italian term for the practice of posing a sculpture's weight on one foot, throwing the shoulders and hips into opposition. For example, if the right shoulder is angled downward and the left shoulder is upward, then the right hip would be angled upward and the left hip downward. This gives the simultaneous impression of dynamism and relaxation — half of the body seeming to be in action while the other half is not. This pose is often perceived as beautiful by audiences, and sculptors throughout history have used it when presenting goddesses of love and the like.

The contrapposto pose can also convey psychological information about the state of mind of the subject, implying that he or she is unsure or "in two minds," while poses with even feet and level shoulders and hips can convey a calmness or certainty, which we find less visually interesting. This technique has been used since the very beginning of western classical sculpture and was employed by many of the old masters, but it was really cemented in our creative minds by many of our contemporary Japanese sculpting heroes including Takayuki Takeya and Yasushi Nirasawa. We would study their pieces and struggle to understand how the character could seem relaxed, while simultaneously appearing as if it was about to move, with stored potential movement inside it — kinetic and yet still. The discovery of the concept of contrapposto posing was the key to unlocking this mystery for us.

COMPOSITION

We aspire to always have a good sense of balance in our sculptures. There is physical stability to consider — engineering a piece so that it doesn't fall over onto its side or face is incredibly important! But another form of balance is compositional, and it takes place within the figures themselves. Pay attention to the axis of the figure — the vertical line bisecting the character right down the middle. Do the perceived weights in the piece balance each other? Could a human or an animal actually stand as he, she, or it, is depicted in the sculpture? We not only ask ourselves whether the pose is possible and well-balanced, but whether it is visually pleasing and will work in the context of the design.

Something else we think about early on when assessing the composition of a new sculpture is the silhouette. If the interior of the piece couldn't be seen, would the outline or outer shape of the piece work compositionally? Does it still look strong design-wise, and does it convey the story of the character? Sometimes we add a feature that negatively impacts our sculpture's silhouette, and once we realize this fact, we change it back to the original form to keep the preferred silhouette intact. Another trick for improving the composition of a sculpture comes from our study of comic-book artists' techniques. When designing a cover for a comic book, they will often create a thumbnail drawing of the cover, just slightly larger than a postage stamp. The thinking is that if the art still works compositionally at that tiny size, then it will definitely work at a larger size. For sculpture, we often view the piece from afar, especially in the early stages of production. We walk perhaps twenty or thirty feet away from the piece, shrinking it down to a much smaller scale in our view, much like a comic artist creating a thumbnail. From a significant distance, does the design and composition of our sculpture still appear effective and tell the story that we want it to tell? If so, we have a good indication that our design is progressing as desired.

This page and opposite: *Dragon Division: Egg Appropriations Unit*, originally sculpted by the brothers in Aves Apoxie Sculpt and featured in *ImagineFX* magazine. Photography by Joe Winston.

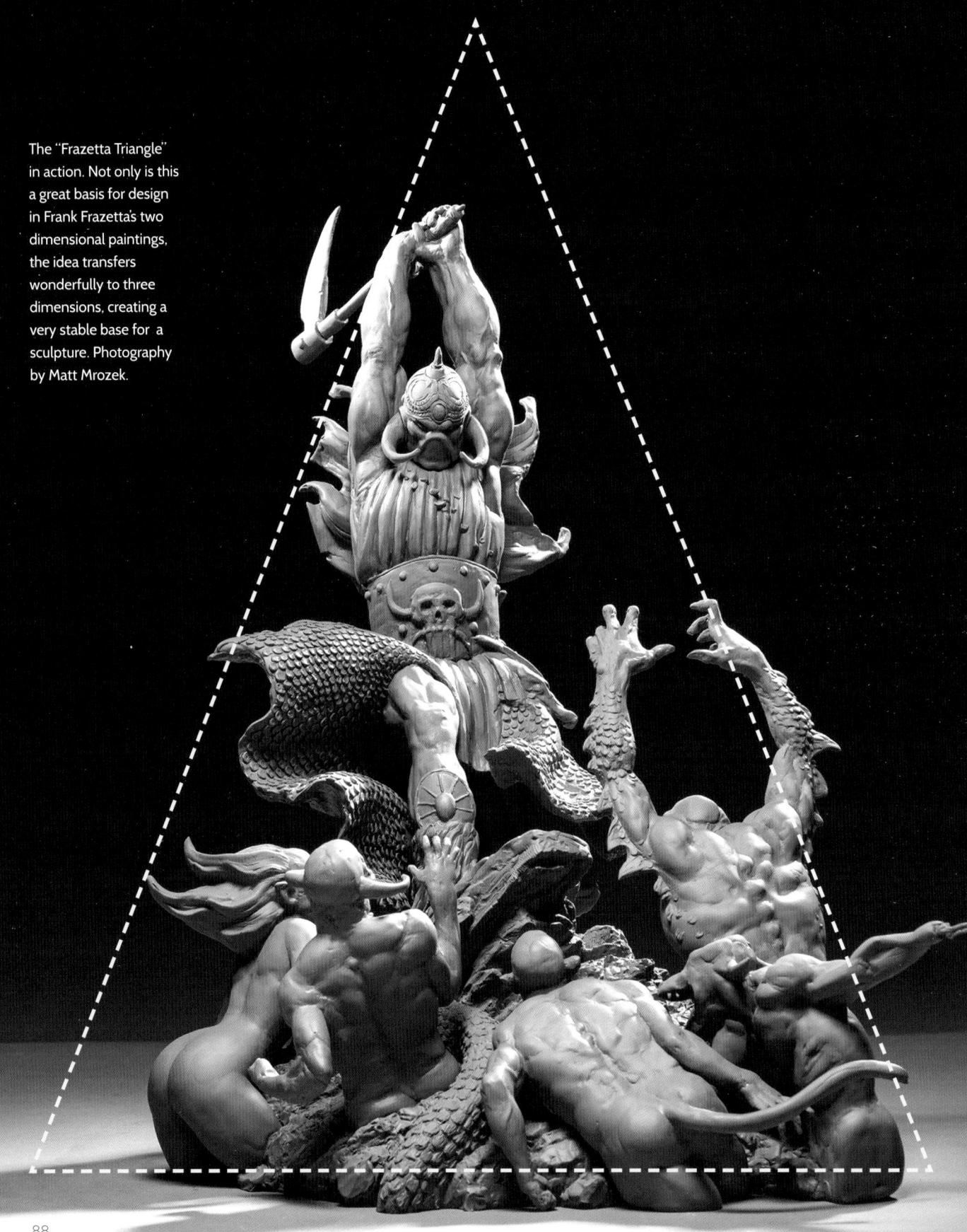

The "Frazetta Triangle" in action. Not only is this a great basis for design in Frank Frazetta's two dimensional paintings, the idea transfers wonderfully to three dimensions, creating a very stable base for a sculpture. Photography by Matt Mrozek.

THE VIEWER'S FOCUS

When sculpting human-type characters, a focal area of the piece is framed by the triangular shape made up of a character's two hands and face (as mentioned on page 77). In any human-based design, the viewer's eyes naturally gravitate toward the action of the hands and face, and the expression or emotion they convey. The viewer's reading of these three elements creates a small triangle within the piece that is automatically a focus of interest. As well as ensuring the face and hands portray the chosen story, we work hard to detail and add interest to the area of the sculpture contained within this smaller triangle. Upon stepping back from the composition, the theory of the "Frazetta Triangle" can also be applied.

When studying the paintings of Frank Frazetta, many artists and designers mention the "Frazetta Triangle," referring to the artist's tendency to create a large triangular form as the basis of the composition (especially prevalent in his book covers). No major forms destroy the triangle, but minor forms and elements do subtly break the frame to create visual interest without obscuring the overall triangle. This design idea transfers perfectly to sculptural work. The base of our pieces is often the widest point, with a general triangle shape leading up to the highest point of the sculpture. This works especially well with single-character pieces. Of course, the Frazetta Triangle concept can't (and shouldn't) be used on every sculpture, just as it isn't appropriate for every painting. But we believe where it works, it *really* works.

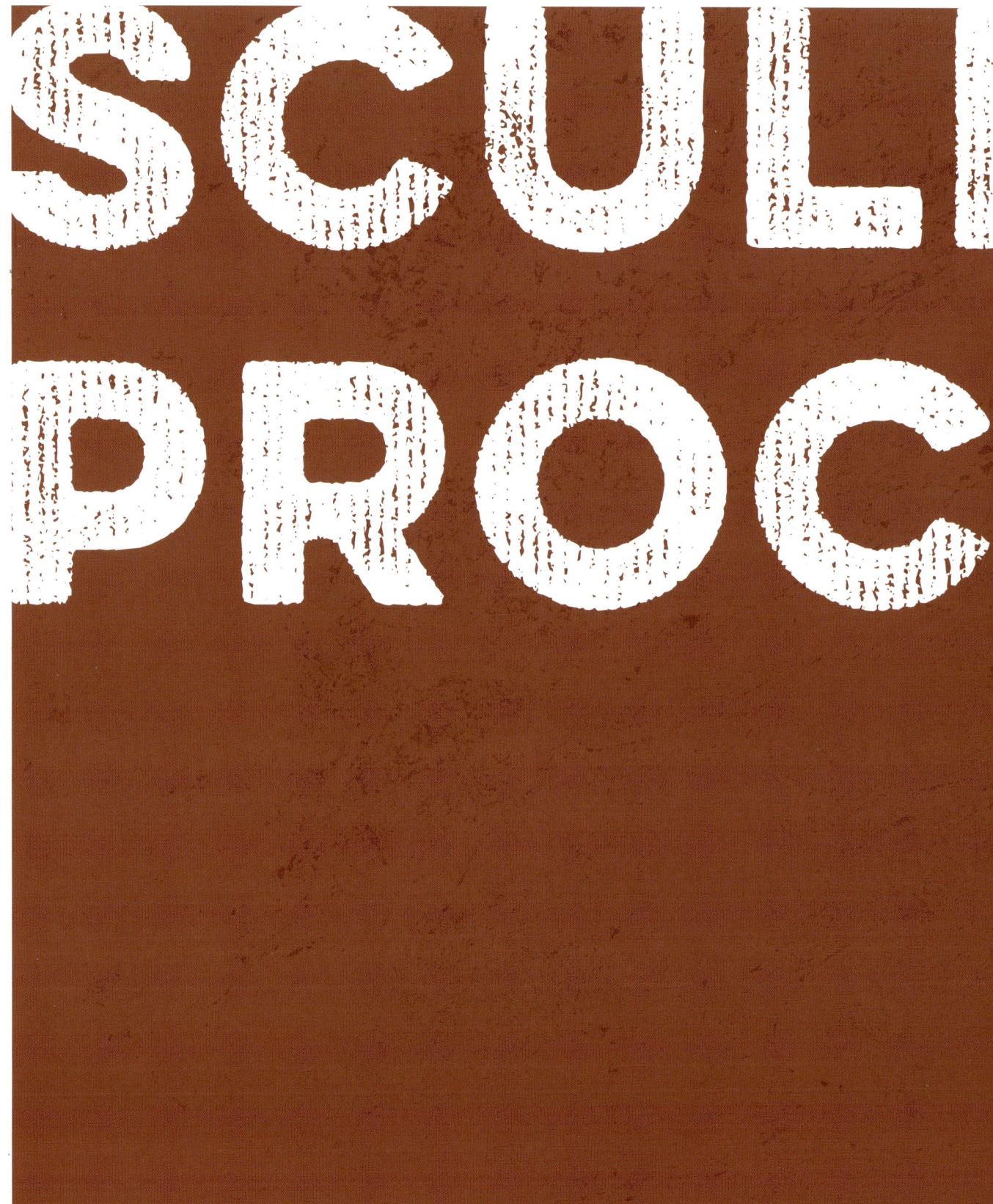

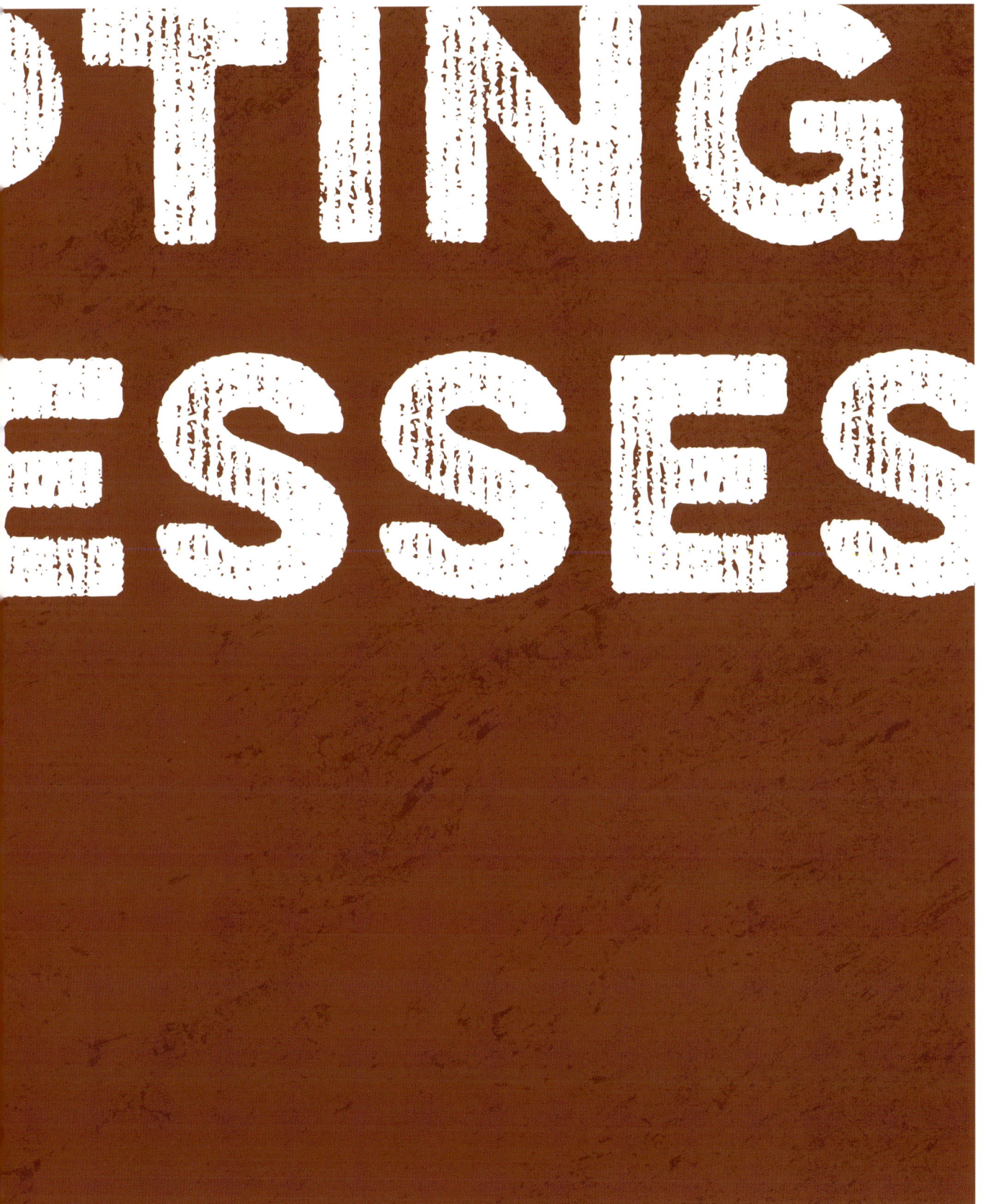

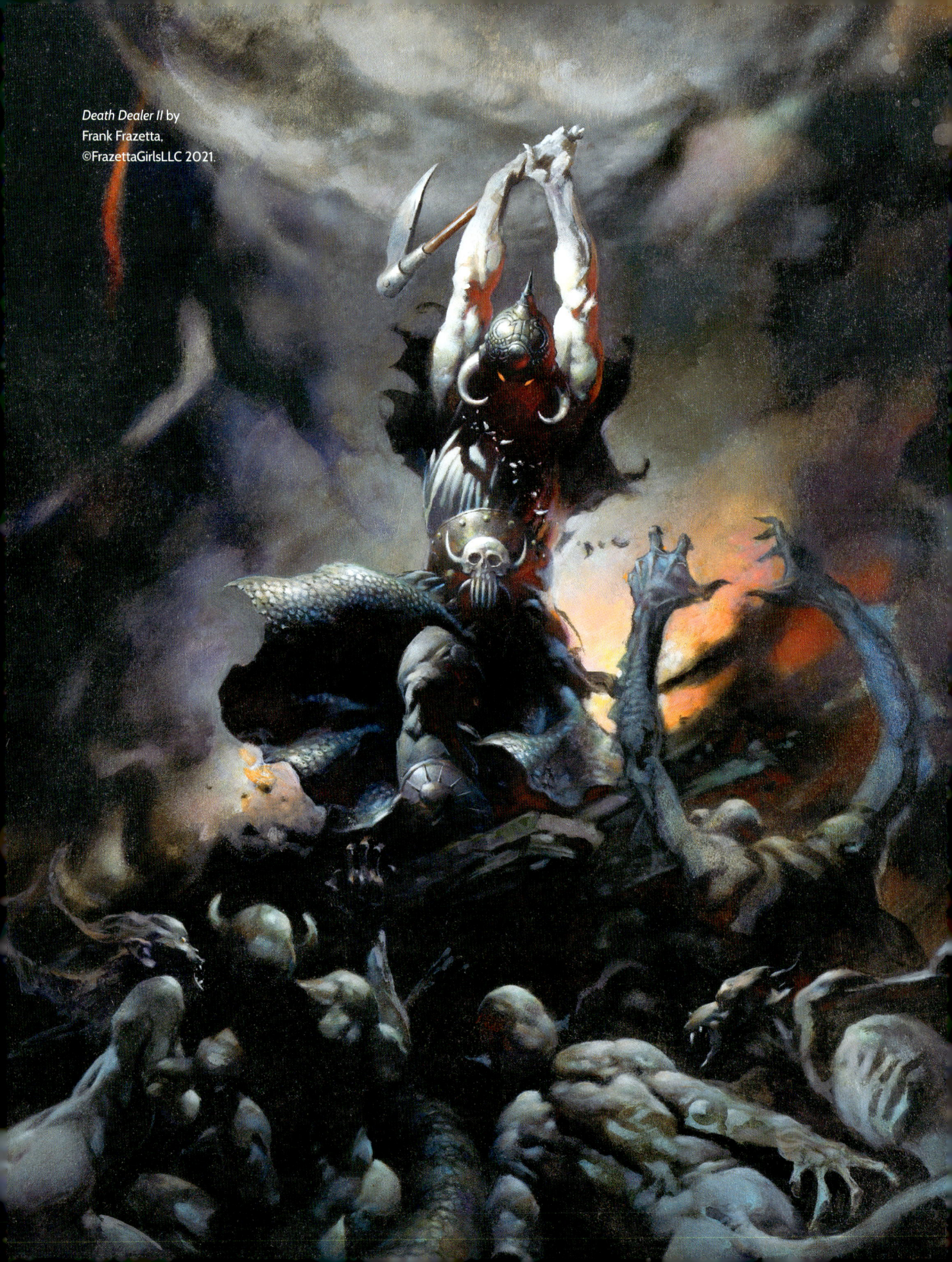

Death Dealer II by
Frank Frazetta,
©FrazettaGirlsLLC 2021.

SCULPTING DEATH DEALER II

It's no secret that the artwork of fantasy painting legend Frank Frazetta is a huge inspiration for us, so the chance to sculpt a statue based on his iconic 1978 painting *Death Dealer II* is a dream come true. This is the second piece Frazetta painted featuring this character, the first being the original *Death Dealer*, in which the character was posed atop his horse (see page 32). *Death Dealer II* has a much more dynamic feel to it, and capturing that movement and excitement is one of our chief goals. Unlike our personal work, where we want every sculpture to result in a Shiflett Brothers-style piece, here we most definitely want the result to look like a Frank Frazetta piece.

We sculpt this barbarian at exactly 1/6 scale, meaning a six-foot-tall human will be 12 inches tall when sculpted. We start with the armature, which is a sculpture in and of itself when creating a piece as complicated and with as many characters as this one. Then we bulk out the main form, refine the anatomy of the piece, and add details. Throughout this process, we make sure we aren't deviating from the overall form and silhouette of the original painting. We have our armature wire, our tools, and our clay... let's dive in!

BY THE SHIFLETT BROTHERS

MATERIALS & TOOLS

MATERIALS

ARMATURE
Almaloy aluminum alloy
armature wire (15-gauge/1.5 mm)
Aluminum foil
Aluminum wire mesh
Floral wire

CLAY
Super Sculpey Firm
Aves Apoxie Sculpt
Plumber's epoxy putty

GLUE AND SOLVENT
Wood glue
Super glue
91% Isopropyl rubbing alcohol

OTHER
Wooden base
Wood chunks/offcuts
PVC pipe
Styrene tubing

TOOLS
Cutting wire
Hobby knives
Wire-cutting pliers
Needle-nose pliers
Rake tools
Needle files
Loop tools
Ball tools
Burnisher
Scraper
Brushes
Heat gun

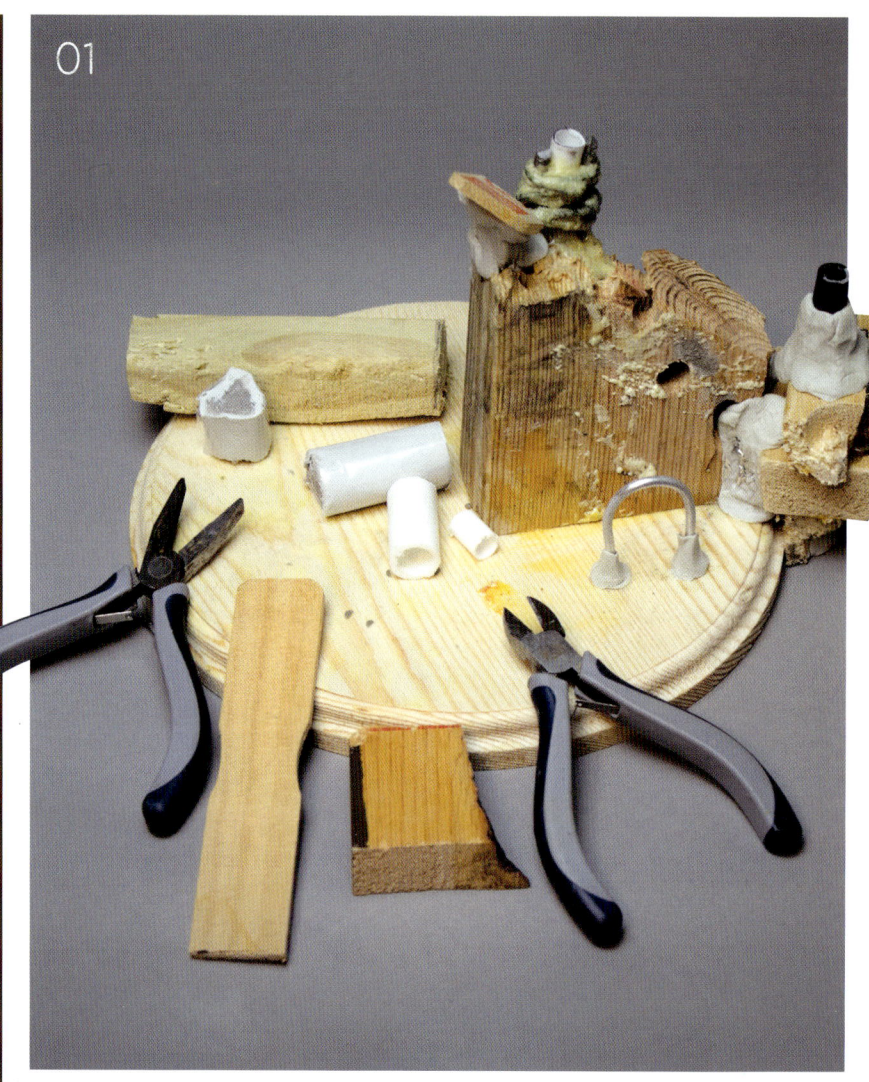

01

BUILDING THE ARMATURE

STEP 01

To start the piece, we build a large base to support the subsequent scene. Even at this early stage, we visualize the demons and bodies that will feature on the outer edges, surrounding the main character. We use chunks of wood to form a hidden sub-base in the general shape of the rocks, affixing them to the wooden base piece using wood glue. We then use plumber's putty to secure small curved lengths of PVC pipe on each side of the rocks. These will hold the armature wire that makes up the legs of the main character.

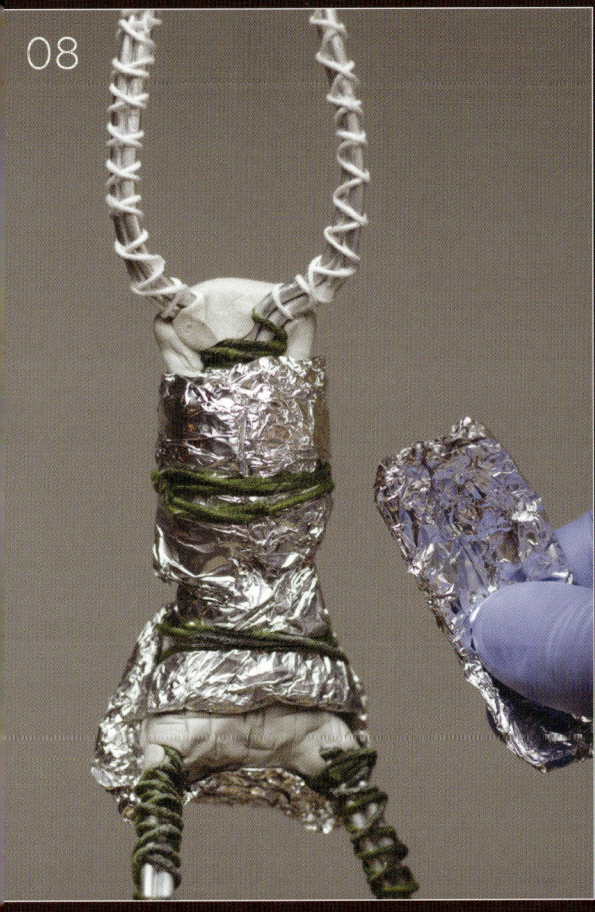

Remember that plumber's putty sets hard in just a couple of minutes, so you need to plan exactly where and how you are going to apply it once you mix it up.

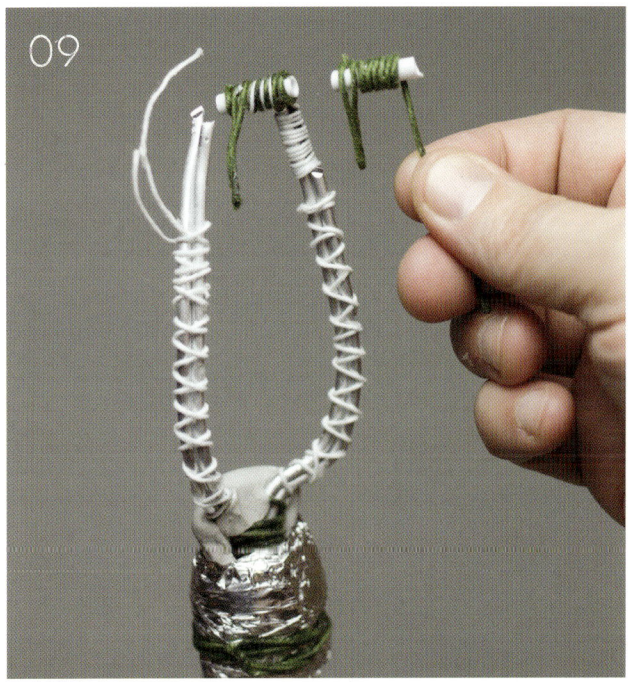

STEP 08

Aluminum foil is added to what will become the biggest part of the body, the torso. Using aluminum foil to pack out the torso and hips lightens the overall weight of the piece and prevents cracking after the completed sculpture is baked.

STEP 09

In the original painting, the Death Dealer wields an axe, so we create a special element in the armature by attaching tiny styrene tubing to the main armature with floral wire. This is approximately where the axe handle will be located, with the hands eventually gripping around it. We plan to use a smaller wire as the actual axe armature to slip into this styrene tube.

STEP 10

We bind the foil to the armature, again using floral wire. We then add super glue to this as well, cementing the whole structure in place.

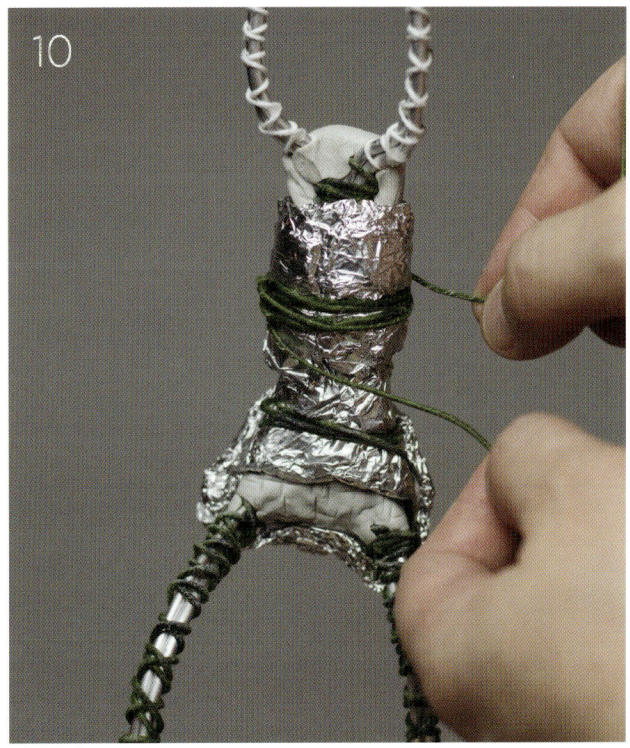

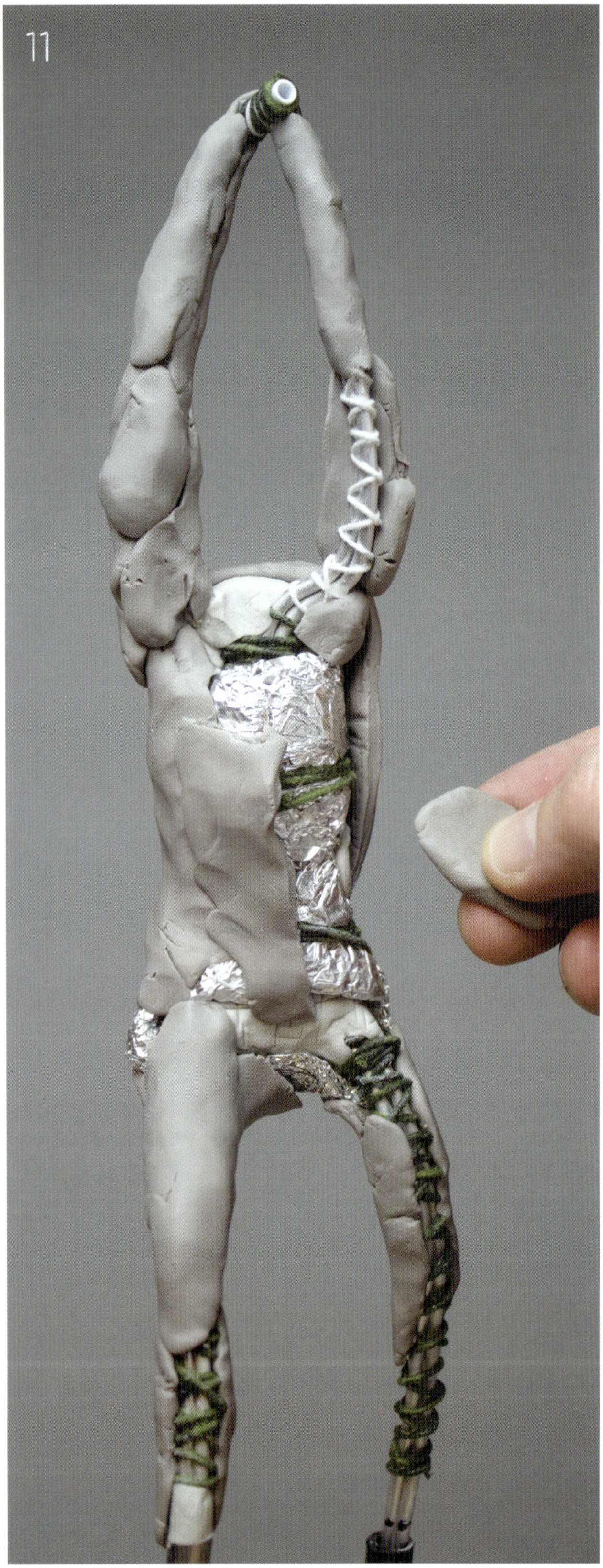

APPLYING CLAY

STEP 11

When bulking out the form of the piece, we begin as a painter might approach a large canvas — large, broad strokes first, moving on to more detailed work later. At this stage, we work with small pieces of clay. We have anatomy in mind, but focus mainly on form and proportion. We make any minor adjustments that are needed, such as adding or subtracting a few millimeters, and if the armature needs to be adjusted, then we do that at this point too. From the second you begin a piece, you are correcting and refining it along the way.

STEP 12

We continue to add Super Sculpey one small piece at a time, and sometimes draw lines in the clay to give us an idea of where the abs will be. We build the musculature — very rough triceps and elbows can be seen here. These little landmarks help us to place other features, such as anatomy, clothing, or armor.

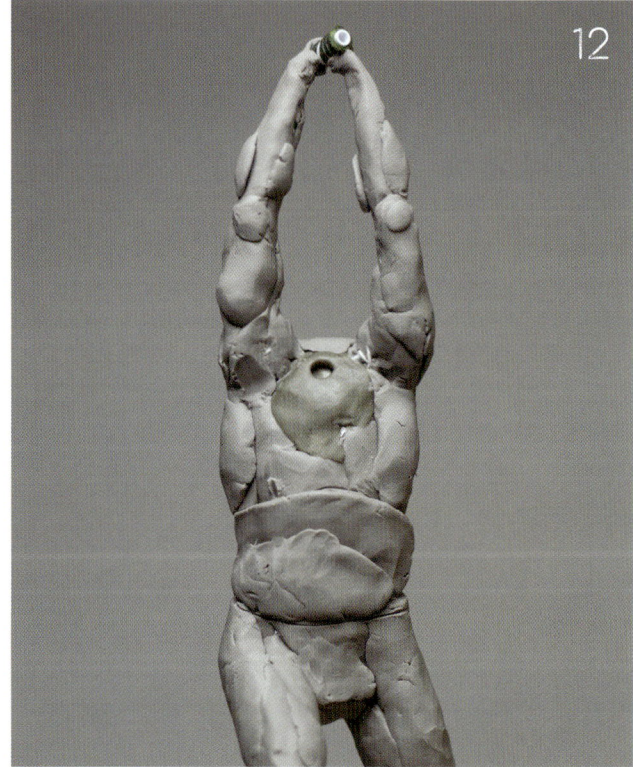

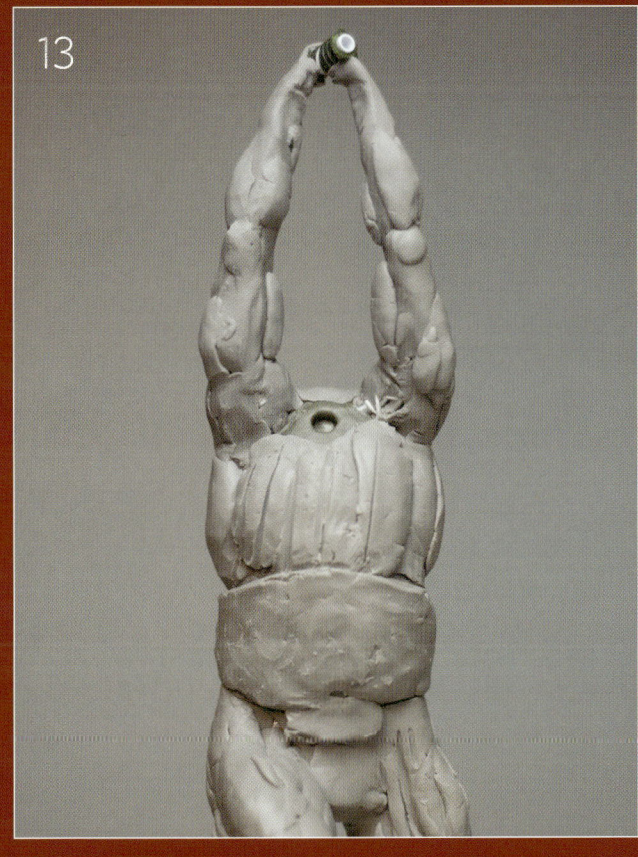

STEP 13

Next, we insert plumber's putty into the neck and add a hole, to later hold a removable head. We engineer this feature now instead of sculpting the entire piece and *then* cutting it up. But both options are viable. More bulk is added to the arms and legs, and the shape of the thighs begins to form. At this stage we also begin to sculpt the character's belt and tunic. We attempt to place folds in the fabric in the same positions as they are depicted in the original painting.

STEP 14

This view shows the back of the piece, much of which will eventually be covered by the tunic and pelt at the top and a chainmail skirt farther down. For now, the temporarily exposed aluminum foil bulks out the back.

STEP 15

Now, we add the head armature. Aluminum wire secured in the hole we made previously, forms the neck. Around this, we wrap floral wire to form the beginning of the head area. Separately, we form a basic head using plumber's putty. This stable skull-shaped ball acts as the base onto which we will sculpt the head using clay.

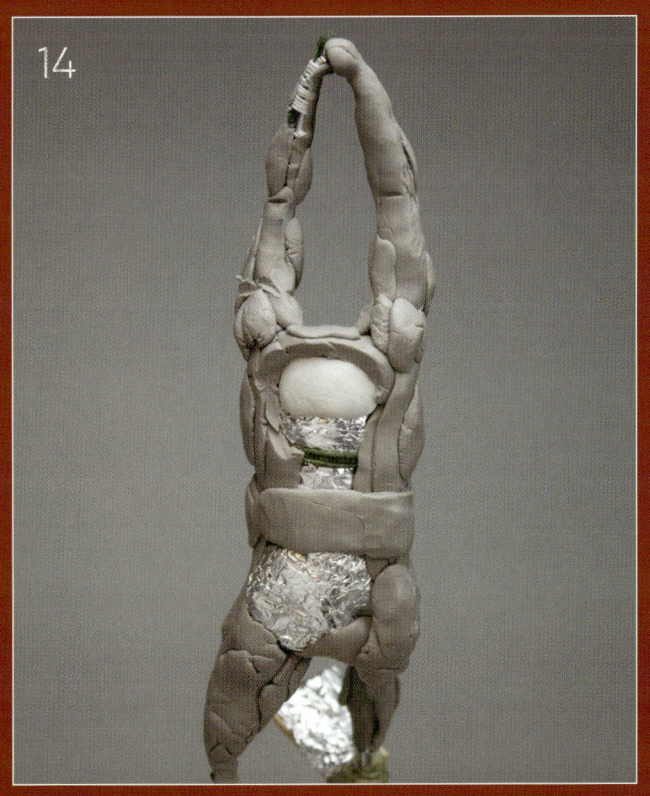

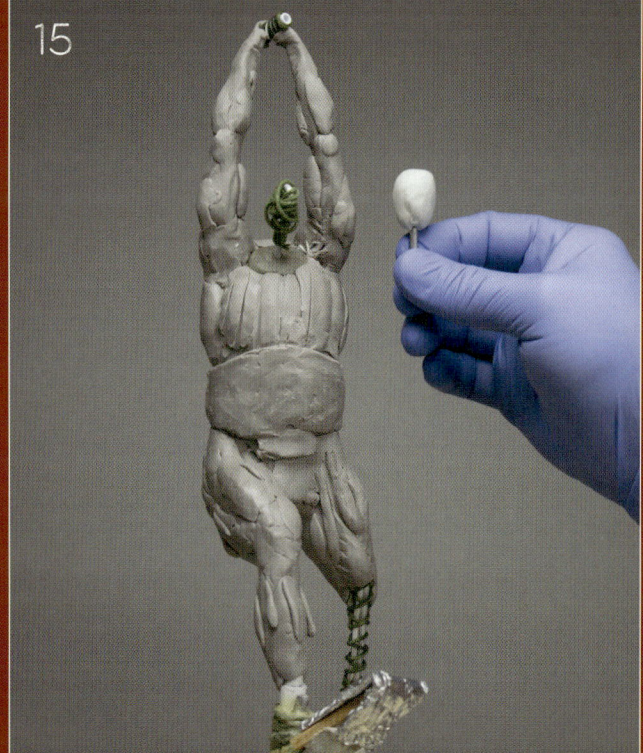

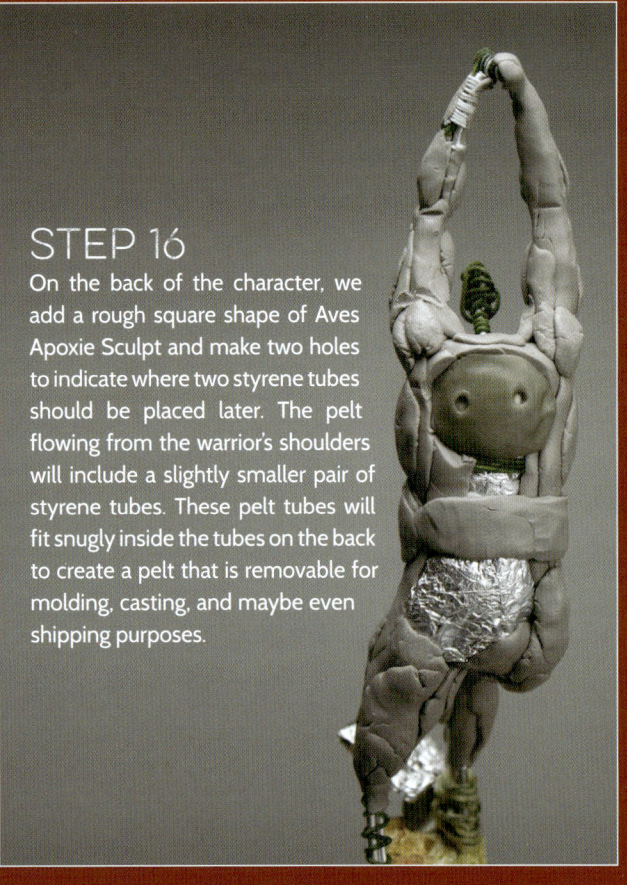

STEP 16

On the back of the character, we add a rough square shape of Aves Apoxie Sculpt and make two holes to indicate where two styrene tubes should be placed later. The pelt flowing from the warrior's shoulders will include a slightly smaller pair of styrene tubes. These pelt tubes will fit snugly inside the tubes on the back to create a pelt that is removable for molding, casting, and maybe even shipping purposes.

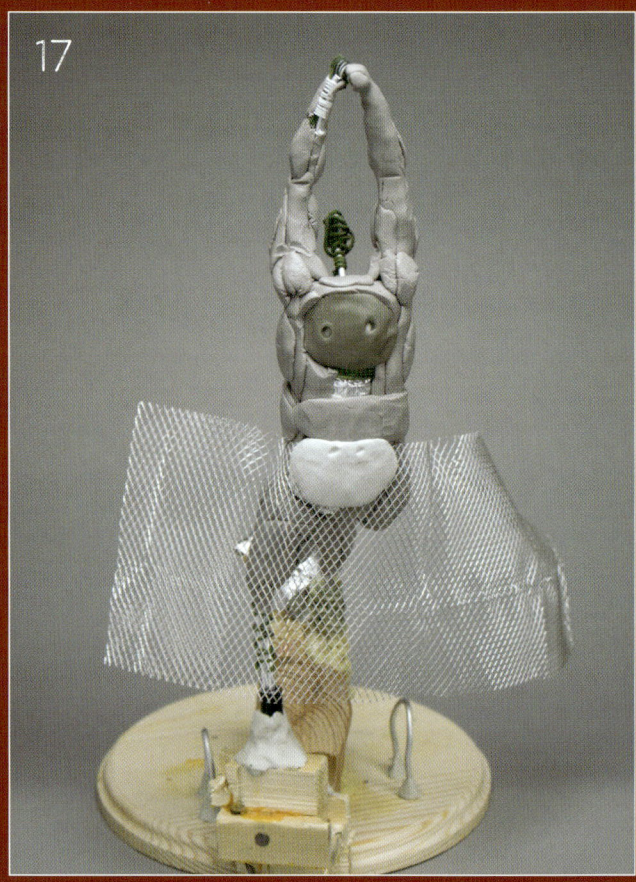

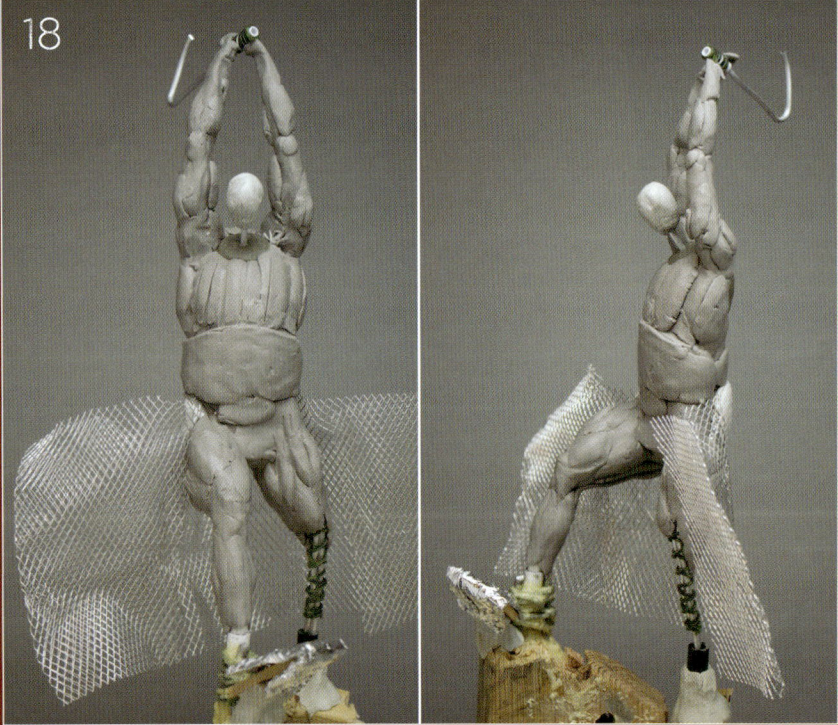

STEP 17

Further down the back of the sculpture, we add a second square to hold two styrene tubes, this time made of white plumber's putty. This will secure the skirt section while also making it fully removable. We also begin to apply the wire mesh, and will later shape this into the base layer (effectively the armature) for the chainmail skirt.

STEP 18

Next, we add the simple aluminum wire axe armature and the base for the character's head. With the head tilted down and leaning forward, the character has a more aggressive and powerful silhouette. The dynamic action pose begins to take shape.

STEP 19

Here, our male/female styrene tubing method to create removable parts can be seen. The tube coming out of the base of the head is a bit smaller than the tube that rests inside the body, allowing it to fit snugly. To make the potentially delicate horns strong and durable, we connect a couple of floral wire pieces, attaching them to the head with small pieces of plumber's putty.

STEP 20

As we block in the helmet, the look of the character really begins to come together. We also start to shape the chainmail skirt in clay on top of the wire mesh armature. We want to replicate the way the skirt looks in the painting, but we also want its flow to look natural from all angles. Therefore, we make sure to continually check progress from all sides.

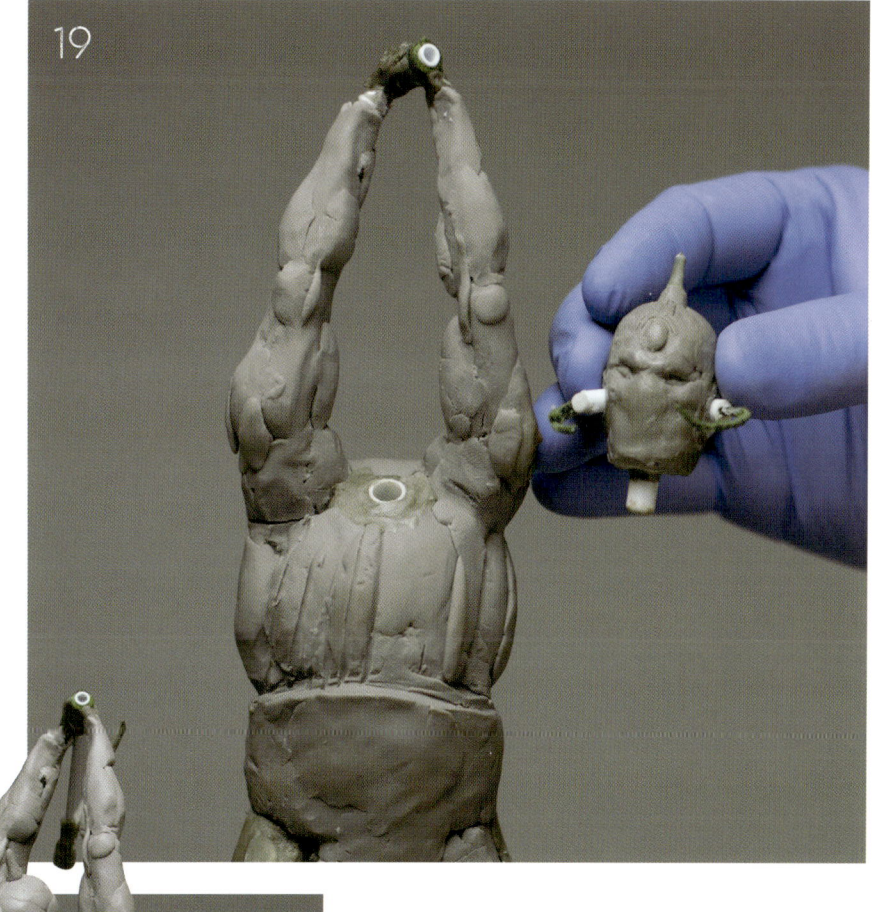

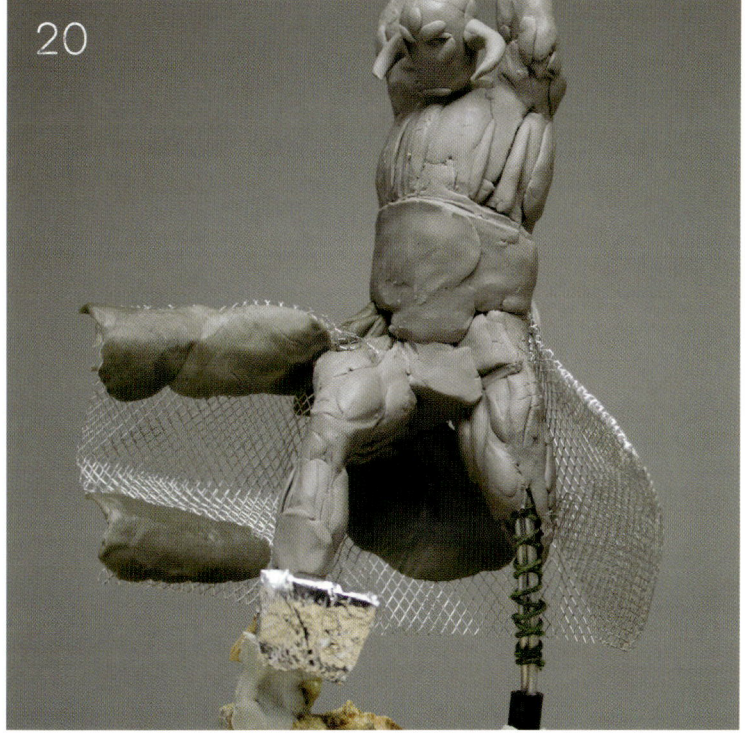

WITH THE HEAD TILTED DOWN AND LEANING FORWARD, THE CHARACTER HAS A MORE AGGRESSIVE AND POWERFUL SILHOUETTE

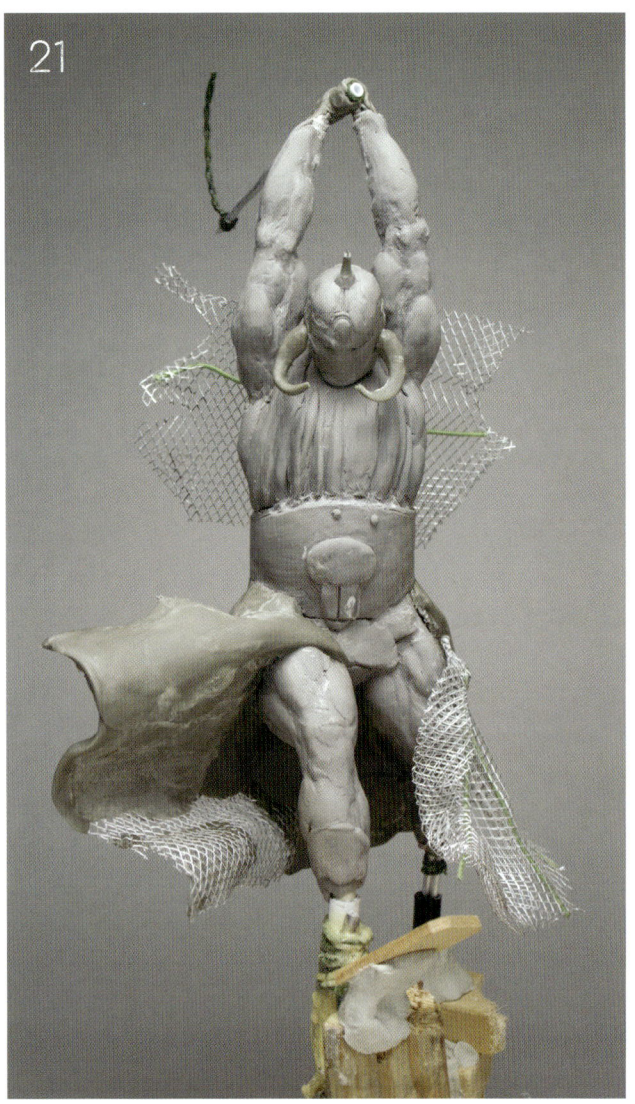

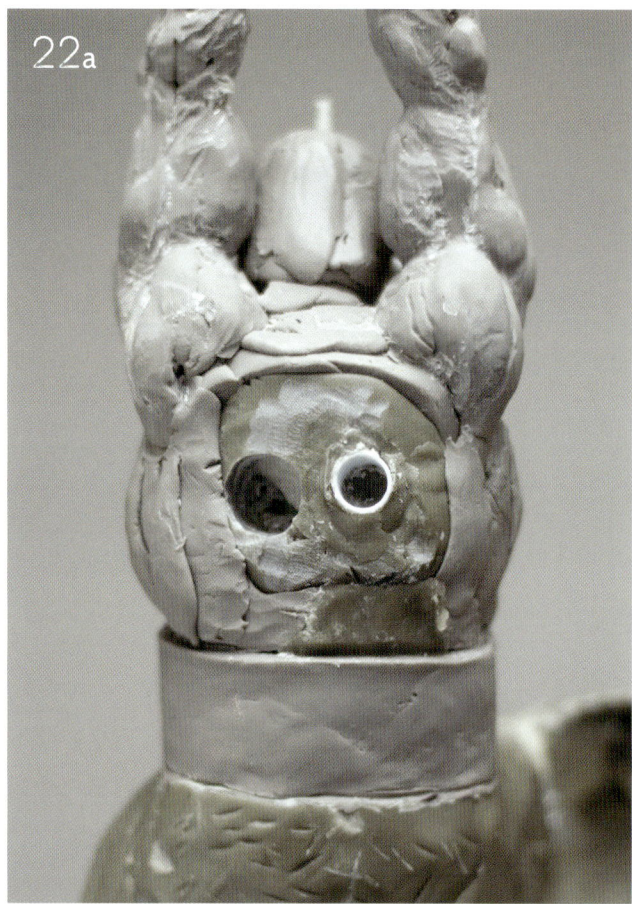

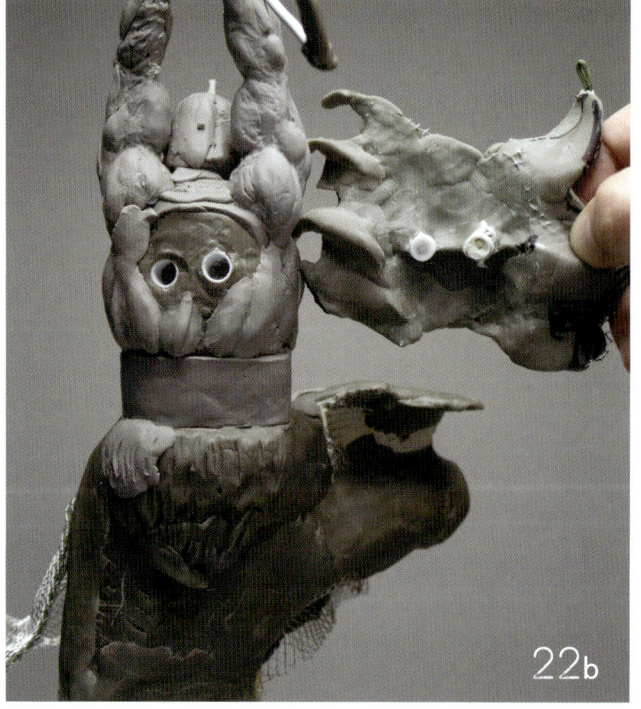

STEP 21

We refer to the shape of the pelt the Death Dealer wears on his shoulders in the painting, then cut and fold wire mesh into the general form before adding it to the sculpture. In addition, the sword armature is recreated, and the skirt filled out with more clay. We also begin to outline the general shape of the skull design adorning the belt.

STEP 22

Next, we drill into the Aves Apoxie Sculpt section on the back of the piece and insert styrene tubing, again slightly larger than the tubing that will protrude from the pelt section, so that the two can slot together (22a). Here, you can see how the pelt section can be connected, removed, and replaced all thanks to the magic of our plastic tubing connection method! (22b)

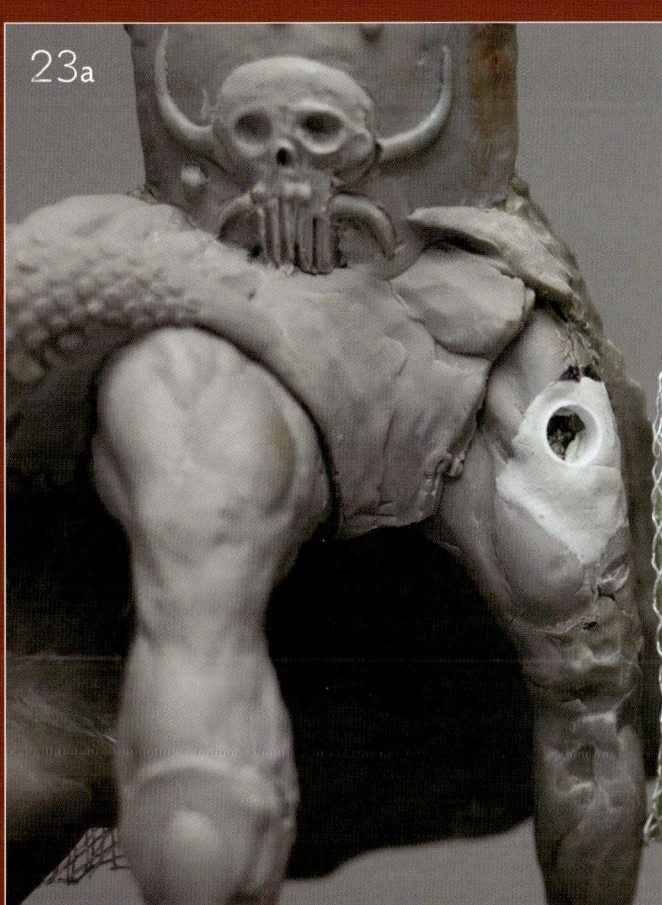

23a

STEP 23

We begin to build the left side of the skirt from clay and construct the armature for the flowing section of the skirt from mesh. We also drill holes in the upper thigh and fit tubing in the holes as well as on the armature of the flowing skirt section. Once built from clay and detailed, the flowing skirt section will fit into the corresponding tubing on the upper thigh. At this point, we judge the shape, flow, and proportion of it compared to the original Frazetta art. We want our sculpture to match up as closely as possible.

23b

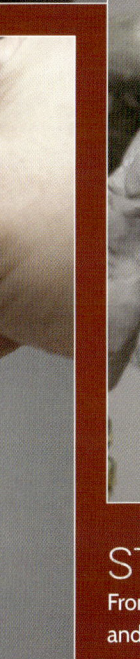

24

STEP 24

From this side view, it is clear to see how the horns can be removed and replaced in the helmet. We engineer the connections as we work, as opposed to sculpting the entire piece and then cutting it up at the end. We've done the latter before and find it to be a different but still viable method.

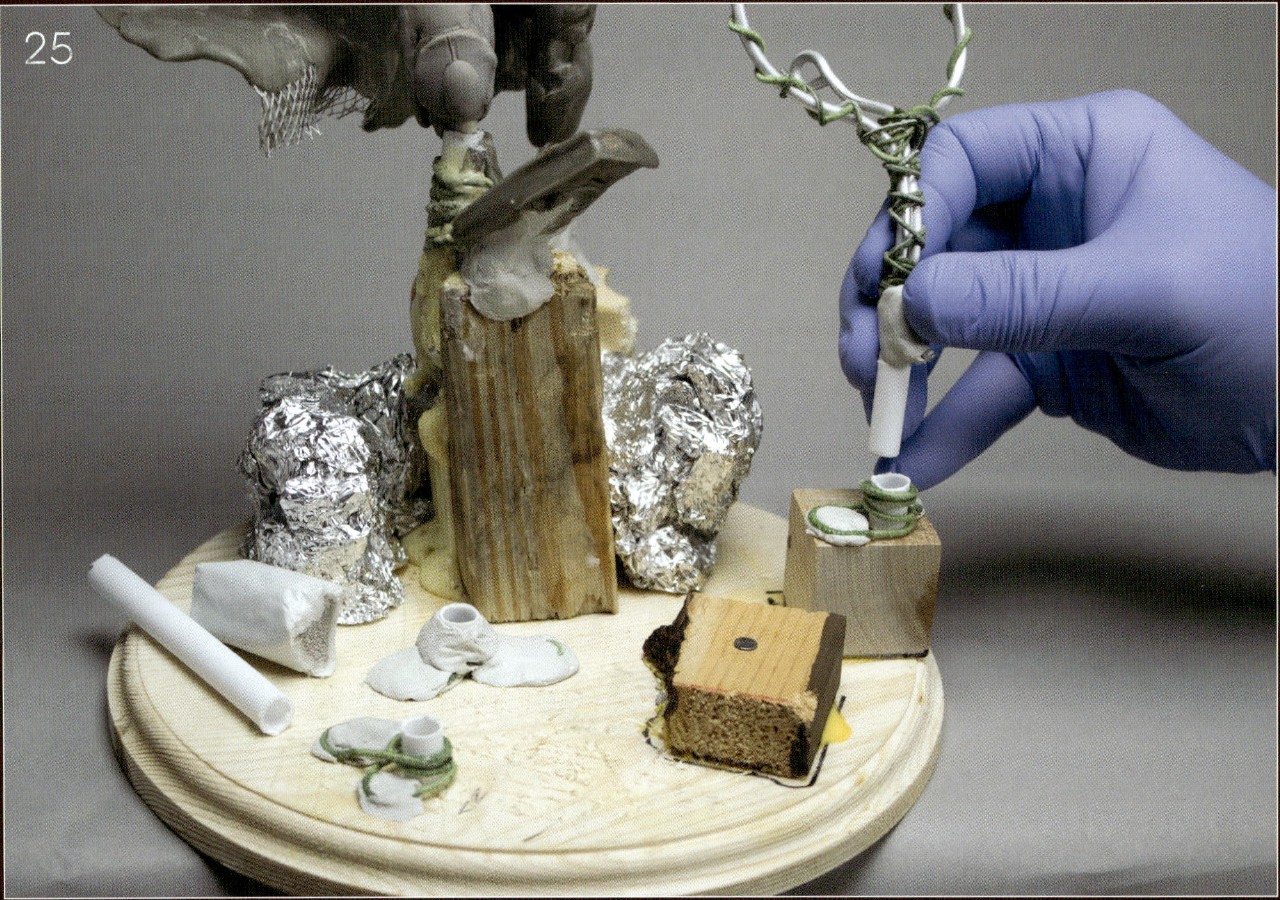

25

CONSTRUCTING THE BASE

STEP 25

Next, we focus our attention on the base of the piece. We begin with the armature for the demon who rises up with his arms aloft, to the Death Dealer's left. The armature is made of our usual combination of aluminum wire wrapped in floral wire. We strengthen the bottom of the demon's armature with plumber's putty and create a system of tubes so that the demon will be removable.

STEP 26

We then bulk out the base using a lot of aluminum foil and secure it in place with plumber's putty. At this stage, we remove the Death Dealer from the base so as not to compromise any of the work on him so far.

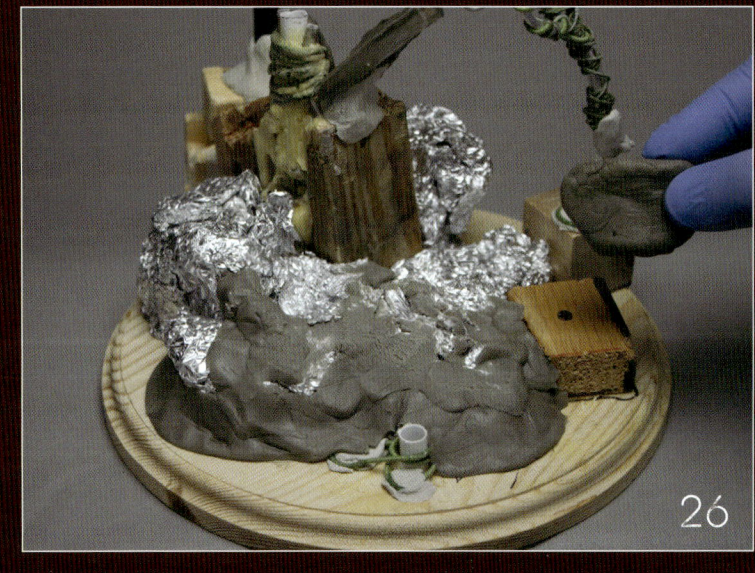

26

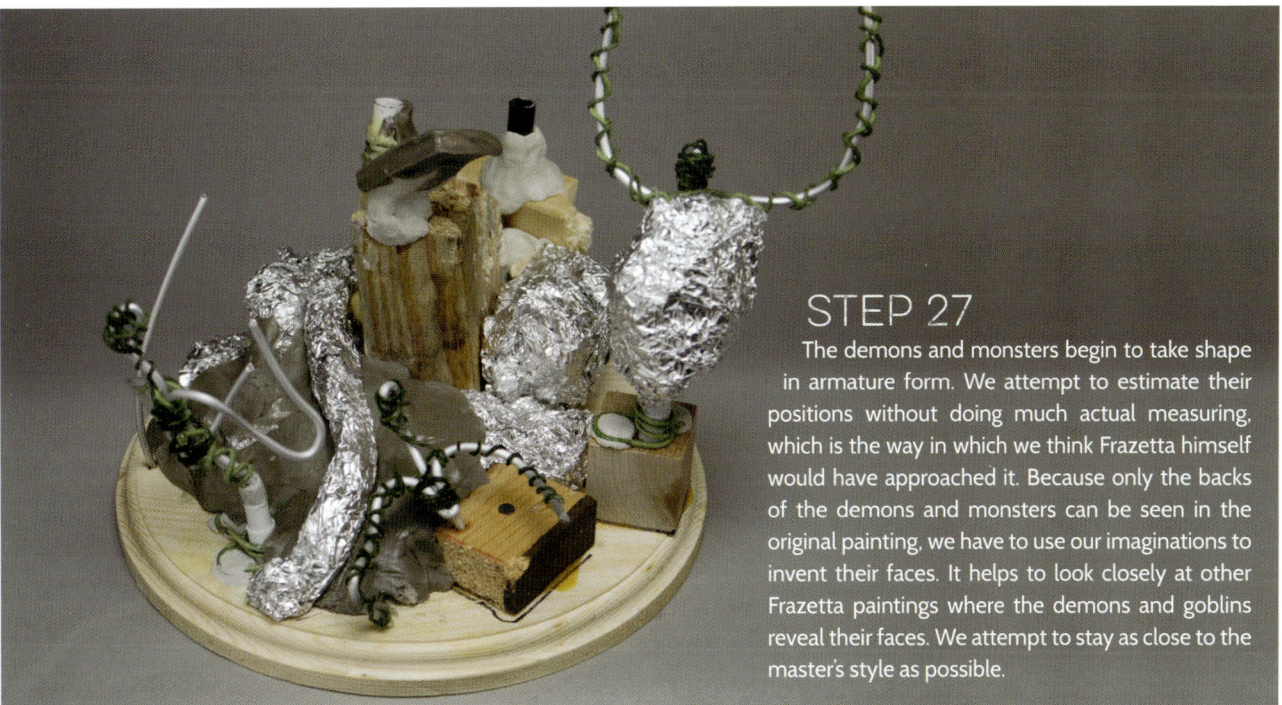

STEP 27

The demons and monsters begin to take shape in armature form. We attempt to estimate their positions without doing much actual measuring, which is the way in which we think Frazetta himself would have approached it. Because only the backs of the demons and monsters can be seen in the original painting, we have to use our imaginations to invent their faces. It helps to look closely at other Frazetta paintings where the demons and goblins reveal their faces. We attempt to stay as close to the master's style as possible.

STEP 28

As we add clay to their bodies, the Death Dealer's nemeses begin to emerge from the rocks. We also work on sculpting the rocks, which always sounds easy to beginners, but it is actually tricky to create realistic rocks and cliffs. We use lots of references of real-life rocks and cliff edges.

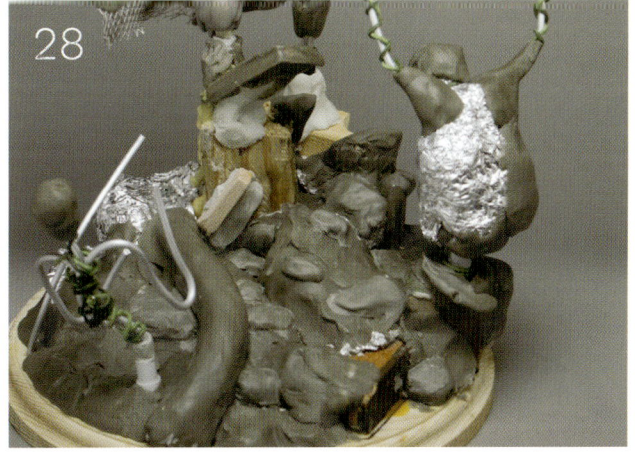

STEP 29

Clay is applied to the foil used to bulk out the demons' thicker spots (29a). The clay should not be more than half an inch thick because of the stress and weight it can put on the armature, so building the bulk with foil is beneficial. At this point, we also start work on the large snake form which runs down the center of the base (29b).

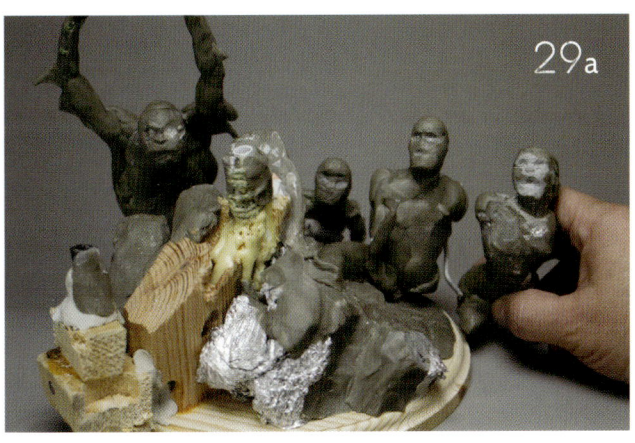

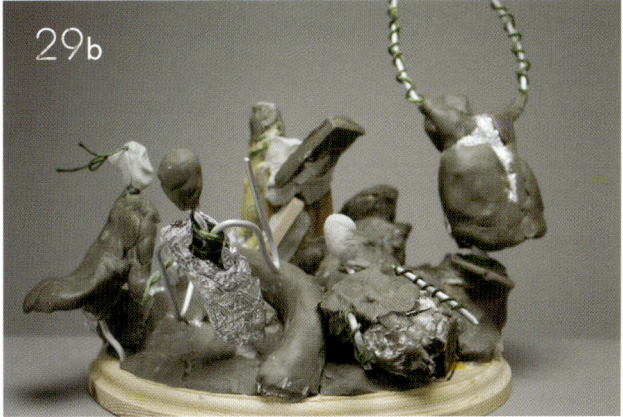

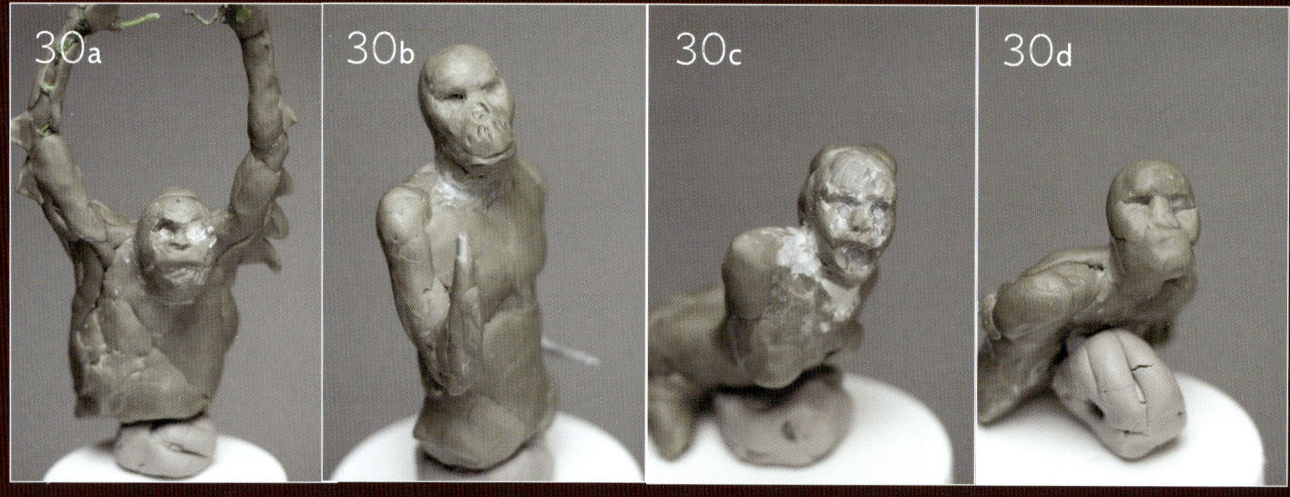

STEP 30

Here is the line-up of demons. The first, largest creature features on the right side of the sculpture and we consider him the most important character on the base as he is the biggest and highest up in the air, with his lifted arms (30a). As such, we give him extra care and attention in the form of refined details. The remaining creatures are in their very early forms, simply bulked out at this point, with more detail to come. The third creature is the female monster (30c). Her face appears to be monstrous in the painting, but some of the tell-tale signs of a typically shaped "Frazetta Woman" can be seen.

STEP 31

With the addition of more clay and sculpting, some of the anatomical detail of the demons starts to take shape. The clearest example can be seen on the main demon's back and shoulders.

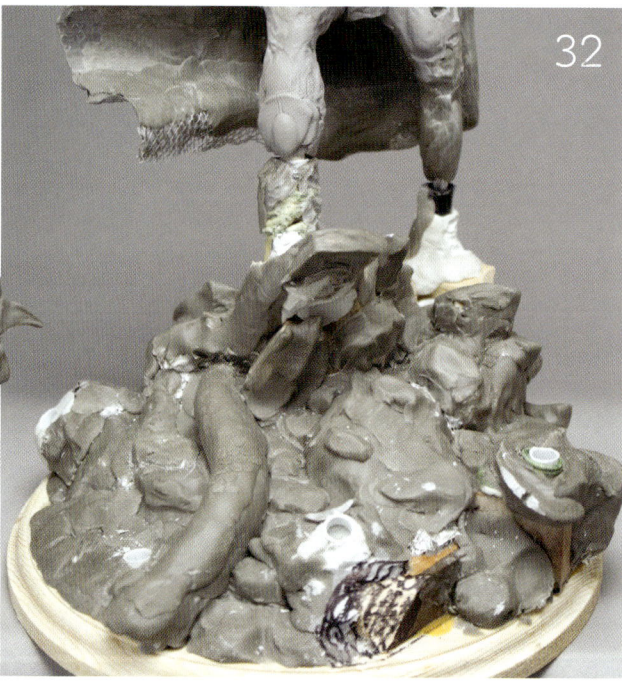

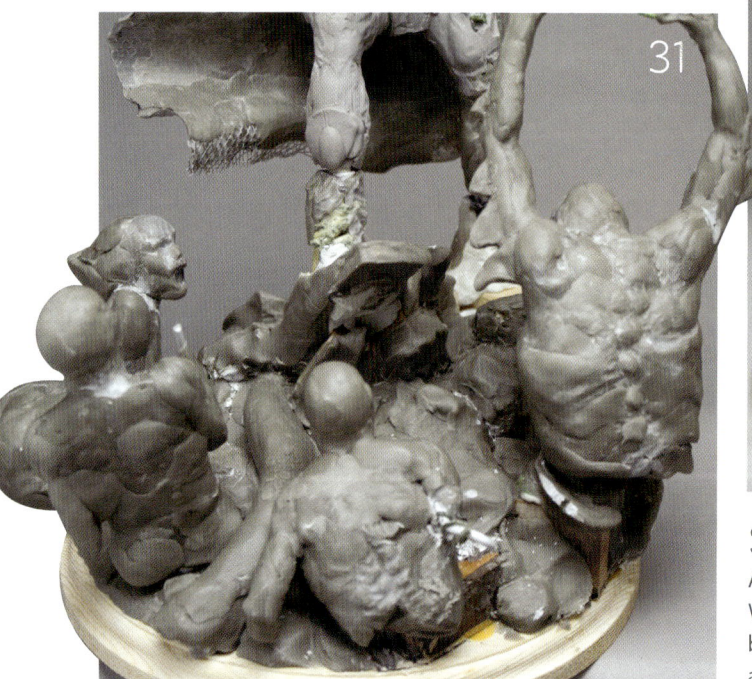

STEP 32

As shown, all demon characters can be removed from the base. We again utilize plastic tubing to allow the individual creatures to be detachable. This allows us to work on each demon individually and to access otherwise hard-to-reach zones of the sculpture.

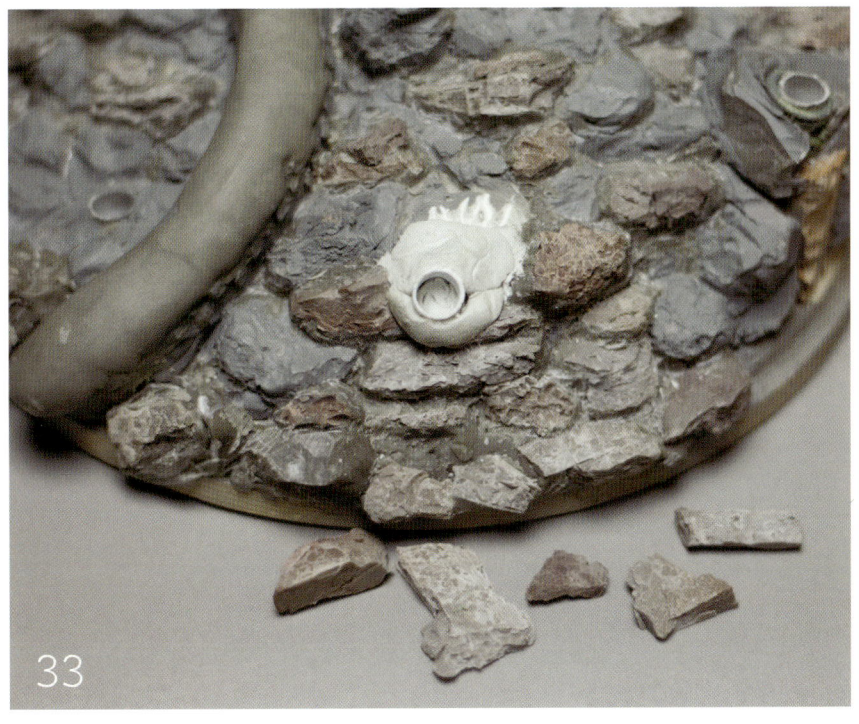

33

STEP 33

To create rocks on the base, we create slabs of different types of hardened clay and smash them with a hammer. We can take all of our frustrations out on baked and cured clay! The smashing creates little bits of clay with rock-like striations and angles in it. We select the best-looking pieces and fit them into our base. We're happy with the forms and think they look convincing as a rocky outcropping. We then apply a layer of gray primer paint to unify the rocks.

STEP 34

We add scales to the big snake whose body runs down the middle of the base (34a). We take the time to detail each individual scale with tiny lines running their length (34b). It isn't clear in the painting where this snake begins or ends but the size of his reptilian body is imposing.

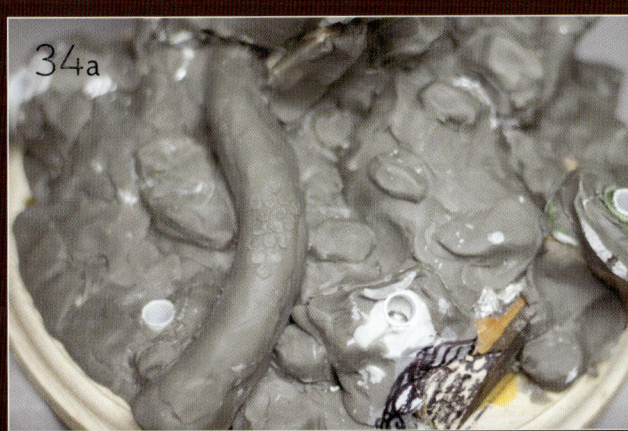

34a

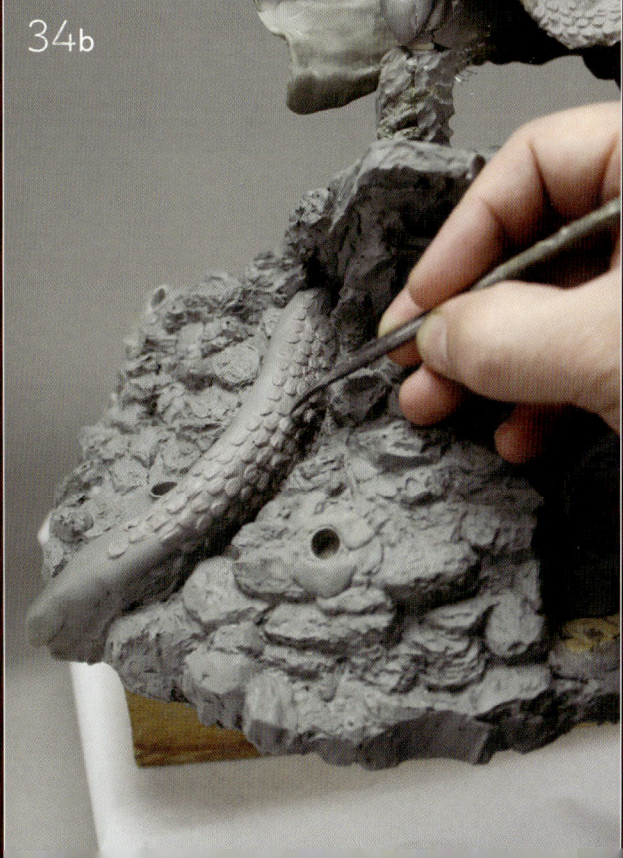

34b

WE TAKE THE TIME TO DETAIL EACH INDIVIDUAL SCALE WITH TINY LINE SHAPES RUNNING THEIR LENGTH

DETAILING THE DEATH DEALER

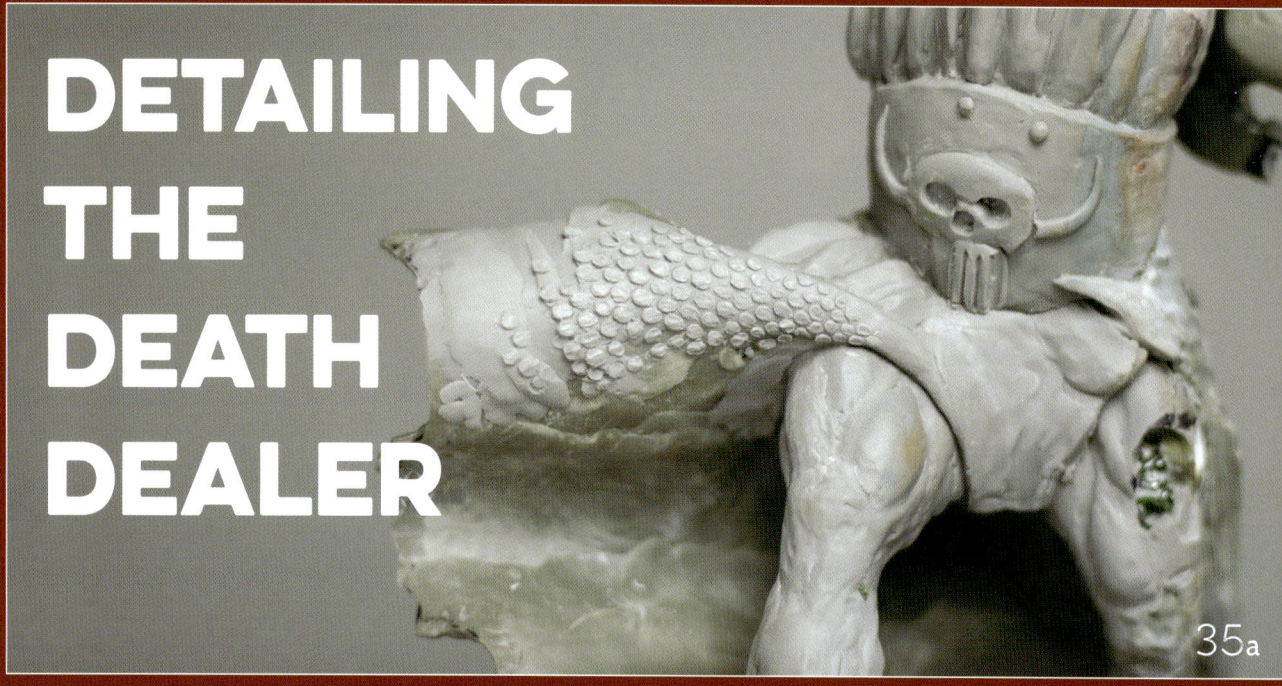

35a

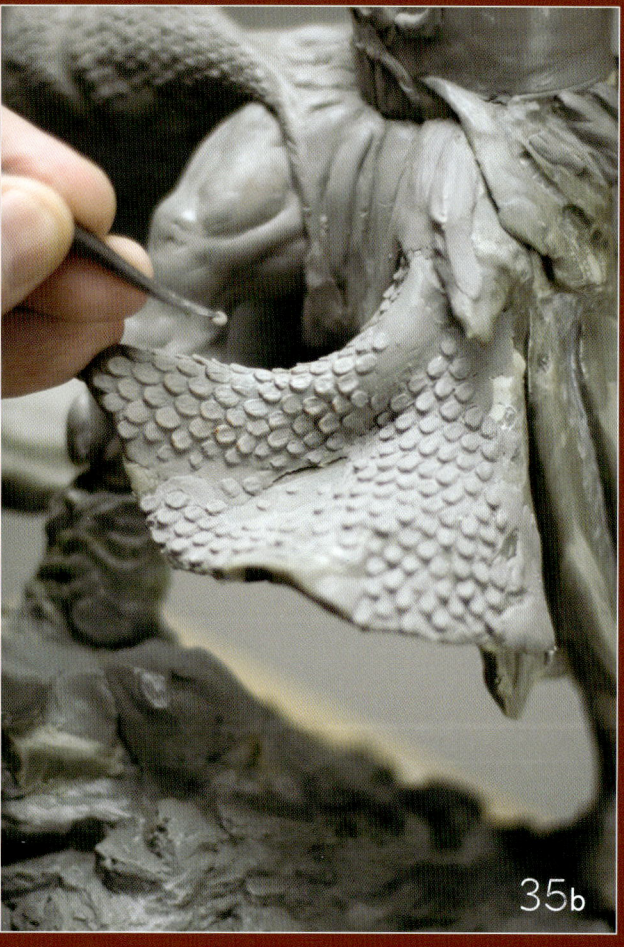

35b

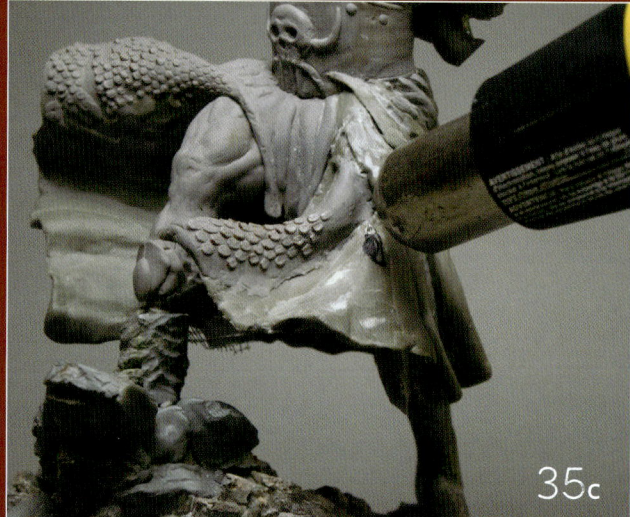

35c

STEP 35

Next, we work on building the flowing chainmail skirt. After constructing the wire mesh armature and applying a thin layer of plumber's putty to provide a stable base on which to sculpt, we add tiny balls of clay and smooth them into place to try to mimic the look of chainmail (35a). Sculpting at this scale often means creating many little illusions. For instance, we can't actually recreate chain mail at this size, but we can create a good enough approximation that it fools the eye (35b). To "lock in" the details of the chainmail and avoid damaging the intricate work as we progress, we gently cure the clay with a heat gun (35c).

36

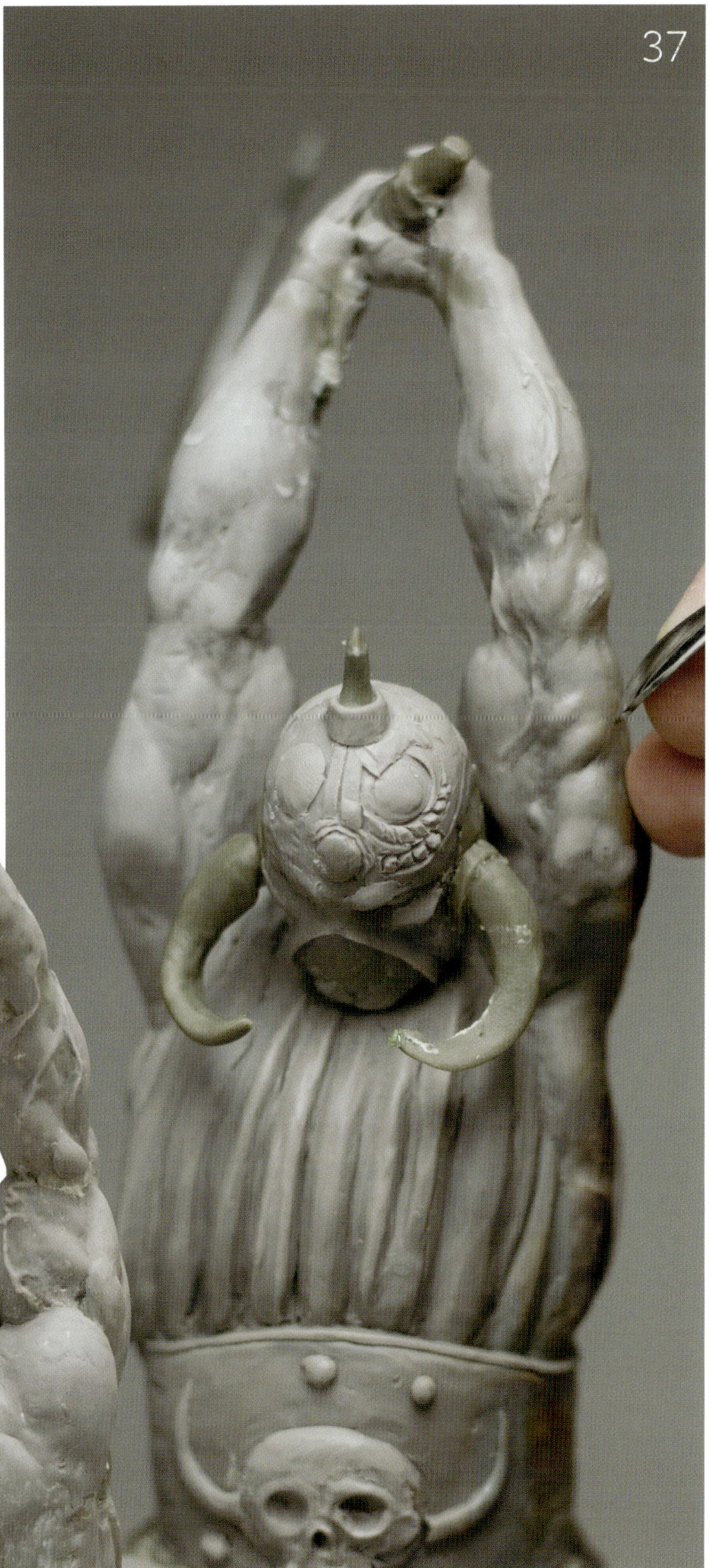

37

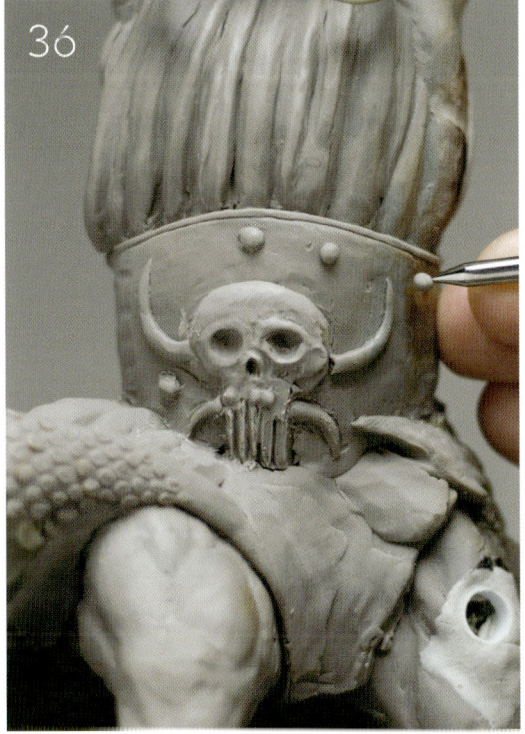

STEP 36

Rivets are added to the Death Dealer's massive metal belt. We place the balls of clay on as placeholders for now, but soon we will endeavor to make these details and the belt itself look like real metal. The key will be looking at references of hammered metal items similar to those depicted in the painting.

STEP 37

Now we get back to the fun parts: arm anatomy! We work on the musculature under the arm and, as always, use photographic references to guide us — bodybuilder magazines to the rescue! We manipulate the clay with the spoon end of our trusty burnisher.

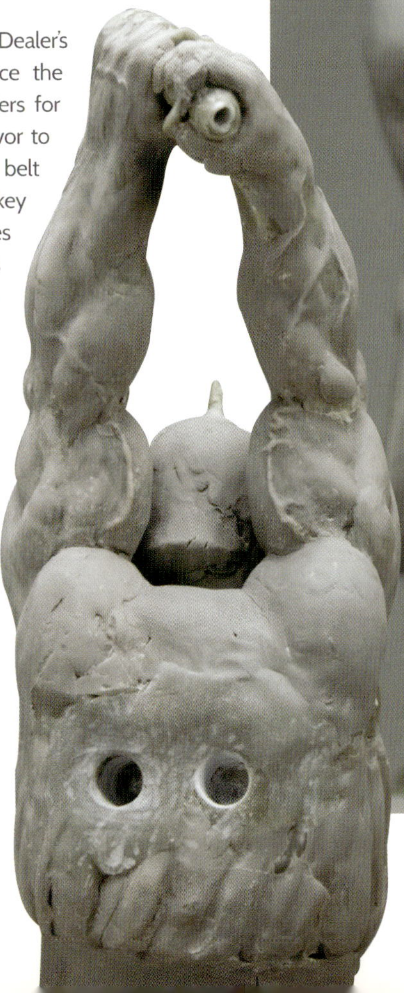

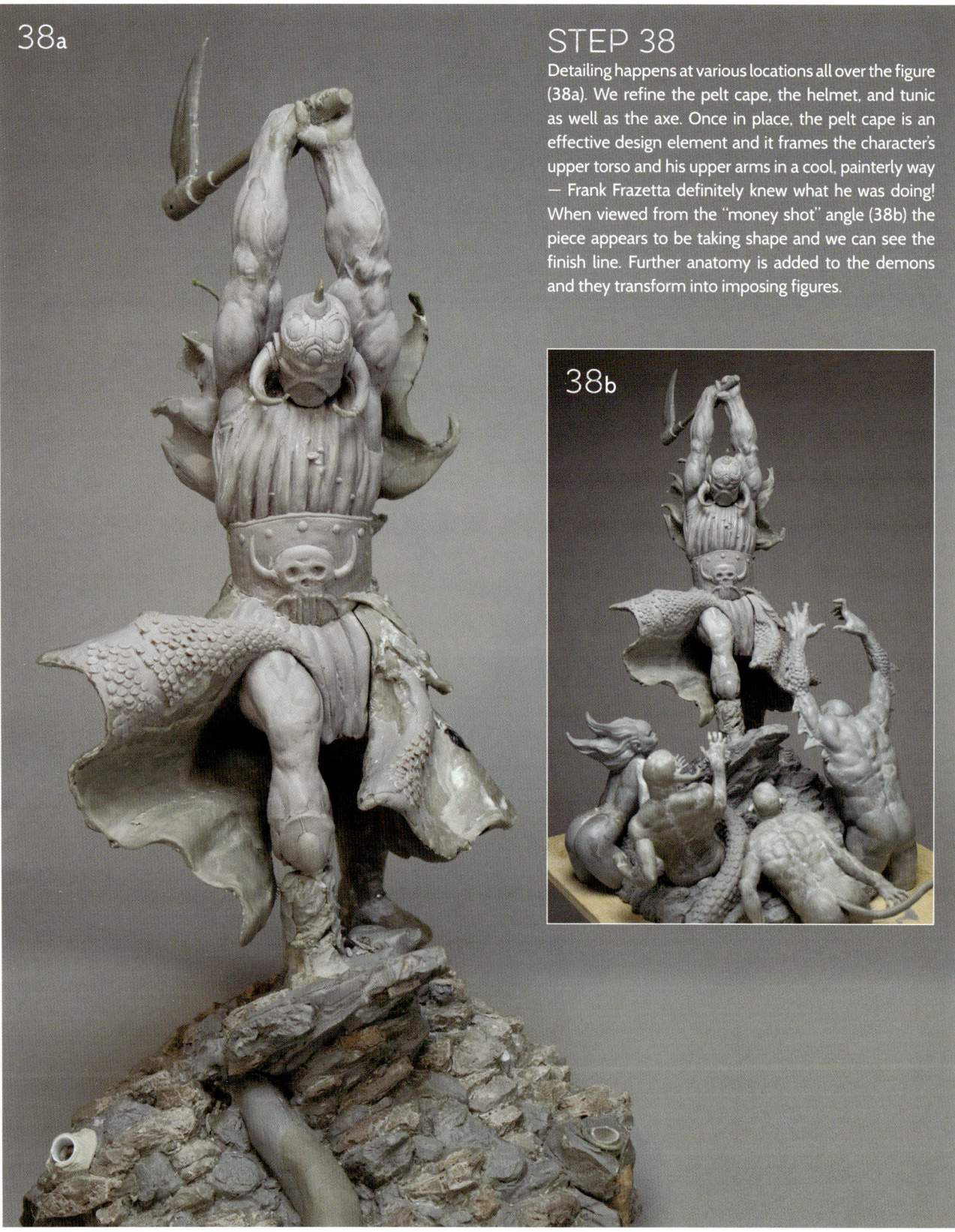

38a

STEP 38

Detailing happens at various locations all over the figure (38a). We refine the pelt cape, the helmet, and tunic as well as the axe. Once in place, the pelt cape is an effective design element and it frames the character's upper torso and his upper arms in a cool, painterly way — Frank Frazetta definitely knew what he was doing! When viewed from the "money shot" angle (38b) the piece appears to be taking shape and we can see the finish line. Further anatomy is added to the demons and they transform into imposing figures.

38b

STEP 39

Once we are happy with the overall forms of the demons, we then move on to adding definition and character. As Frazetta's original painting doesn't show the faces of most of the demons, we decide to take the most imposing demon in a more simian direction, with angry ape-like facial features and expression (39a). One of the demons in the foreground is depicted bent over, almost lying down, and again his face cannot be seen, so we invent a menacing face with demonic skeletal features (39b).

39a

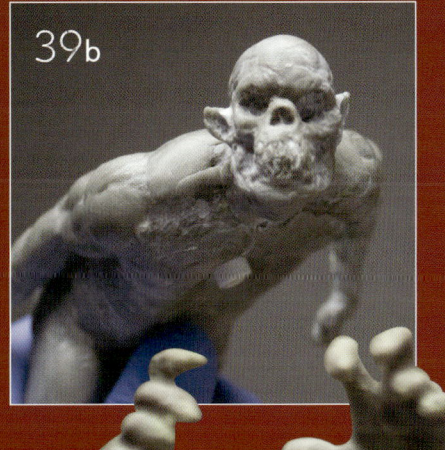

39b

WE DECIDE TO TAKE THE MOST IMPOSING DEMON IN A MORE SIMIAN DIRECTION, WITH ANGRY APE-LIKE FACIAL FEATURES AND EXPRESSION

STEP 40

To finish the whole piece, all elements are assembled and secured in place. At this point we make any last finishing touches to perfect the piece while retaining its slightly raw aesthetic and leaving just enough to the viewer's imagination.

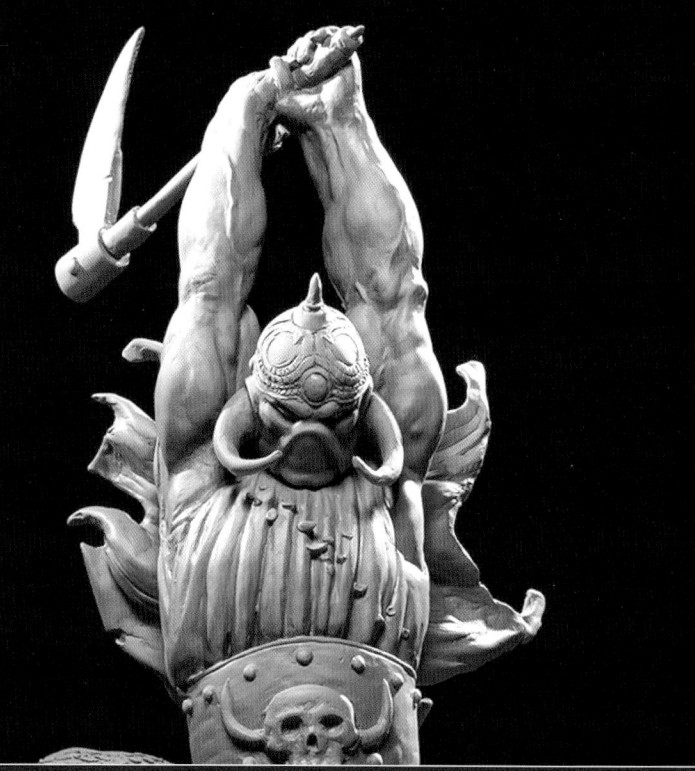

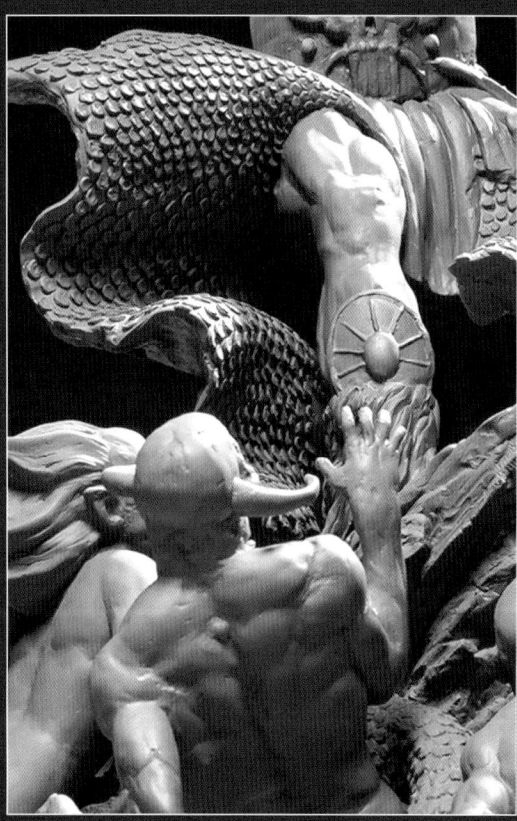

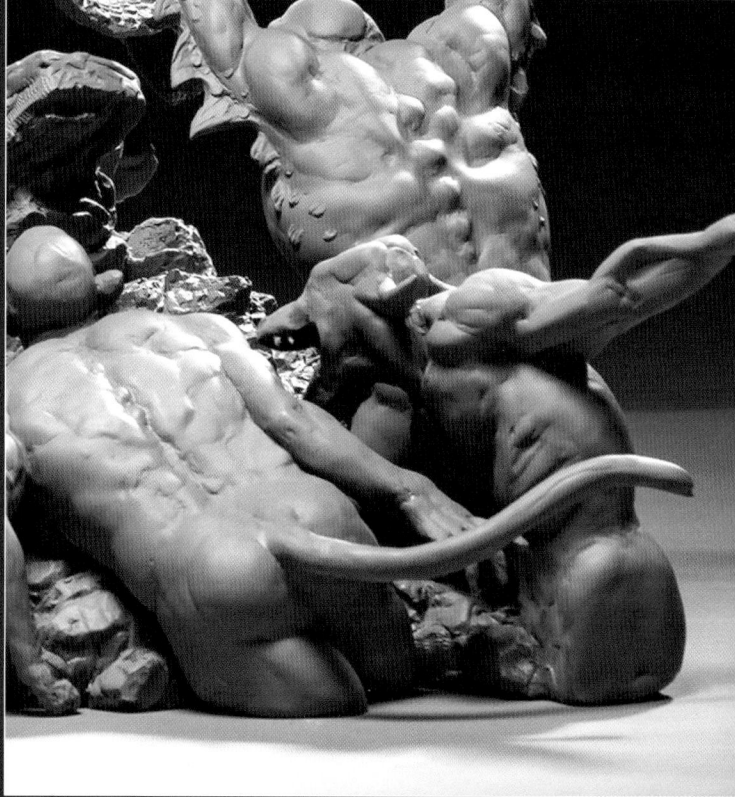

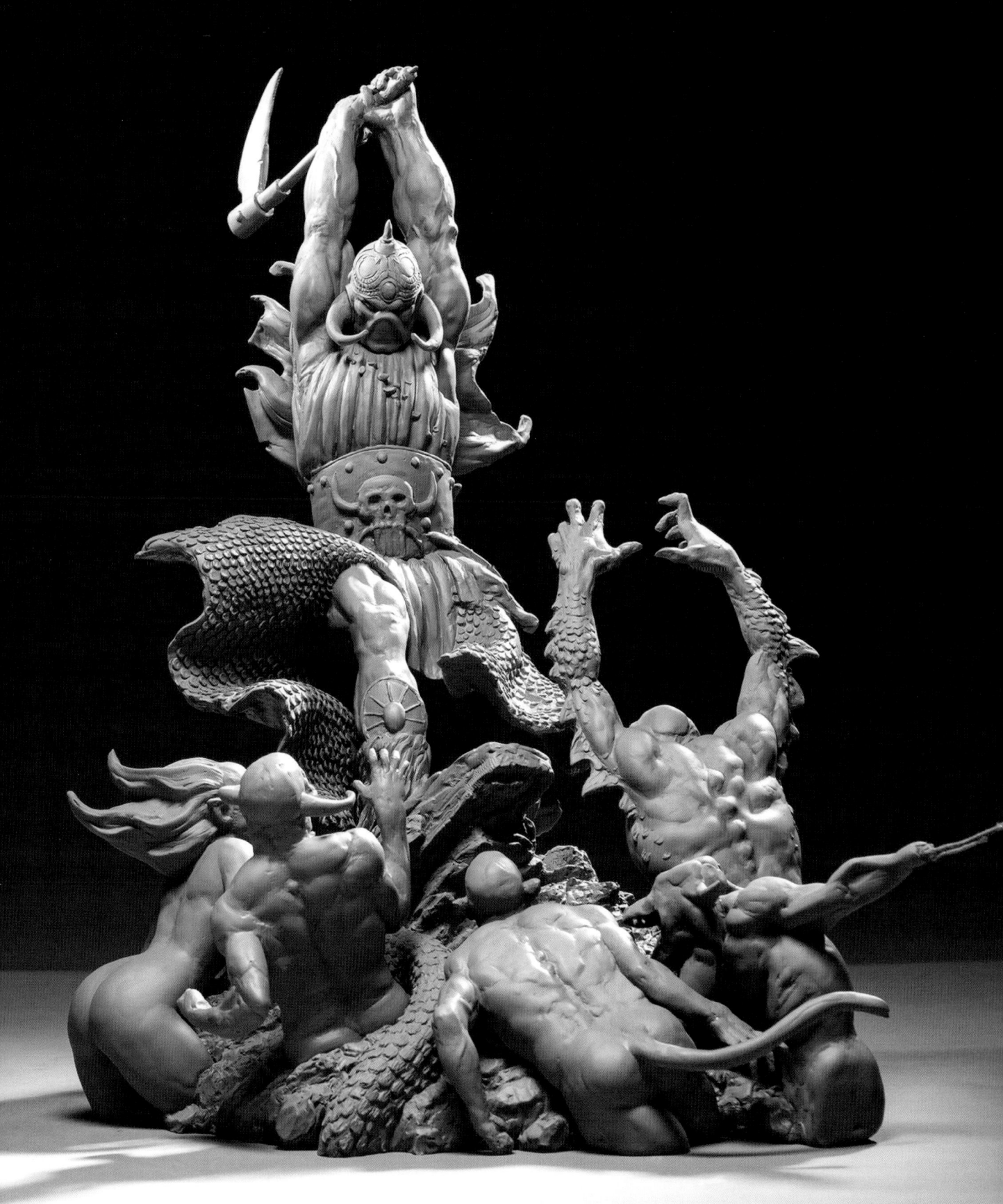

Photography by Matt Mrozek.

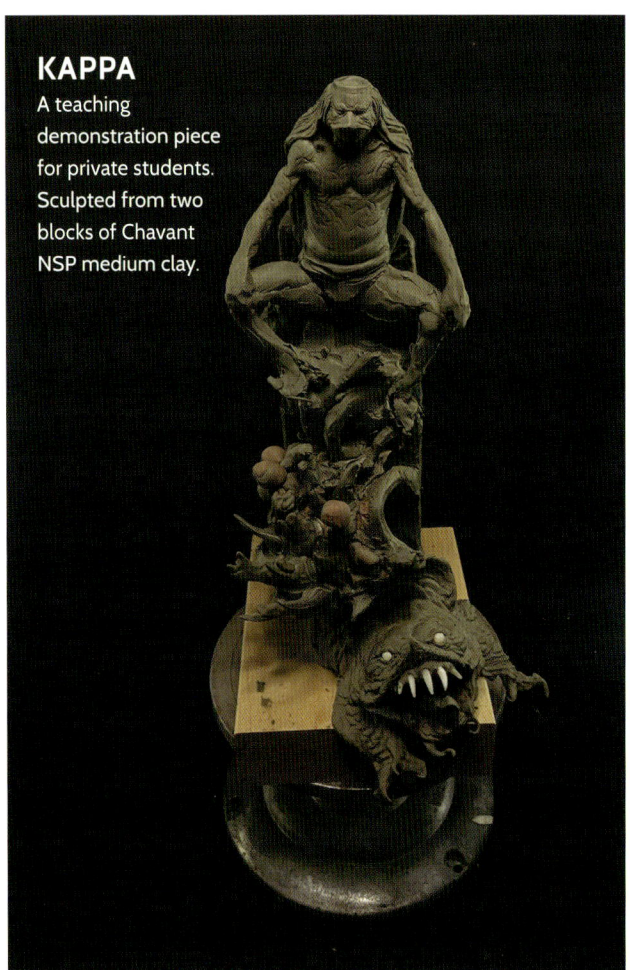

KAPPA
A teaching demonstration piece for private students. Sculpted from two blocks of Chavant NSP medium clay.

ARTIST SPOTLIGHT

SIMON LEE
Concept artist
bigbluetree.com

Based in Los Angeles, Simon Lee is a concept designer for feature films and games. Self-taught, with over thirty-five years of experience, some of his more notable film design works include King Ghidorah from *Godzilla: King of the Monsters*, the skullcrawler from *Kong: Skull Island*, and the vampire creatures from Guillermo del Toro's *The Strain*. In addition to working professionally as a designer, Simon has taught and coached many professional artists for over a decade.

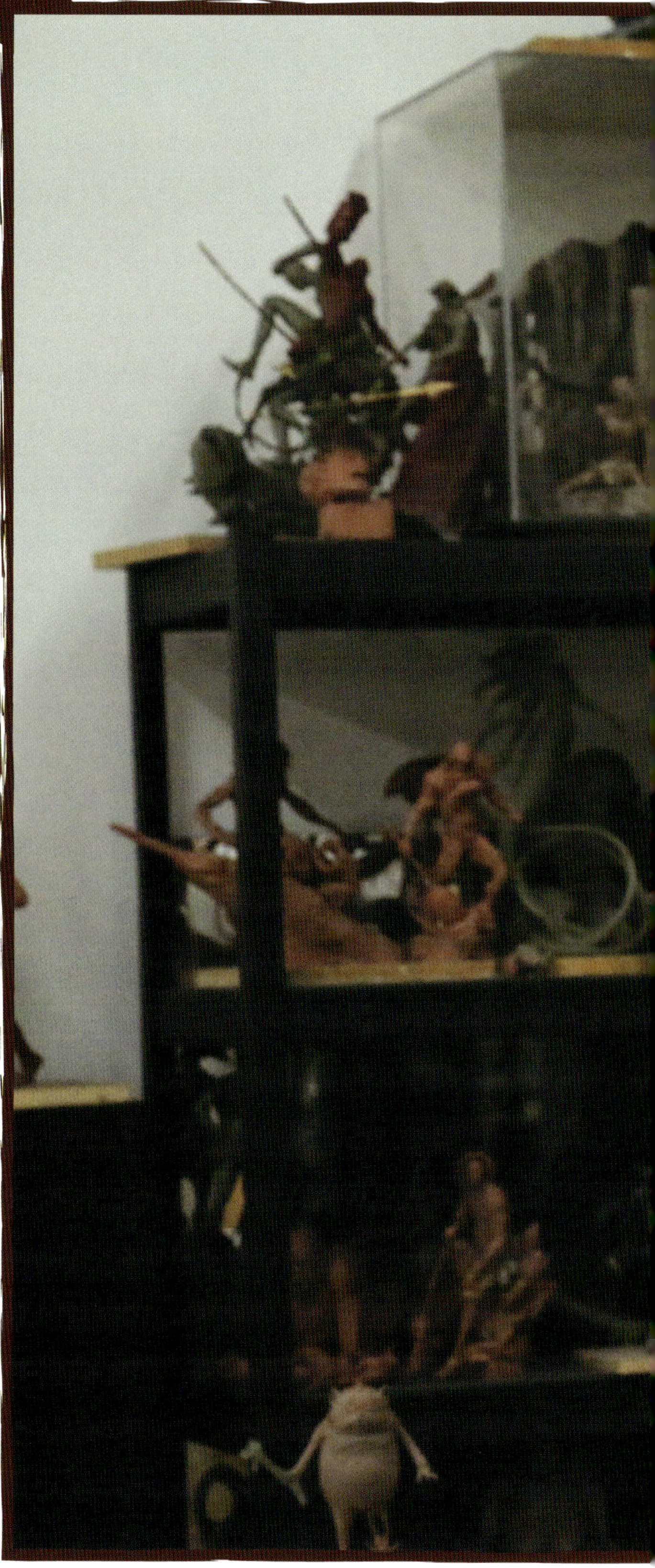

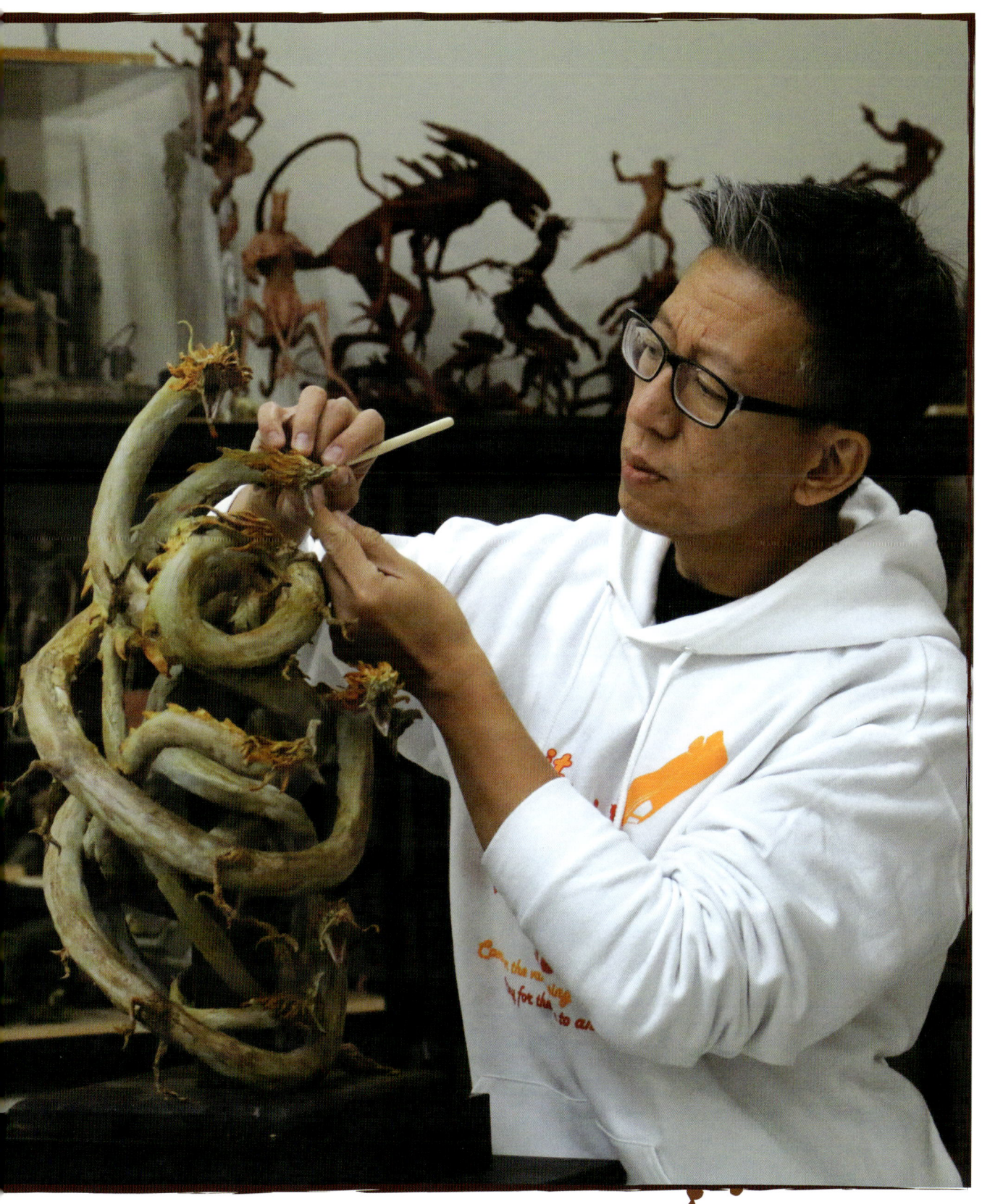

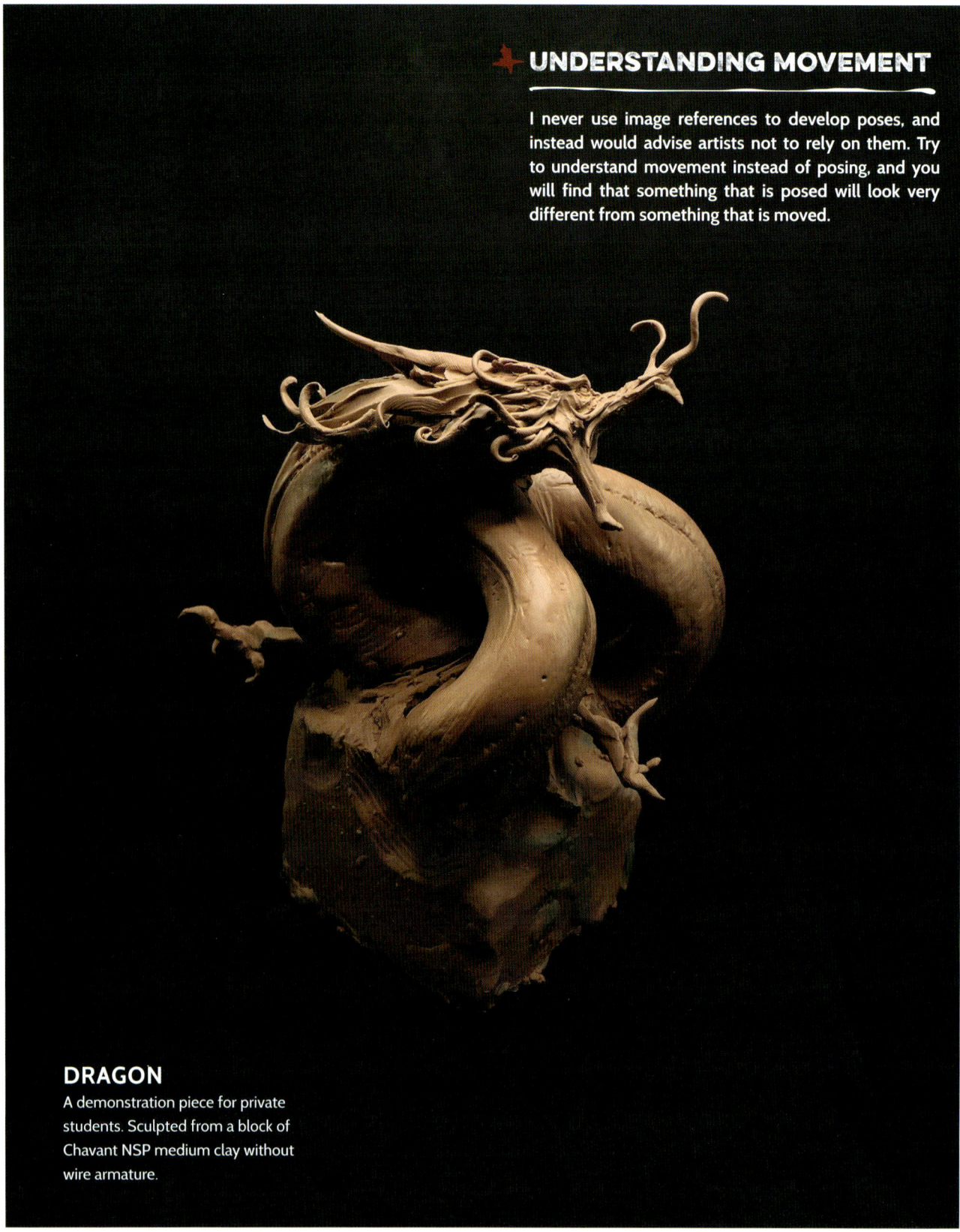

UNDERSTANDING MOVEMENT

I never use image references to develop poses, and instead would advise artists not to rely on them. Try to understand movement instead of posing, and you will find that something that is posed will look very different from something that is moved.

DRAGON

A demonstration piece for private students. Sculpted from a block of Chavant NSP medium clay without wire armature.

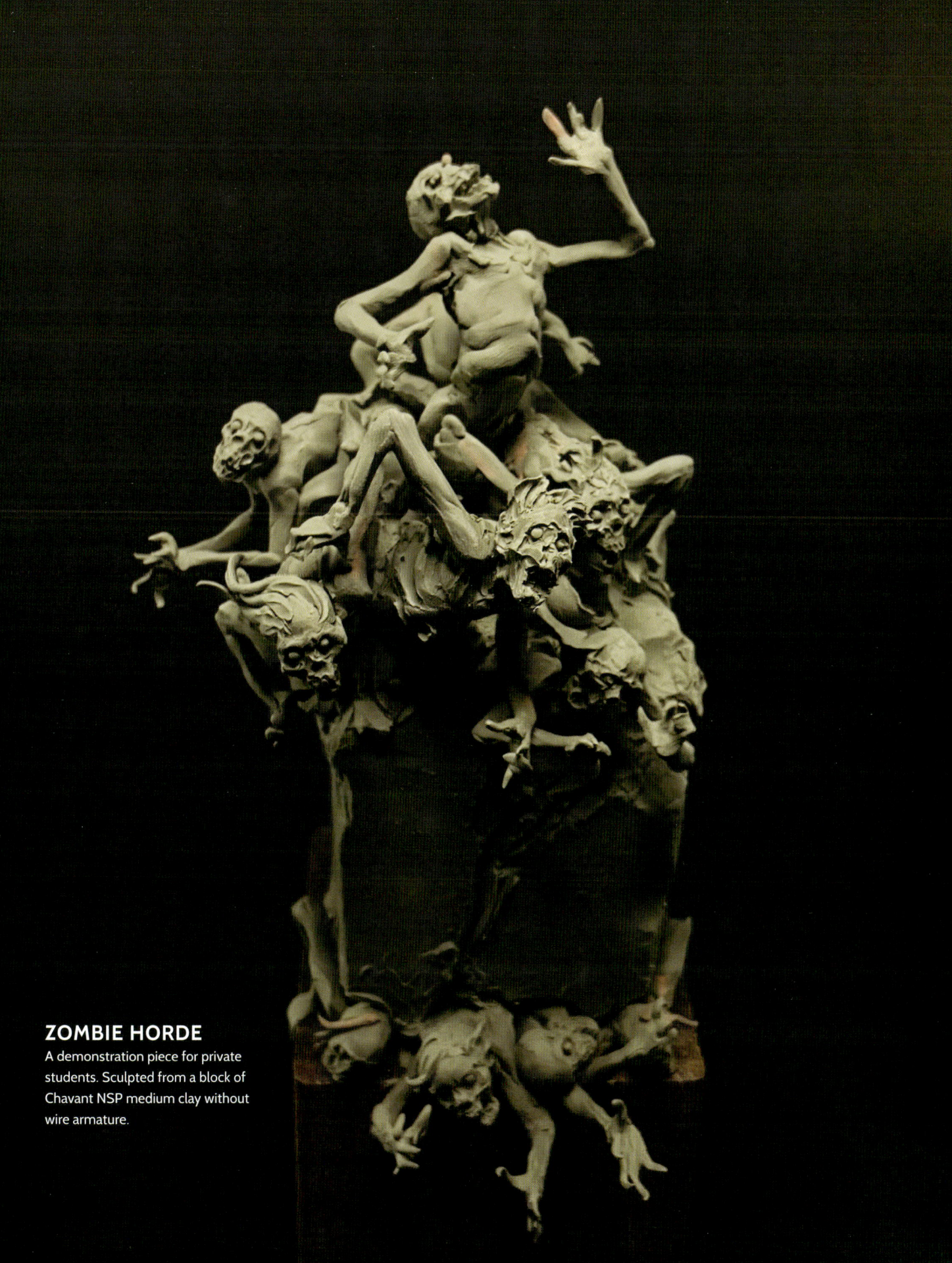

ZOMBIE HORDE

A demonstration piece for private students. Sculpted from a block of Chavant NSP medium clay without wire armature.

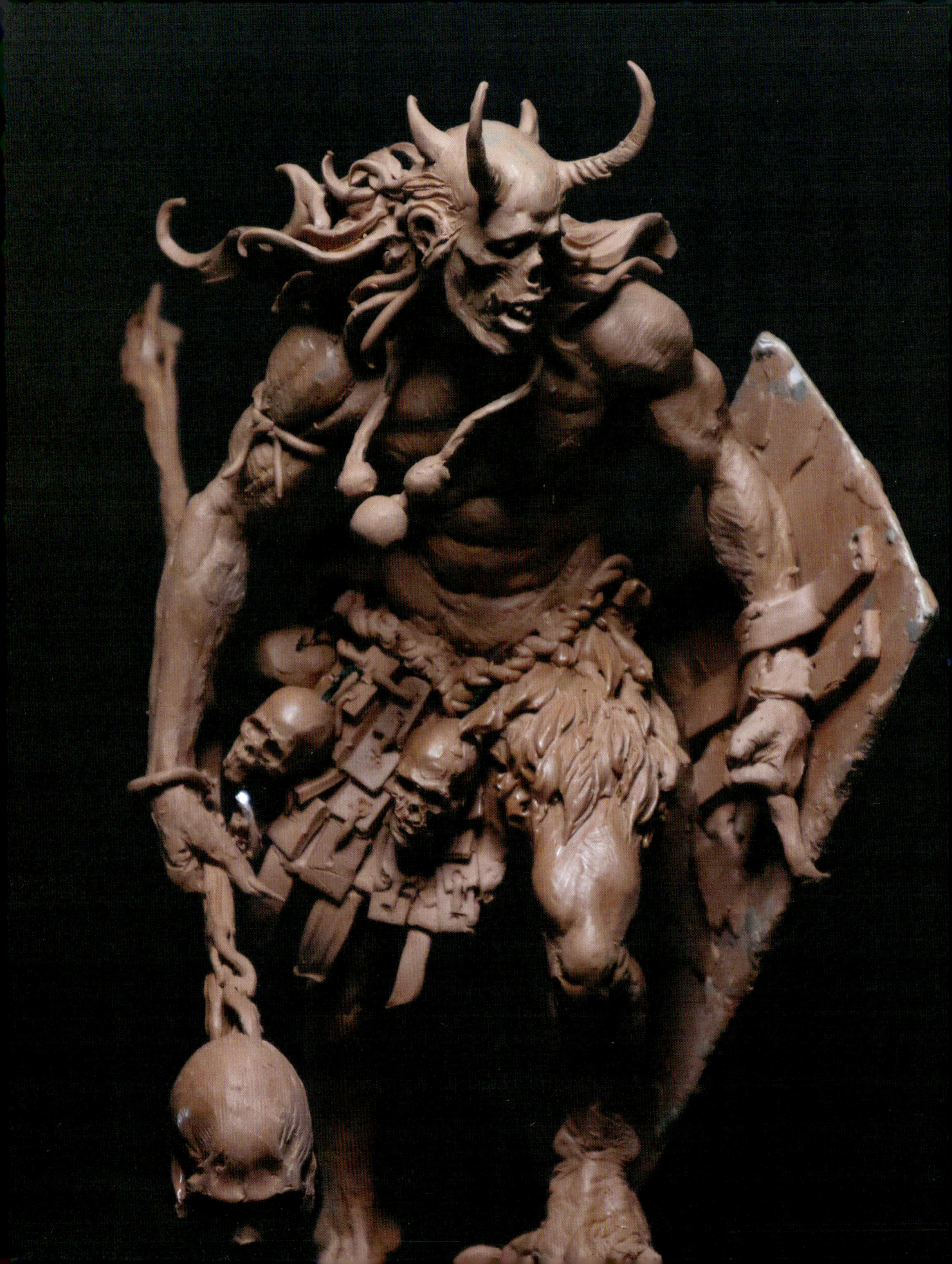

DESIGNING THE BARBARIAN

In this tutorial, I demonstrate how I design a character directly in clay. Professionally, I work mostly in the concept-design phase of pre-production in films, so my job is to come up with fresh design ideas for characters and creatures in a timely manner. Here I explain one of my more typical processes of creating a character — working directly in three-dimensional form. The focus is not about the making of a sculpture, but more about creating a visual design through the use of a sculpture. My design process almost always happens directly in clay. When designing, I always try to let my process unfold with as few restrictions as possible. The design is not only about the visual qualities of a character, but also about the three-dimensional composition of the entire concept presentation.

BY SIMON LEE

MATERIALS & TOOLS

MATERIALS

Aluminum wire (14-gauge/1.6 mm)
Floral wire (22-gauge/0.6mm)
Chavant NSP oil-based clay
(medium density)
99% Isopropyl rubbing alcohol
Cardboard

TOOLS

Wire cutter
Guitar string loop tools
Rake tool
Ball-point stylus
Paintbrush

STEP 01

For this demonstration, I use Chavant NSP medium oil-based clay and two different sizes of armature wire. My tool kit for this design includes standard sculpting tools as well as some home-made tools.

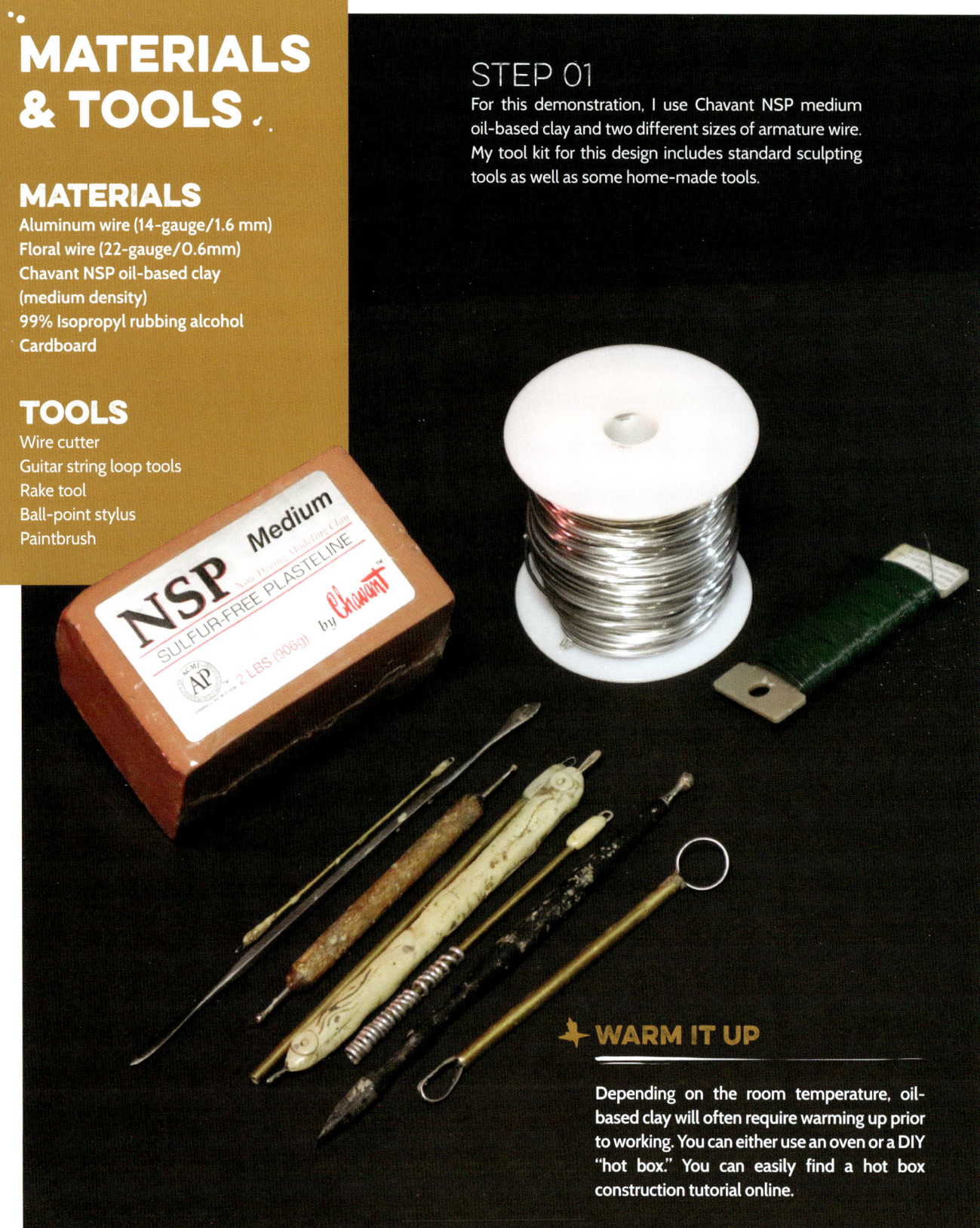

✦ WARM IT UP

Depending on the room temperature, oil-based clay will often require warming up prior to working. You can either use an oven or a DIY "hot box." You can easily find a hot box construction tutorial online.

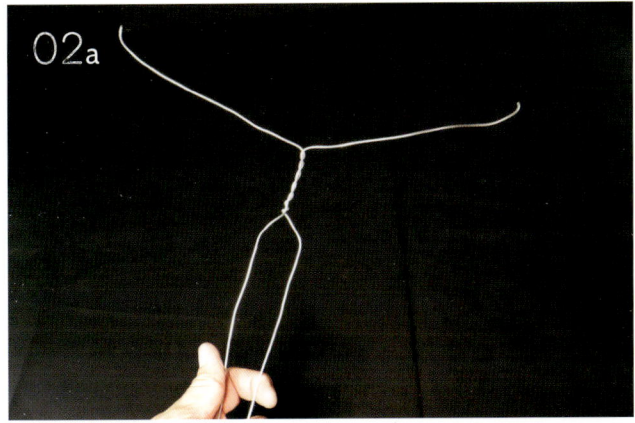

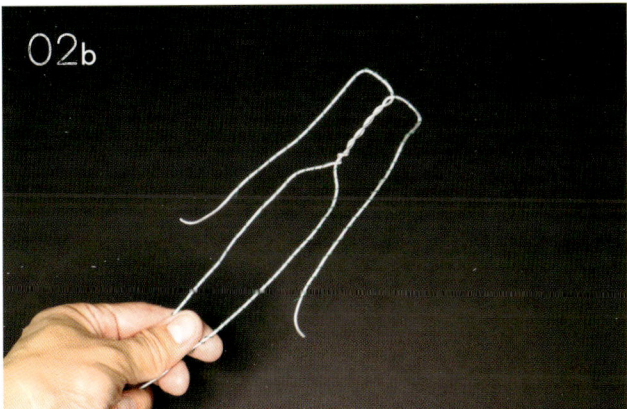

STEP 02

To begin, I make a generic wire armature of a human form in a neutral pose, almost like a stick-figure drawing (02a). Next, I create the basic shoulder and arm shapes, and wrap floral wire over the entire armature to prevent clay breaking away from the aluminum (02b). (Added to bare aluminum wire, the clay can shift and may eventually come off.) This type of armature is at the core of almost all of my sculptures. As a designer, I always use the most basic armature as much as possible; whenever I can manage, I use no armature at all.

STEP 03

Once the basic armature is ready and the human form is secured into a base, I start to add clay to the armature to build a generic human form. I always start my character build-up from a skeletal base. The character's body type might change as I progress, but in the beginning, I always keep things anatomically generic.

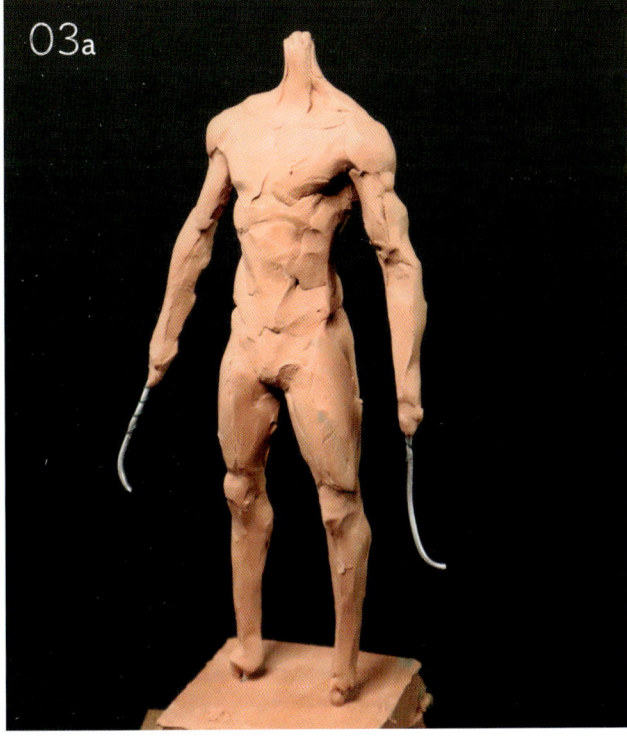

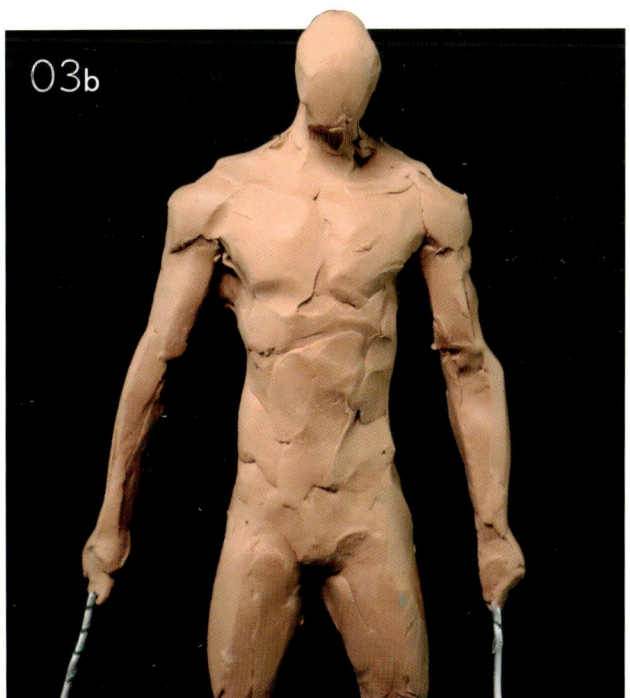

✦ WEAK VERSUS STRONG ARMATURE

I use weak wire for my armature, which forces me to achieve balance through proper weight distribution rather than relying on the strength of the wires. Weak wires allow flexibility and a natural sense of movement. Strong wires, on the other hand, are suitable for building a more rigid and solid-looking sculpture.

STEP 04

I begin moving the figure as a warm-up process — this is how I develop a "feel" for the character. At this stage, I am not too concerned with how the character will look, but instead focus on what the character would do. The movement and behavior help me determine what the character should eventually look like. If it is a warrior character, it should move in the way a warrior would before it can look like one.

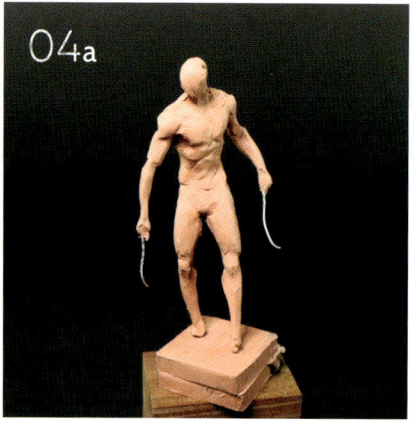

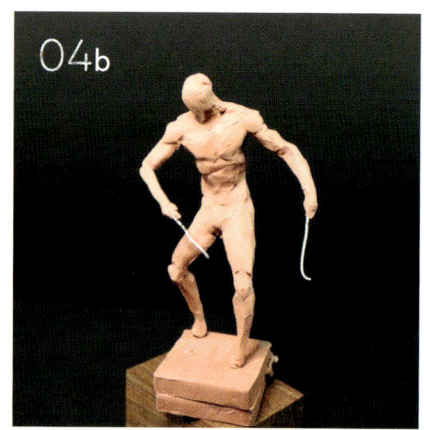

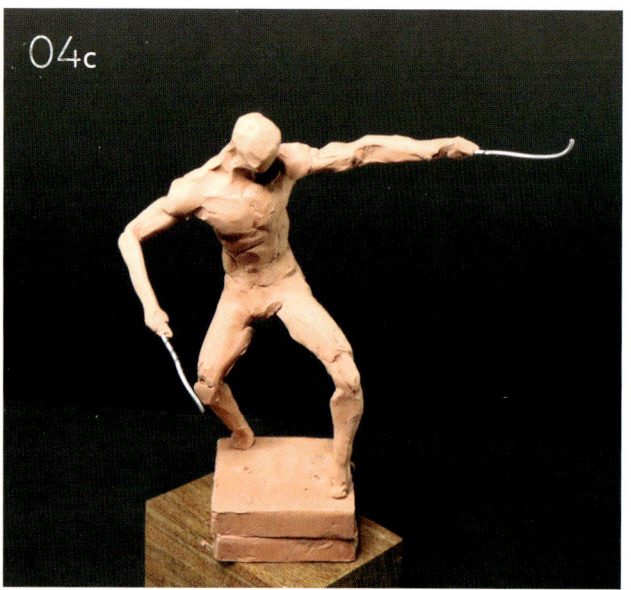

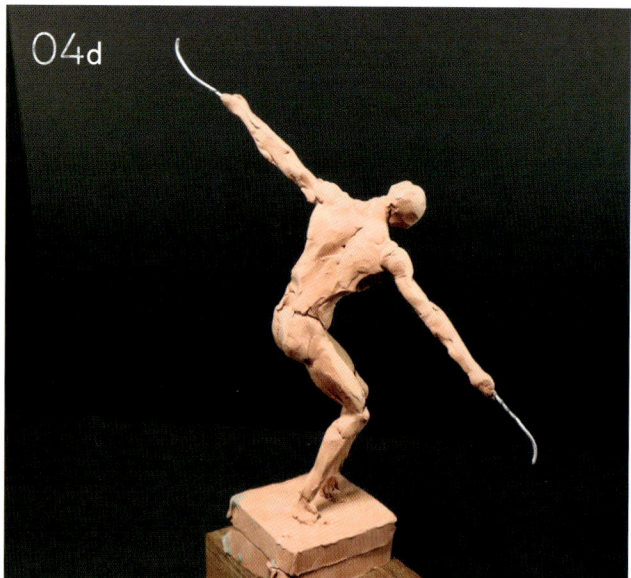

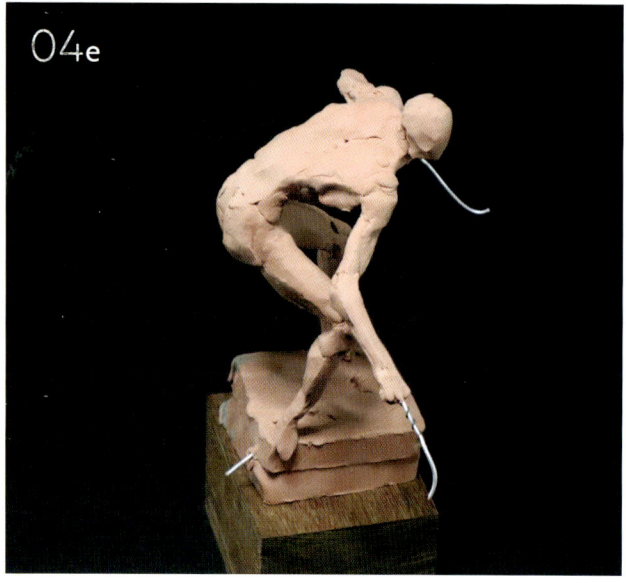

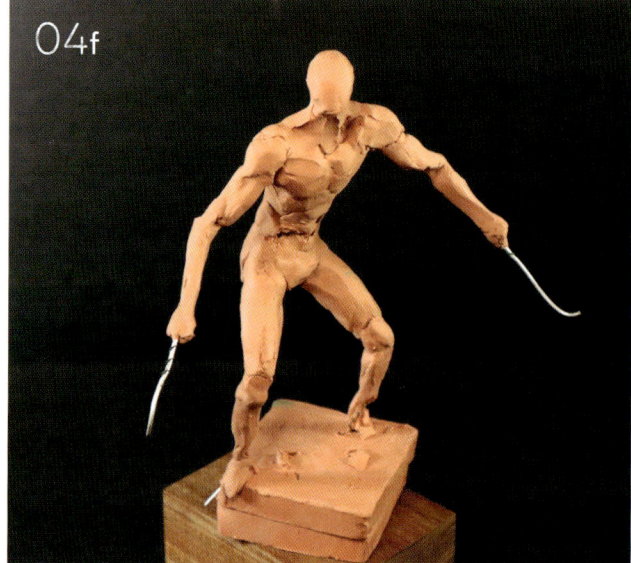

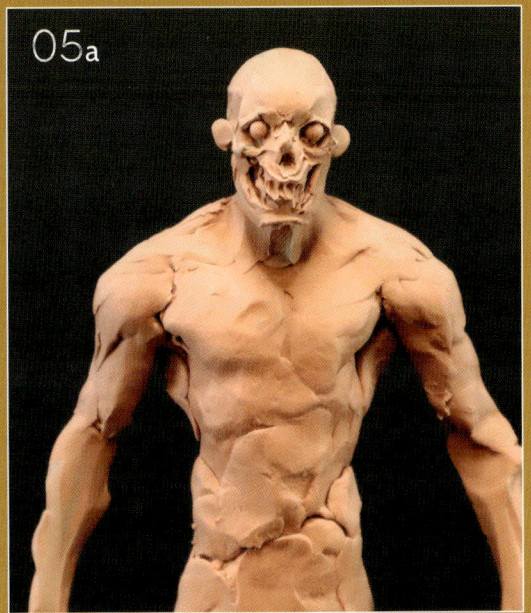

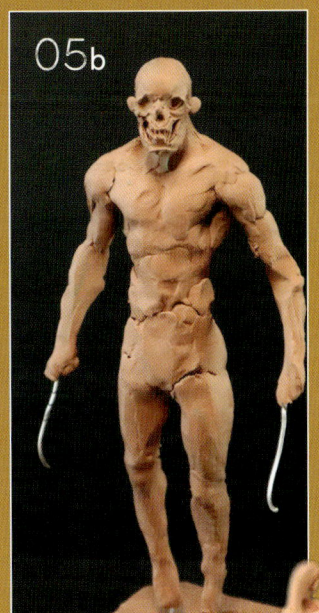

STEP 05

The warm-up process in the previous step gives me some idea of what this character could be, so next I begin to direct the idea toward realization. I move the figure back to a neutral pose for easier access to the parts, then start to detail the head to give the character more context.

STEP 06

While my attention remains on the character's head, I begin to add hair. A different hairstyle will shed more light on the character's background in terms of culture, environment, and so on, all of which help me narrow down the overall design direction.

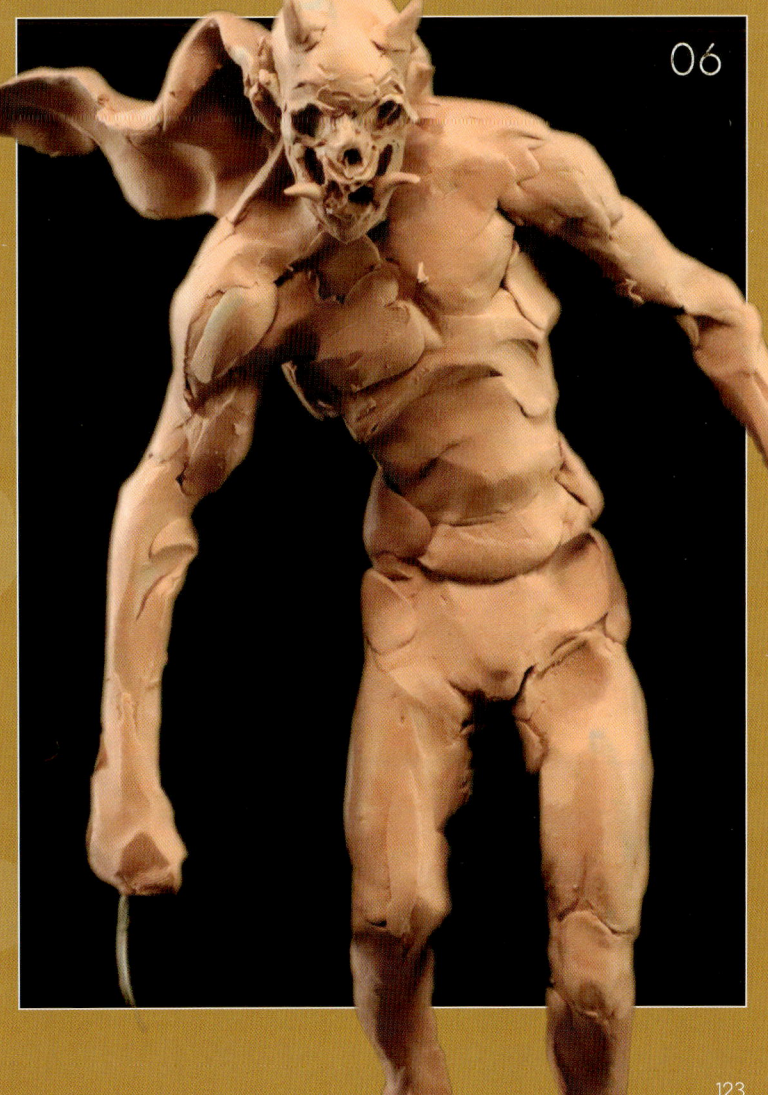

✦ ADAPT AND EVOLVE

Because I am creating an idea rather than a character, the process should unfold fluidly. I need everything, from the armature to the anatomy, to be highly adaptive.

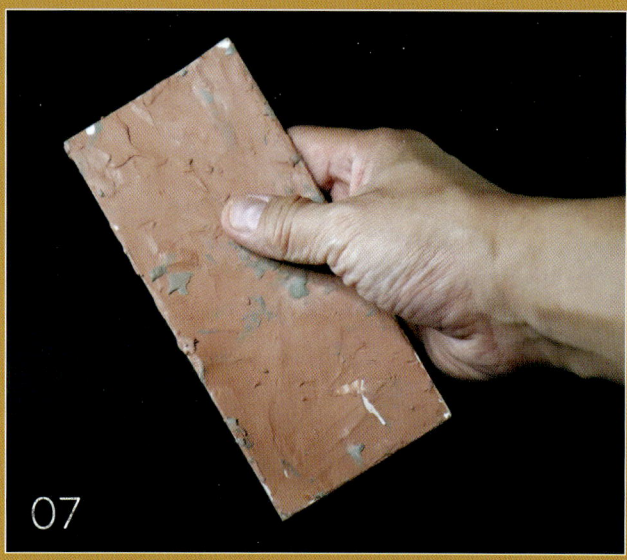

07

STEP 07

I decide to introduce a shield, which I create by covering a piece of cardboard in clay. It's a little too large to be realistic, but the scale offers some very interesting visual possibilities for the composition.

STEP 08

Based on the character's body language, I begin to incorporate design elements that will enhance the overall composition. I test the idea of adding a weapon. Because my design ideas are constantly evolving, there's no way for me to anticipate what's needed in the beginning at the armature building stage. As mentioned previously, I rely on the character's posture to balance all added weight, instead of relying on strong wires for support.

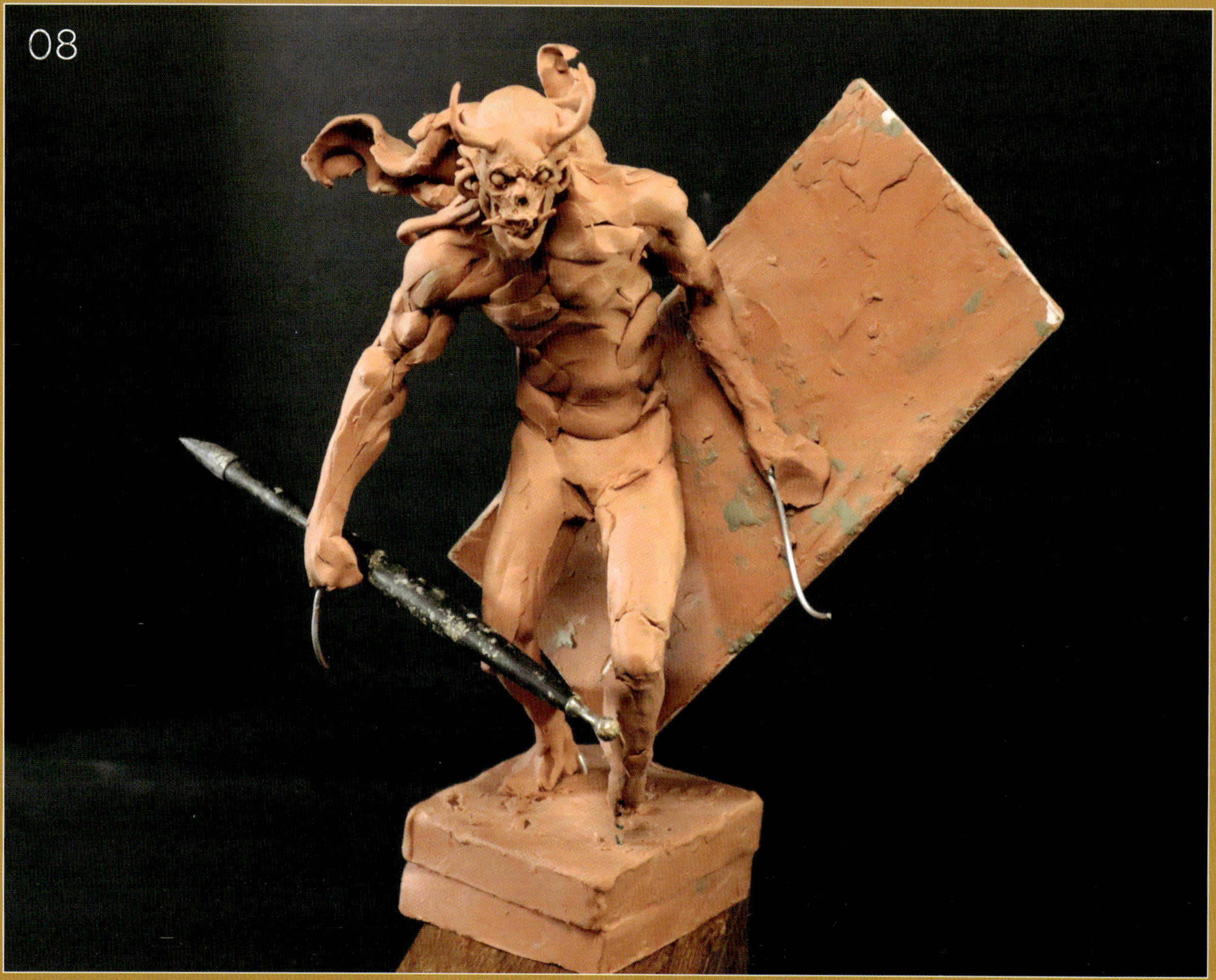

08

STEP 09

With the key visual elements in place, everything else comes together quickly. I bulk up the anatomy in proportion to the head, build the beginnings of clothing, and develop the hair and base to enhance the overall composition.

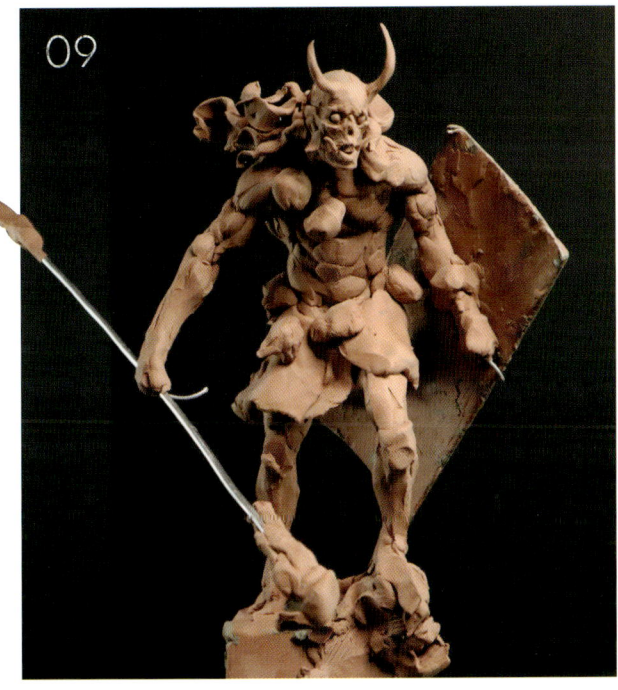

STEP 10

The shield occupies a large piece of visual real estate on the sculpture, so I decide to create a version of the shield with a design motif similar to the character itself. Much like the hairstyle, any weapons and accessories that the character carries will reflect their culture, which once again will help me narrow down the design.

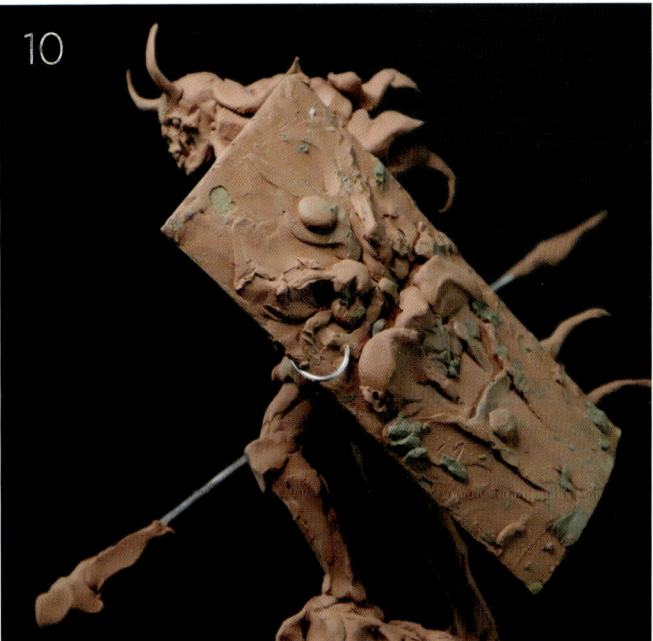

STEP 11

I remove the shield to add an unusual fish tail to the back of the character (11a). The tail enhances and diversifies the composition and adds a hidden surprise element for the viewer (11b). Once I am happy with the progression of the overall visual design elements, I start refining the sculpture.

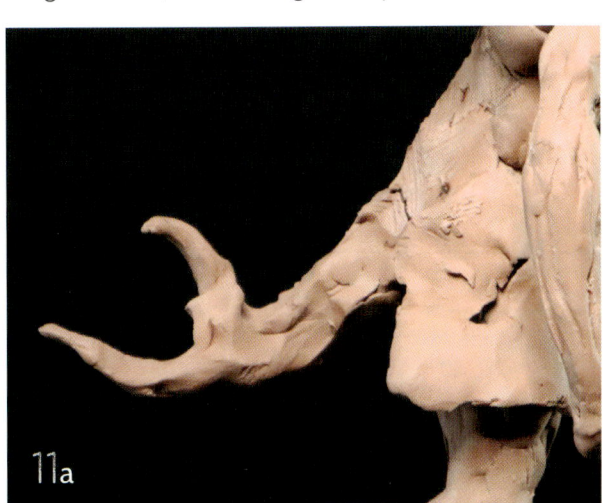

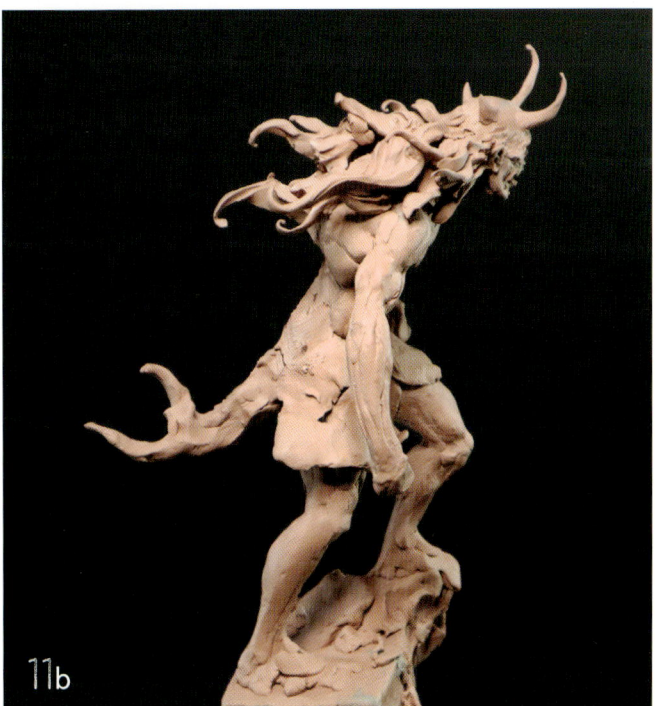

STEP 12

The goal in this step is to clean up the overall sculpt and further define the character. To start cleaning up the head and redefine the facial planes, I use a variety of loop tools. A guitar-string loop tool works almost like a small rake tool. I can remove clay more aggressively and prepare the areas for the following stage of more refined work (12a). A more delicate loop tool is suitable for cutting and reshaping areas that are more fragile and without armature support, such as hair (12b). For a more aggressive approach to bulkier areas, a heavier rake tool is ideal, allowing me to work quickly while still maintaining the level of detail needed (12c).

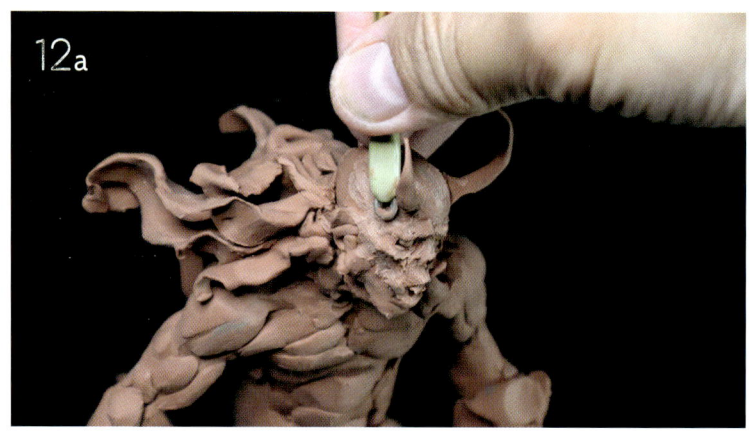

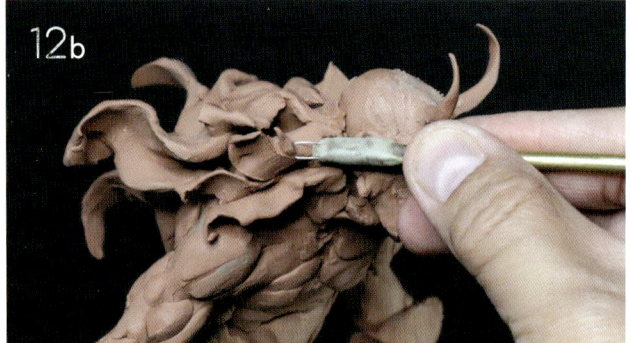

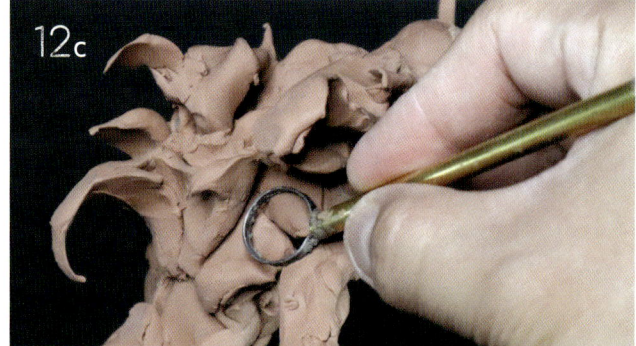

STEP 13

I undertake further work on the hair arrangement to enhance the sense of both movement and environment. It's important that I check the hair from different angles. The movement and aesthetics should work no matter where the audience is placed. I don't use armature when designing hair – if I like the design, I can commit to the arrangement and retrofit armature support where necessary.

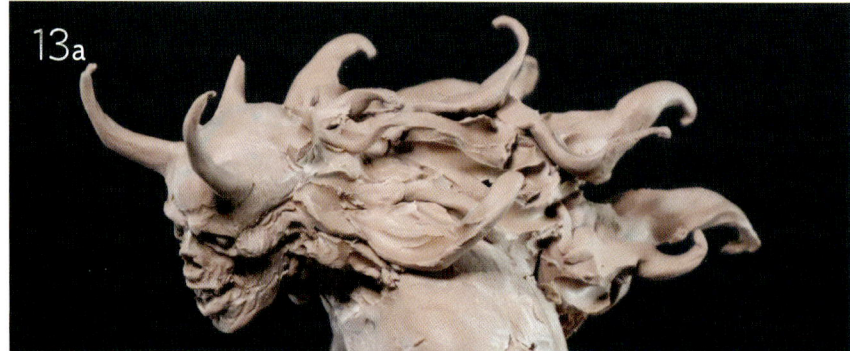

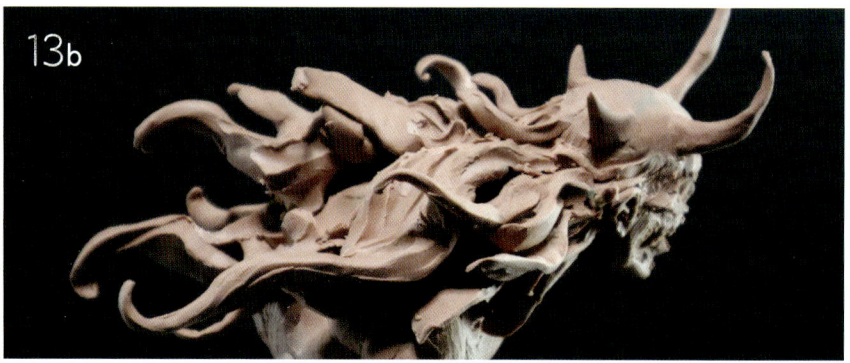

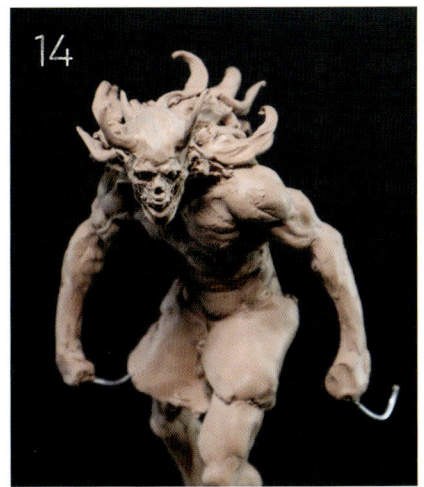

STEP 14

As the overall clean-up progresses, I move on to defining the character's anatomy. I employ the same process as used previously — using various tools to remove and shape the clay to give further definition to the arms, facial structure, and torso. When cleaning up different parts of the character, I remove any parts of the sculpt that I believe are in the way. I may even re-pose the character as needed for easier access.

STEP 15

Next, I start to develop the costume design. I first add armor plating to the skirt-like clothing around the character's waist and adorn it with skull trophies to introduce further interest and a sinister narrative to the figure. The armor plates and weapons reflect the character's occupation, and the skull trophies reveal a different side of his hunter-warrior culture. Because these accessories were added as I progressed, I retrofit armature support as needed to hold the parts in place. In this instance, I attach the skulls to the waist using lengths of floral wire.

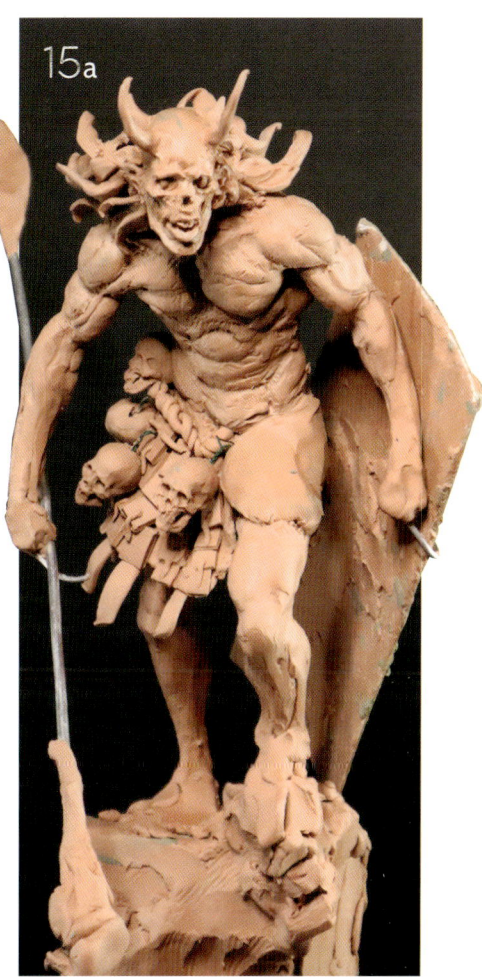

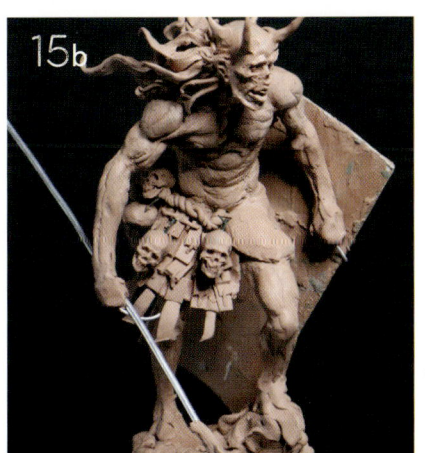

STEP 16

I work further on the design of the shield and weapon, the motifs of which bear a close resemblance to the character itself. I also use a second block of clay for the base of the sculpture. The blocky shape of both the shield and the base complement each other and help to guide the audience's attention when viewing the design.

STEP 17

Revisiting the costume, I consider what the remaining half of the skirt will be made from. Instead of repeating the plated armor on the other side of the character's skirt-like clothing, I opt for fur to break up the design and add variety. The fur is depicted by layering up individual chunks of clay.

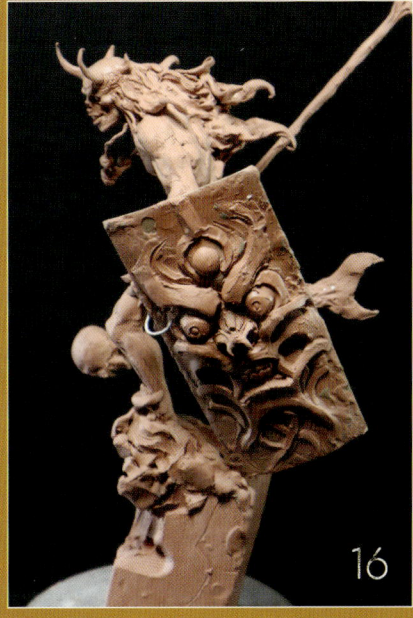

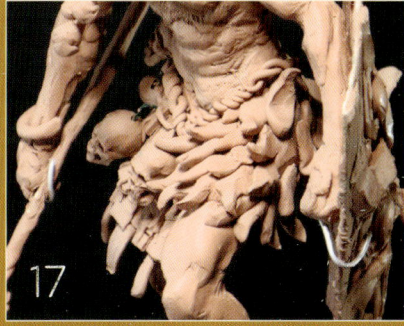

THE DEVIL'S IN THE DETAILS

To ensure all details are considered, check my designs from all sides continuously while I work. On this piece, I made time to address the design aesthetics on the back.

STEP 18

After cleaning up the sculpture using sculpting tools, I use solvents to refine and smooth the surfaces. One of the common solvents that I use for Chavant NSP clay is 99% isopropyl rubbing alcohol (18a). There are chemicals that are harsher on the clay and can create very smooth results, but I prefer to use tools and rubbing alcohol to avoid other potential health hazards. I brush the alcohol onto the sculpture with a paintbrush (18b). The alcohol itself will not melt the clay, but instead smooth the surface. Brushing the sculpture with a solvent will also remove most of the clay crumbs left behind from tools. For better results, repeat these steps several times.

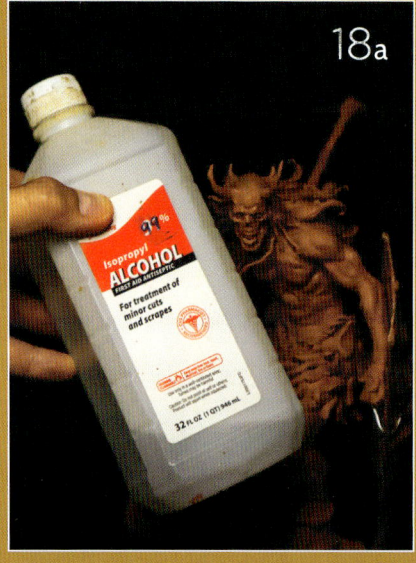

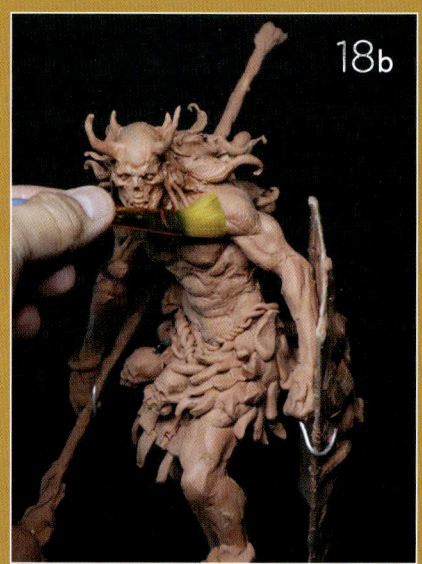

STEP 19

During the finishing stages, I also create and perfect any final embellishments, such as a necklace, and revisit the detailing of the entire piece, including the horns, weapon, and clothing. These details add finesse and refinement to the sculpture, taking it one step closer to completion.

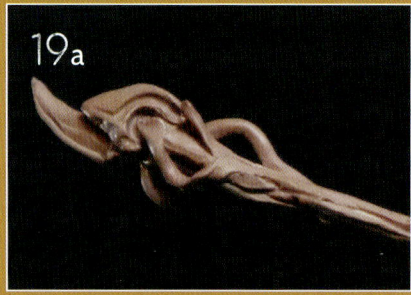

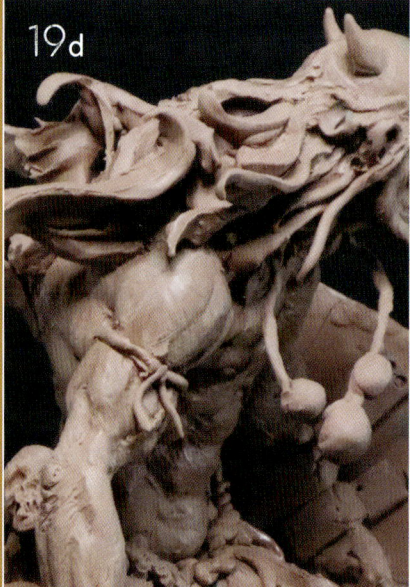

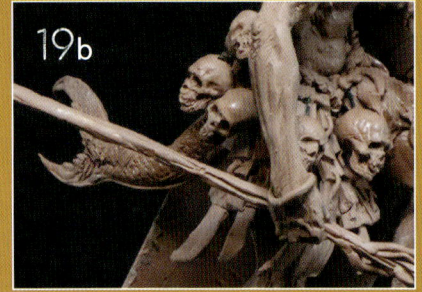

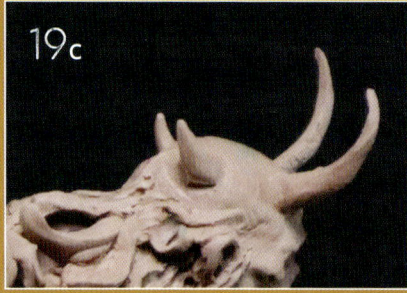

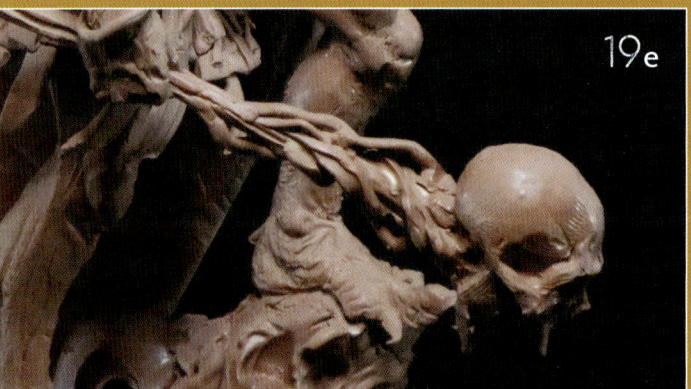

✦ KNOWING WHEN TO STOP

I choose the number of clean-ups depending on the project. If the project is for a collectibles company or a product release, I would put in more time and make sure that the final sculpture is as smooth as glass; but if it is a design project for idea exploration, I would only take the clean-up process as far as my budget and time allow.

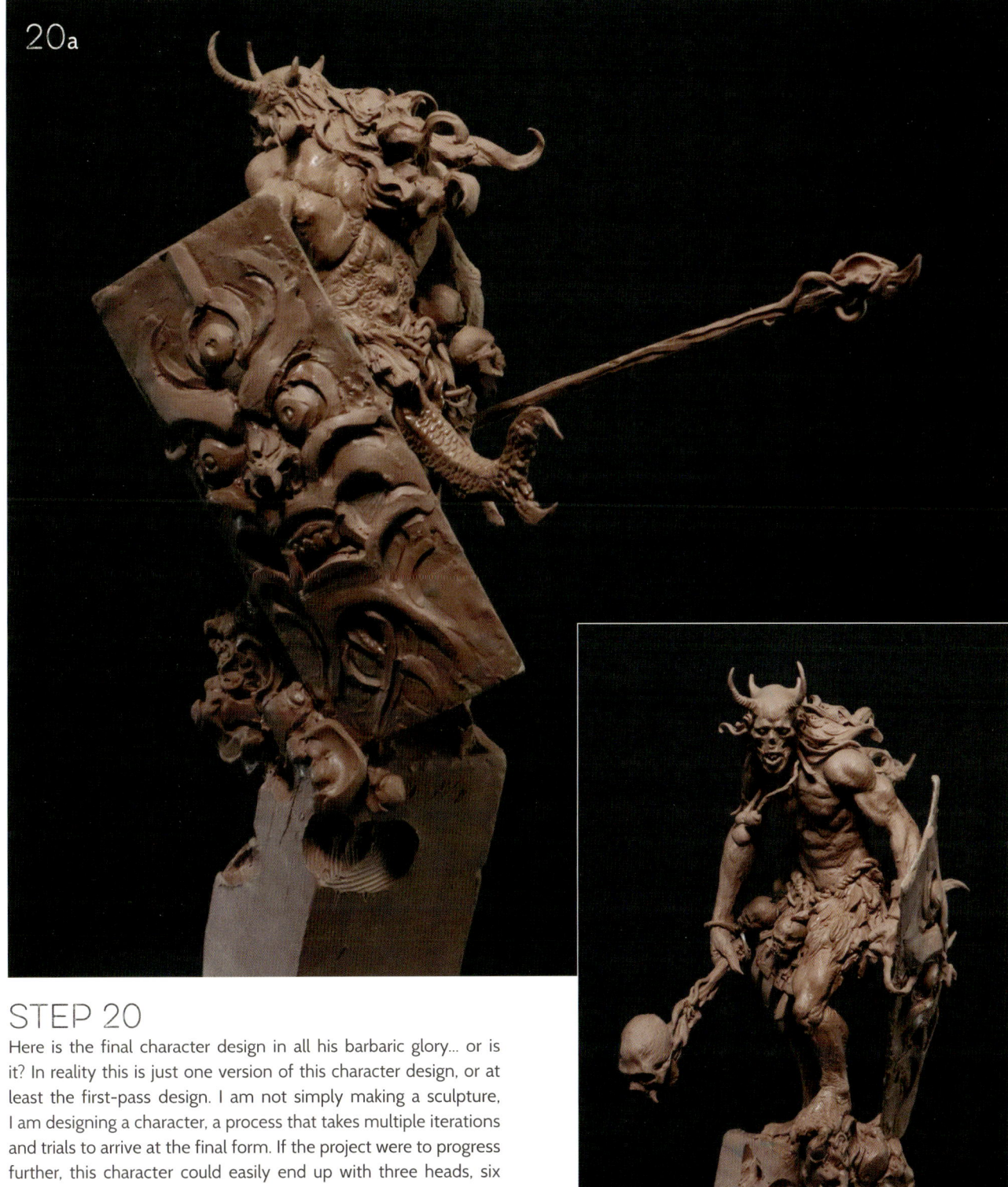

20a

20b

STEP 20

Here is the final character design in all his barbaric glory... or is it? In reality this is just one version of this character design, or at least the first-pass design. I am not simply making a sculpture, I am designing a character, a process that takes multiple iterations and trials to arrive at the final form. If the project were to progress further, this character could easily end up with three heads, six arms, or could even mutate into a completely different beast altogether! If I like this design enough, I could use this sculpture as reference and start to build a larger version as the finished piece for presentation to the client.

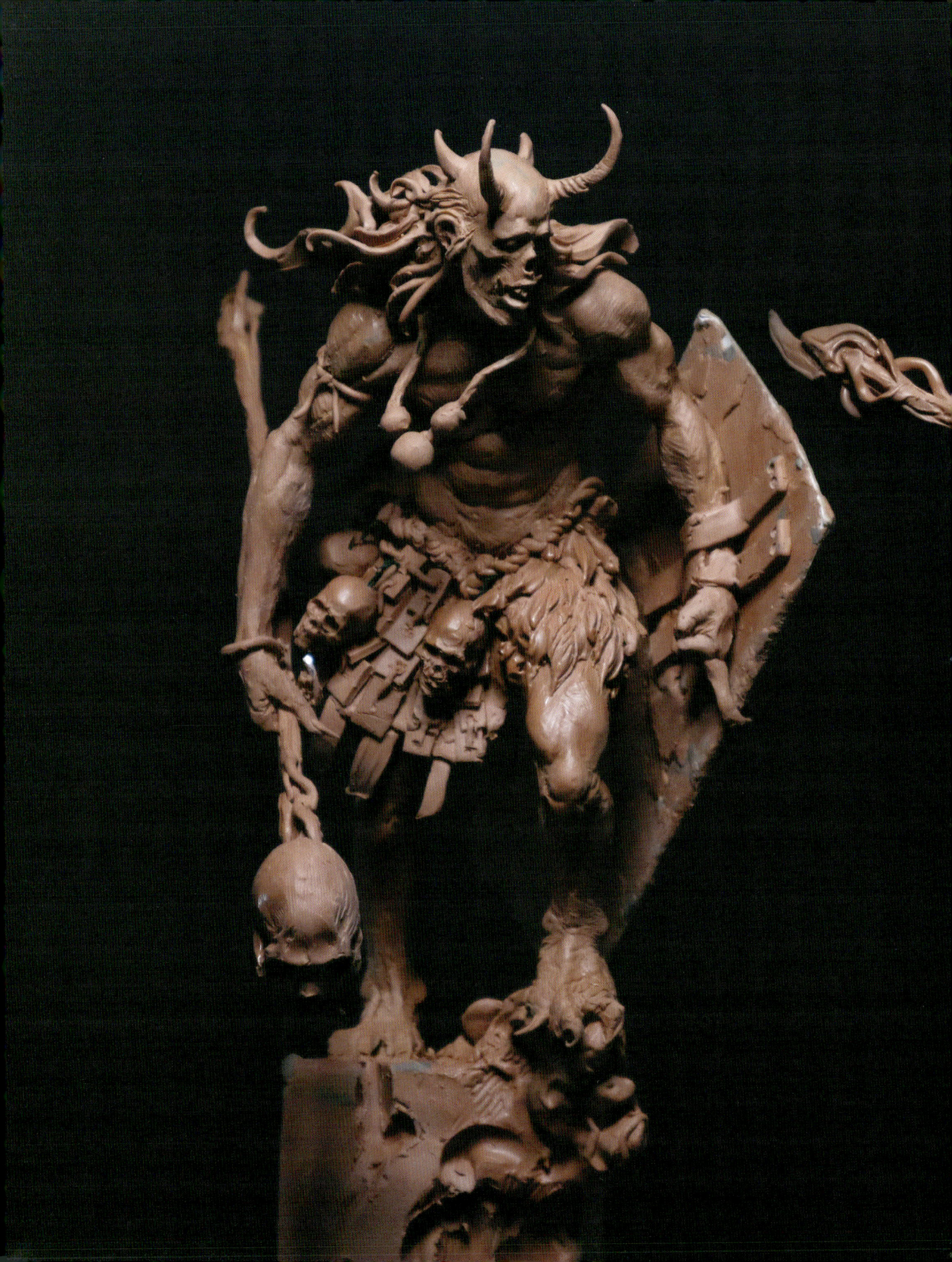

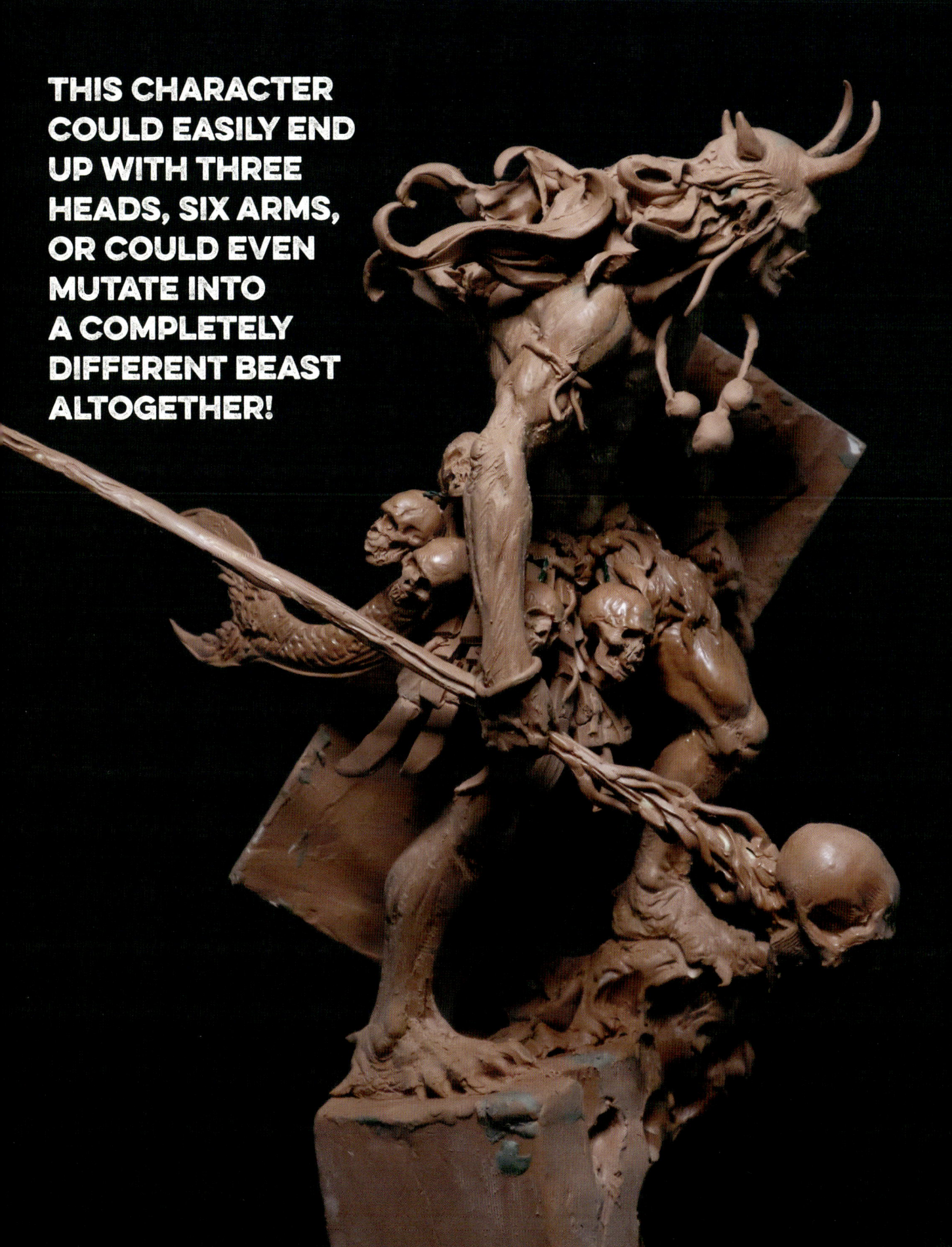

THIS CHARACTER COULD EASILY END UP WITH THREE HEADS, SIX ARMS, OR COULD EVEN MUTATE INTO A COMPLETELY DIFFERENT BEAST ALTOGETHER!

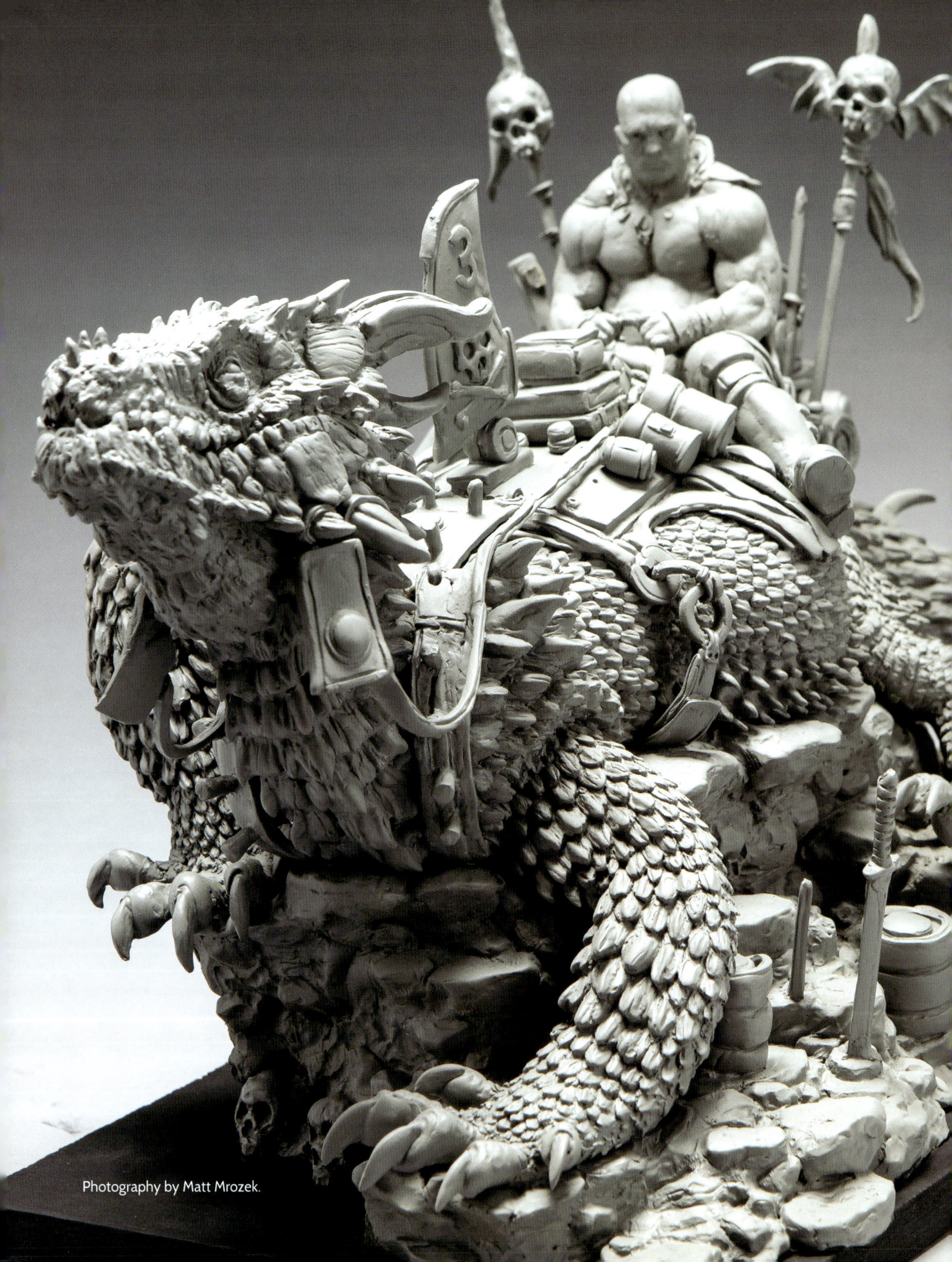

IMAGINING THE PIRATE KING

For this demonstration, we create a commanding pirate character riding on the back of a majestic dragon, Shiflett Brothers style! While we craft, we aim for a fat-bellied lizard-like dragon, and take much inspiration from imagery of real-life large lizards and iguanas to add a level of authenticity. Sometimes, when studying anatomy and creature parts for a proposed fantastical creature, we fall in love with the creatures that exist here on this planet... and this is one of those occasions.

BY THE SHIFLETT BROTHERS

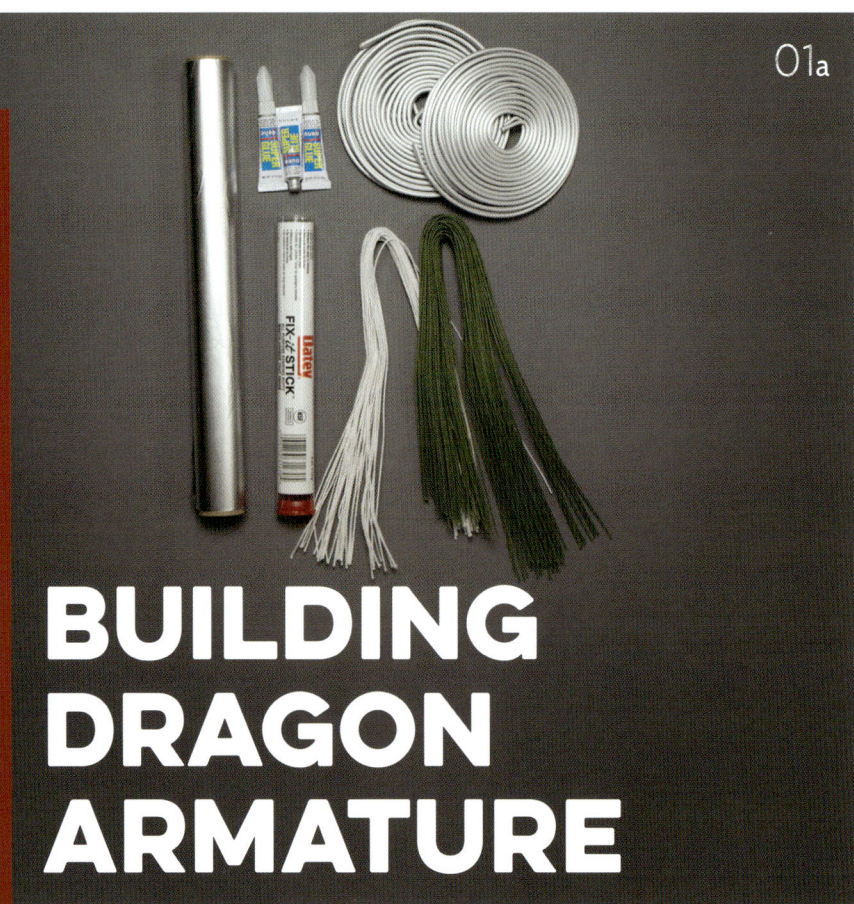

01a

MATERIALS & TOOLS

MATERIALS

ARMATURE
Almaloy aluminum alloy
armature wire (15-gauge/1.5 mm)
Aluminum foil
Aluminum wire mesh
Floral wire

CLAY
Super Sculpey Firm
Aves Apoxie Sculpt
Plumber's epoxy putty

GLUE AND SOLVENT
Wood glue
Super glue

OTHER
Wood chunks/offcuts
Styrene tubing
Nails

TOOLS
Sanding sponges
Cutting wire
Hobby knives
Wire-cutting pliers
Needle-nose pliers
Rake tools
Needle files
Loop tools
Ball tools
Burnisher
Scraper
Brushes

BUILDING DRAGON ARMATURE

STEP 01

To begin, we gather the materials we require to create the armature, which will be made up of floral wire, aluminum wire, and plumber's putty (01a). We also find offcuts and cut short lengths of wood to form the base for the rocky ground (01b). Also pictured below are two pieces of plumber's putty, and a length of plastic tubing that will allow the dragon to be detached from the base.

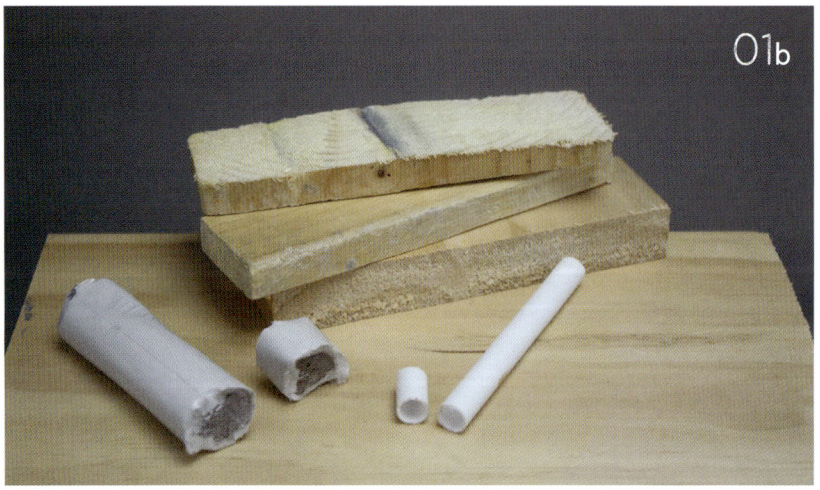

01b

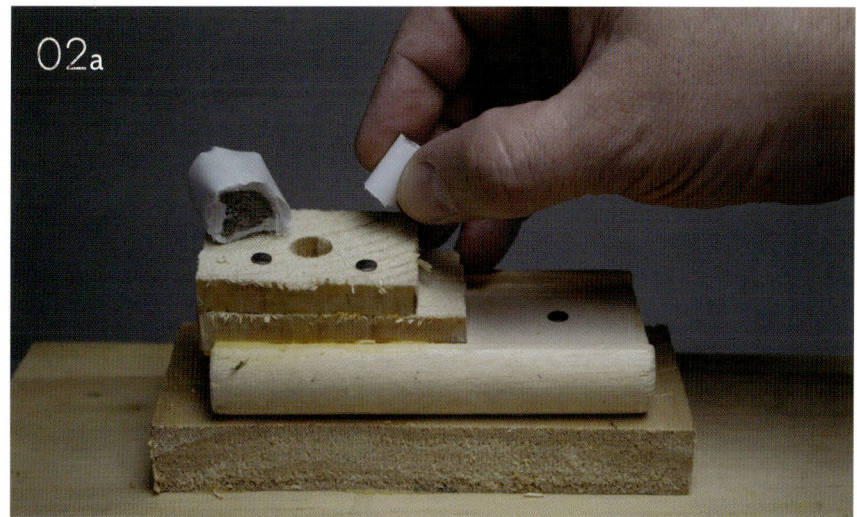

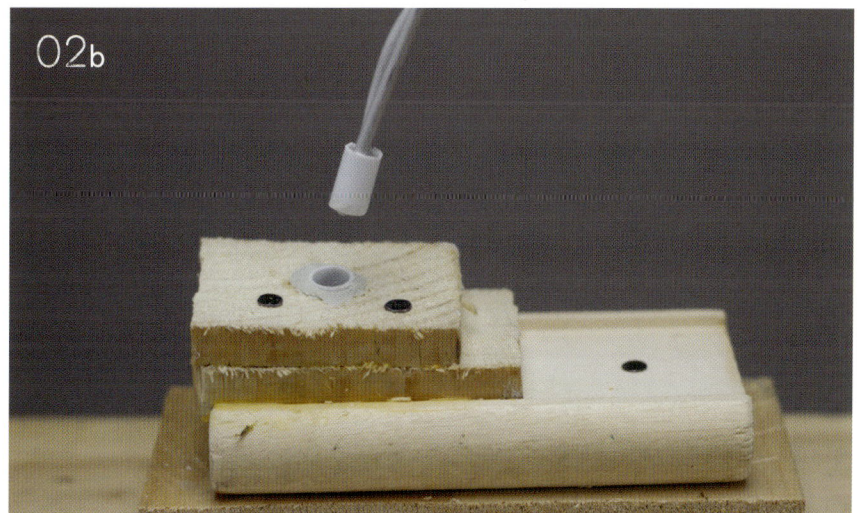

STEP 02

We envision a large rocky base rising up to meet the dragon's belly, so start by nailing the wooden pieces into place to create the approximate shape and height. We then drill a hole down through the top of the base into which we insert a piece of plastic tubing (02a). The tubing is trimmed to sit flush with the wooden block then stabilized with a small amount of plumber's putty around the top (but not inside the tube).

We then attach the smaller tube section to the bottom of two long lengths of aluminum wire, and fit the tube tightly into the slightly larger tube located in the base (02b). The aluminum wire will compose the dragon's skeletal structure, while the male/female rig of the tubing allows the entire body of the dragon to be removed from the rocky base.

✦ EASY SHIPPING

Even if a sculpture is destined to be a one-off, creating separate pieces makes for lighter and easier shipping if and when needed.

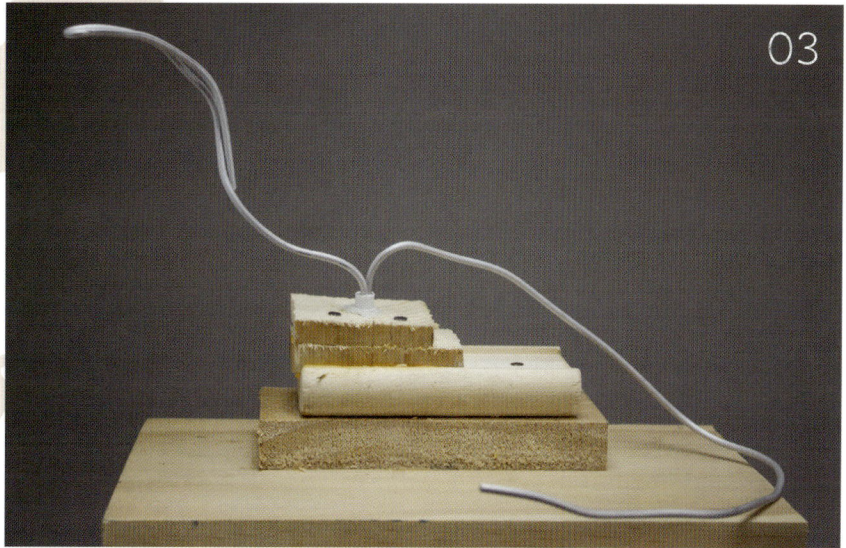

STEP 03

We shape the wire form to rise up from the base and point in two different directions — the raised front is doubled over to form the dragon's head, while the opposite end becomes the tail. These are only the first two wires in what will become a fairly complex armature.

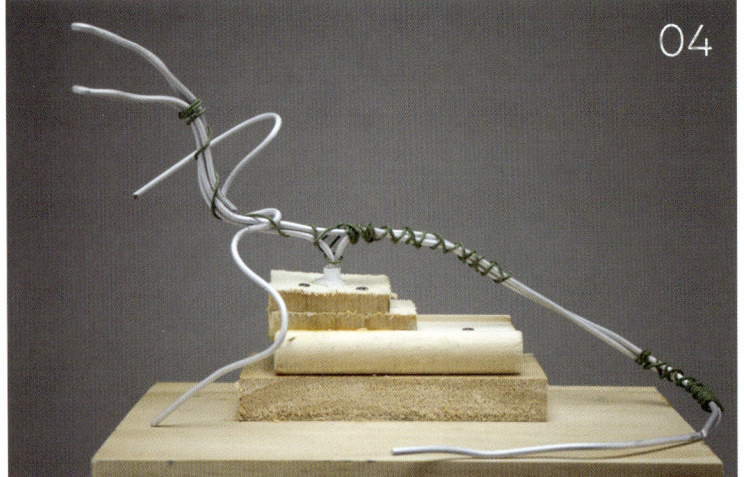

STEP 04

To strengthen the basic structure, we add a second aluminum wire to the full length of the main form, starting at the head (again folding the wire over to double it up) and ending where the tail touches the wooden base. We then tie the two aluminum wires together with floral wire. At the front end of the piece, we also position wire for the front two legs and hold it in place with more floral wire.

STEP 05

To bulk out the dragon's middle section, further floral wire is wrapped around the body. Here we use two different sizes of floral wire, the white colored wire being the finer of the two. Note the "crisscross" wrapping pattern on the front left leg, which helps the clay stick to the armature wire.

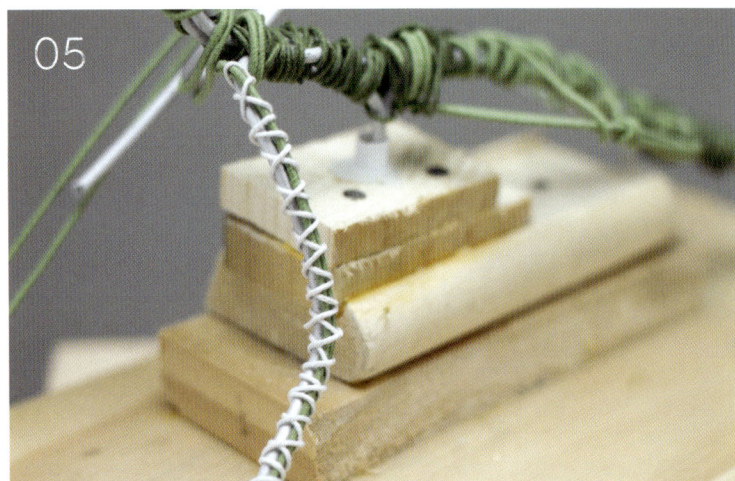

STEP 06

Next, we add back legs to the dragon using the same method as used for the front legs. We also construct a round middle section, composed of multiple pieces of floral wire, to create a much more rounded shape (06a). Once we are completely satisfied with the armature, we use plenty of super glue to bond the floral wire together and set everything in place (06b).

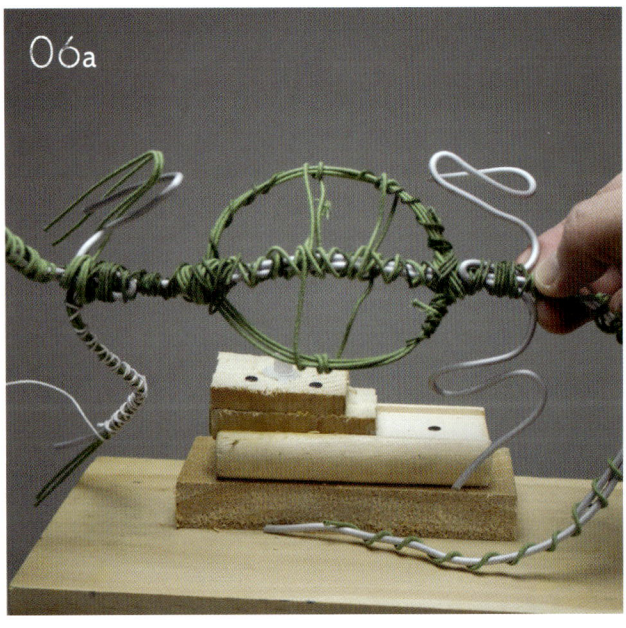

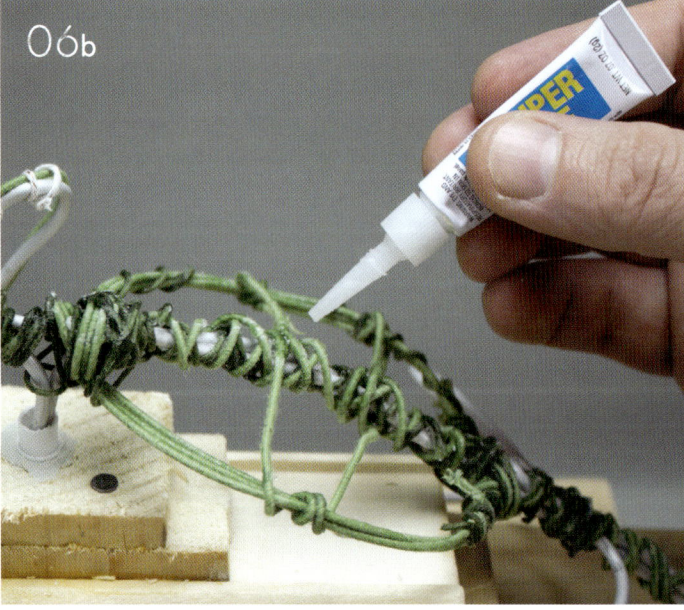

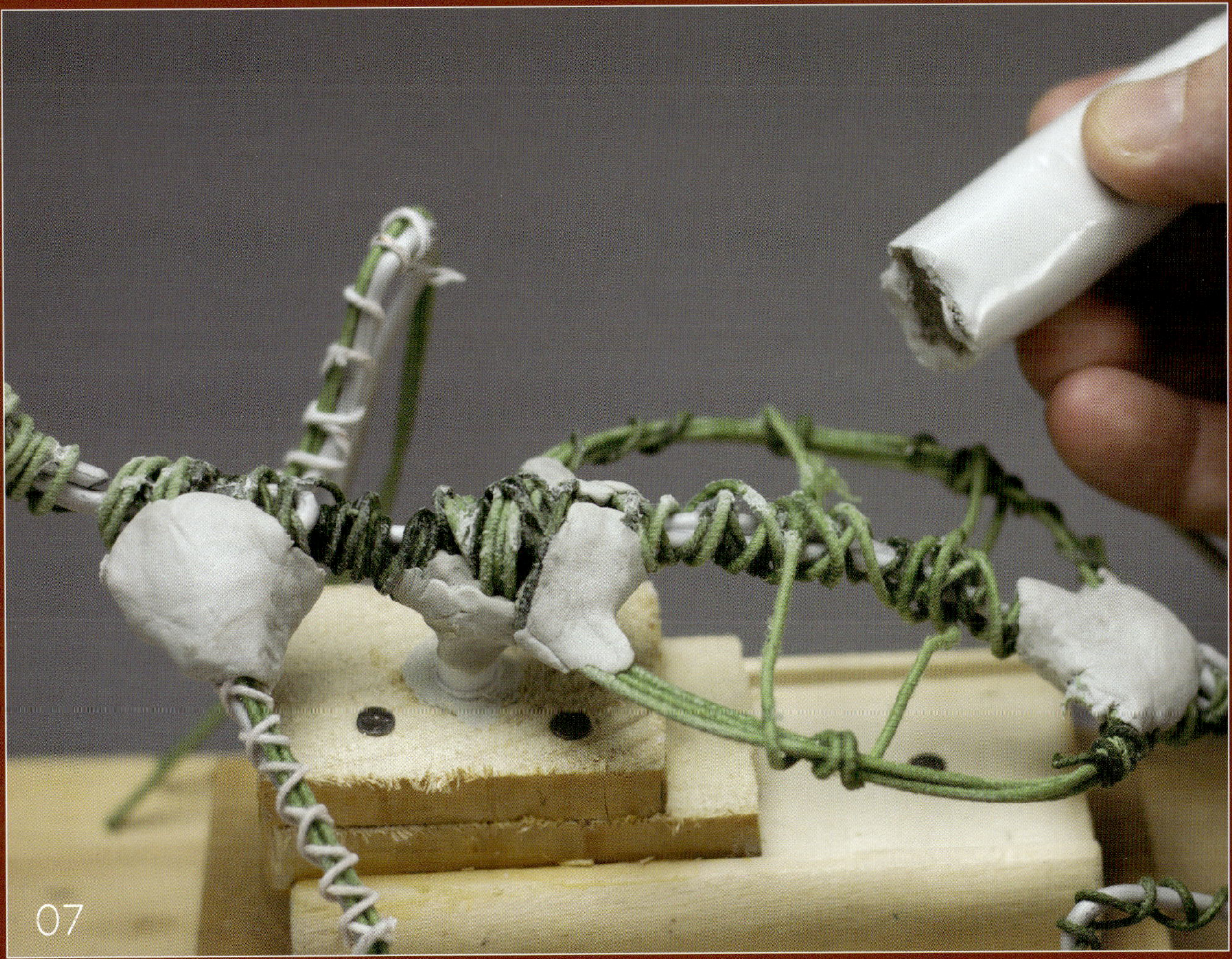

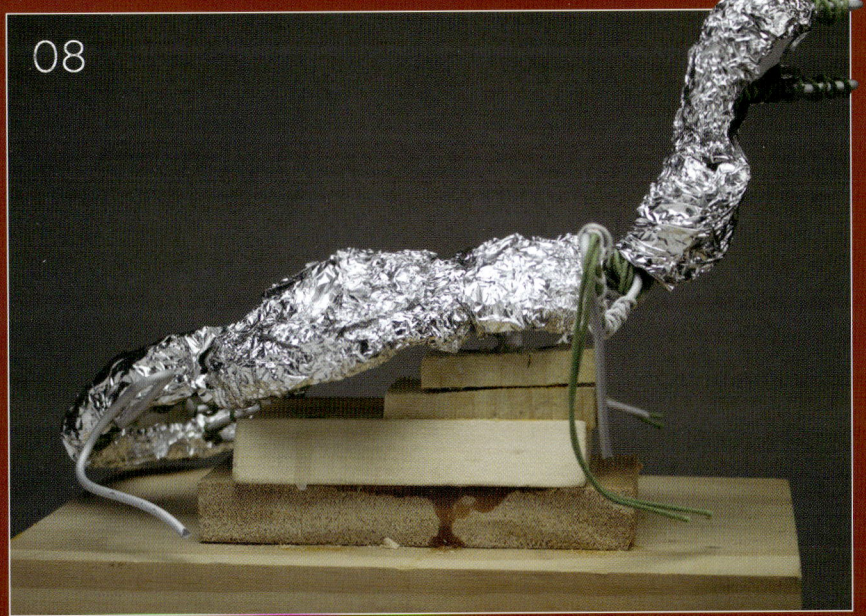

STEP 07

To add further structural support and strengthen any potentially weak points, we add plumber's putty to strategic spots on the armature joints. Once set hard, the putty holds the wire components firmly in place, ready for subsequent layers.

STEP 08

Now it's time to add the aluminum foil. We twist foil around the parts of the sculpture that we envision to be thick with clay, then squeeze it as tightly as possible so that it is extremely compact and sturdy. Using foil in this way not only makes the finished piece lighter, which inhibits cracking, but it is also cost effective because foil is much cheaper than Super Sculpey!

DRAGON SCULPTING

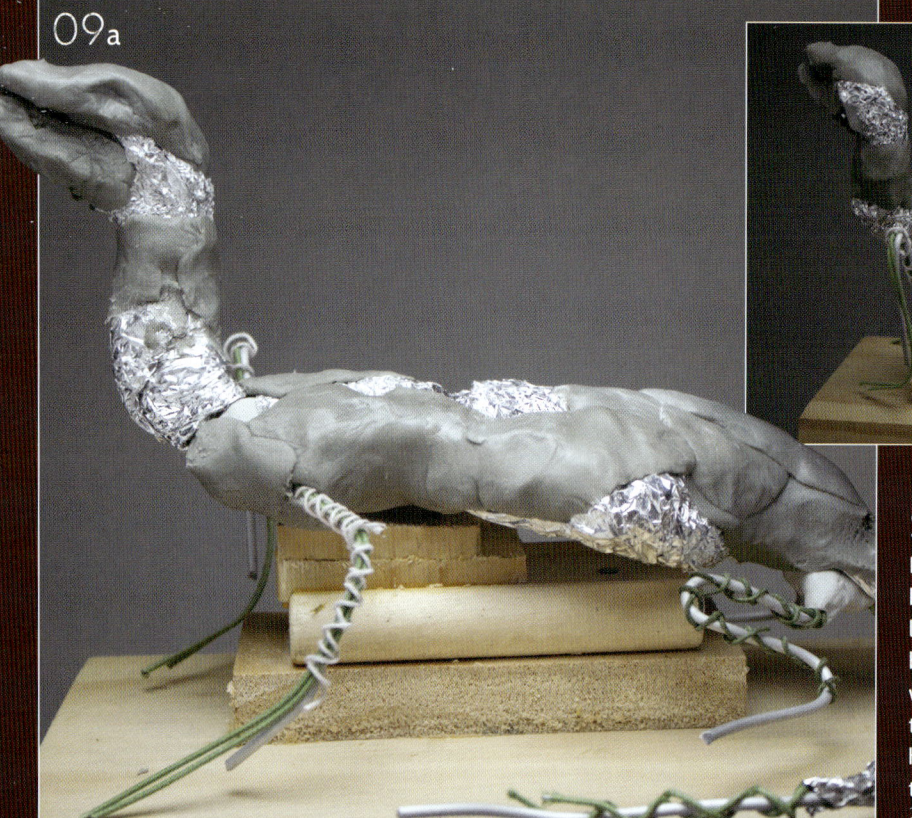

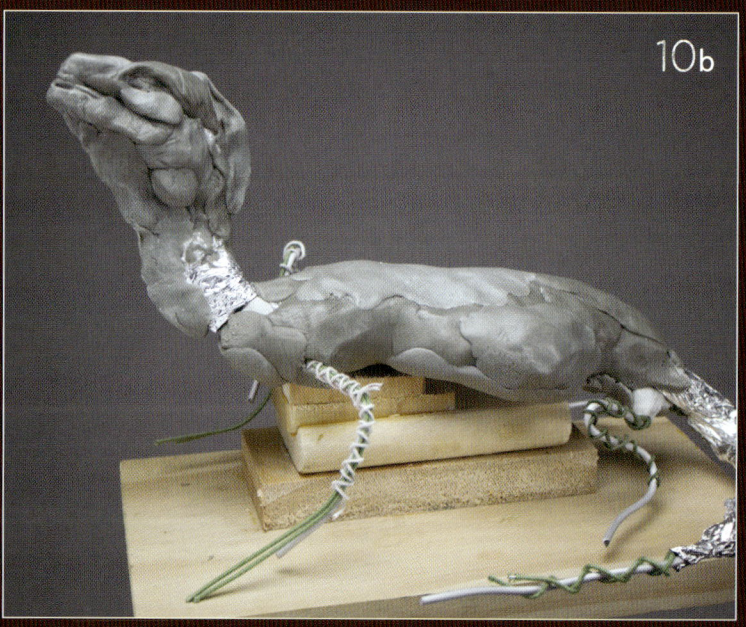

STEP 09

Finally, we introduce clay to our piece! To begin, we block out the dragon's upper and lower jaw, and start to bulk out the dragon's body. At this stage the legs still consist of wire only (09a). When photographed from the back, the angle of the head can be seen, highlighting that the head is turned towards the front of the piece to create a more engaging pose (09b).

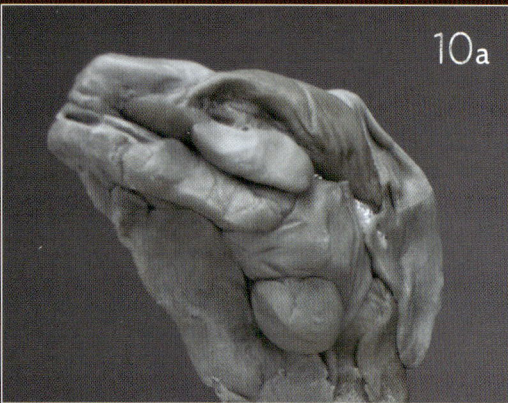

STEP 10

Next, we start to build and sculpt the head with more layers of clay (10a). Getting the size of the head correct at this point is important as it will dictate the size and proportion of the dragon's other body parts (10b).

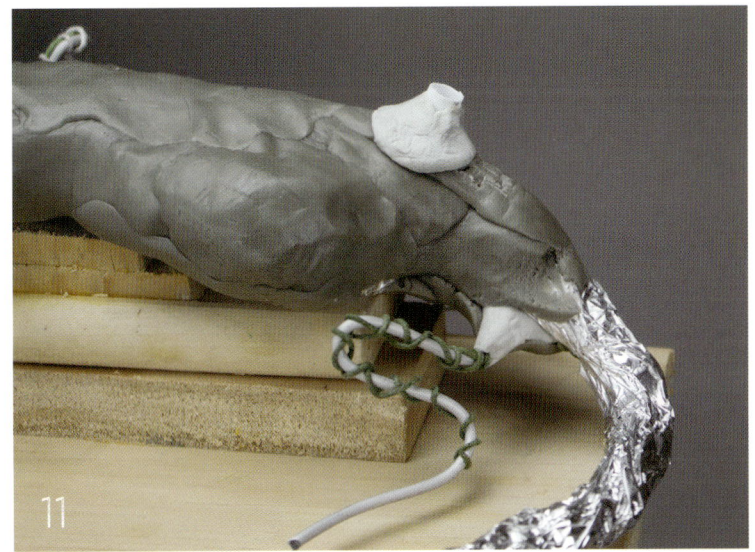

STEP 11

Next we plan how the rider will be attached to the dragon's body. Toward the back of the dragon, just before the start of the tail, we introduce a tube rig to allow for the rider to be attached (and become detachable). We secure a piece of tubing simply with plumber's putty. As we progress, we also score the hardened Aves Apoxie Sculpt with a sharp tool to allow the next application of clay to grip on to it more easily.

STEP 12

We rough out the human form using floral wire; as you can see, we aim for a very relaxed, casual position. The basic human armature form will act as a guide to help us gauge proportion and composition until we make the final, more refined, rider later.

THE BASIC HUMAN ARMATURE FORM WILL ACT AS A GUIDE TO HELP US GAUGE PROPORTION AND COMPOSITION

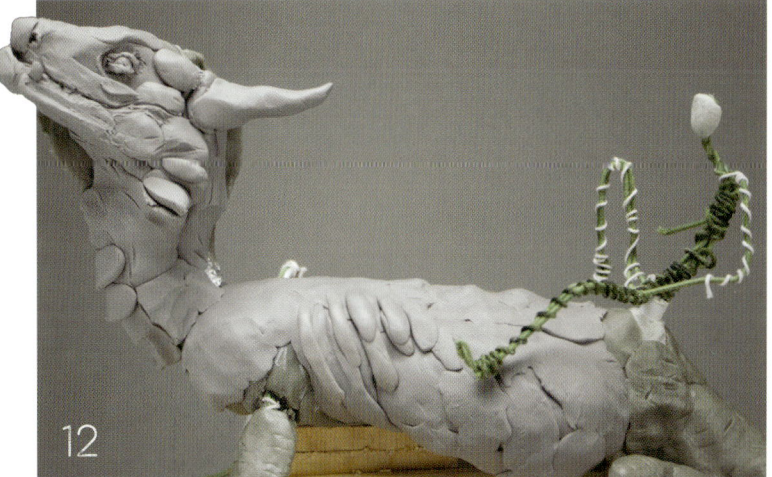

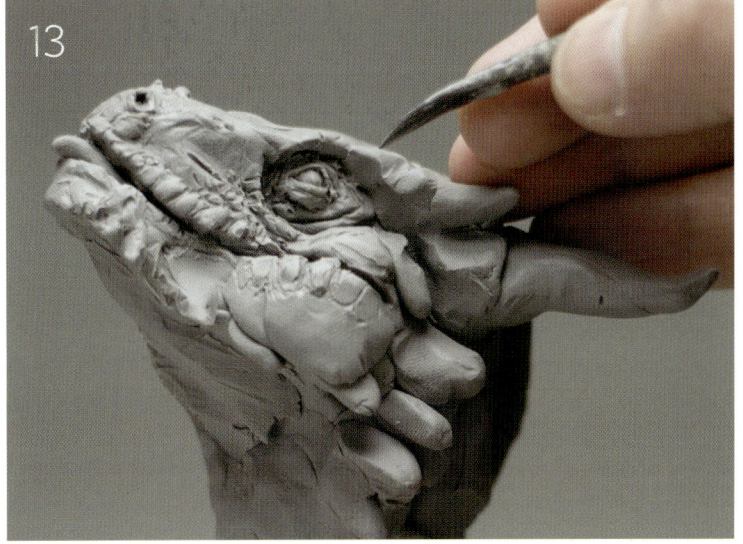

STEP 13

We move on to blocking in and detailing the face of the dragon with Super Sculpey using various tools. Notice how we use our favorite tool, the burnisher, to add shape and detail to the top of the head. We add bulk to the horns using a small, rolled piece of Super Sculpey. We love Super Sculpey's malleability and texture — at this scale its ability to hold detail is exactly what we need.

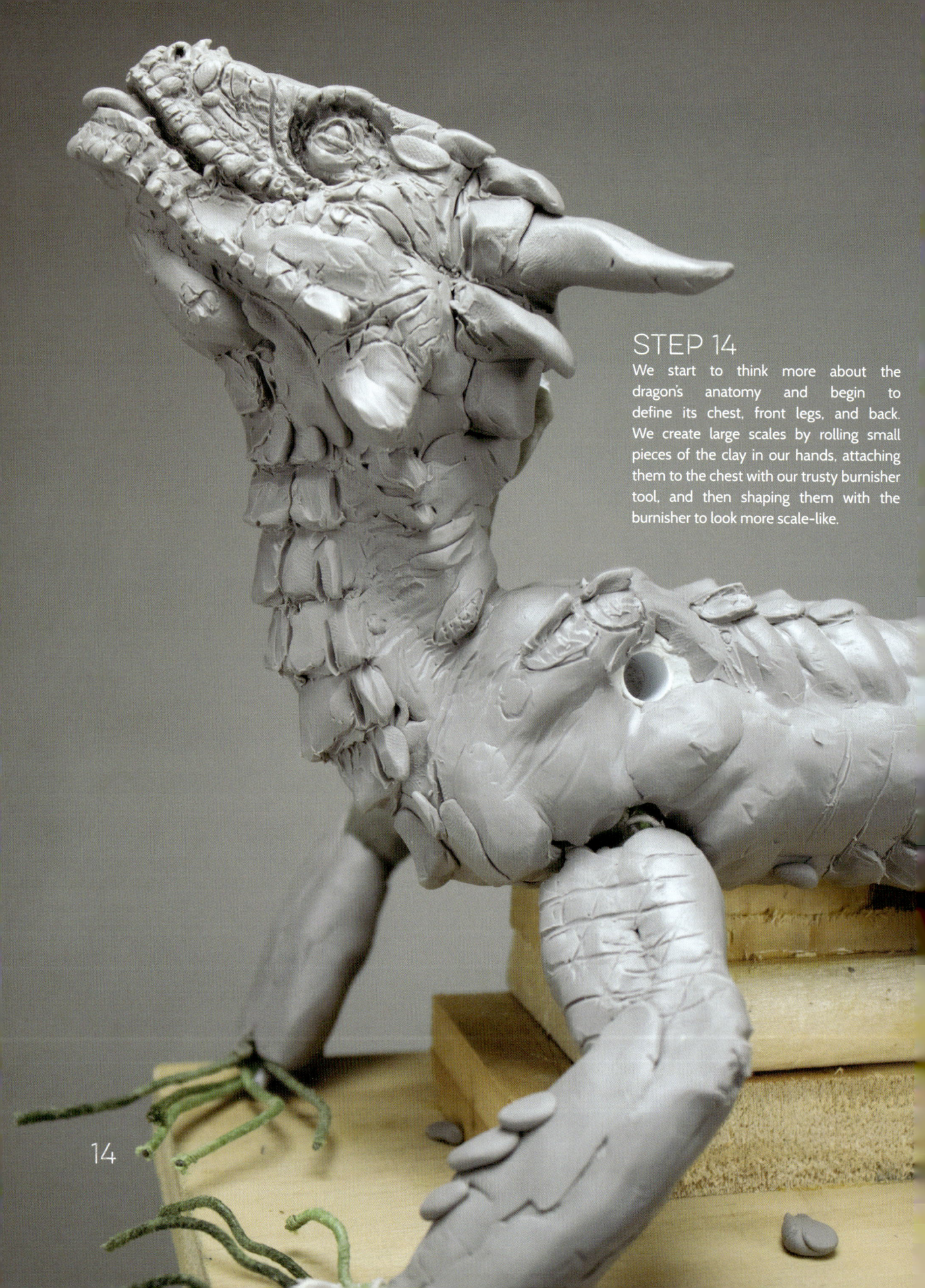

STEP 14

We start to think more about the dragon's anatomy and begin to define its chest, front legs, and back. We create large scales by rolling small pieces of the clay in our hands, attaching them to the chest with our trusty burnisher tool, and then shaping them with the burnisher to look more scale-like.

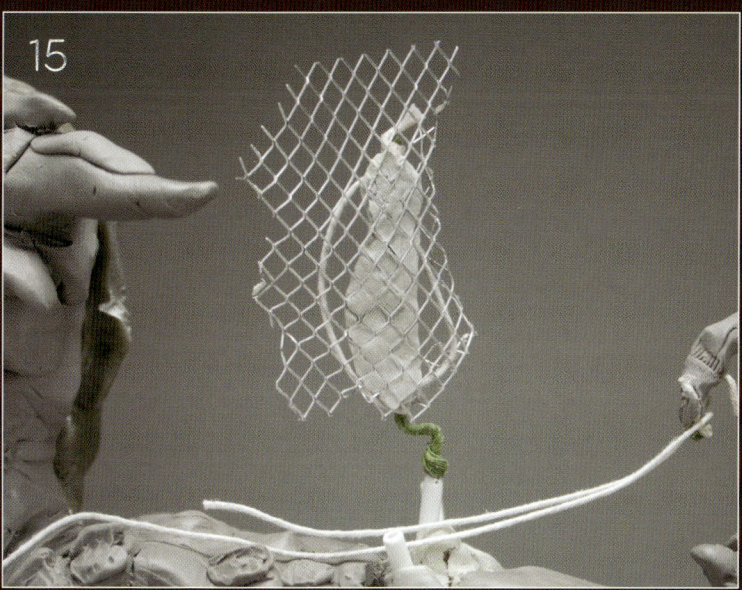

STEP 15

Wire mesh is very effective for creating flat, thin elements. In this case, we create some little flags and banners that hang from our dragon, the same way in which ceremonial accessories hang from a horse. We simply cut out a small rectangle of wire mesh and attach it to a standing floral-wire structure with a piece of plumber's putty. We then cover the mesh with a thin layer of Super Sculpey, creating a lightweight flag.

STEP 16

We consider the construction of the dragon's bridle and reins next. As they will be detachable elements, we create yet another male/female connection from plastic tubing, fixing the large piece of tubing into the jaw area of the dragon with plumber's putty.

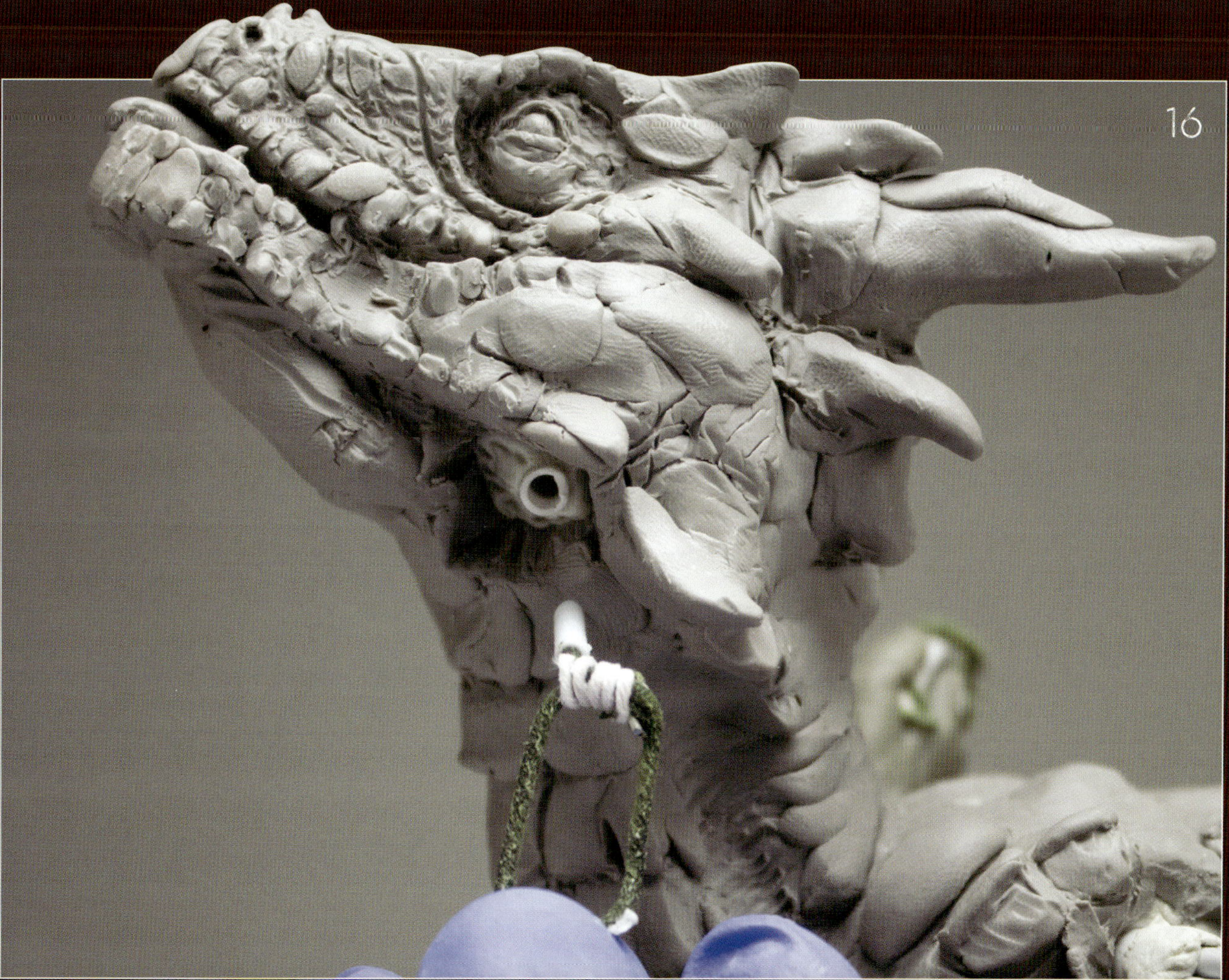

STEP 17

To focus on the base of the piece, we first carefully detach the dragon. We add foil to bulk it out and start to build the rocky plane for our desert rock setting. We imagine that this big lizard will lie on his belly on a flat rock, the way many iguanas and big lizards do in real life.

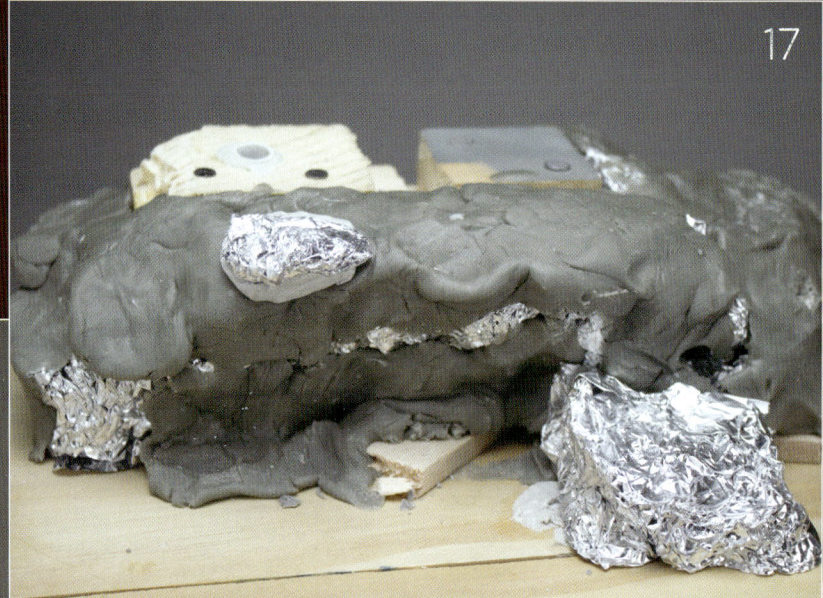

17

STEP 18

Now we concentrate on creating detail on the dragon's belly, removing the flag to give us easy access. Again, we create scales by rolling tiny balls of Super Sculpey, then attaching them and shaping them with the burnisher. Adding each scale individually by hand is time-consuming work, but this detailed work that might seem monotonous to some is actually one of the joys of the process. We also make progress on the base of our saddle contraption, building it up in epoxy putty to ensure a sturdy result in preparation for the next stage.

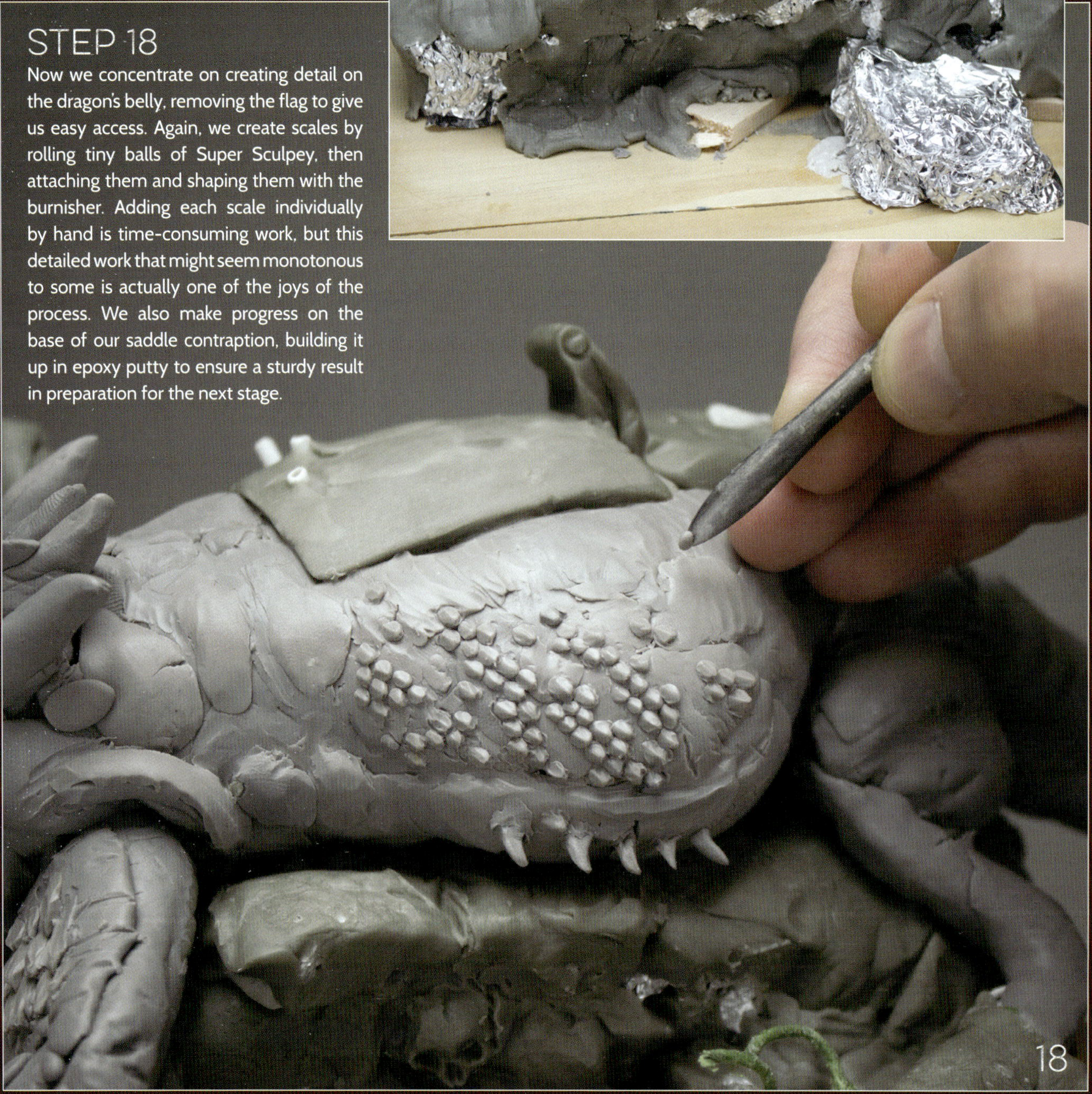

18

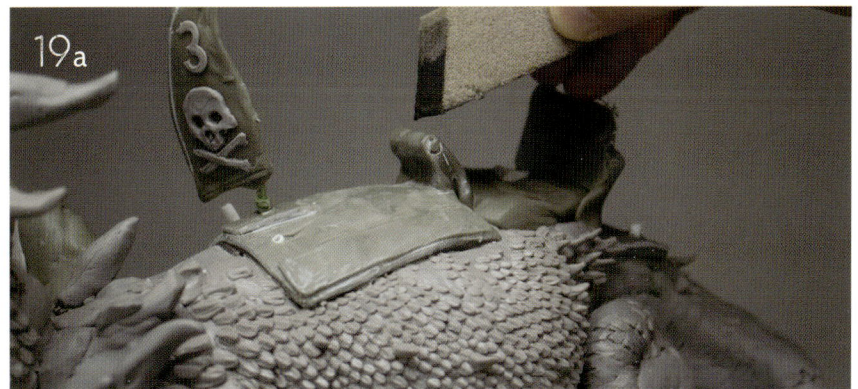

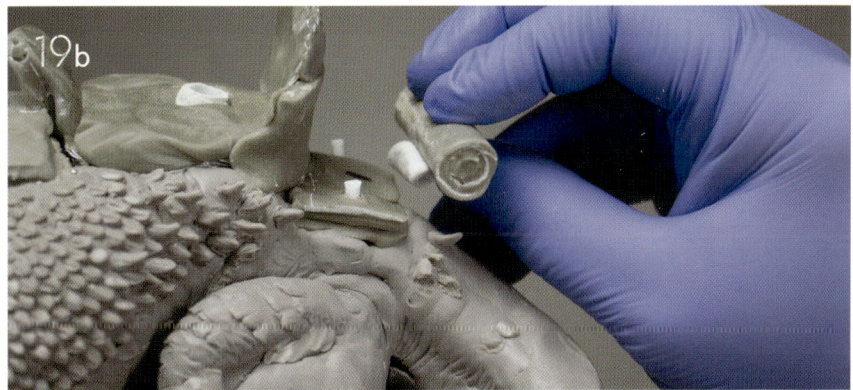

STEP 19

Using a sanding sponge, we lightly sand the saddle (19a) and then add a rolled pack to the back of it (19b). This is the type of detail we think of spontaneously and is probably mostly inspired by certain examples of the art of Moebius, who would draw desert travelers weighed down with various packs and tools for long voyages.

STEP 20

Detailing on the body and scales continues. We now have the rough form of the tail blocked in, but at this point we aren't entirely sure what we are going to do with it. It is strictly a design decision — we often use features such as tails and pieces that fly off from the main form to add movement to the piece as a whole. We study the piece and try to decide on the tail shape that will best accomplish that goal.

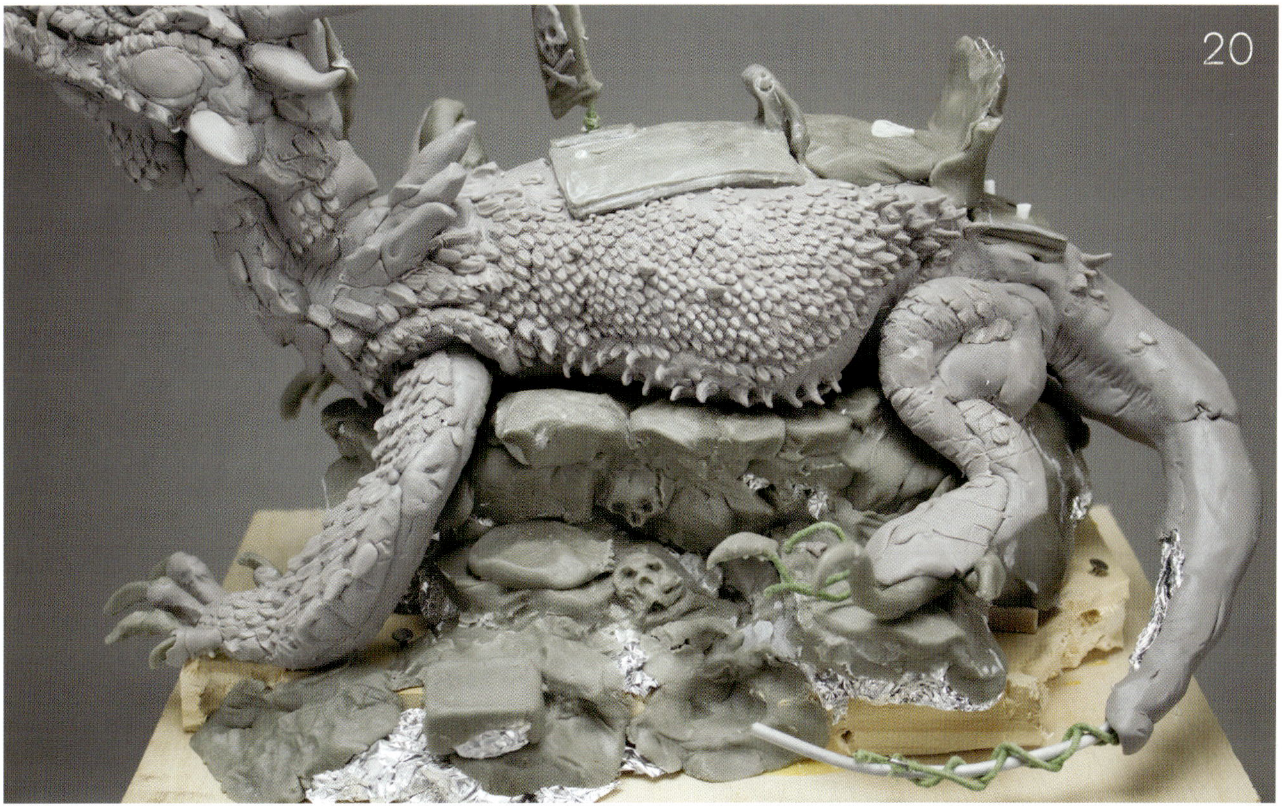

BRINGING THE RIDER TO LIFE

STEP 21

While waiting for inspiration for the dragon's tail, we create the final version of the rider. We start by placing two floral wires into a section of tube that inserts into the piece we have fixed into the saddle. We bend the wires down to create the shoulders of the rider. We also spontaneously decide to add more packs, created from Aves Apoxie Sculpt, behind the rider.

STEP 22

The rider's skeletal structure takes shape as we add legs, a neck, and a coiled head to the armature (22a). As always, we tie the basic structure together with floral wire and soak the structure in super glue. We then completely wrap the armature in more floral wire to help the clay adhere. This is much easier to do when the figure can be lifted from the dragon's body (22b).

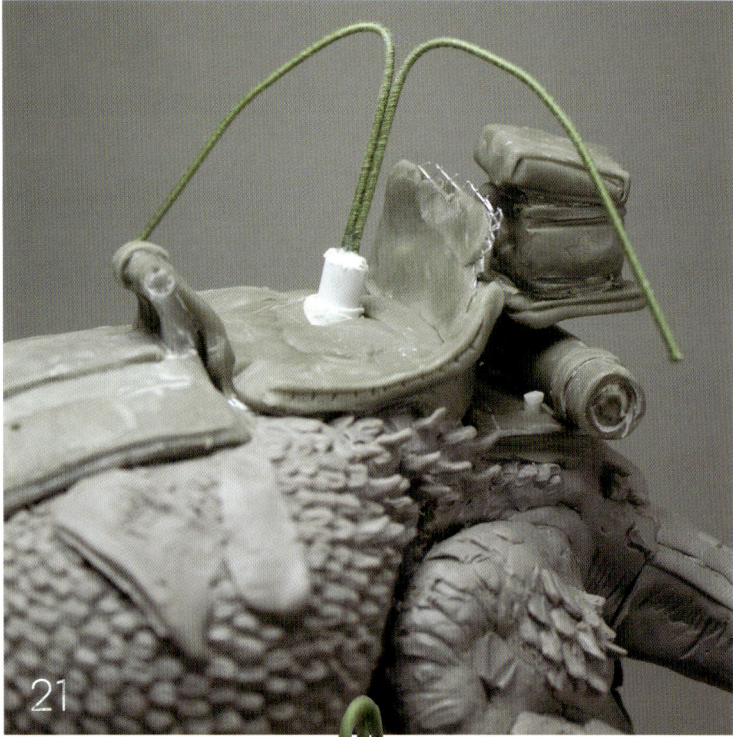

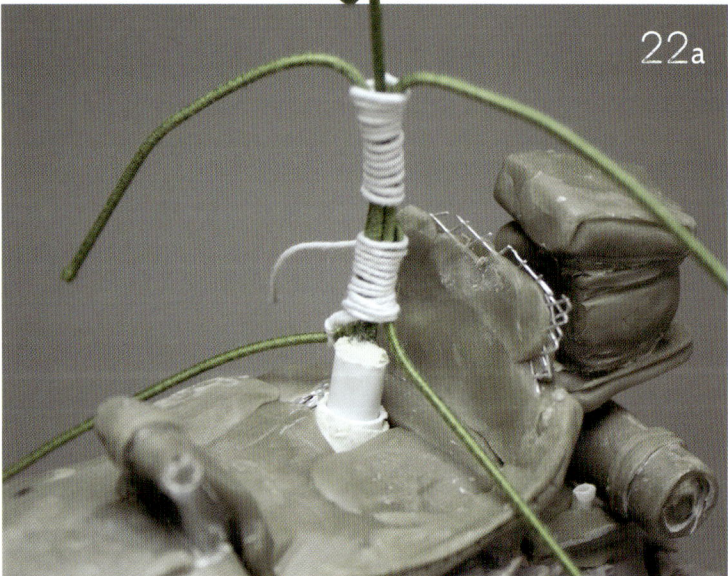

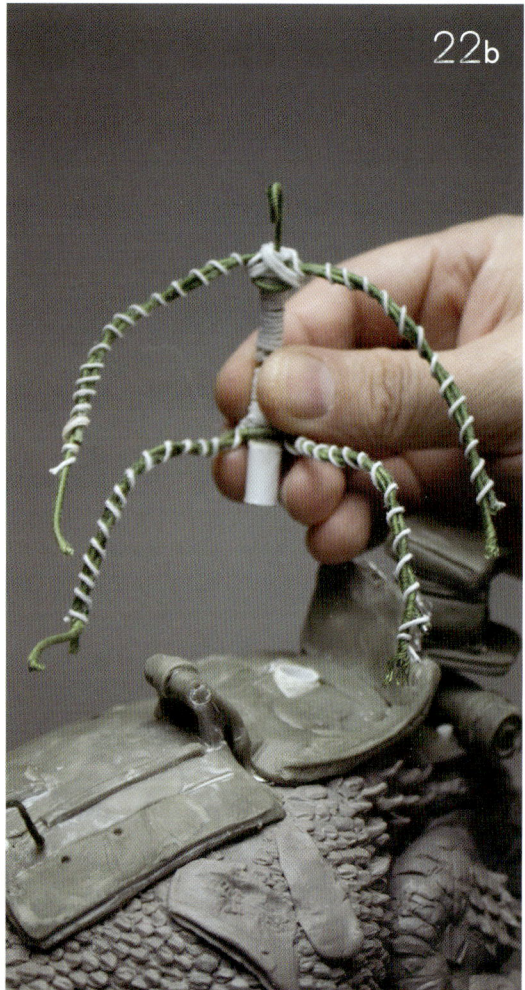

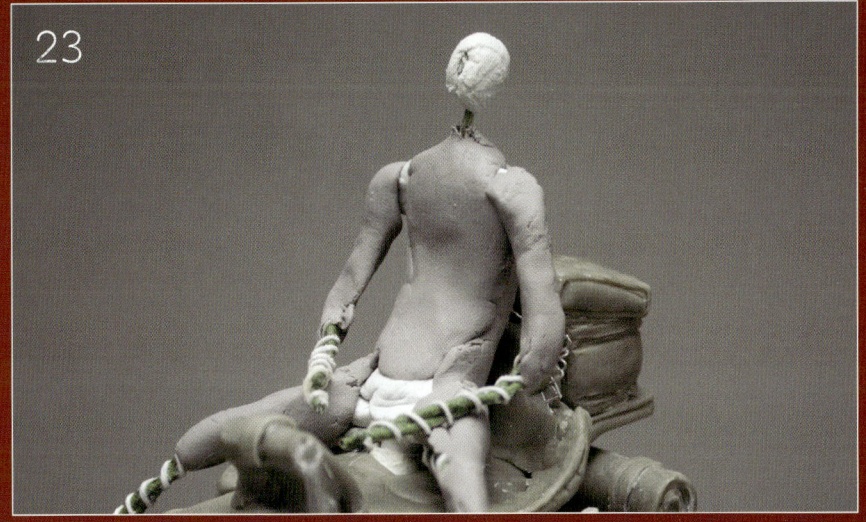

STEP 23

Next, we block in the form of the rider and add a little skull shape in epoxy putty. When the putty hardens, it gives us a stable surface onto which we can easily sculpt the face. We envision a very relaxed, casual pose for the rider, and so we push his shoulders into a slightly slumped position and add the very beginnings of basic musculature to guide our proportions and placement of the anatomy.

STEP 24

To help guide us when approaching the anatomy of the rider, we draw temporary lines in the clay bisecting both the face and the midsection. We also mark out where the eyes will sit, halfway down the length of the head (24a). We then add the eyes, which we consider extremely important in terms of directing the feel of the piece (24b). The emotion in the (eventually finished) eyes and the direction they are looking affects the entire sculpt.

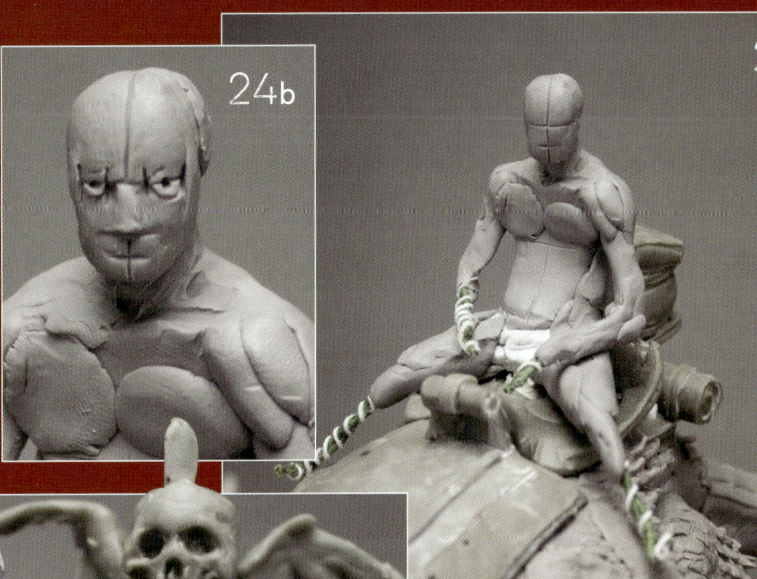

STEP 25

We work on the face and refine the expression. Even though we are of course very familiar with faces, we still use lots of photo reference when sculpting facial features. We also start work on the skull-topped spears which stand behind the rider. Lastly, we lay down more strips of Super Sculpey to denote the chest anatomy.

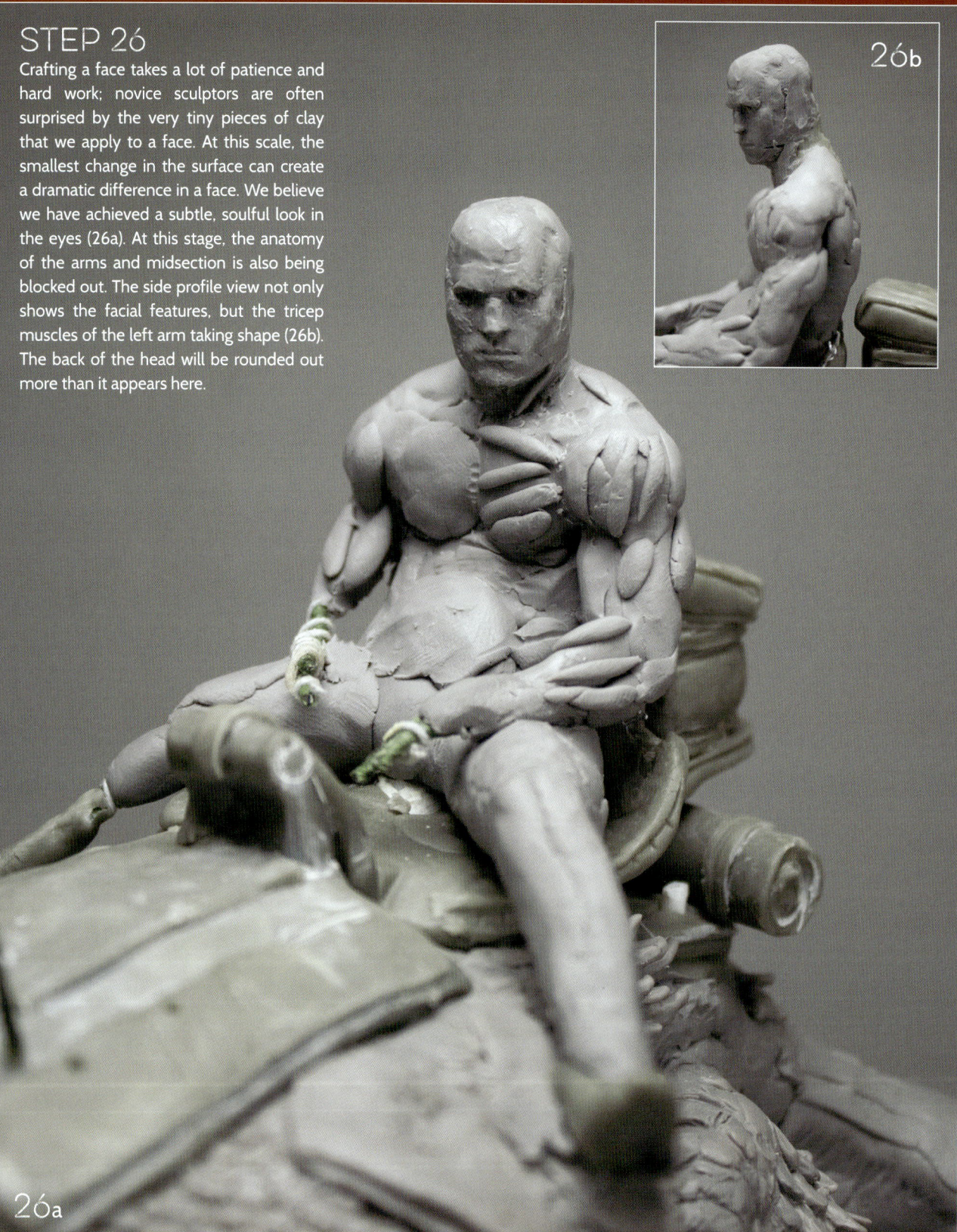

STEP 26

Crafting a face takes a lot of patience and hard work; novice sculptors are often surprised by the very tiny pieces of clay that we apply to a face. At this scale, the smallest change in the surface can create a dramatic difference in a face. We believe we have achieved a subtle, soulful look in the eyes (26a). At this stage, the anatomy of the arms and midsection is also being blocked out. The side profile view not only shows the facial features, but the tricep muscles of the left arm taking shape (26b). The back of the head will be rounded out more than it appears here.

26b

26a

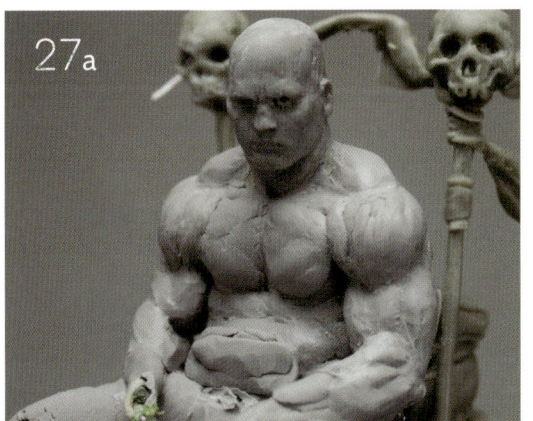

27a

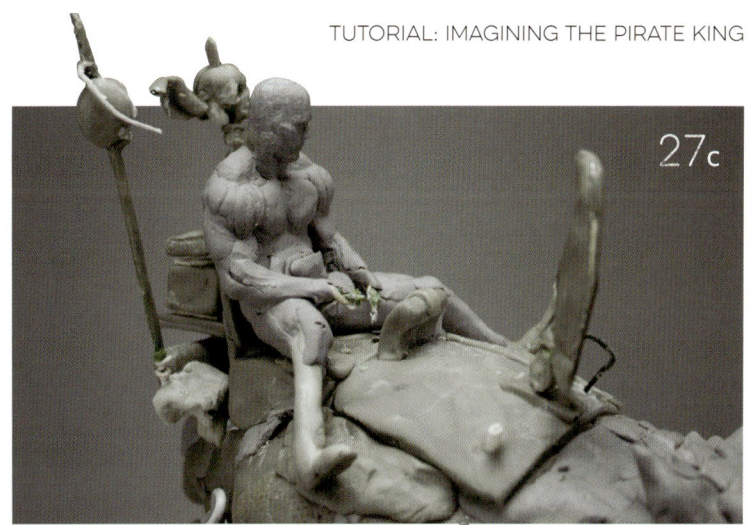

27c

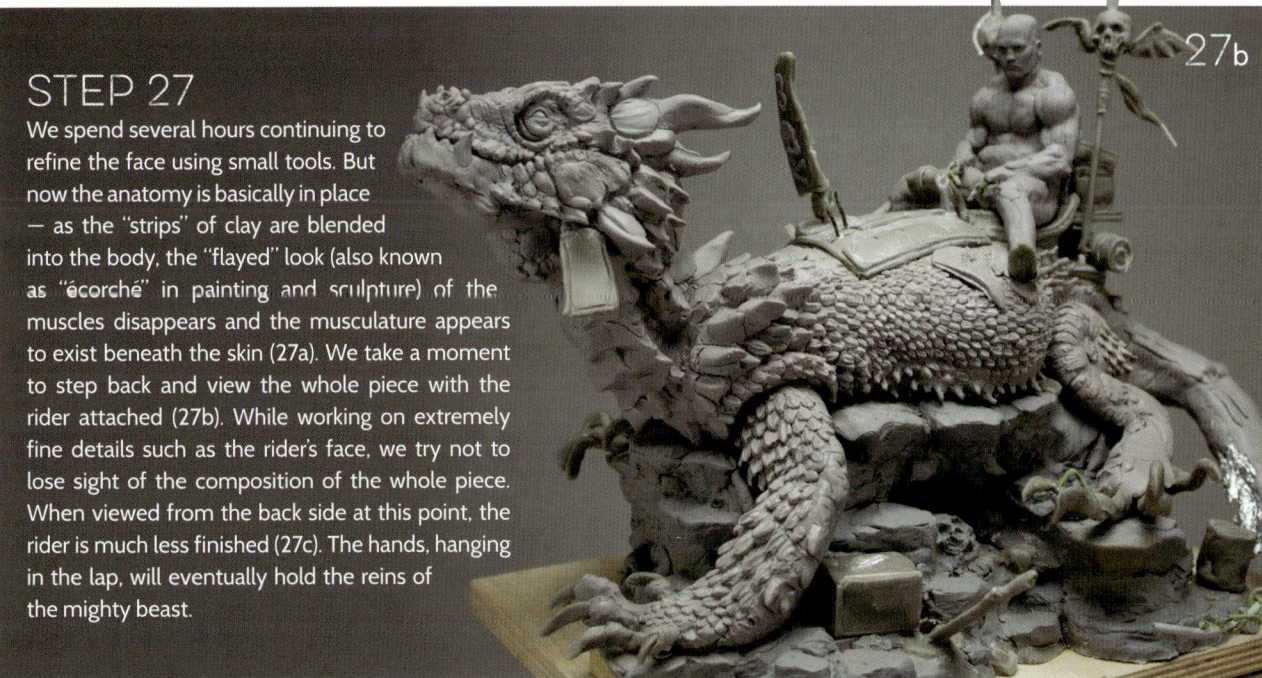

STEP 27

We spend several hours continuing to refine the face using small tools. But now the anatomy is basically in place — as the "strips" of clay are blended into the body, the "flayed" look (also known as "écorché" in painting and sculpture) of the muscles disappears and the musculature appears to exist beneath the skin (27a). We take a moment to step back and view the whole piece with the rider attached (27b). While working on extremely fine details such as the rider's face, we try not to lose sight of the composition of the whole piece. When viewed from the back side at this point, the rider is much less finished (27c). The hands, hanging in the lap, will eventually hold the reins of the mighty beast.

27b

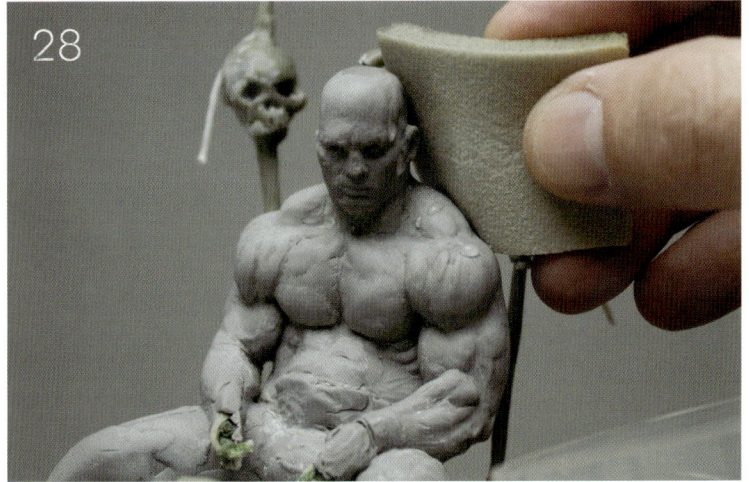

28

STEP 28

The muscles and anatomy have been advanced considerably with detail now, and we do a small amount of sanding to further define these details. At this scale, accurate musculature is so important when creating a believable-looking figure. Clothing, kneepads, and a belt are all roughed in with Super Sculpey.

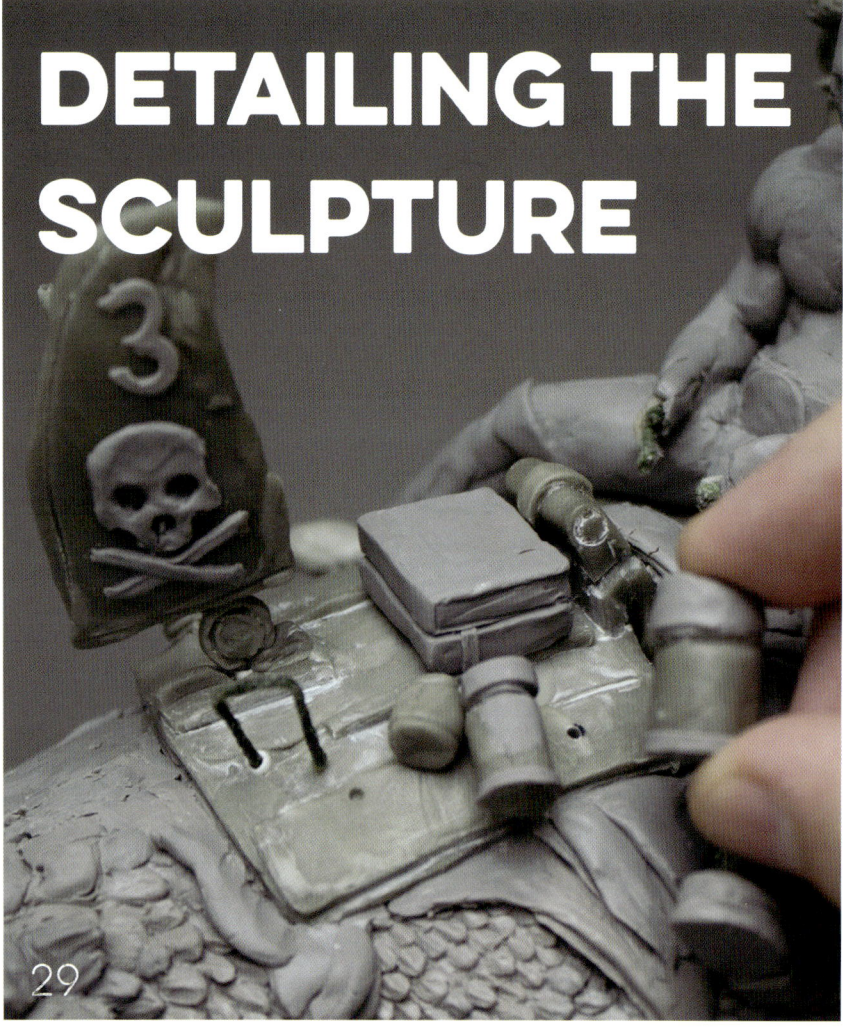

DETAILING THE SCULPTURE

STEP 29

Again, we imagine the type of packs and containers a desert-crossing beast like this would carry. We sculpt some of these items directly onto the piece, and some we sculpt in our hands and then attach to the sculpture. We create a skull and number embellishment on the little pirate flag that sits in front of the rider. We always think about detail and visual interest in certain areas of our sculptures.

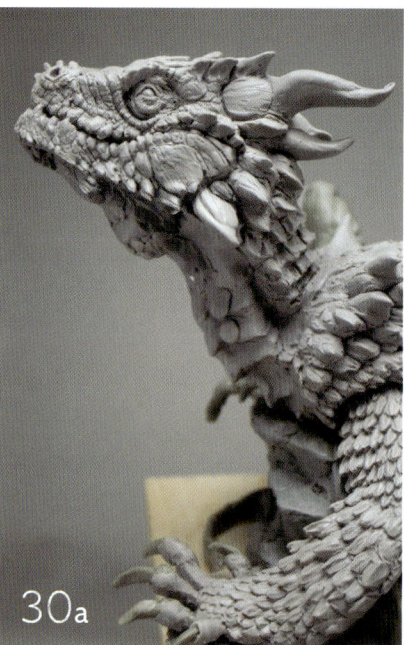

STEP 30

We now finish the detail and scales on the dragon's head and forelegs (30a). Using the tip of a small paintbrush handle, we place more tiny spikes on the dragon's belly (30b). We simply roll tiny pieces of Super Sculpey into a spike shape and then attach them.

✦ GROUNDED IN REALITY

By referencing the scale patterns of real-life lizards, a sculpture which has an overall sense of fantasy and whimsy seems just a bit more possible. Working on reptile anatomy and detail can be a lot of fun!

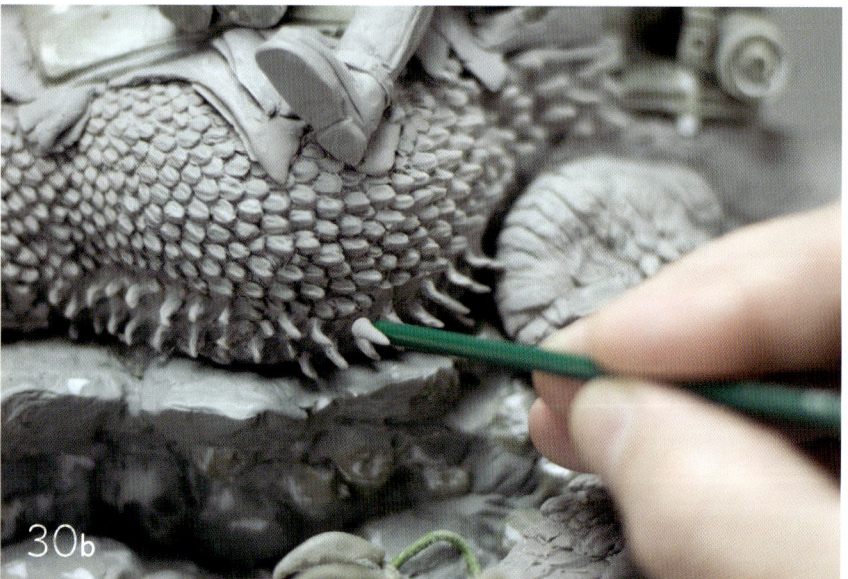

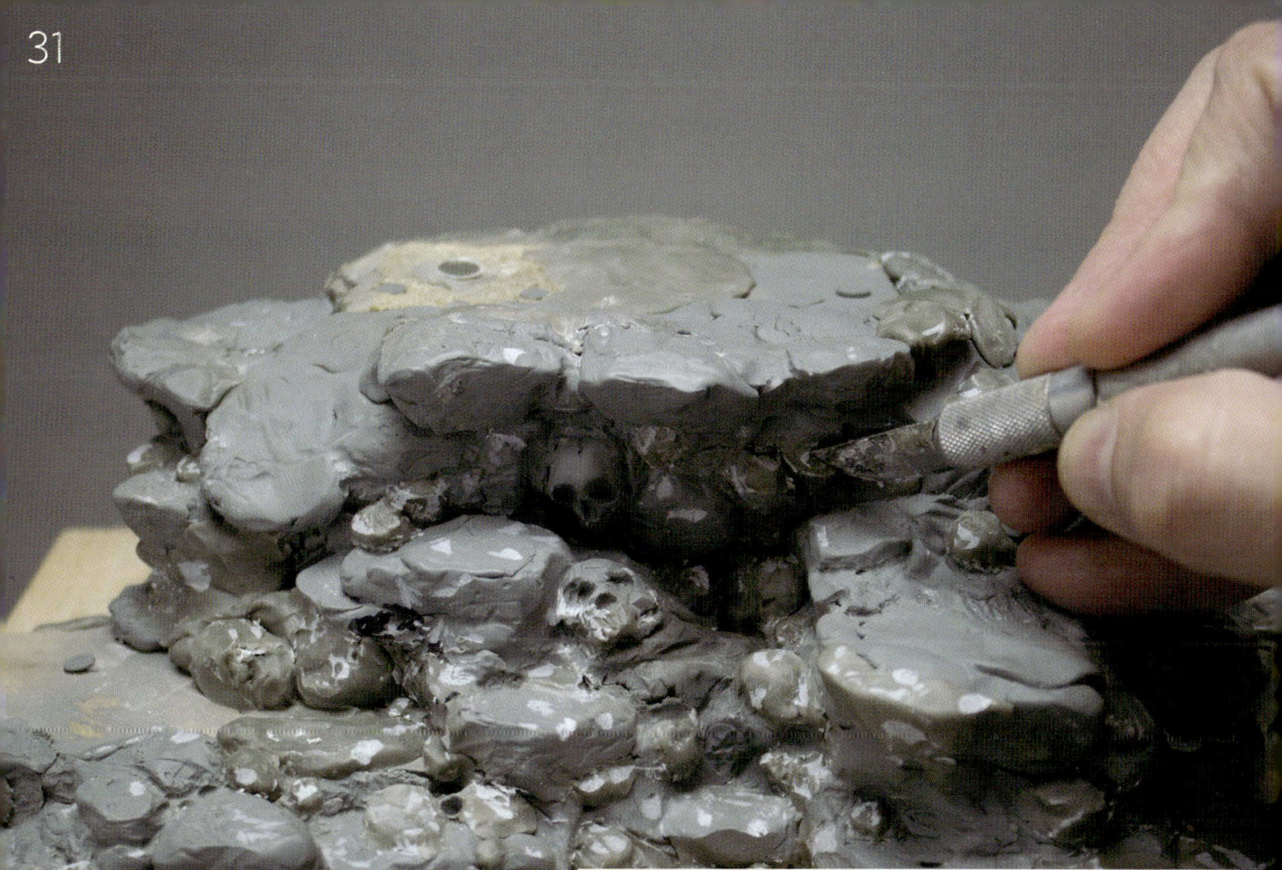

31

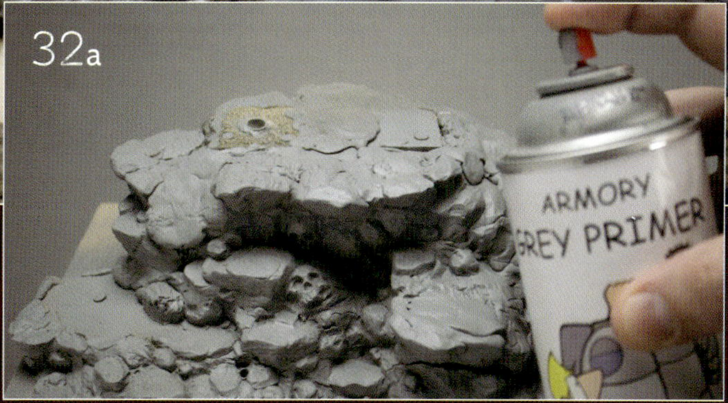

STEP 31

Revisiting the base, we use a scalpel to carve out chunks of clay, creating a more rock-like look. Rock forms might seem easy to the create, but we use references just as we do for other parts of the sculpture. Our sculptures may be fantastical, but we want them to feel believable.

STEP 32

We sometimes apply gray primer to parts of a sculpture, even before completion. The result is that we can see what we refer to as the "true surface." Different colors, textures, scoring, and marks cause our eyes to strain to see the actual shapes that make up this base. The coat of grey primer paint creates a uniformly colored surface and now we can see the base more clearly as a whole. To finish the base beneath the rocks, we paint it black.

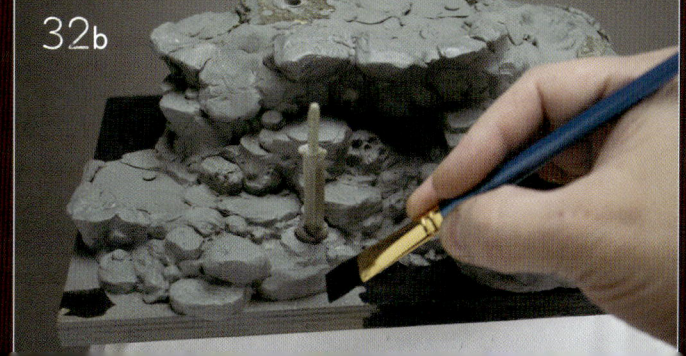

32a

32b

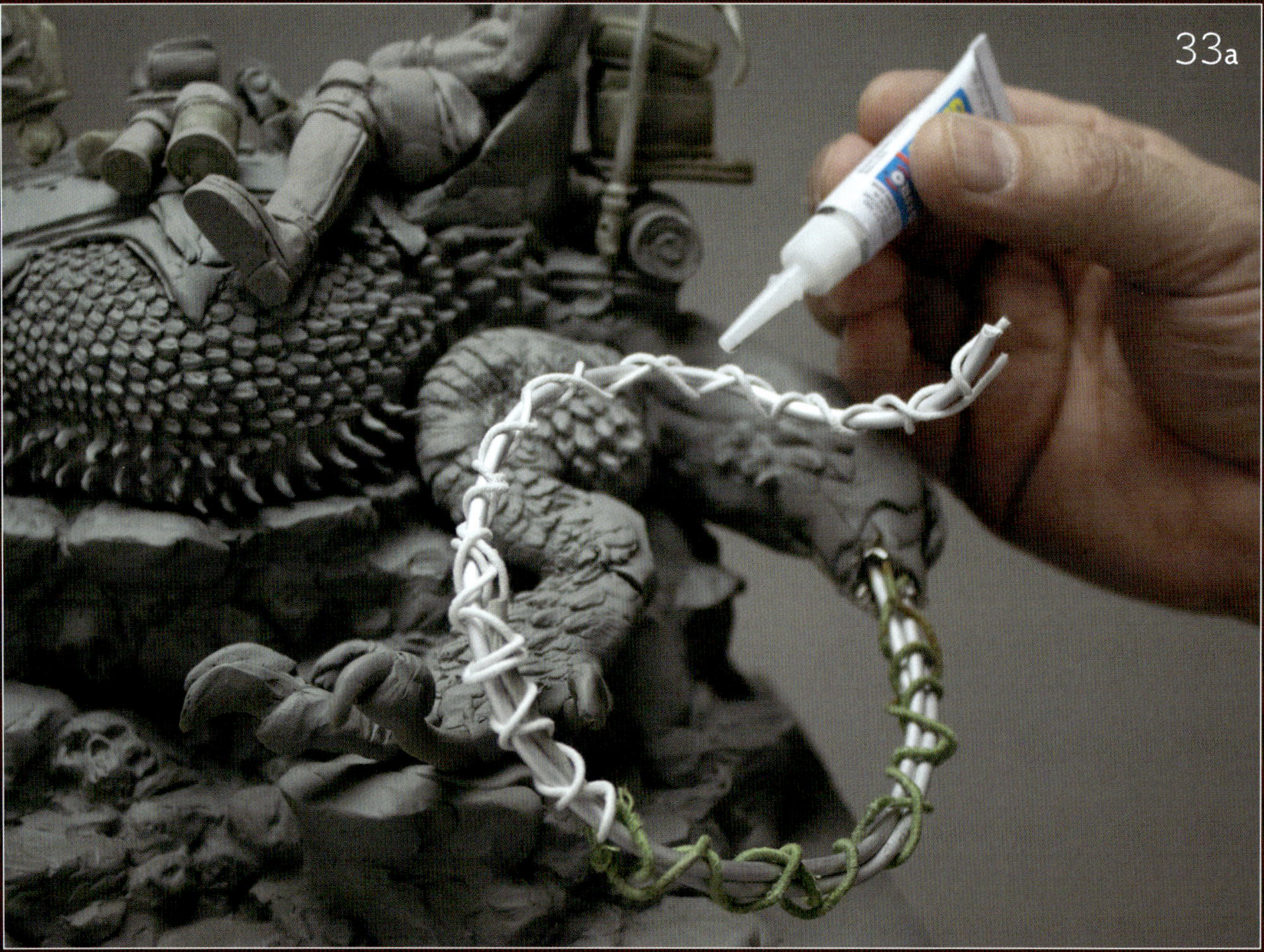

33a

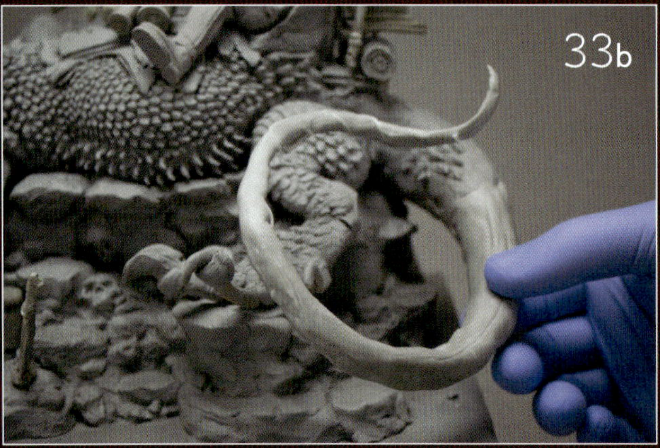

33b

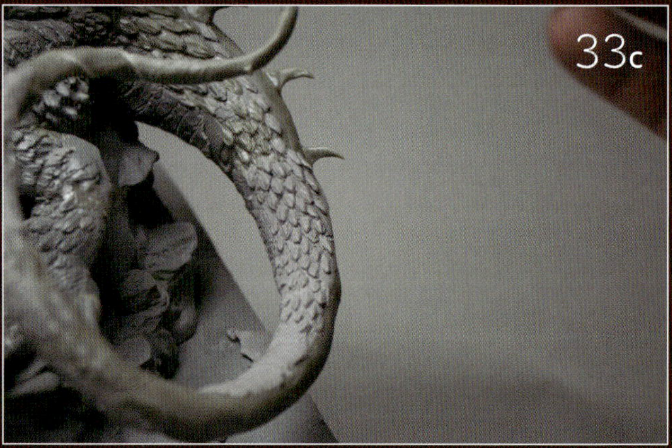

33c

STEP 33

We decide to make the tail more dramatic by creating a flowing shape, so extend the armature by attaching a little more aluminum alloy wire tied on with floral wire. Then we twist the wire up the length of the tail to help the clay adhere to it, preventing it from spinning around the aluminum wire (33a).

With the armature covered with clay, we are more satisfied with the general shape of the tail (33b). It extends out into space in front of the piece, from our "money shot" angle, making the overall sculpture appear more three-dimensional. As scales are added, it seems to truly become part of our dragon (33c).

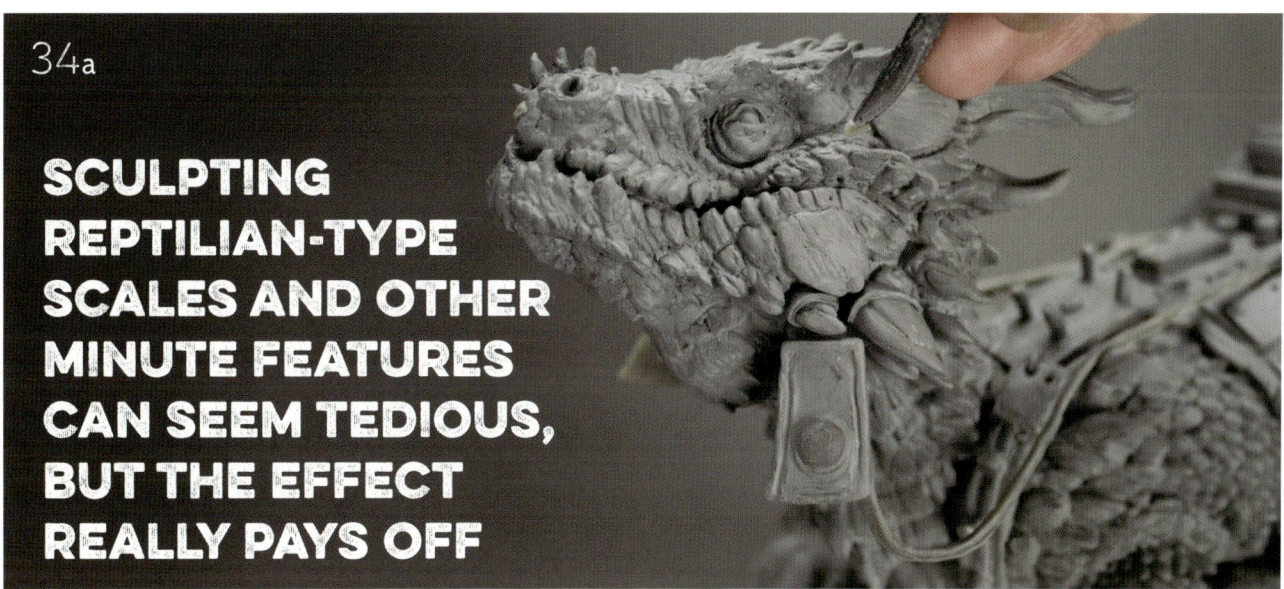

34a

SCULPTING REPTILIAN-TYPE SCALES AND OTHER MINUTE FEATURES CAN SEEM TEDIOUS, BUT THE EFFECT REALLY PAYS OFF

STEP 34

Tiny details in the form of very small pieces of Aves Apoxie Sculpt are added to the dragon's face (34a), and to the saddle rigging (34b) using our favorite tool, our burnisher. We concentrate on making these details as three-dimensional as possible, with small pieces projecting out toward the viewer. Sculpting reptilian-type scales and other minute features can seem tedious, but the effect really pays off in the end, impressing viewers both at the very first glance and later upon closer inspection.

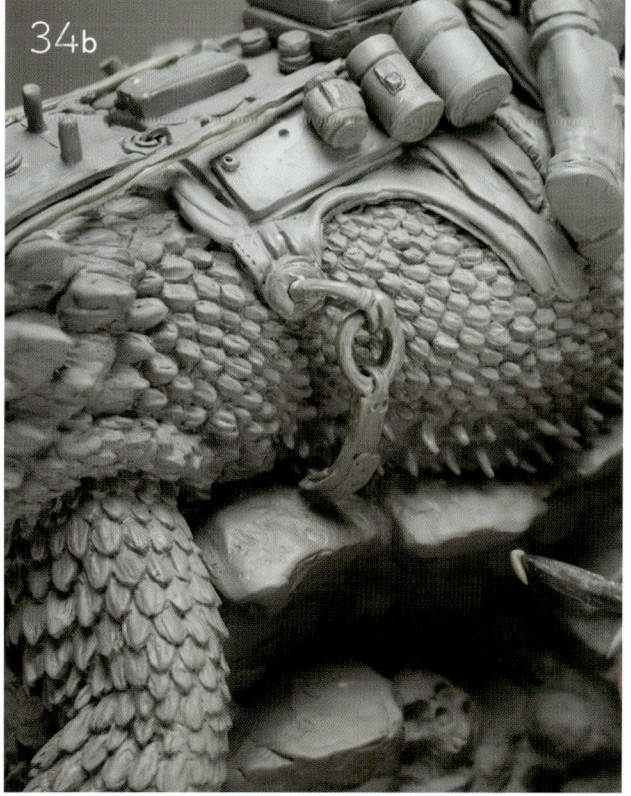

34b

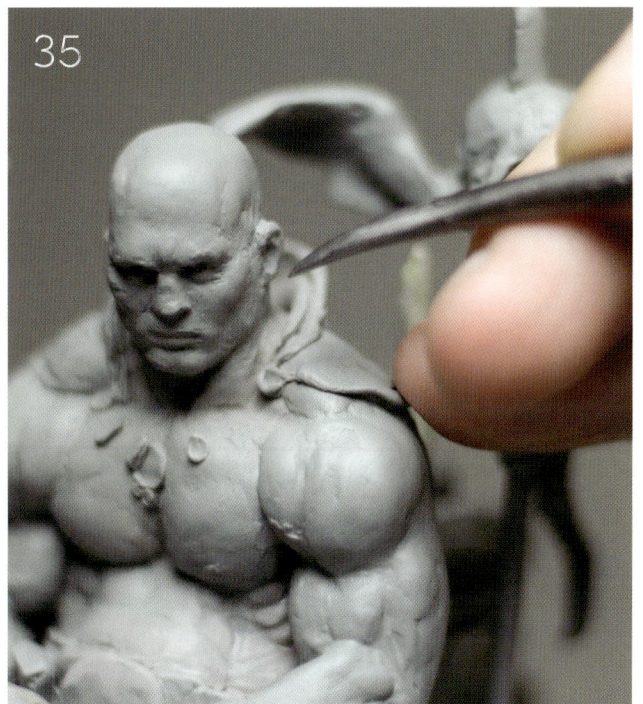

35

STEP 35

We work on faces at such a small scale that the very tiniest adjustments can transform them. A stray touch here or there can completely alter a face for the best *or* the worst. Here, we make excruciatingly small last-minute adjustments to our Pirate King's visage and call the piece complete.

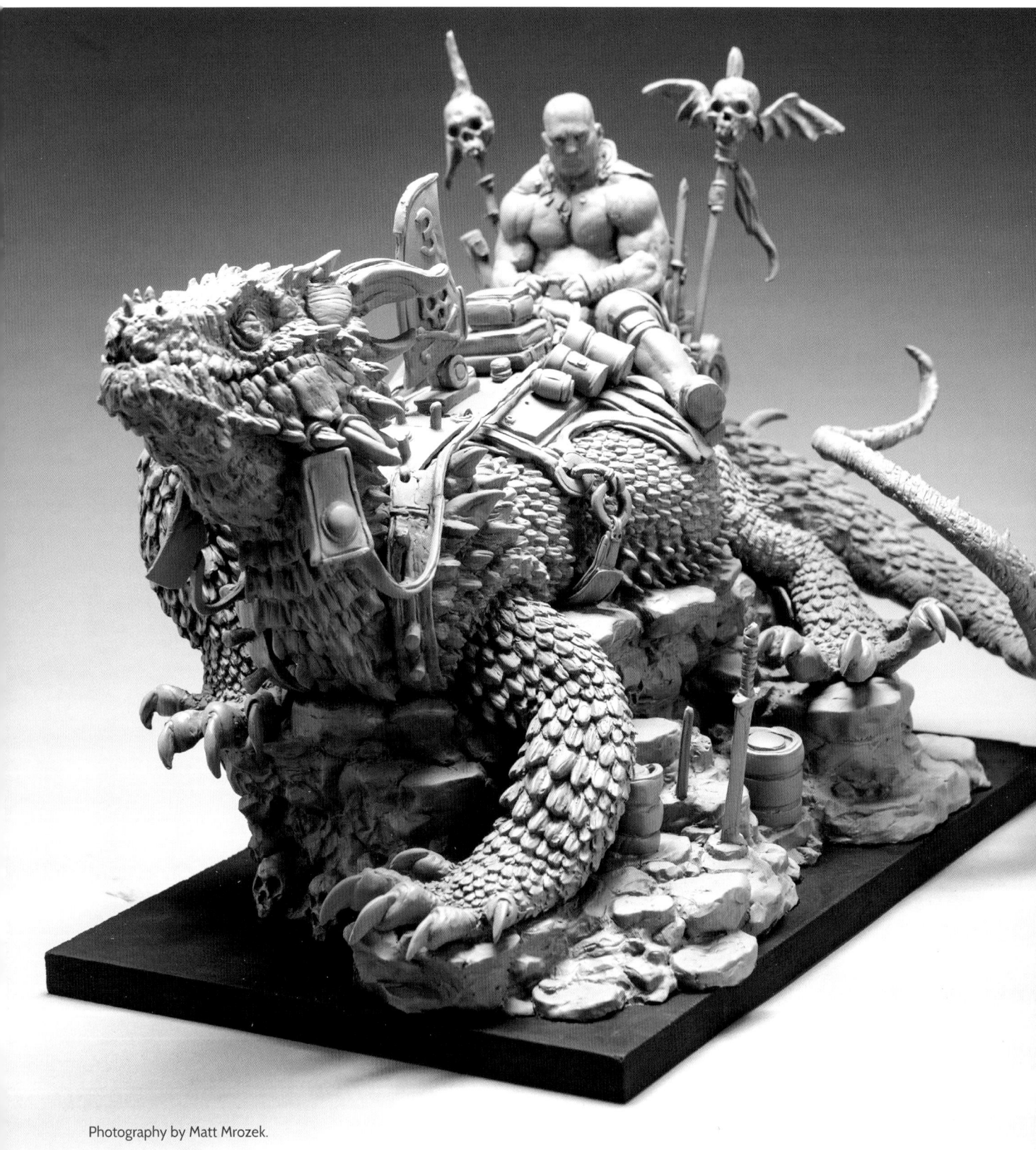

Photography by Matt Mrozek.

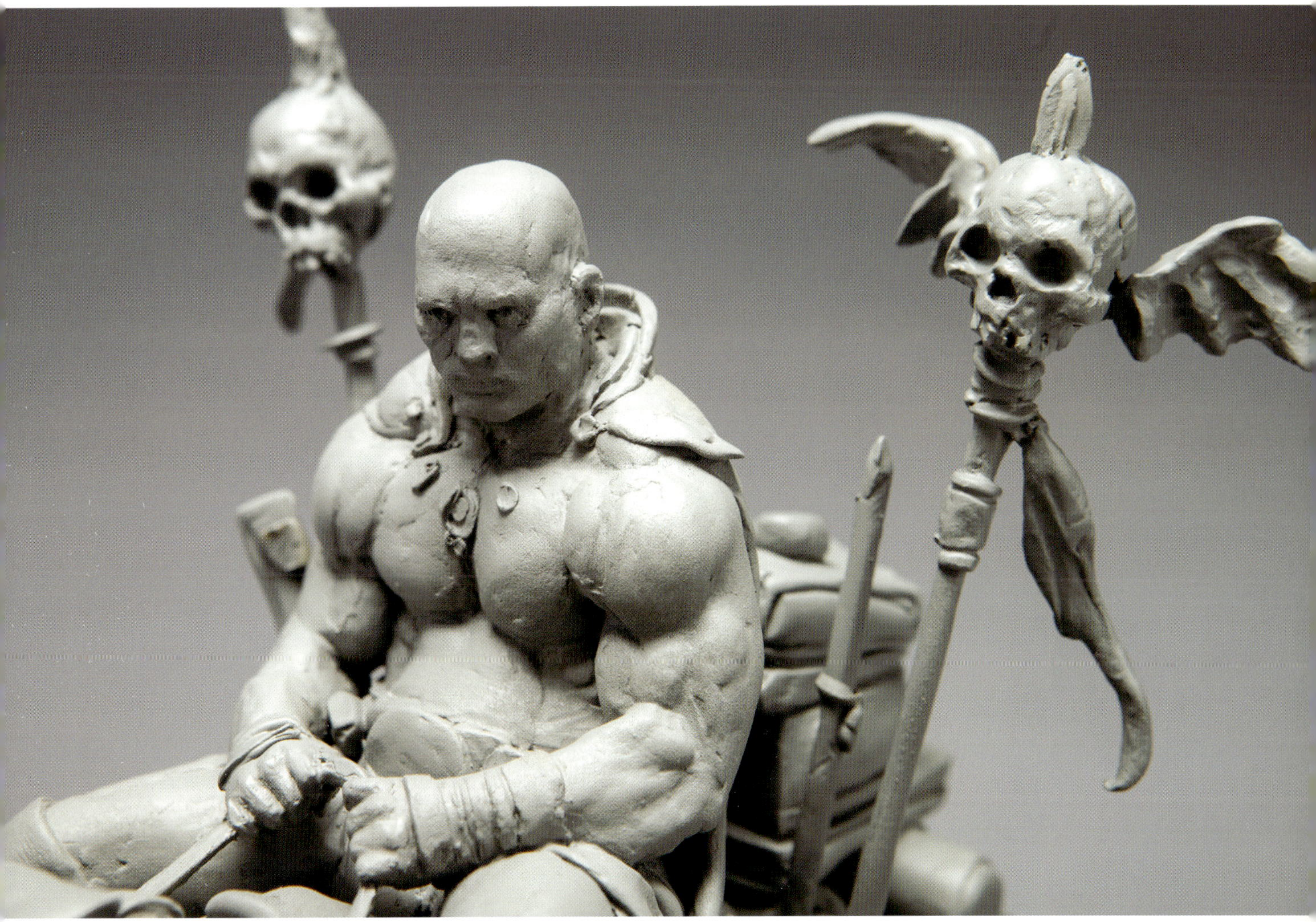

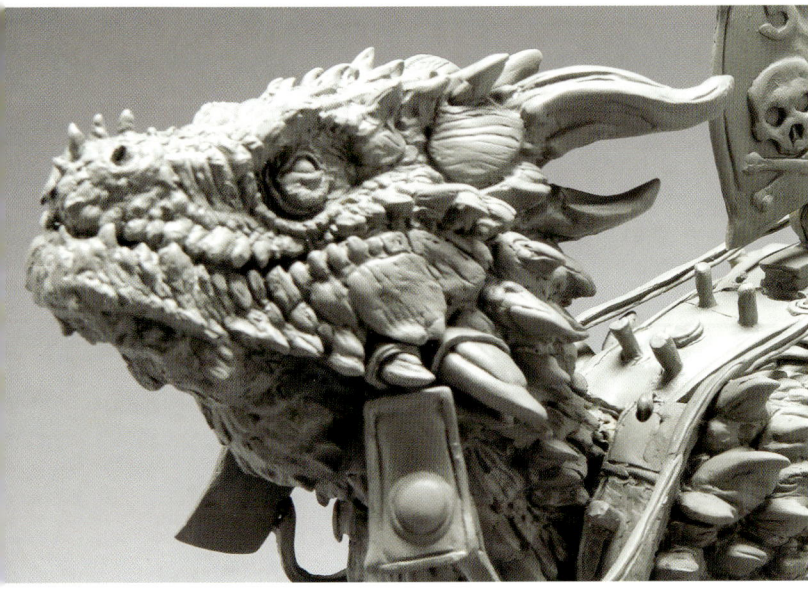

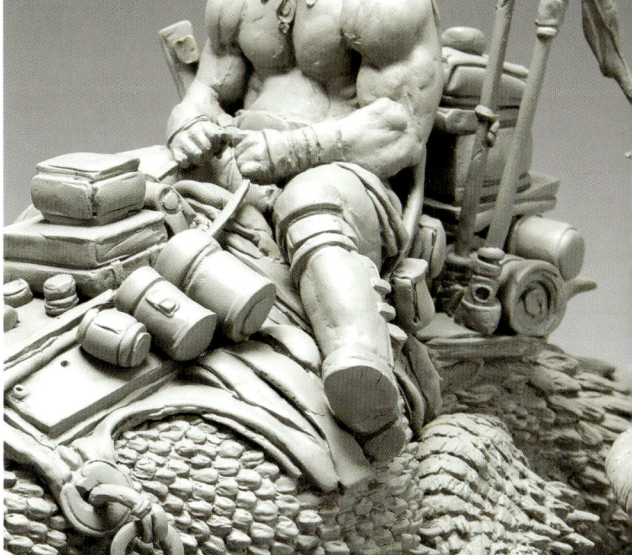

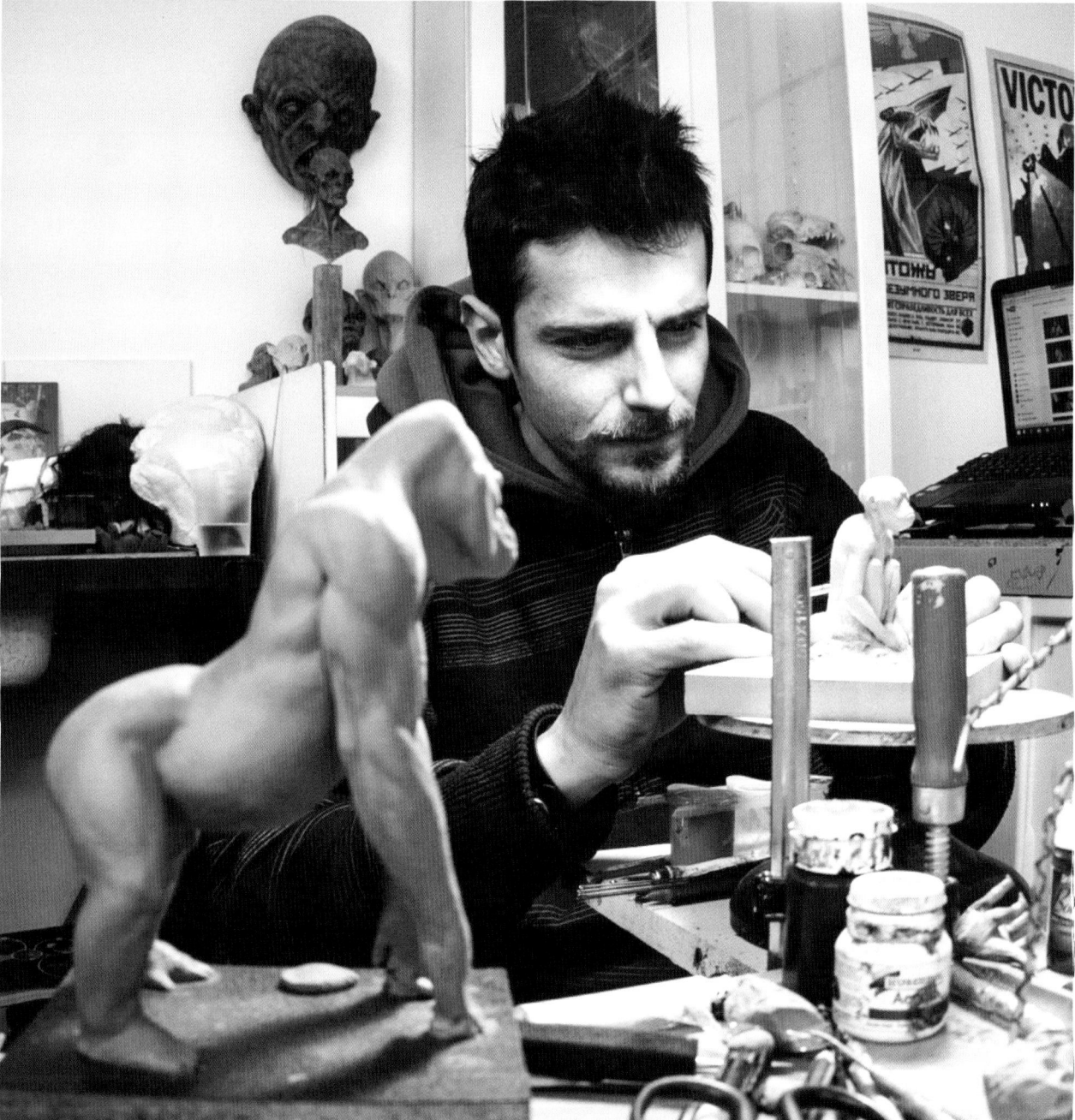

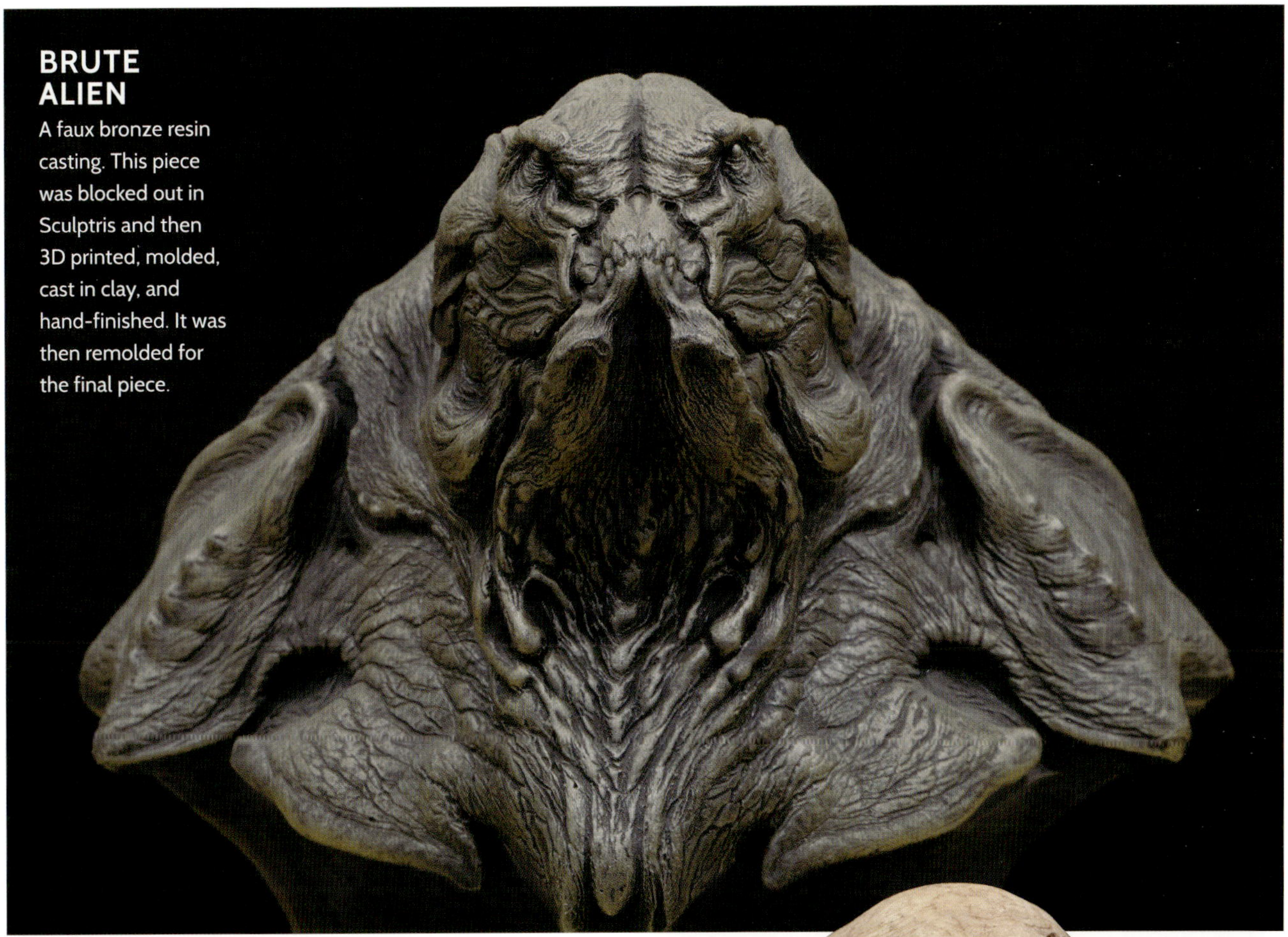

BRUTE ALIEN

A faux bronze resin casting. This piece was blocked out in Sculptris and then 3D printed, molded, cast in clay, and hand-finished. It was then remolded for the final piece.

ARTIST SPOTLIGHT

ARIS KOLOKONTES

Creature & character designer and sculptor

ariskolokontesart.blogspot.com

With a childhood interest in fantasy and sci-fi movies, Aris started experimenting with clay at age sixteen and fell in love with modeling creatures and characters. Twelve years later, he progressed into the world of special effects makeup, and shared an online portfolio alongside practicing his skills. He has undertaken work for film, TV, and art books since 2008, working on exciting projects such as *The Hobbit* trilogy, *Alien Covenant*, and *Victor Frankenstein*. He also teaches creature and character design in clay.

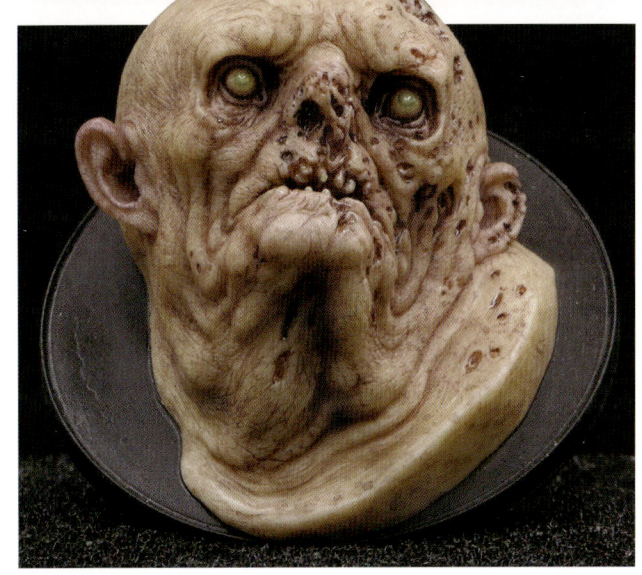

ZOMBIE

Polyester resin casting of a 1/5 scale zombie face coloured with acrylic paint.

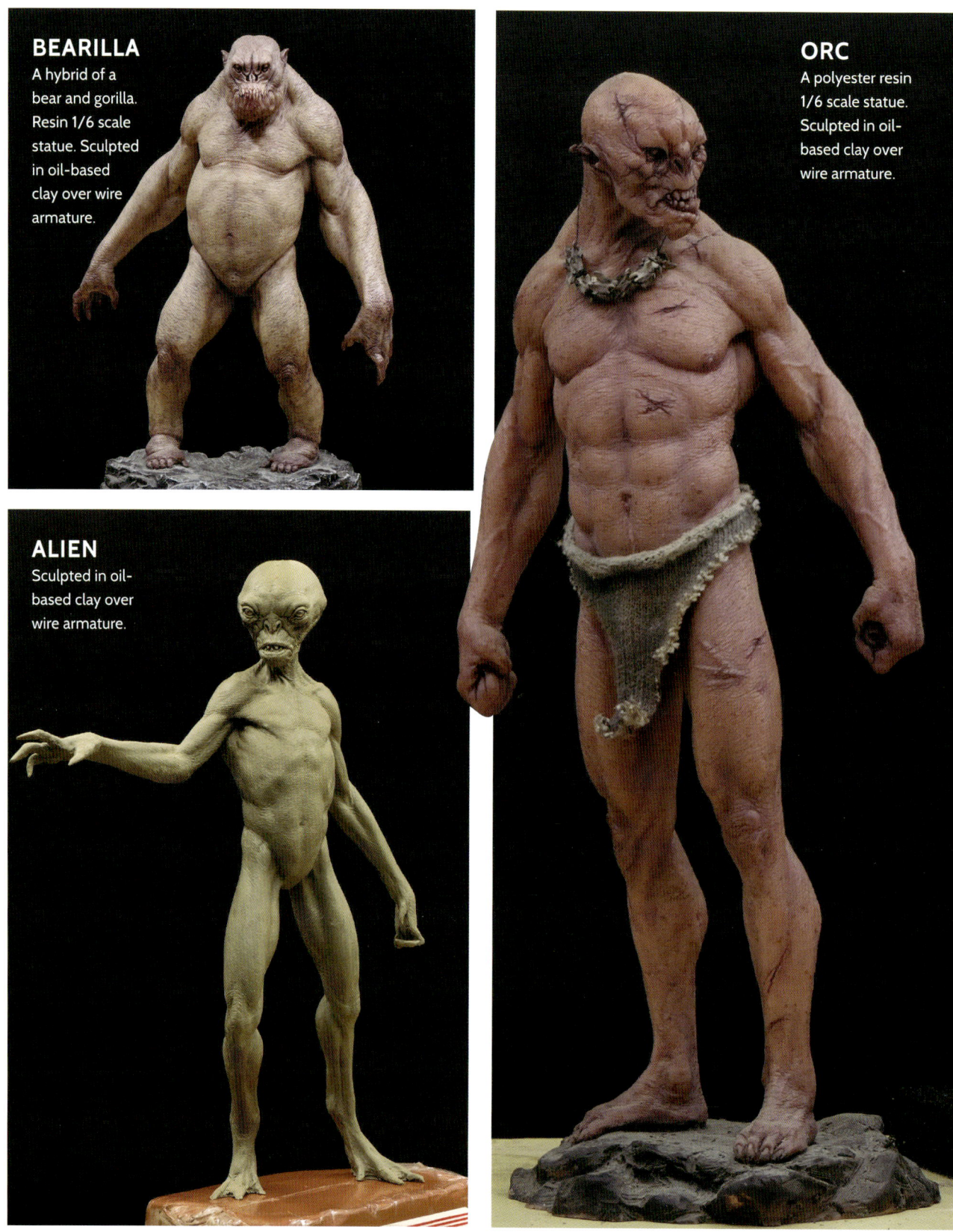

BEARILLA
A hybrid of a bear and gorilla. Resin 1/6 scale statue. Sculpted in oil-based clay over wire armature.

ORC
A polyester resin 1/6 scale statue. Sculpted in oil-based clay over wire armature.

ALIEN
Sculpted in oil-based clay over wire armature.

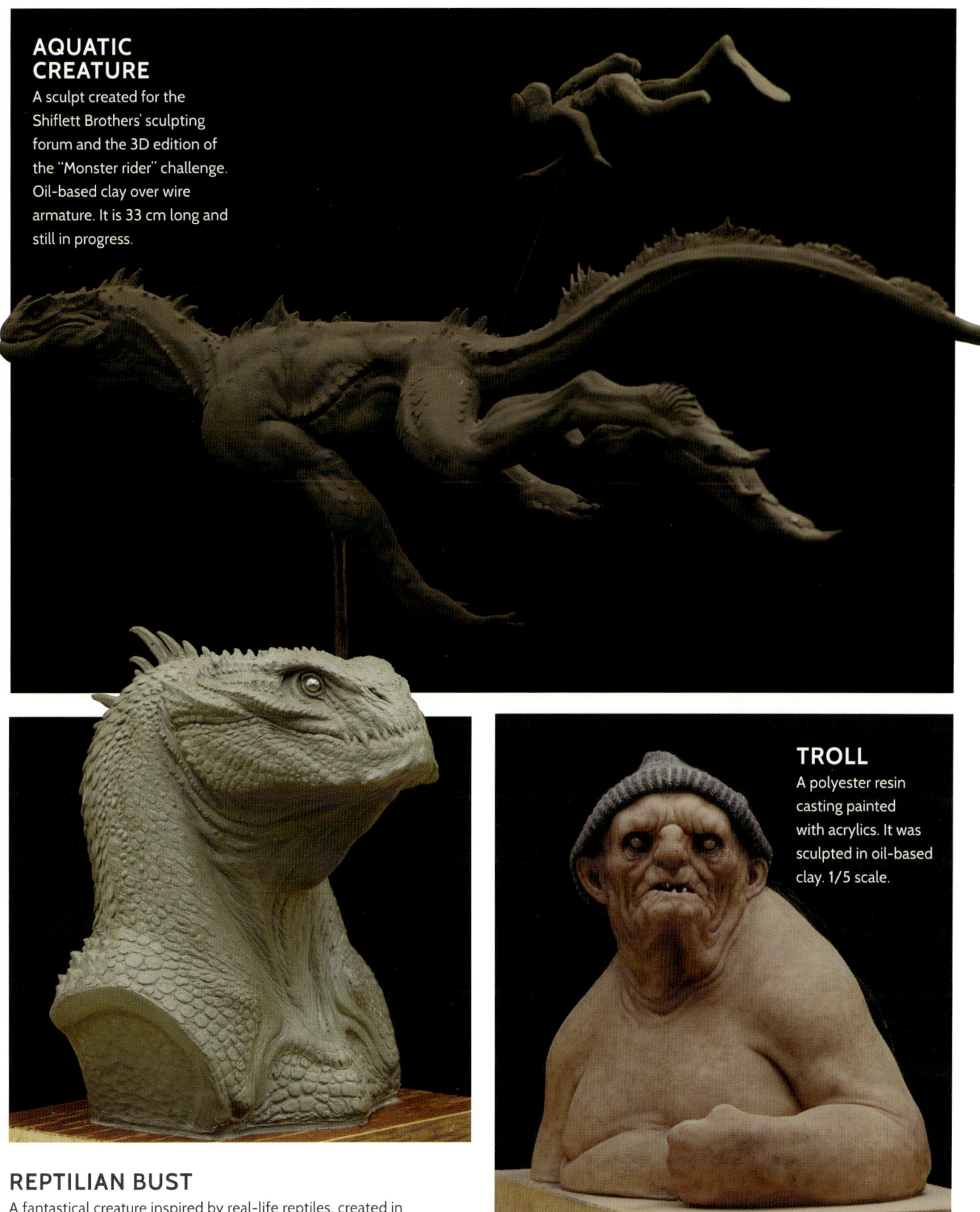

AQUATIC CREATURE

A sculpt created for the Shiflett Brothers' sculpting forum and the 3D edition of the "Monster rider" challenge. Oil-based clay over wire armature. It is 33 cm long and still in progress.

TROLL

A polyester resin casting painted with acrylics. It was sculpted in oil-based clay. 1/5 scale.

REPTILIAN BUST

A fantastical creature inspired by real-life reptiles, created in oil-based clay.

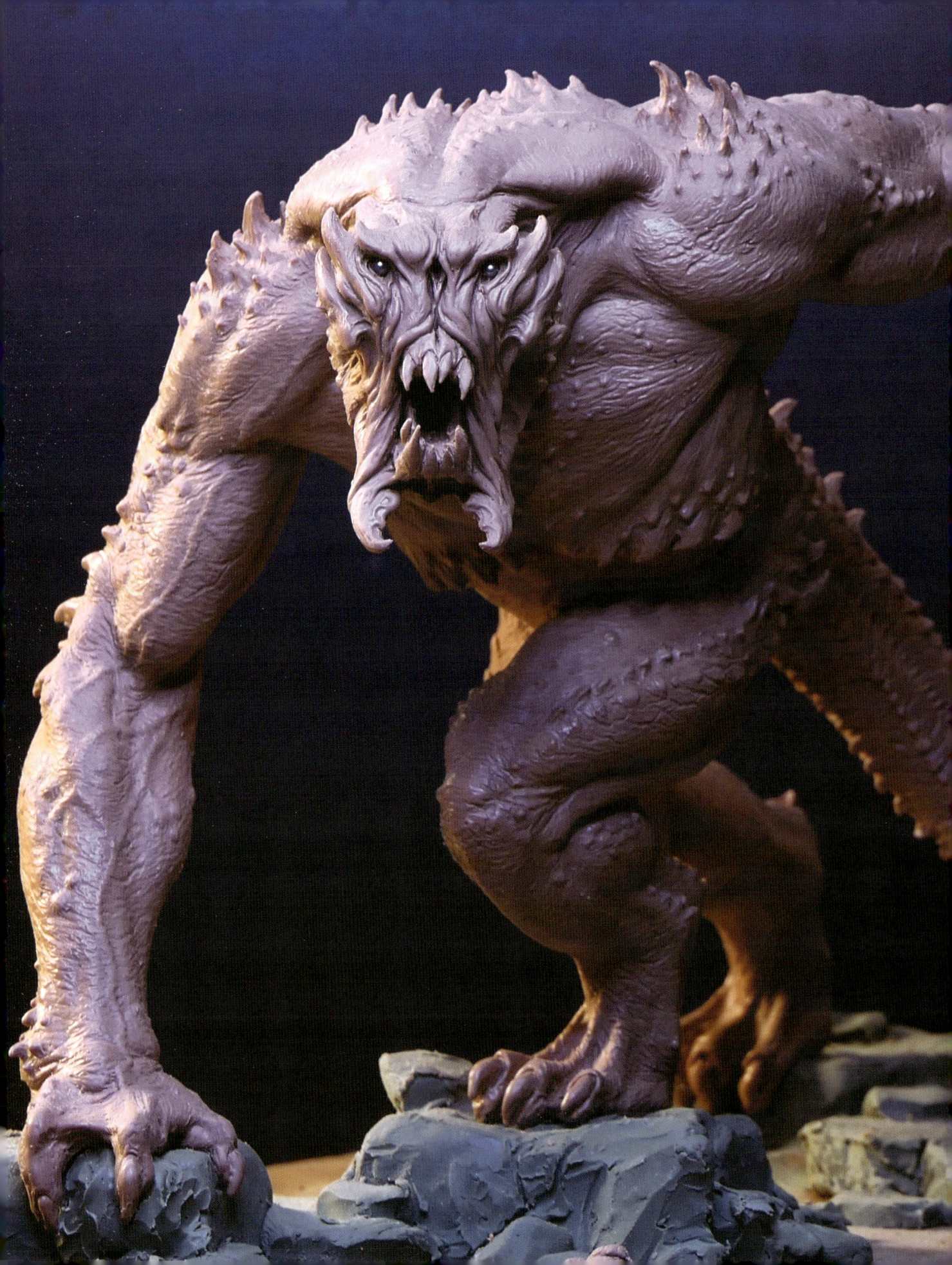

CREATING THE GATEKEEPER

For this tutorial, my initial thought is to sculpt a kaiju-type monster (giant monster, such as Godzilla) running in rage and about to crash into a building. But, while sculpting I move in a different direction. I have no design drawn out before I start; I design intuitively as I work. While constructing the piece, I find a dynamic pose and create a demon-like creature that I imagine being the guard of something, hunting trespassers, similar to the Balrog character from *The Lord of the Rings*. From the beginning, I just know that I want to convey a sense of motion and ferocity in the creature.

BY ARIS KOLOKONTES

MATERIALS & TOOLS

MATERIALS

Aluminum wire (7-gauge/3.5 mm)
Galvanized wire (18-gauge/1mm)
Oil-based clay (medium density)
Super glue
Benzine and lighter fluid
99% Isopropyl rubbing alcohol
2 mm ball bearings
Wooden base

TOOLS

Wire cutter
Pliers
Shapers and scrapers
Loop tools
Ball tools
Rake tools
Paintbrushes (thin and coarse)
Drill

STEP 01

I cut and straighten a piece of 3.5 mm wire. The length of the piece depends on the scale of the sculpture. In this tutorial it is a 1/6 scale figure, so I cut approximately 31 in (80 cm). Next, I create the basic armature shape using that single length. First, I bend the wire in half until the ends meet, then cross the ends to create a loop shape (01a). Holding the loop, I twist the two ends about ten times, making each twist as tight as possible to achieve the result shown (01b). The twisted length will be the torso area of the armature. I then cut the loop in the center, resulting in four limbs plus the torso. The longer pair of limbs will be the legs — the extra length is useful because I'll later insert the legs into the base. I straighten out the two curved wires that will be used as arms to make the next stage easier (01c).

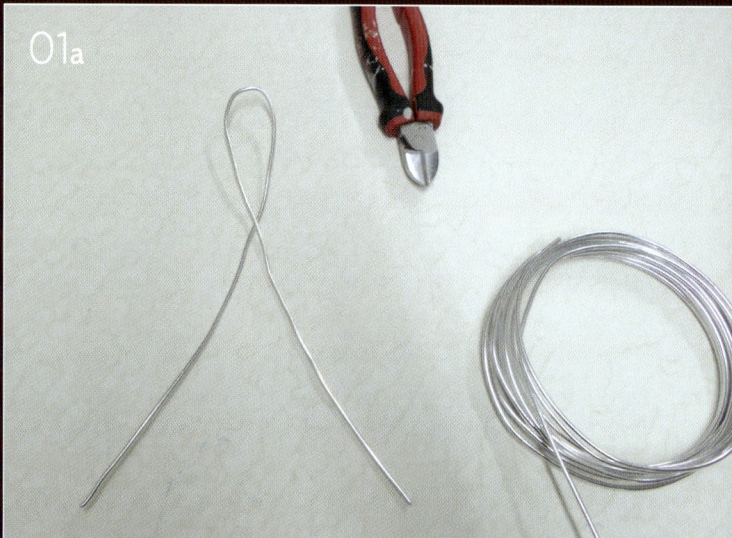

01a

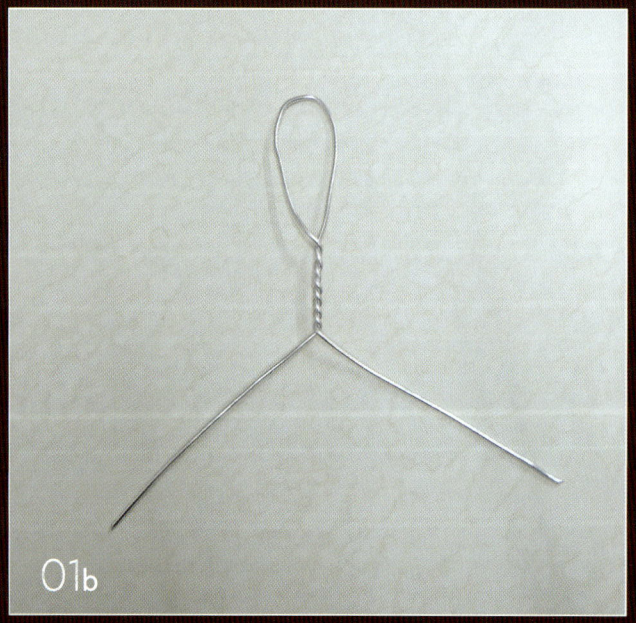

01b

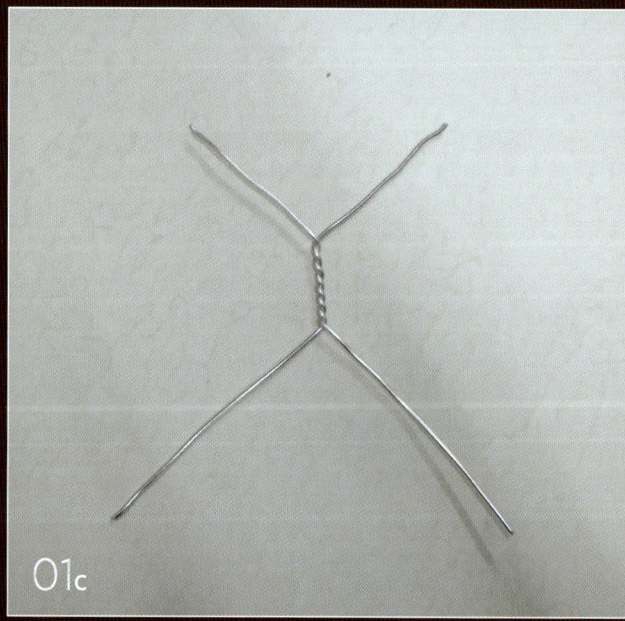

01c

STEP 02

Next, I begin to wrap 1 mm galvanized wire around the whole armature — this will help the clay adhere to the armature. Starting each limb from the torso, I wrap along each to the end (02a), then back again to create the "X" pattern as shown in 02b. I complete this step with one single piece of wire until everything is covered, including the torso.

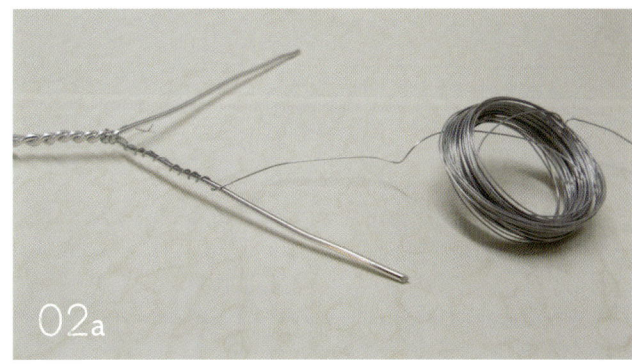

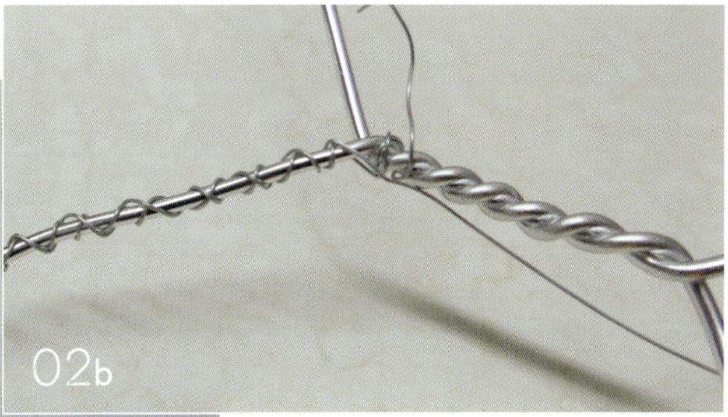

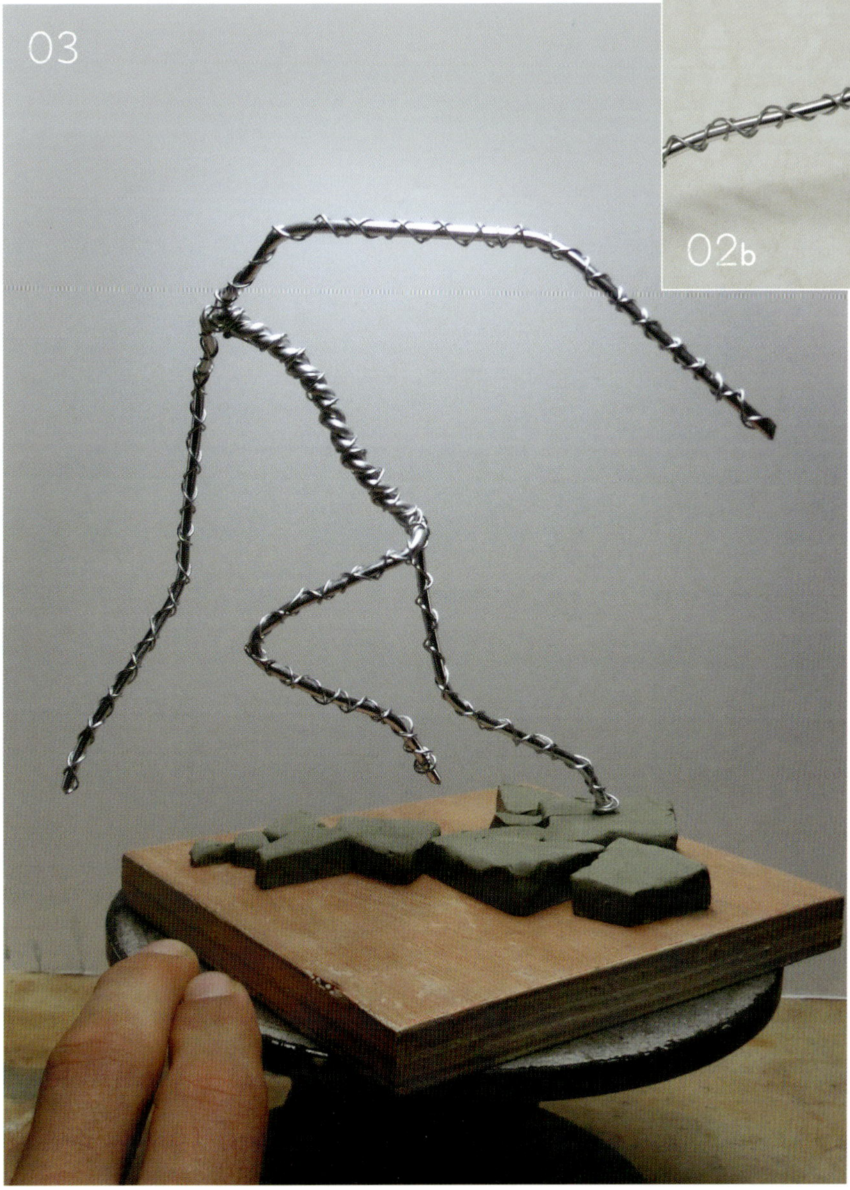

02a

02b

03

STEP 03

To pose the armature, I use pointed pliers or my hands to bend the joint areas such as elbows, knees, and shoulders. The bending points should be as precise as possible to avoid exposing armature later when sculpting the clay. I temporarily attach the armature to the base using chunks of clay and make more adjustments while turning the base to ensure the armature looks right from all angles.

At this scale and using this clay, I don't need to use wire for the neck, head, hands, and fingers if they can support themselves. This saves a lot of time and allows me to try several different versions until I'm satisfied.

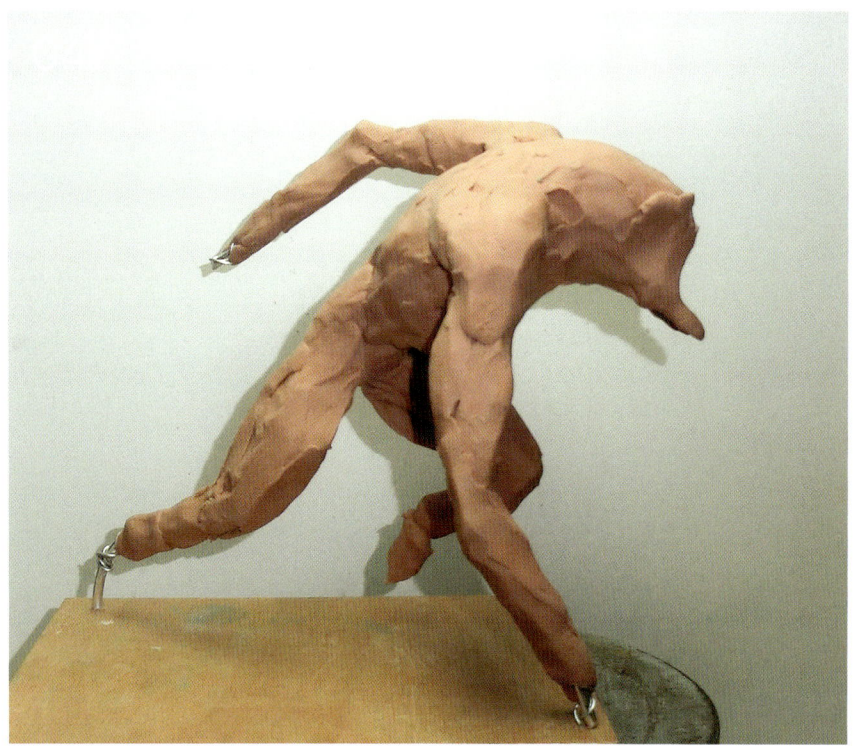

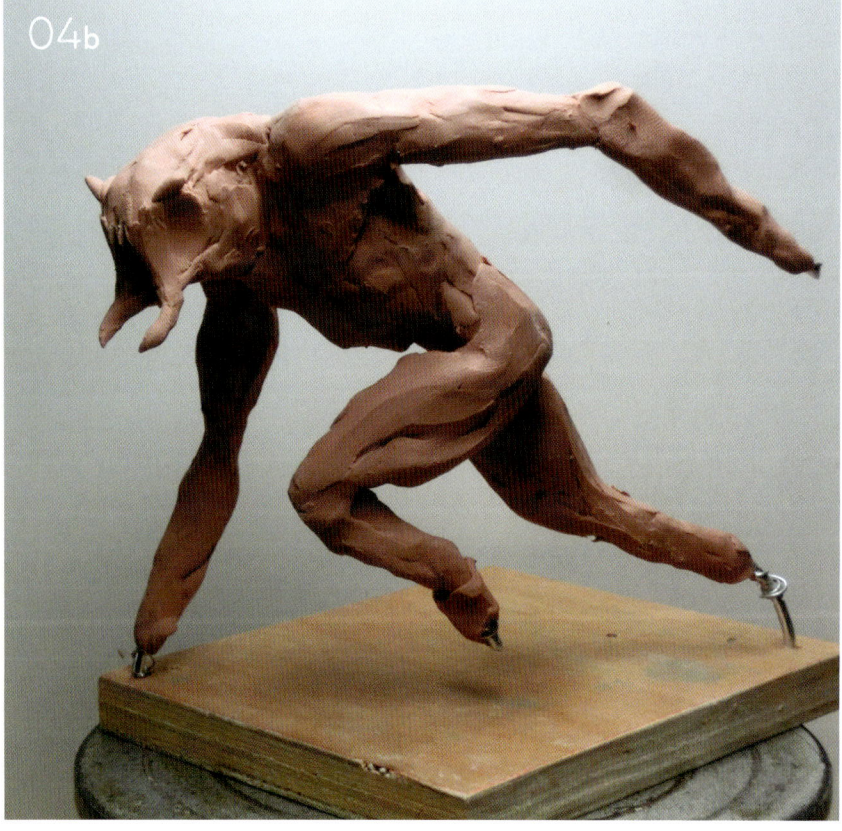

04b

STEP 04

Now I add the first layer of clay to the armature. I use warm clay to ensure good adhesion to the armature and to avoid air gaps. The softness also allows me to work quickly; there is no need to go slowly at this point. Using only my fingers, I add more volume to the torso area and overall musculature. I also add a placeholder head to view the figure as a whole and assess the proportions, composition silhouette, and pose (04a). I turn the figure to check it from every angle (04b).

STEP 05

I establish the basic anatomy using my fingers, and with a spatula tool, make guidelines such as those shown in the shoulder area (05a). I want this figure to have a muscular body type that is also grounded in reality. The limbs and torso have a very human-like anatomy, while other features are inspired by animal anatomy. For example, the dog-like leg joints (05b) as well as the tail I plan to add later. In my mind, the scale of this creature is that of a Tyrannosaurus rex. I refine the anatomy and head by adding progressively smaller pieces of clay, then adjust and blend each piece onto the sculpture using my fingers and a spatula tool (05c).

STEP 06

To get a better overall view of the creature, I move the sculpture onto a larger board, adding blocks of wood to slightly elevate the model from the ground. While exploring ideas about the scale and backstory, I also add a little human stick figure. I use a rake tool to even out the surface of the creature and clean the forms, one of many passes that I do until I get to the detailing stage. On the hip area I create skin folds to give the effect of compression. Details such as this add a lot to the believability factor.

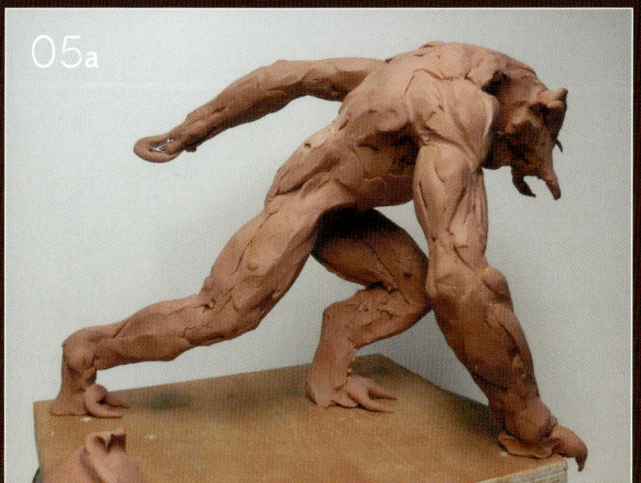

05a

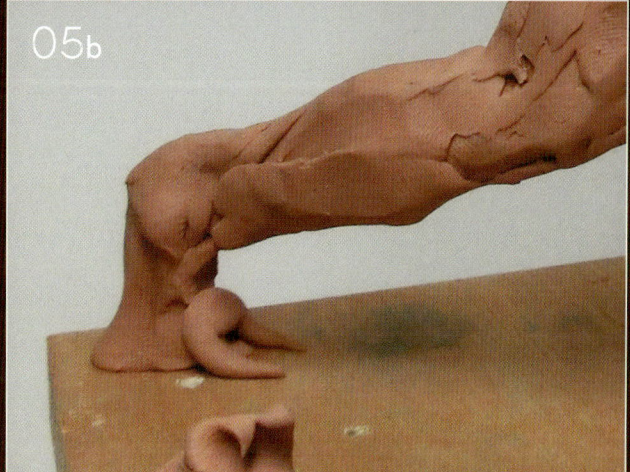

05b

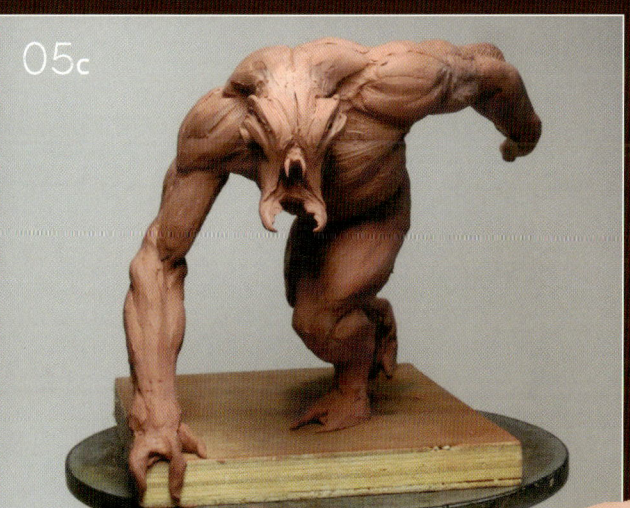

05c

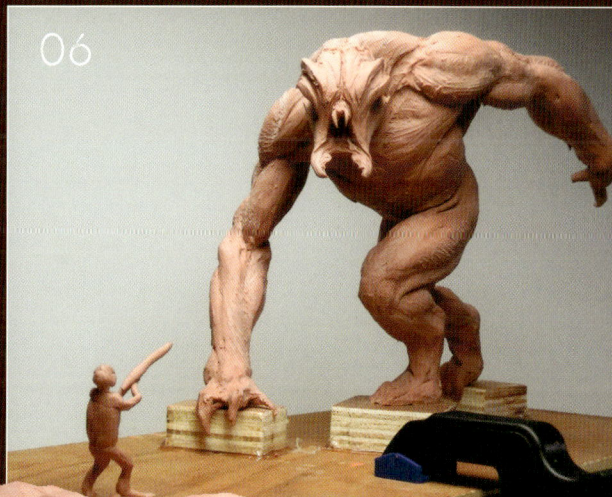

06

CHECK THE ANGLES

Keep turning your sculpture using a turntable or by moving the base in order to work all around it. This helps to highlight any flaws in the form, silhouette, and pose. It also allows you to maintain uniform progress.

163

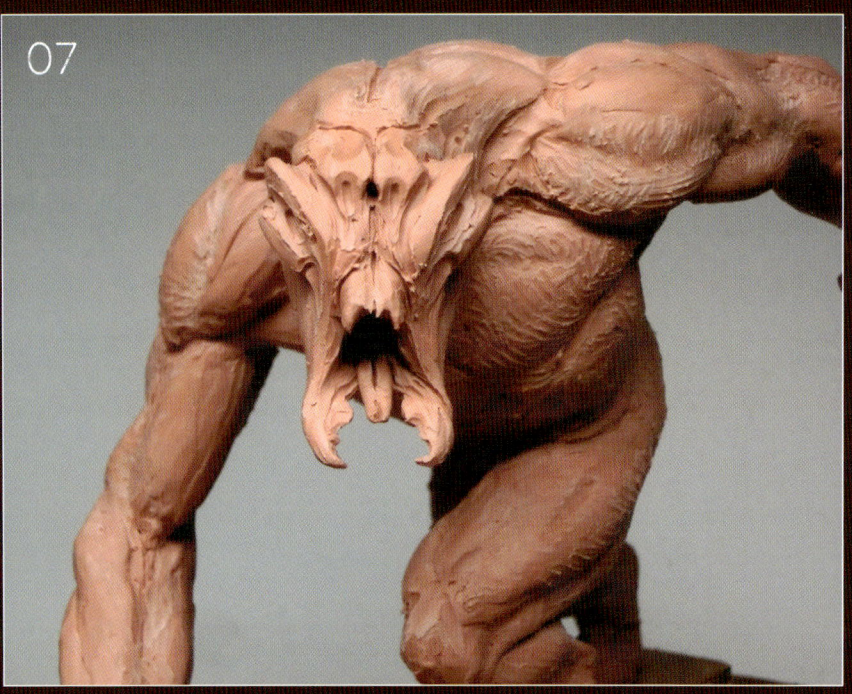

07

STEP 07

Next, I work on defining the face. I add volume to the central top portion of the head to break it down into smaller forms and create a more detailed, otherworldly face. The new facial forms then create interesting shadows and highlights, adding to the dimensionality of the creature. I also consider the overall silhouette the face shape produces and ensure it remains readable from all angles.

STEP 08

I consider the placement of the eyes and press two indentations into the clay to mark their final position (08a). I then adjust the existing forms on the cheekbones and brows to match the eye position and will add ball bearings for the eyes (08b).

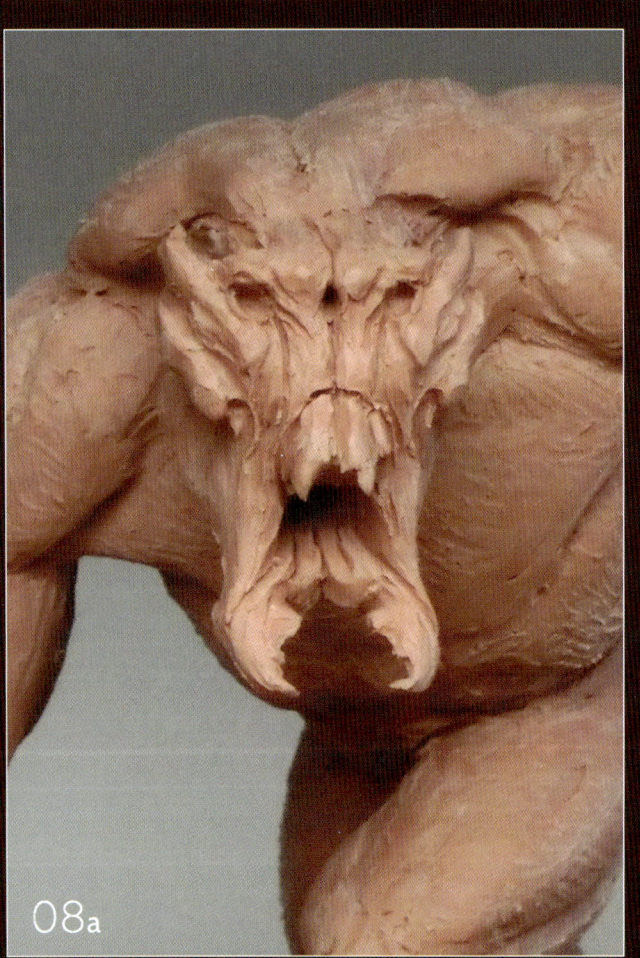

08a

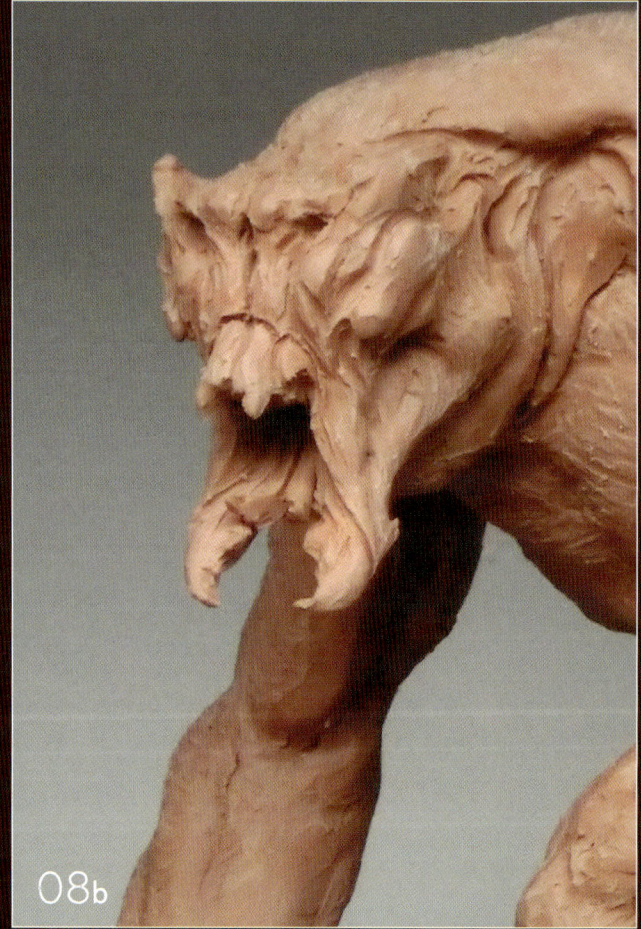

08b

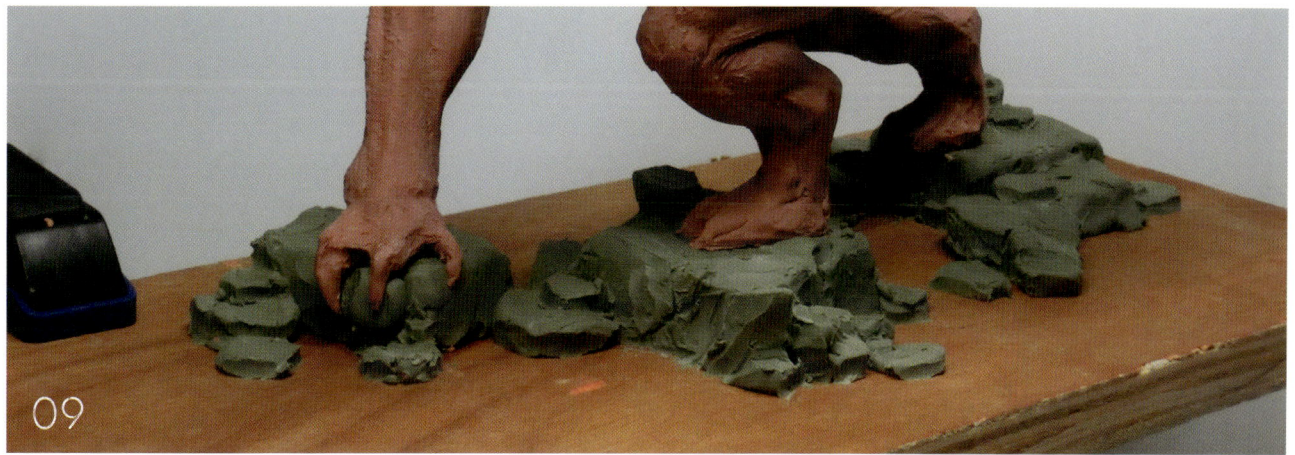

09

STEP 09

Revisiting the base, I cover the small blocks of wood with a thin layer of green oil-based clay and sculpt them to look like rock or stone. The choice of color provides contrast between the creature's feet and the ground.

STEP 10

On the creature, I focus on secondary forms while refining and breaking down the anatomy. First, I create cylindrical worm-like pieces of clay in the desired size and lightly press into position (10a). Then I work over them with either a rake or spatula tool to blend them to the surface (10b). I repeat the process all over the sculpture, using a human anatomy figure for reference. Depending on the form I'm aiming for, I make the appropriate size cylinder or ball or spike to add before I stick it on.

STEP 11

Next, to refine and hone the surface of the whole sculpture, I use rake tools. As the refinements become more subtle, I use a finer rake over the surface and apply less pressure. Pictured are two of the rakes I made at home using brass tubing and saw blades of various sizes. The finest rake I use is also one I made, incorporating a guitar string. The fine texture of the guitar string produces a closer rake pattern than the other tools.

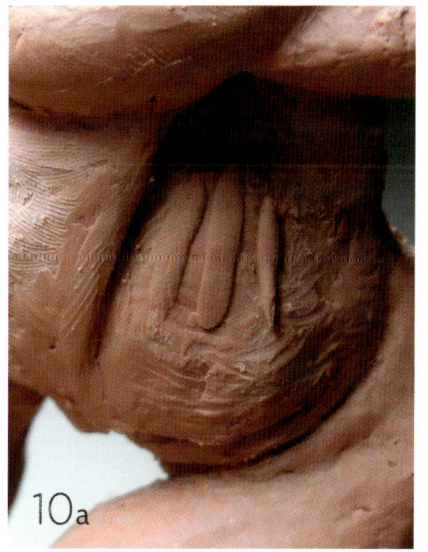

10a

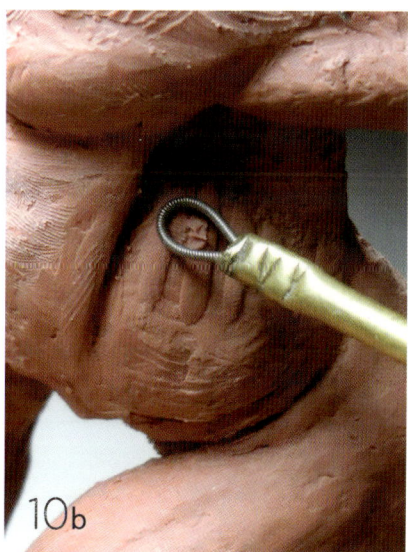

10b

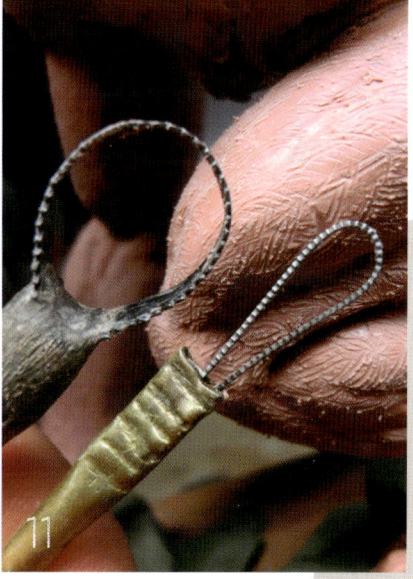

11

✦ TOOL-MAKING

You can make your own tools using brass or aluminum tubing and steel wire, guitar strings, piano wire, saw blades, and so on to accommodate the exact style or scale of work you do.

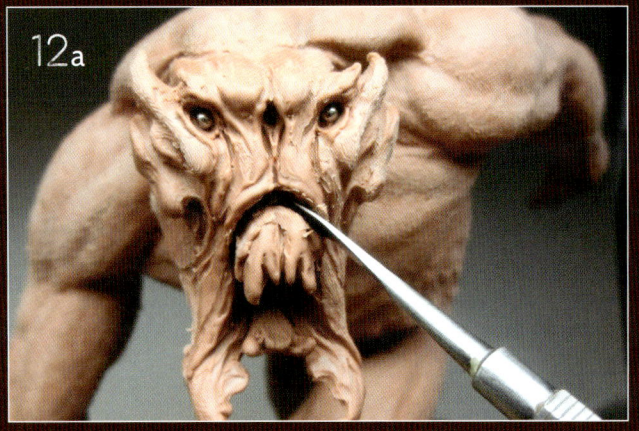

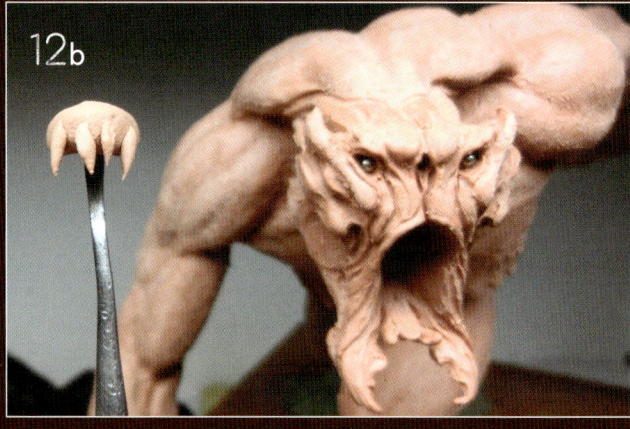

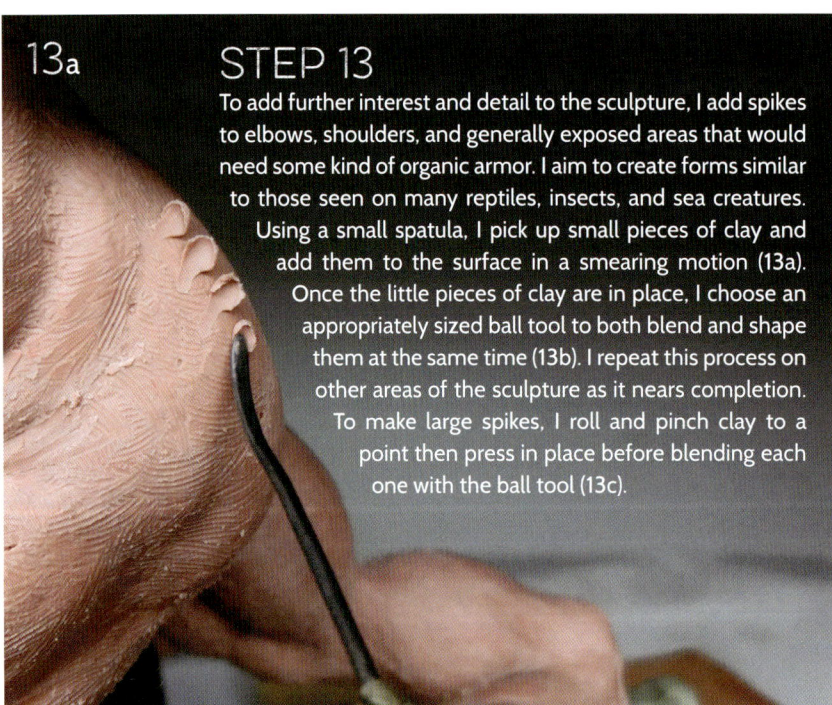

STEP 12

I now focus on the mouth, and in particular, the teeth. With a spatula tool, I cut away the existing teeth and remove from the mouth (12a). Once I'm happy with the design, I make a more refined set using the hard grade of the same clay, which is better for delicate structures (12b). I make adjustments once the teeth are secured in place. For best adhesion, I melt both surfaces to be glued, using a mini heat gun or butane-alcohol torch, then press together while still hot. Once cooled, a few seconds later, the two surfaces are welded together. Sometimes I use a freeze spray to cool it down even more quickly. I decide to add a lower set of teeth as it adds dynamism to the jaw and silhouette of the head, so repeat the same process as for the upper teeth (12c).

STEP 13

To add further interest and detail to the sculpture, I add spikes to elbows, shoulders, and generally exposed areas that would need some kind of organic armor. I aim to create forms similar to those seen on many reptiles, insects, and sea creatures. Using a small spatula, I pick up small pieces of clay and add them to the surface in a smearing motion (13a). Once the little pieces of clay are in place, I choose an appropriately sized ball tool to both blend and shape them at the same time (13b). I repeat this process on other areas of the sculpture as it nears completion. To make large spikes, I roll and pinch clay to a point then press in place before blending each one with the ball tool (13c).

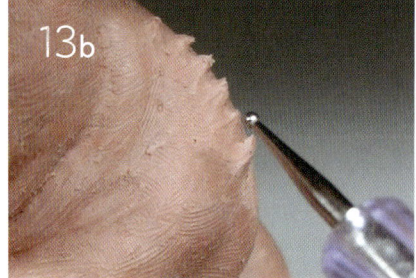

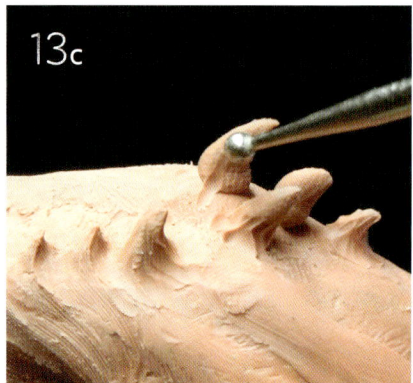

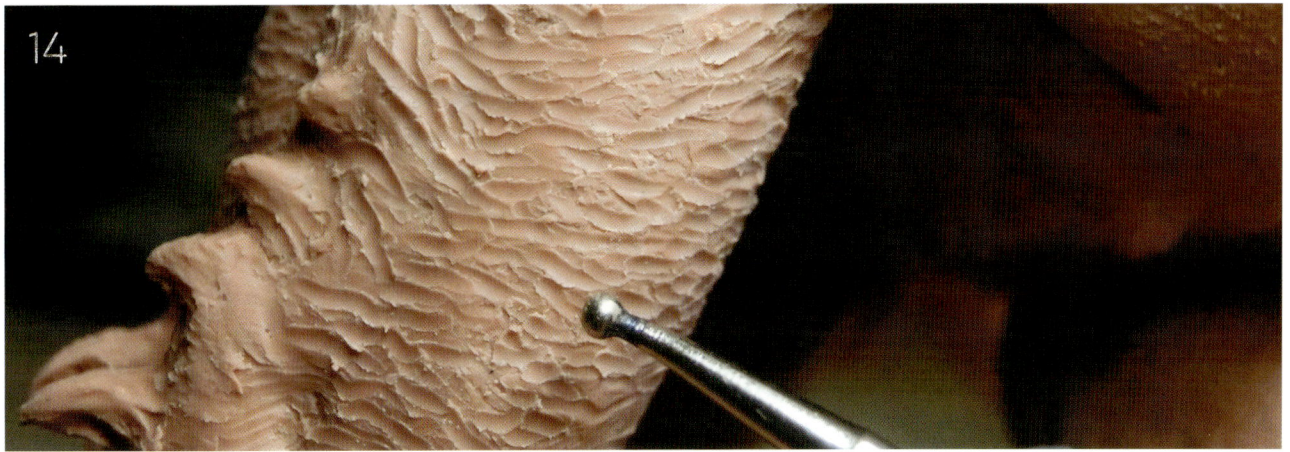

STEP 14

Next, I begin the first pass of texture for the skin using the ball tool with a poke-and-drag motion all over the surface of the sculpture. The dragging has a specific direction depending on the area of the body that it's applied to, following the natural flow of the form and musculature beneath. I can still add more forms on top of the texture later in the process.

✦ ACHIEVING BALANCE

Although it's important to have areas that are busy and full of detail, it's also important to retain areas of simplicity and "rest" on the surface of the sculpture. This gives the design balance, and is commonly seen in nature.

STEP 15

To create veins, I first apply fine clay "worms" of the desired size to the specific areas (15a). I then press and push them around with my fingers, giving them the characteristic pattern also seen in lightning, plant roots, and tree branches. Finally, I blend the shapes into the surface with the ball tool (15b).

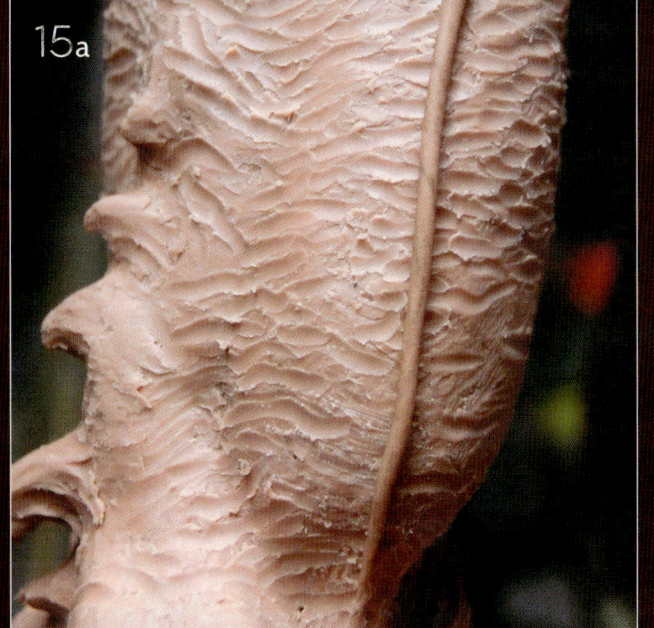

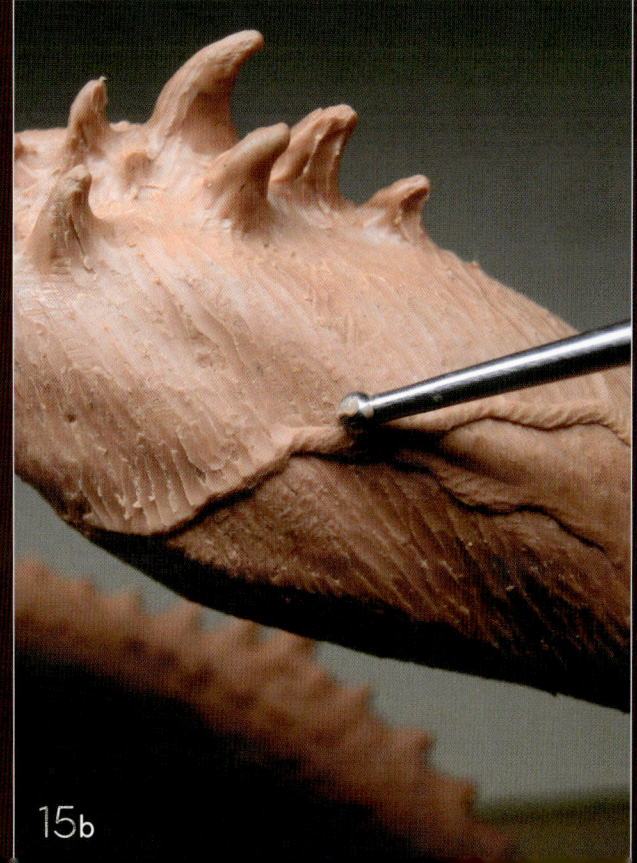

STEP 16

To create the tail, I first roll a piece of warmed clay on a worksurface to create a cylindrical form in the desired diameter and length. I then use a loop tool to carve a central groove down the full length of the tail. To mimic a snake's tail, I taper one end to a point. I pose the tail by twisting it gently to retain a smooth natural curve, then let it cool down to room temperature. Before attaching it to the sculpture, I position the tail in a variety of different ways to decide which works best. Once I feel the positioning is fitting for the creature and its pose, I weld it in place by slightly melting the two areas to be attached and pressing them together. As the sculpture is small, the tail doesn't require a separate wire armature. Instead, I ensure that it is attached firmly and can hold its own weight.

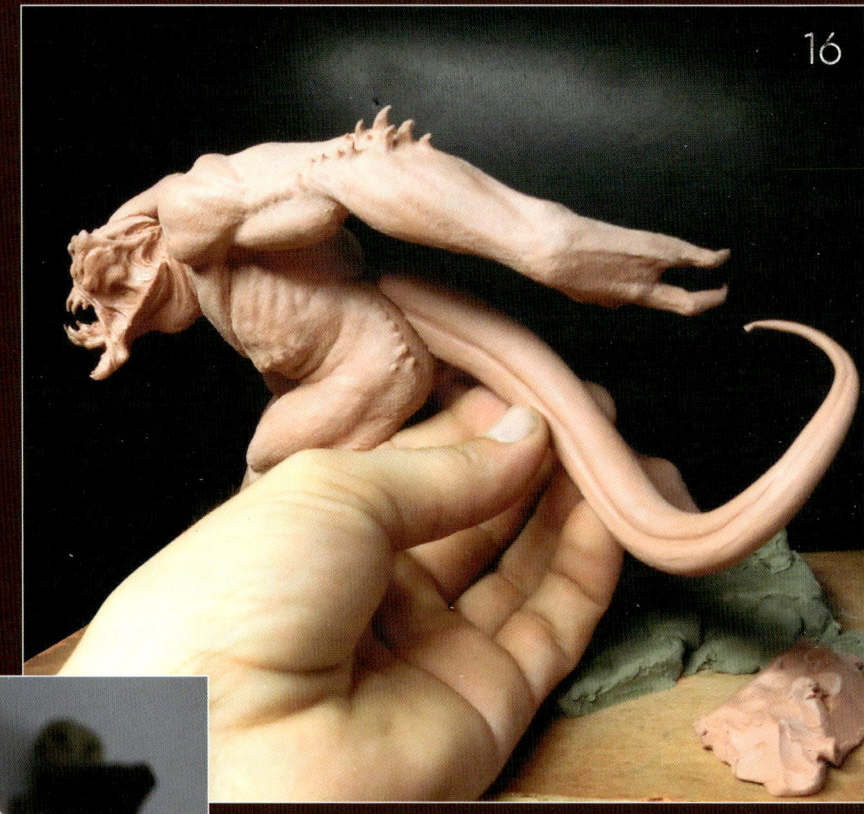

16

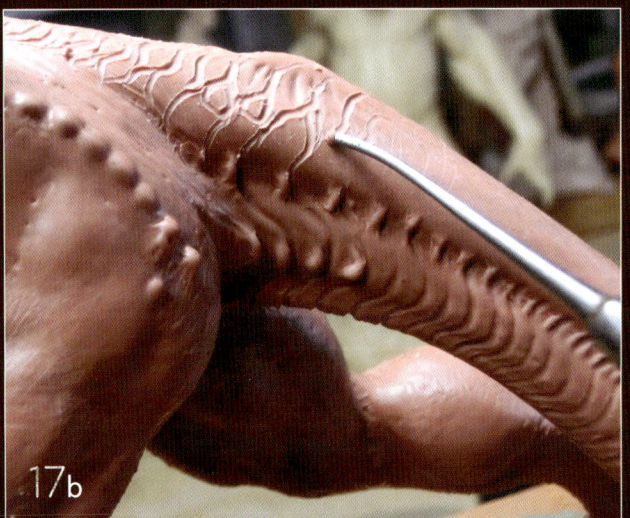

17a

STEP 17

Using a mixture of techniques and tools, I add more interest and texture to the surface of the tail. First, I carve guidelines with a rounded needle tool (17a), then work around those lines to create more dimension and complexity while enhancing the overall look of the creature (17b). I embellish the creature by using little pieces of clay to make bumps and spikes and carving away areas to create dramatic shadows (17c).

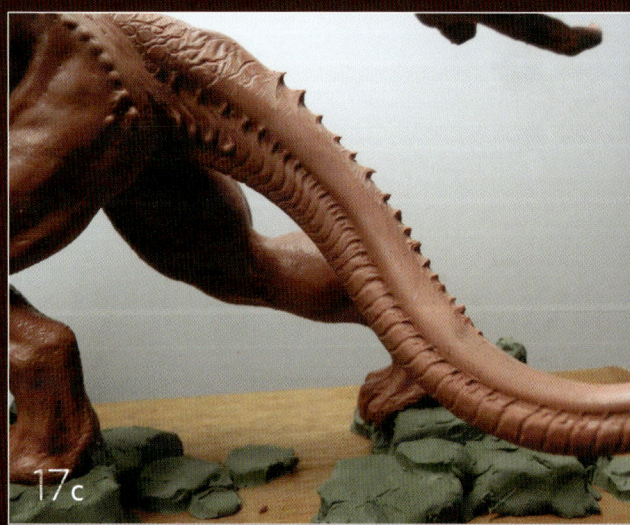

17b

17c

STEP 18

Next, I revisit the surface texture of the entire sculpture. First, I use a small ball tool to add a finer texture (18a) and correct areas that need more definition. I also add subtle irregular forms such as skin imperfections, bumps, and tiny spikes to add to the believability of the creature. Between layers, I smooth the surface either with heat from a butane torch or by brushing on solvents such as lighter fluid or benzene. I then drag a hook tool along the surface (18b). A variety of other tools such as fine loops or ball tools could be used — it's a matter of personal preference.

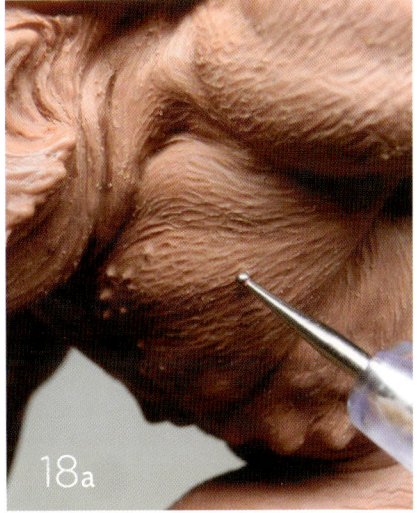

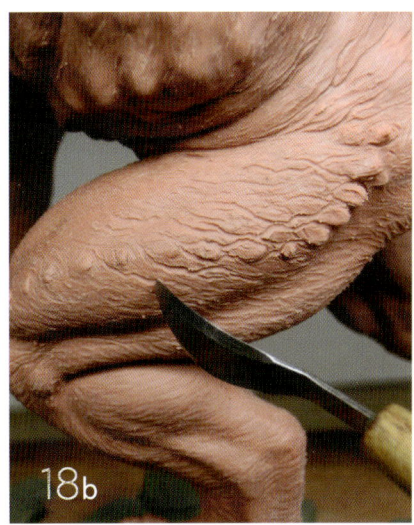

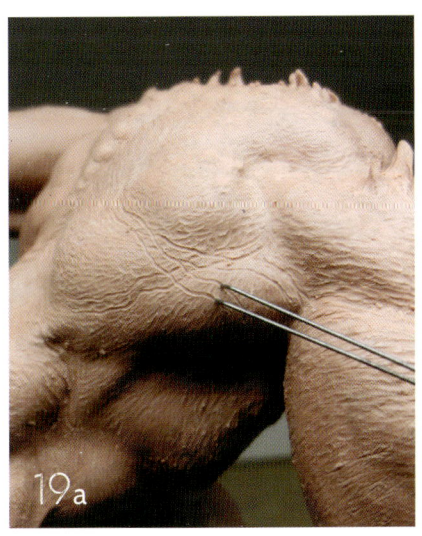

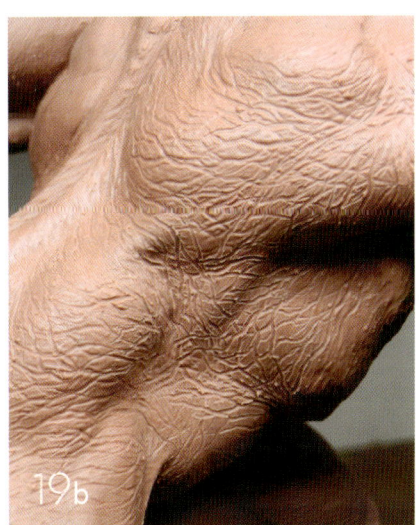

STEP 19

The final layer of texture work is developed using a wire rake made out of two or four wires secured next to each other in a brass tube. I drag the wires across the surface, scratching it in different directions while keeping in mind where and how the skin folds in certain areas of the body (19a). This tool was introduced to me by sculptors at Weta Workshop and I have used it ever since. It's great for creating organic-looking texture that resembles the wrinkled skin of many animals, including a rhino or elephant, which is perfect for this creature (19b).

STEP 20

To finish the piece, I smooth the whole surface using soft brushes and lighter fluid. Smaller brushes work best on the face and in tight, awkward areas, while larger brushes are more suitable for larger surfaces. I move the brush in the direction of the forms and skin texture first, then make circular motions with a very soft, long-haired brush in both directions over the whole sculpture. If I want an area to have an extra smooth, shiny finish, I apply a little heat with the mini heat gun or butane torch.

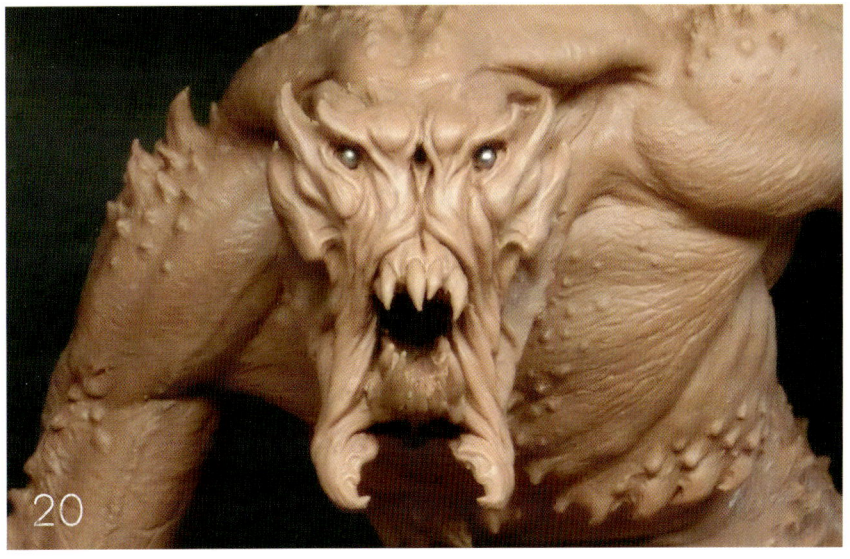

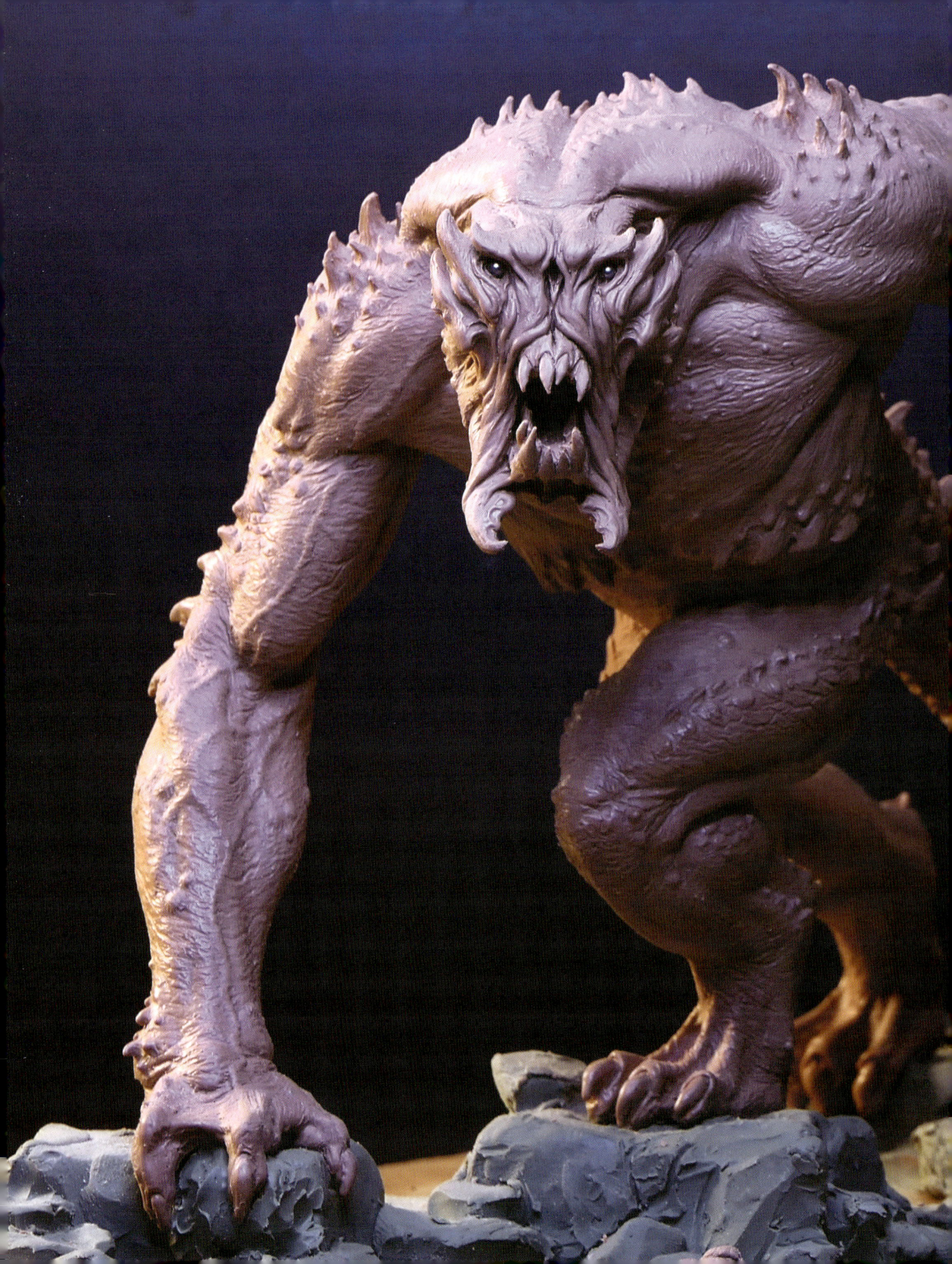

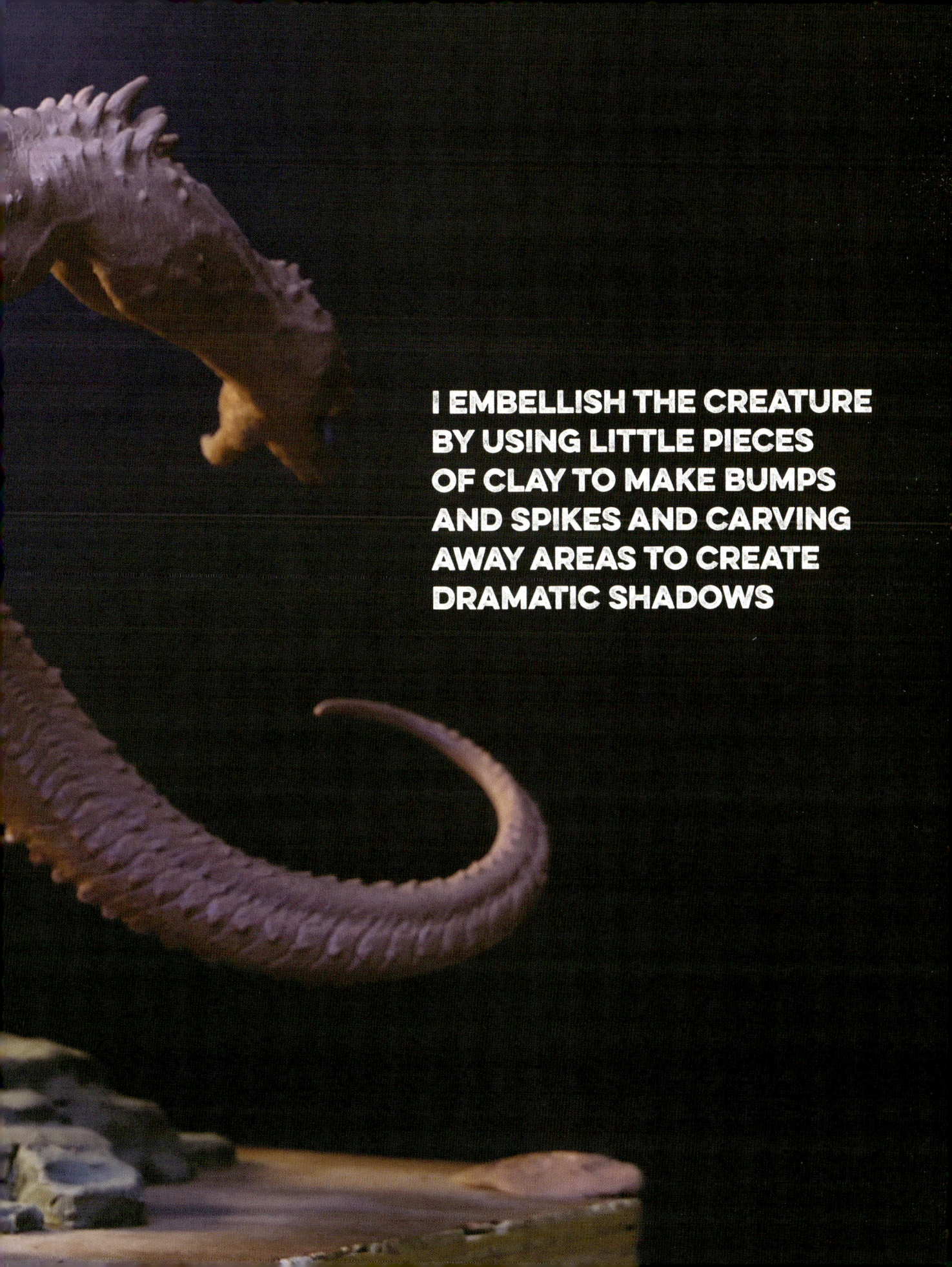

I EMBELLISH THE CREATURE
BY USING LITTLE PIECES
OF CLAY TO MAKE BUMPS
AND SPIKES AND CARVING
AWAY AREAS TO CREATE
DRAMATIC SHADOWS

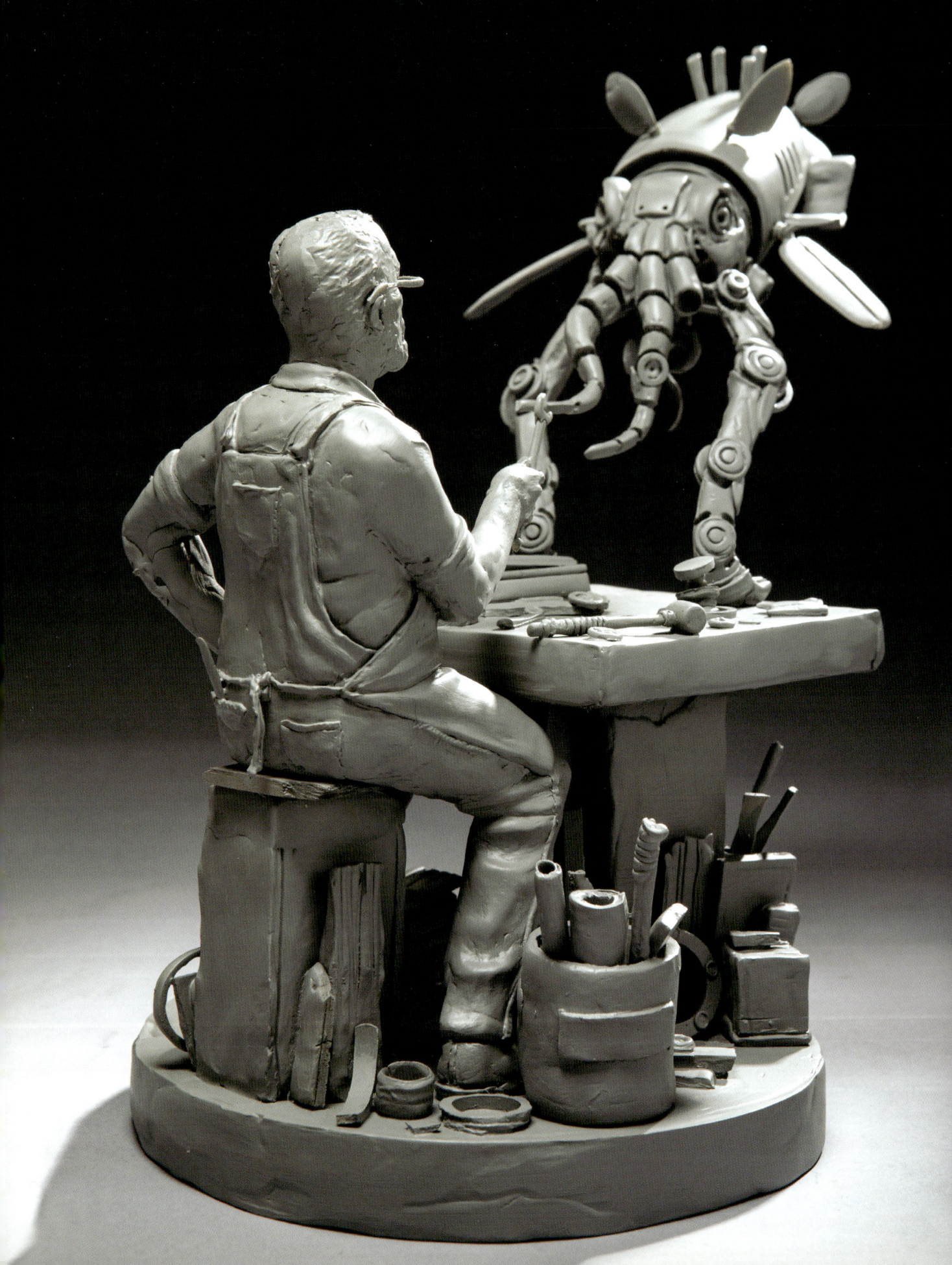

BUILDING PROFESSOR McELROY

The concept for this sculpture originated from our loose idea of main character, Professor McElroy from the late 1800s and early 1900s. As a longtime-builder of junkyard robots with a strange otherworldly aura, he is seen working alone in his workshop creating a smaller version of one of his mechanical monstrosities. We imagine the creation as a mechanical squid-like creature.

We then consider what the scene might actually look like and the details and mood of the moment — the professor working intensely late into the night, tinkering with his newest creation away from the prying eyes of onlookers.

BY THE SHIFLETT BROTHERS

MATERIALS & TOOLS

MATERIALS

ARMATURE
Almaloy aluminum alloy
armature wire ($^3/_{16}$ in gauge)
Aluminum foil
Aluminum wire mesh
Floral wire

CLAY
Super Sculpey Firm
Aves Apoxie Sculpt
Plumber's epoxy putty

GLUE AND SOLVENT
Super glue
91% Isopropyl rubbing alcohol

OTHER
Wooden base
Woodchunks/offcut
PVC pipe
Styrene tubing

TOOLS

Sanding sponges
Cutting wire
Hobby knives
Wire-cutting pliers
Needle-nose pliers
Rake tools
Needle files
Loop tools
Ball tools
Burnisher
Scraper
Brushes
Heat gun

BLOCKING IN THE COMPOSITION

01

STEP 01

We start this sculpture with a round wooden base that can be purchased from almost any arts and crafts store. We're planning to completely cover this base with clay, but for now it will work as an anchor to which we will attach different elements.

02

STEP 02

We first drill two small holes in the wooden base and secure two sections of styrene tubing into the holes using plumber's putty. We then insert a length of aluminum wire with a narrower piece of tubing attached to one end, into one of the holes. By introducing this tube rigging, the figure will be detachable. We start to shape the wire to form a human leg, bending at the knee and the hip.

STEP 03

After securing a second wire in the second hole in the base, we twist floral wire around the two wires to create the waist of the character and reinforce the backbone. One wire continues up to become the character's left arm, which we bend down at the shoulder. We then bend the top of the right leg wire to form a loop that will later become the armature for the skull (03a). Viewing the piece from another angle helps us to judge the proportions of the limbs (03b). The head and neck skeletal structure is in place and we just need to add a right arm.

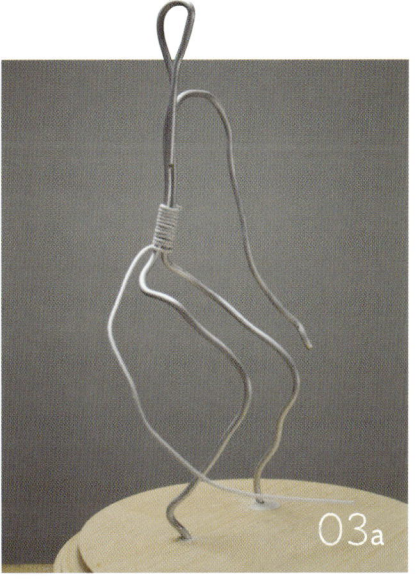

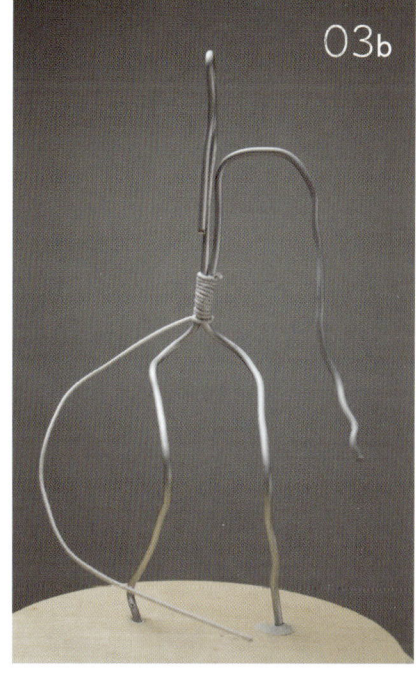

VIEWING THE PIECE FROM ANOTHER ANGLE HELPS US TO JUDGE THE PROPORTIONS OF THE LIMBS

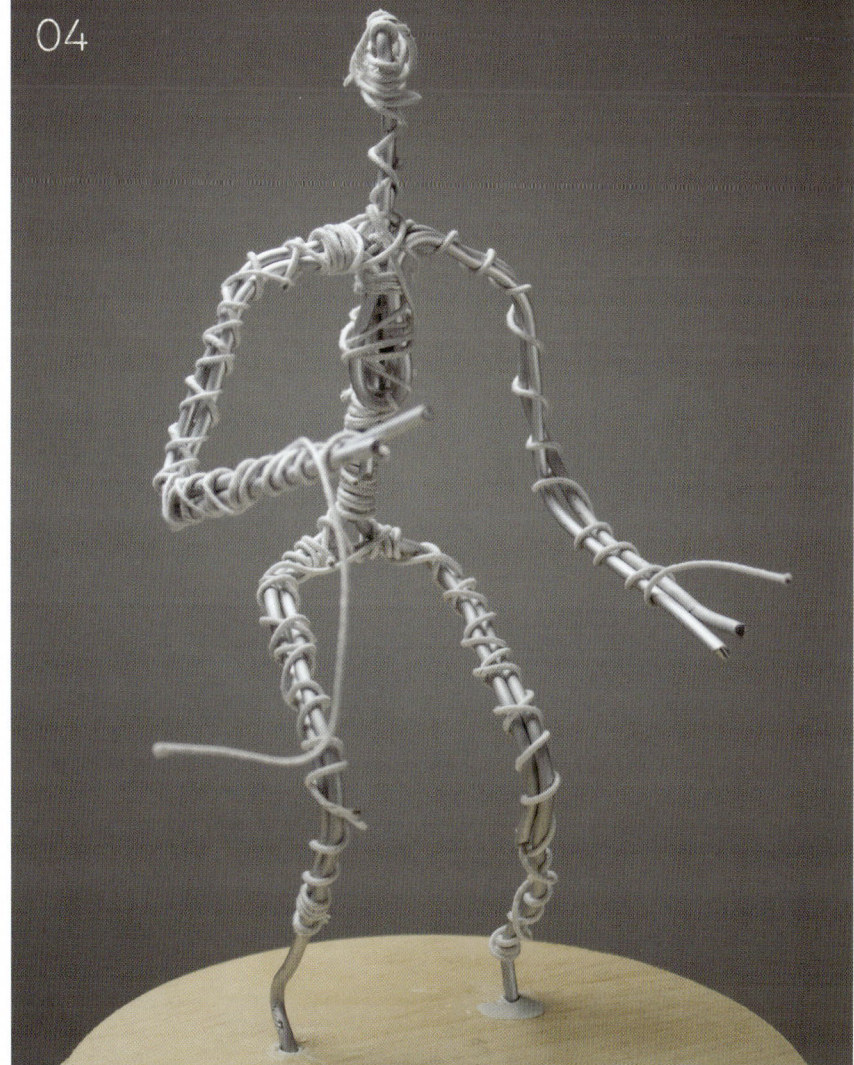

STEP 04

More aluminum wire is added to every limb, to lend more support and strength to the skeletal shape. To secure the additional wires in place, we wrap them tightly with floral wire. The floral wire and aluminum wire structure is then saturated with super glue.

STEP 05

As the character will be seated, we build the base of the stool the character will sit upon by attaching a small piece of wood directly behind the figure (05a). We then construct another tubing connection to allow the character to lock into place on the stool (05b).

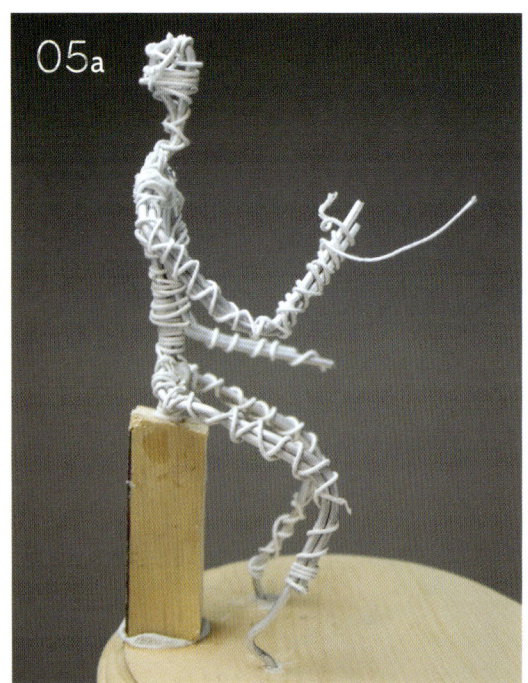

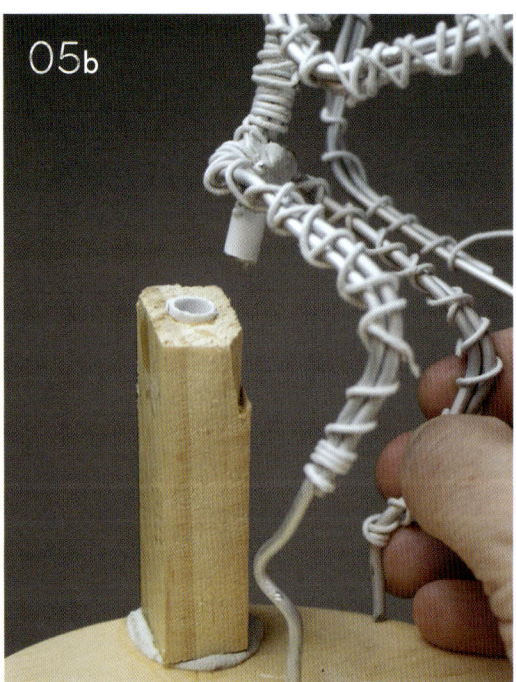

STEP 06

We strengthen the armature at strategic points that tend to carry a lot of the weight of the clay and also need to be wide and thick — for example, the hips and chest. We always add a plumber's putty skull shape to the head so that we can then sculpt onto a relatively sturdy base.

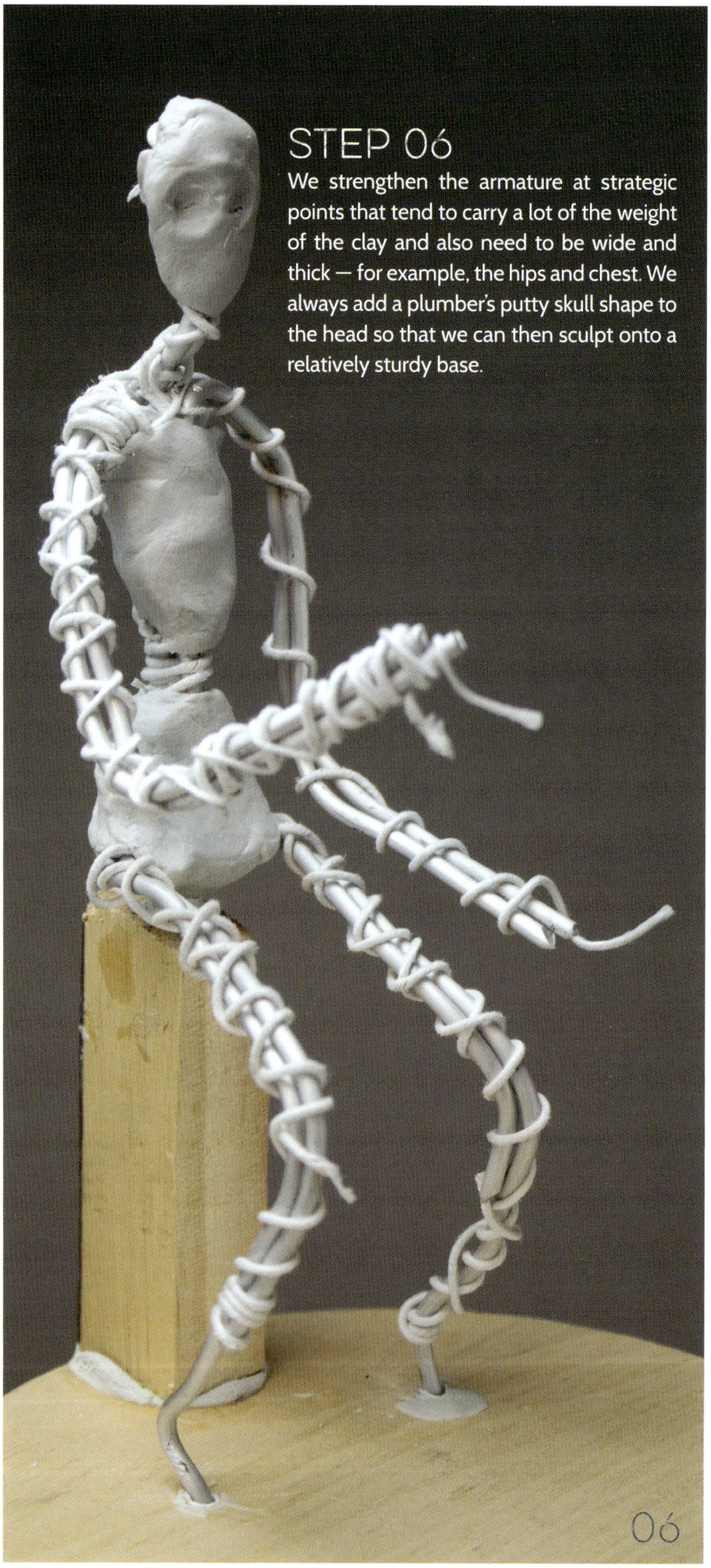

06

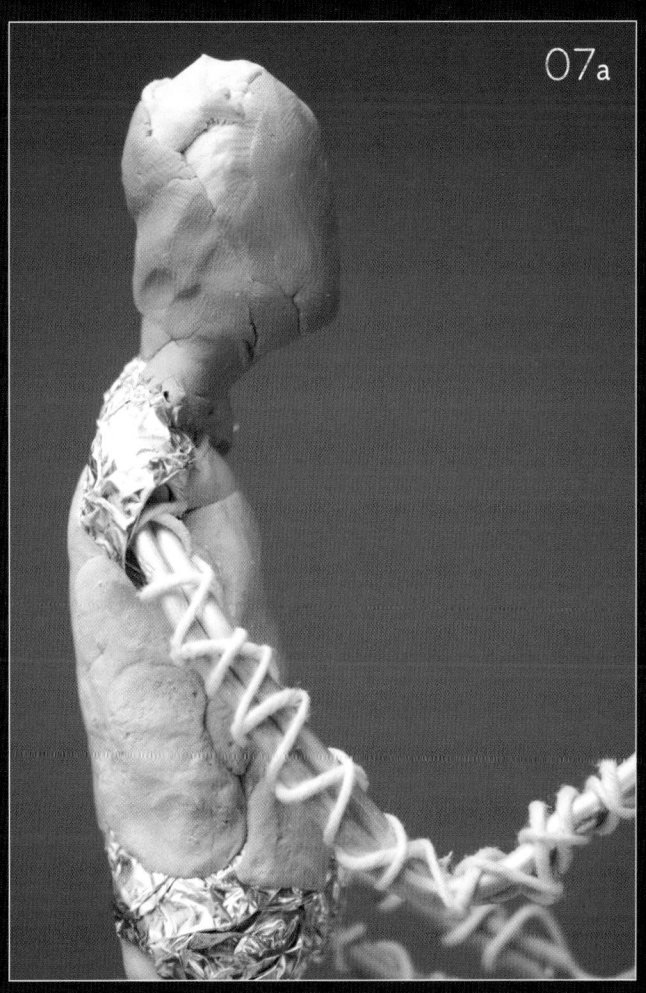

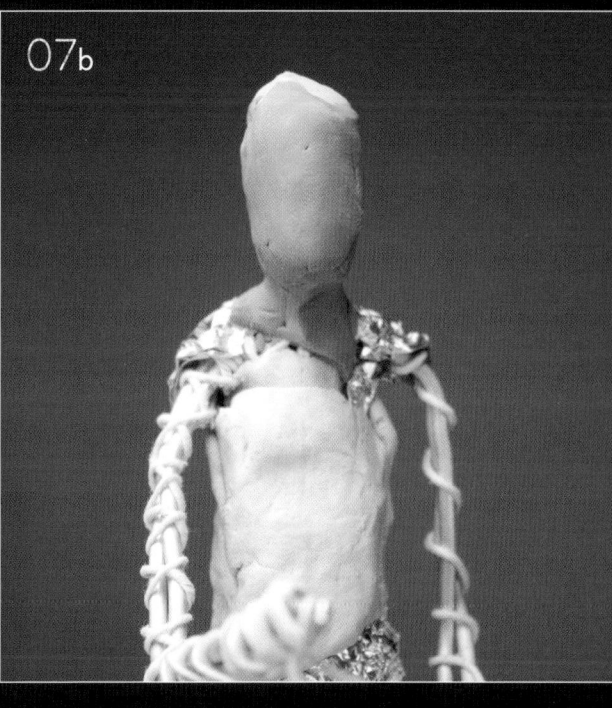

STEP 07

After applying some aluminum foil to the largest parts of the body, we start to add sculpting clay to the piece! This is always a big moment for us. The armature is essential and needs to be made strong and with care, but once clay goes onto the piece, we feel like we can start to have fun. We apply clay to the head and neck area. The profile view will become the "money shot" for this piece. From this angle you can see the general shape of the head.

STEP 08

We often draw lines on the face to mark the midpoints for symmetry both vertically and horizontally — we use our hands to sculpt traditionally rather than computer sculpting programs, so we have no symmetry or mirroring button! We use simple lines to measure out where we believe the eyes, nose, and mouth should be. These only serve as a guide and will not be visible once the face is complete.

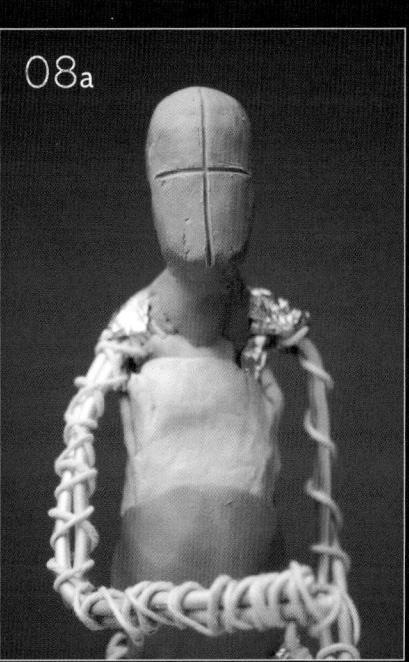

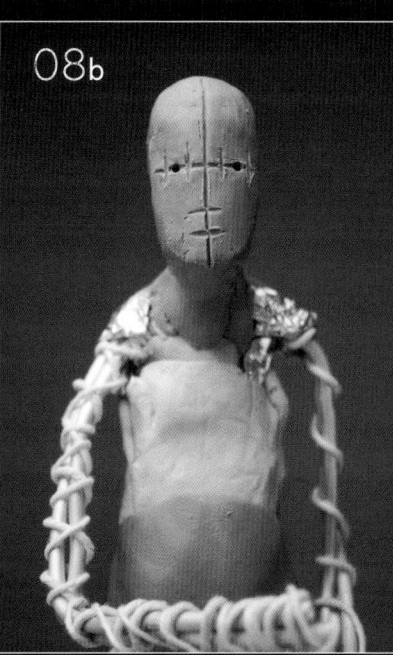

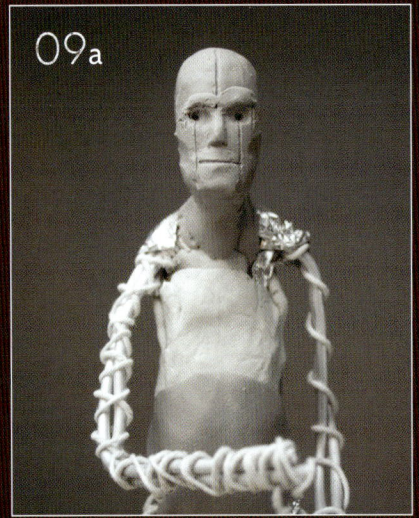

09a

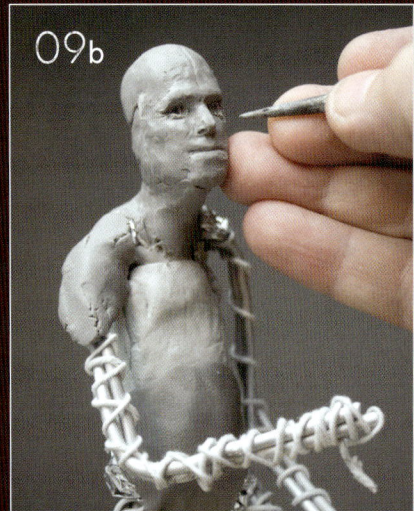

09b

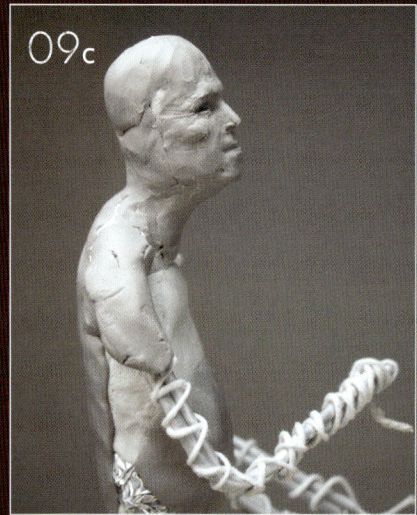

09c

STEP 09

Detail work on the face commences. We hollow out the eye sockets and build up the eyebrow area simultaneously (09a). We also start constructing the nose and mouth. All of this work is completed using the spoon end of our burnisher. Next, we add cheekbones, lips, and nostrils and use the pointed end of our burnisher to add tiny details such as individual eyeballs (09b).

STEP 10

Next, we make the armature for the character's work table out of wood. We wood-glue the bottom piece of the table to the wooden base and nail the table top (made from another piece of wood) to the top of it.

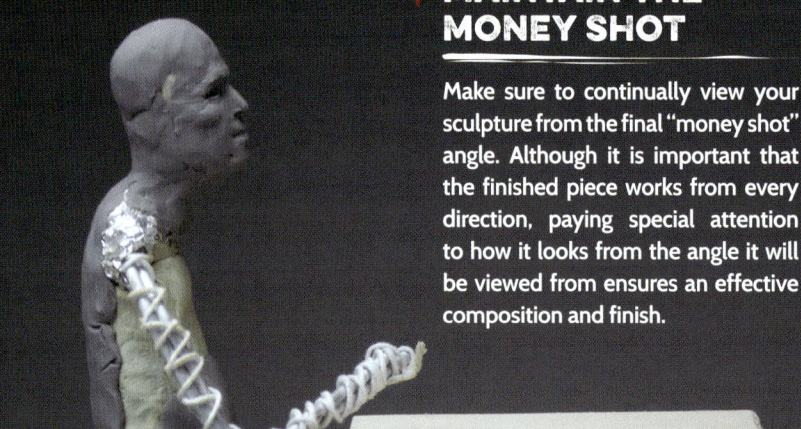

10

✦ MAINTAIN THE MONEY SHOT

Make sure to continually view your sculpture from the final "money shot" angle. Although it is important that the finished piece works from every direction, paying special attention to how it looks from the angle it will be viewed from ensures an effective composition and finish.

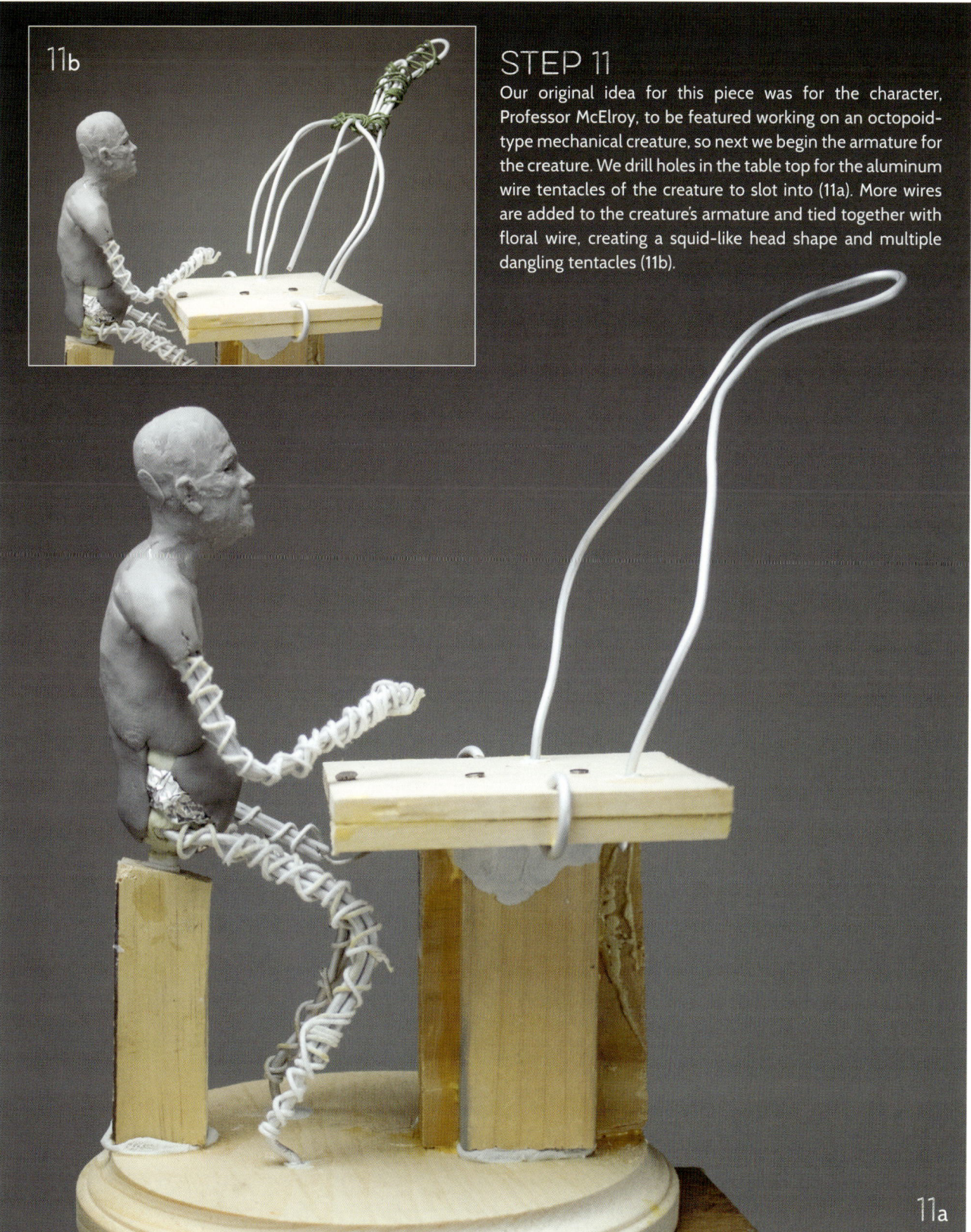

11b

STEP 11

Our original idea for this piece was for the character, Professor McElroy, to be featured working on an octopoid-type mechanical creature, so next we begin the armature for the creature. We drill holes in the table top for the aluminum wire tentacles of the creature to slot into (11a). More wires are added to the creature's armature and tied together with floral wire, creating a squid-like head shape and multiple dangling tentacles (11b).

11a

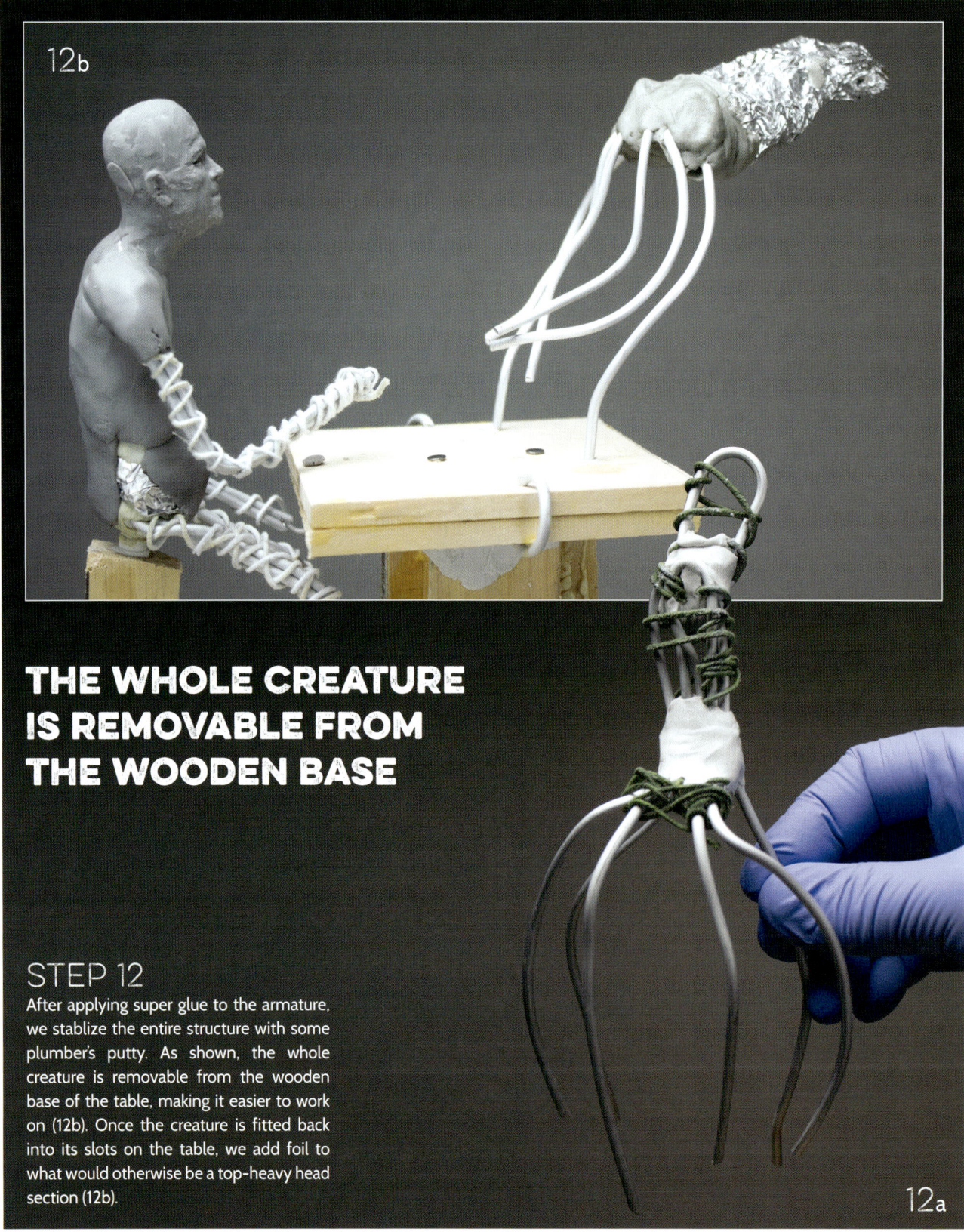

12b

THE WHOLE CREATURE IS REMOVABLE FROM THE WOODEN BASE

STEP 12

After applying super glue to the armature, we stablize the entire structure with some plumber's putty. As shown, the whole creature is removable from the wooden base of the table, making it easier to work on (12b). Once the creature is fitted back into its slots on the table, we add foil to what would otherwise be a top-heavy head section (12b).

12a

STEP 13

Next, we cover both the table and the stool with clay and work on blocking in the forms of both the professor and the creature (13a). We also add further details to the professor's face, including a beard (13b), and attach floral wire extensions to the hands to create armature for a tool in his hand.

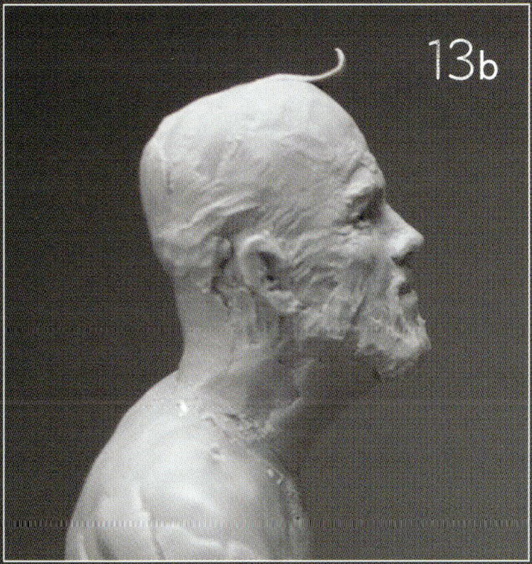

13b

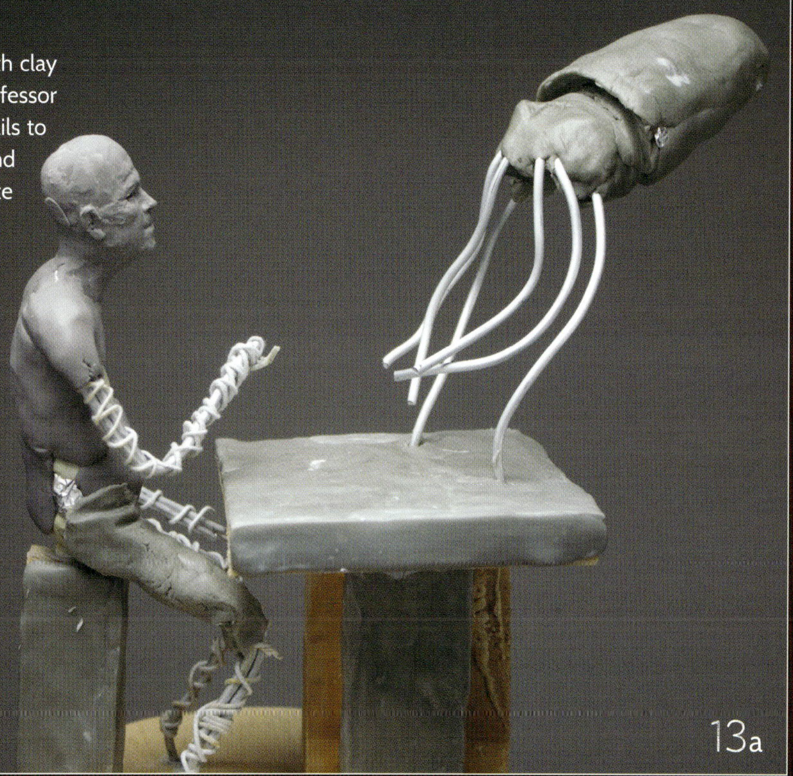

13a

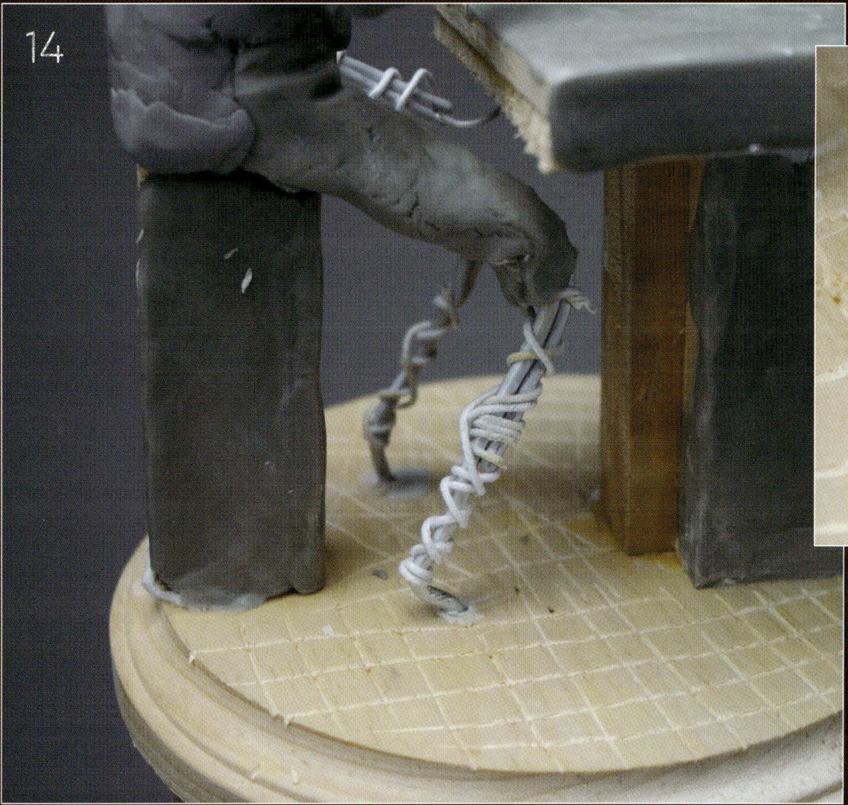

14

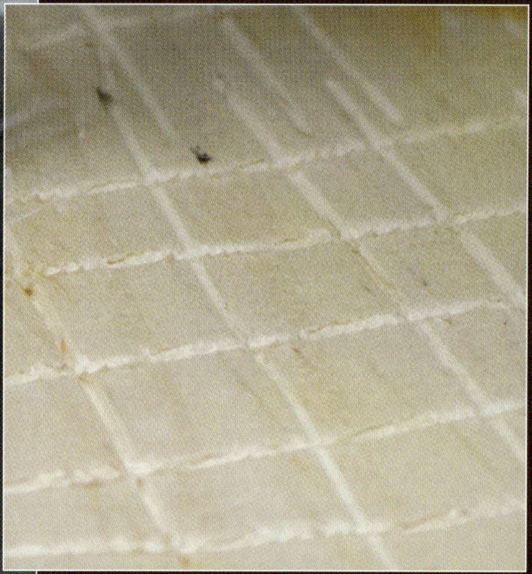

STEP 14

Using a sharp tool, we score the wooden base so that clay grips to it better and sticks in place. We don't want the clay to move around on the slick wood. We need a solid surface of rigid clay on which to sculpt.

CRAFTING THE DETAILS

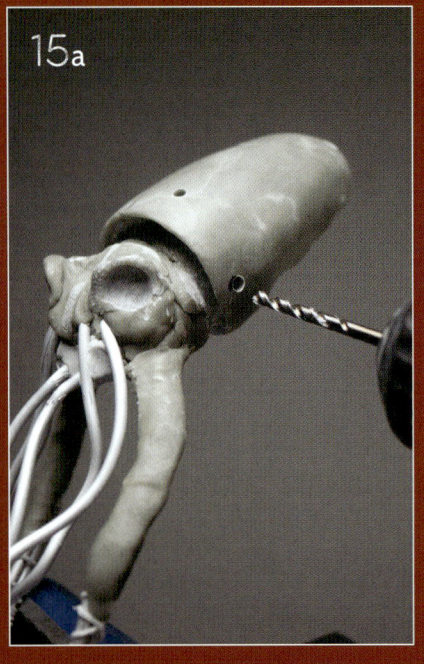

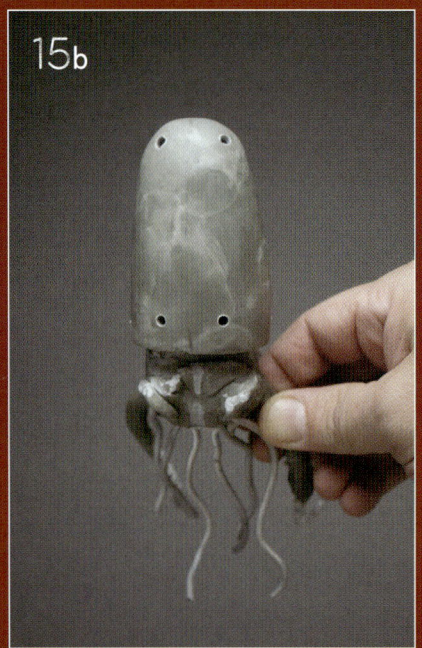

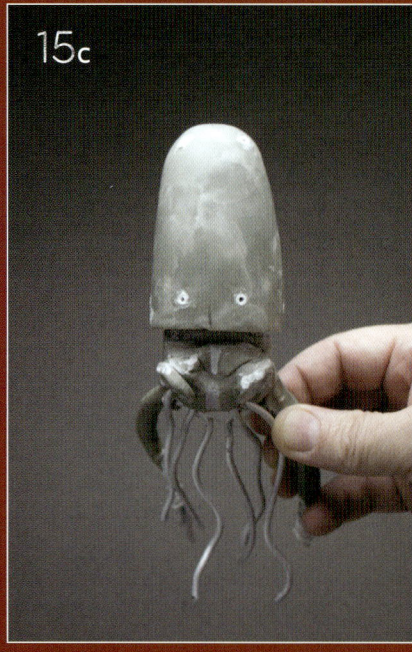

STEP 15

We intend to attach mechanical-looking fins and dimensional details to the creature's head, so first we drill holes into the hardened clay head (15a-15b) and fix small sections of tubing in place with tiny amounts of plumber's putty (15c).

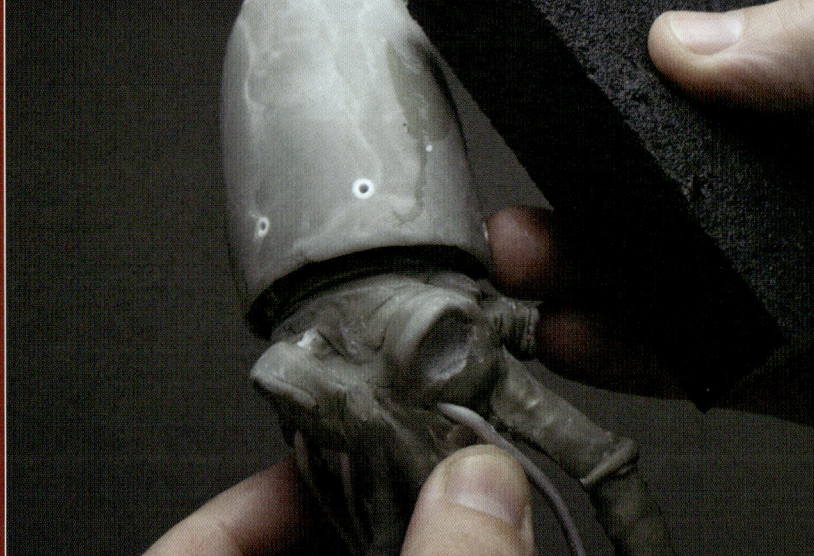

STEP 16

Next, we wet-sand the surface of the creature's head area in an attempt to create a smooth, almost shiny, metallic-looking surface, giving the impression that the creature is in fact mechanical and not organic. The sanding process also refines the shape of the creature's head and makes it appear more rounded and perfected.

STEP 17

To build the fins, we cut out small pieces of wire mesh and affix them to pieces of floral wire using plumber's putty. The lengths of floral wire then fit into tubes fixed in the creature's head. We repeat the process to create a frilled head fin, mimicking the shapes we find in nature on the biological cousins of our bio-mechanical creature.

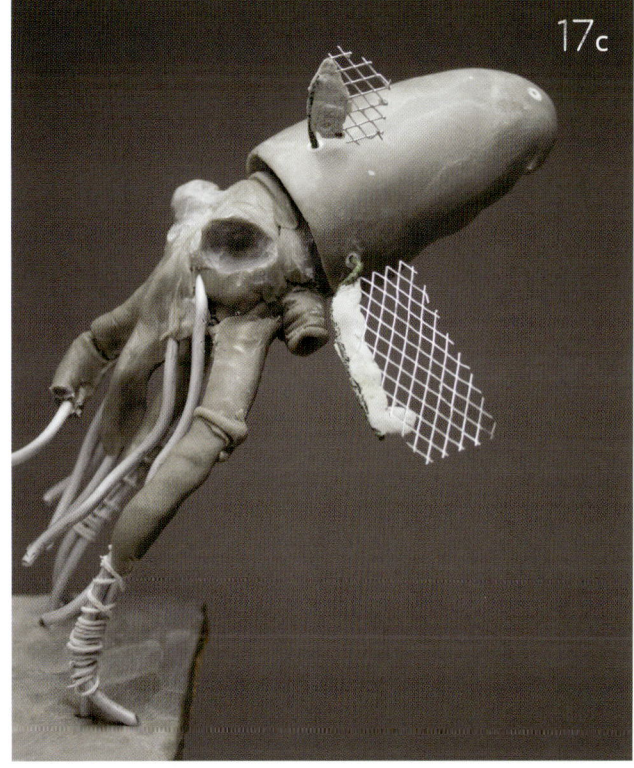

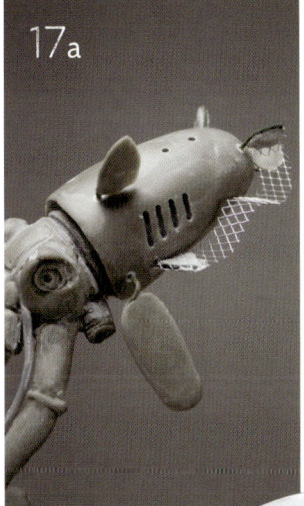

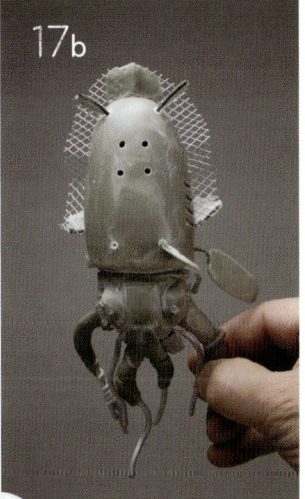

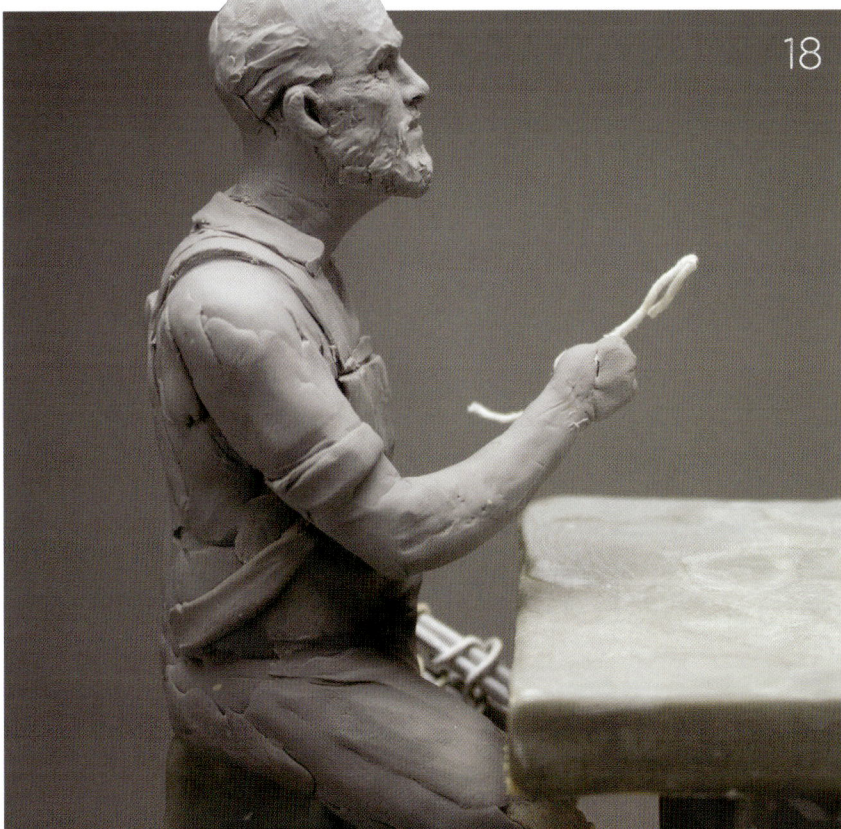

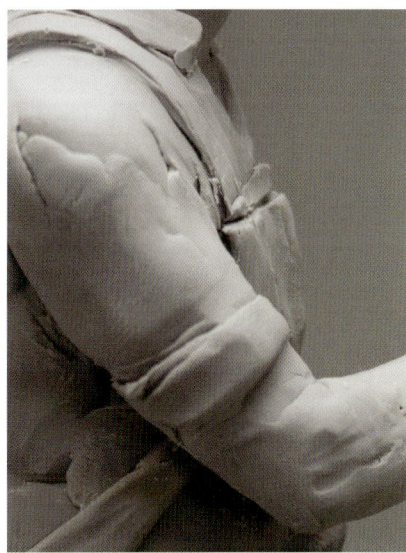

STEP 18

The professor's clothes are built up in clay. For the rolled-up sleeves, we simply roll a piece of clay into a snake-like form and then add it to the arm, attaching it and flattening and shaping it with the spoon end of our burnisher.

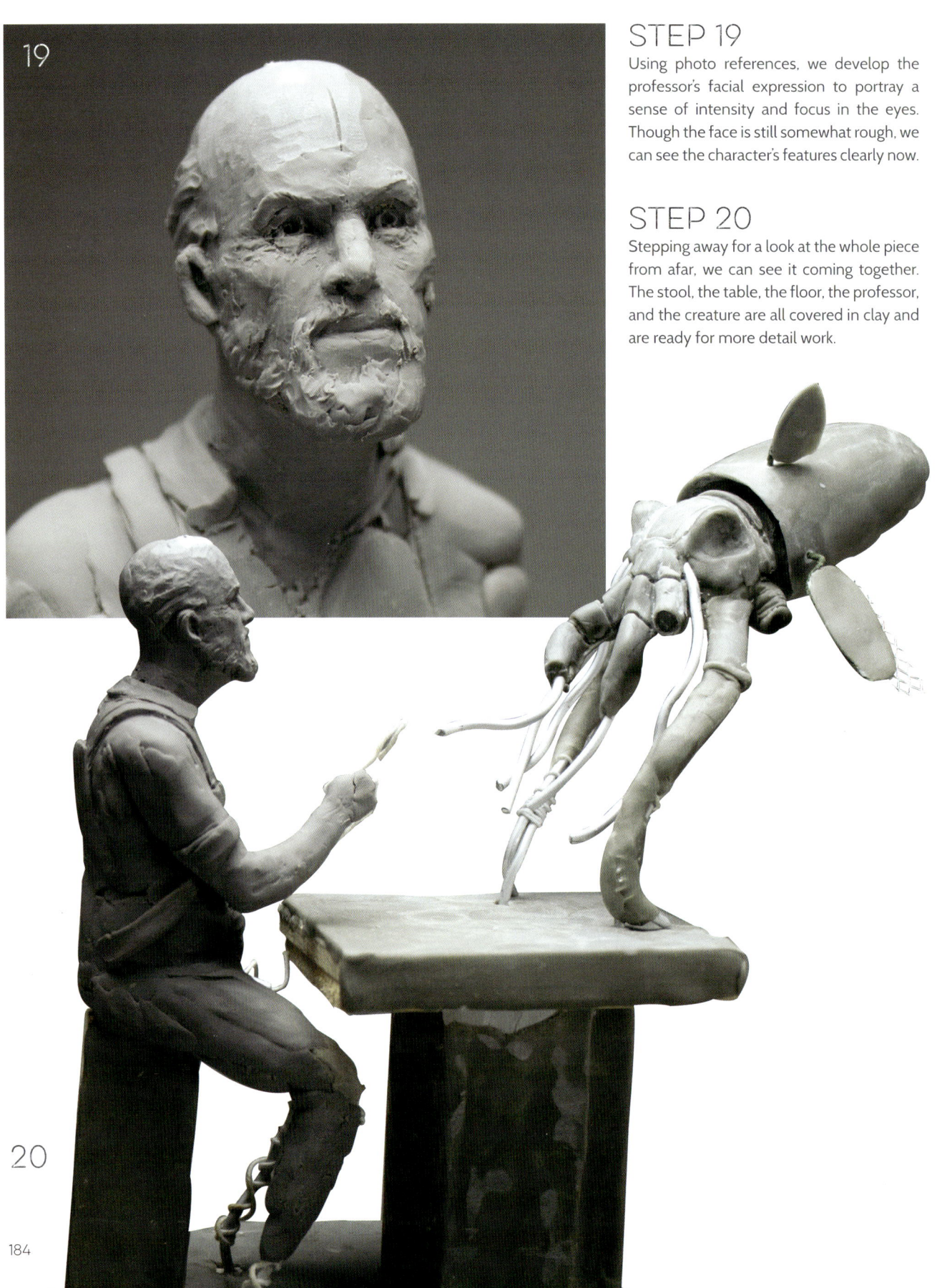

STEP 19

Using photo references, we develop the professor's facial expression to portray a sense of intensity and focus in the eyes. Though the face is still somewhat rough, we can see the character's features clearly now.

STEP 20

Stepping away for a look at the whole piece from afar, we can see it coming together. The stool, the table, the floor, the professor, and the creature are all covered in clay and are ready for more detail work.

STEP 21

The professor's left arm is still only made of armature wire. Because the piece is intended to be seen from the opposite profile, we haven't yet focused on the opposite side of the sculpture. The varying stages of progress can be seen here.

STEP 22

After removing both the creature and the professor from the base of the piece, we file down the base with a metal file. This is just a more heavy-duty form of sanding. There are no details here that we need to protect or preserve, so we file the entire base to create a smooth surface.

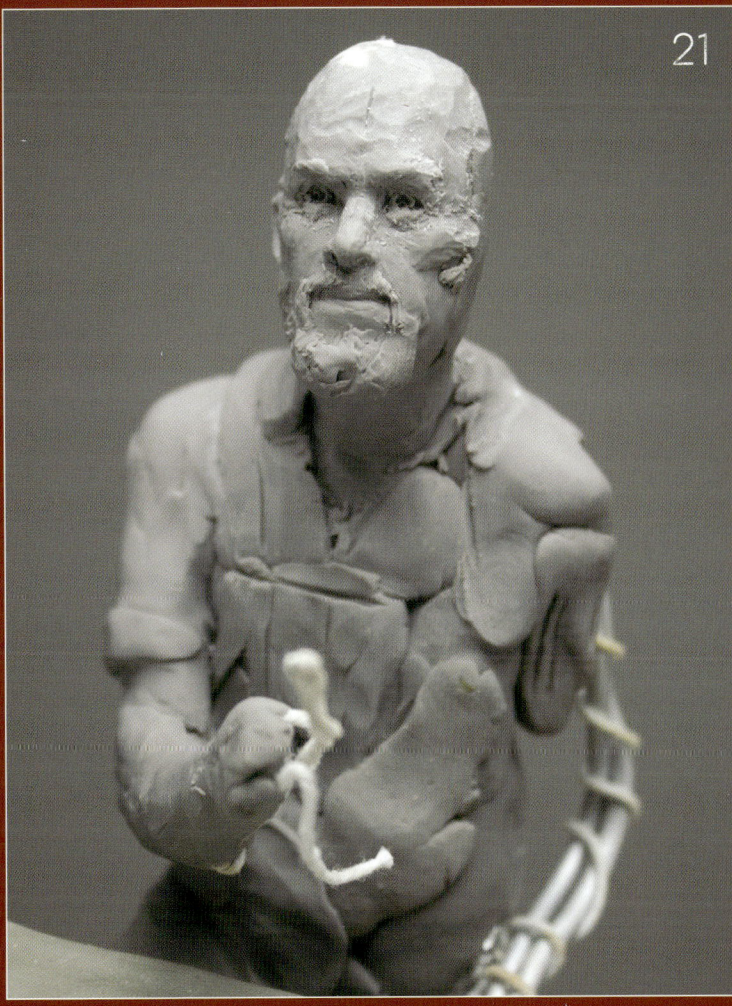

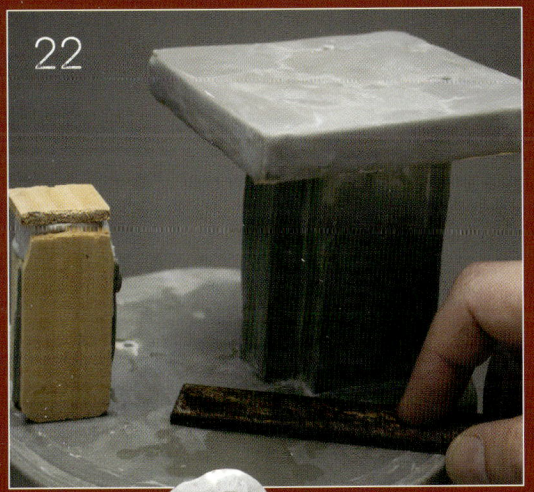

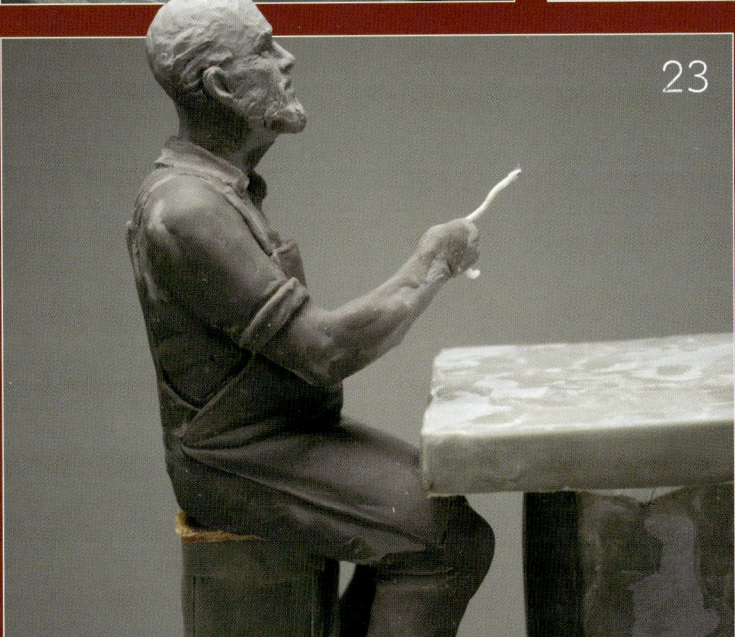

STEP 23

Professor McElroy wears a heavy leather work apron. We use photo references to try to capture how and where the fabric folds. We use small metal tools, including our burnisher, to create these folds. It's important to remember to add "snake" shapes of clay for the convex folds and not just draw lines in the clay. Don't be scared to make things more three-dimensional!

STEP 24

We adjust the position of the professor's left arm to depict his hand resting on his hip as he works (24a). We apply clay and start blocking in the clothing on that arm. At the same time, we return to working on the professor's face — we want his love of these mechanical contraptions to shine through and be evident in his expression (24b).

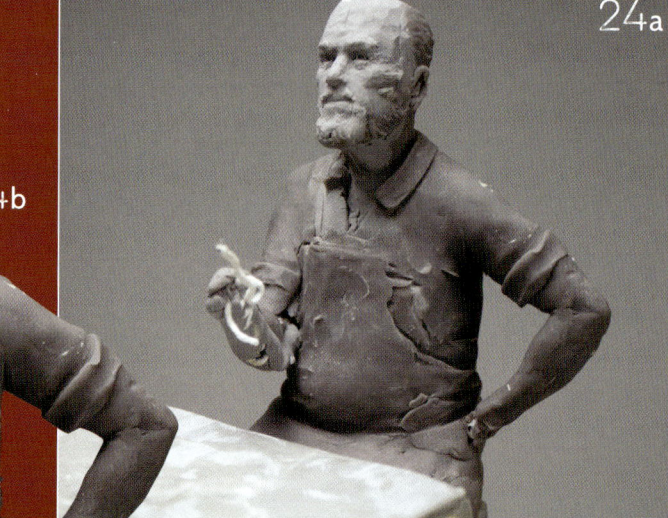

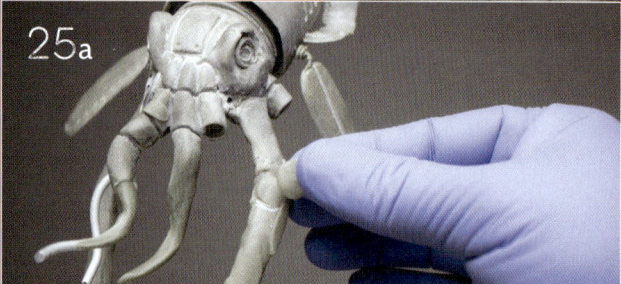

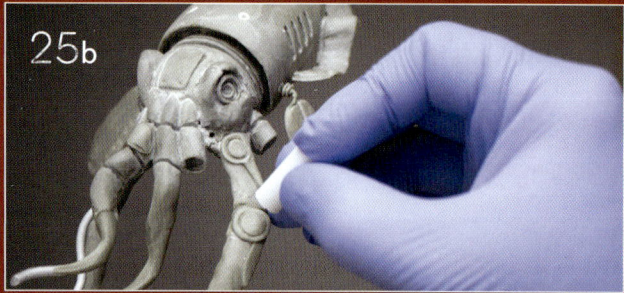

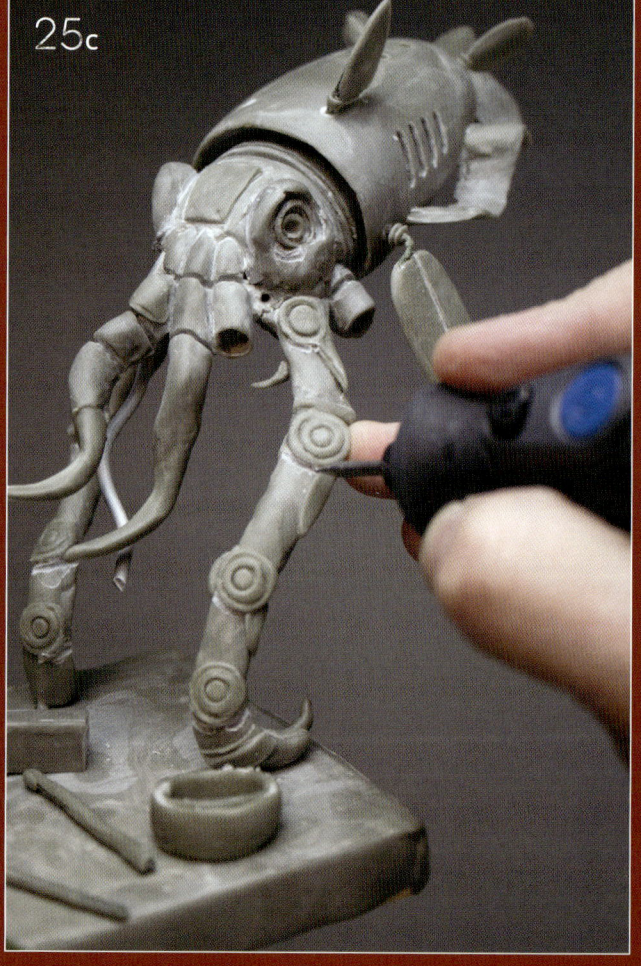

STEP 25

Next, we refine the details on the mechanical squid. Round discs are added to the tentacles to depict joints (25a). We press the circular end of a plastic tube into the small round piece of clay on the tentacle, creating a very round, mechanical-seeming joint (25b). When sculpting pieces of hardware and machinery in clay, clean edges like this circle can go a long way in building a convincing illusion. A Dremel multi-tool with a cutting tip comes in very handy when carving sharp mechanical-looking lines into the joint areas (25c).

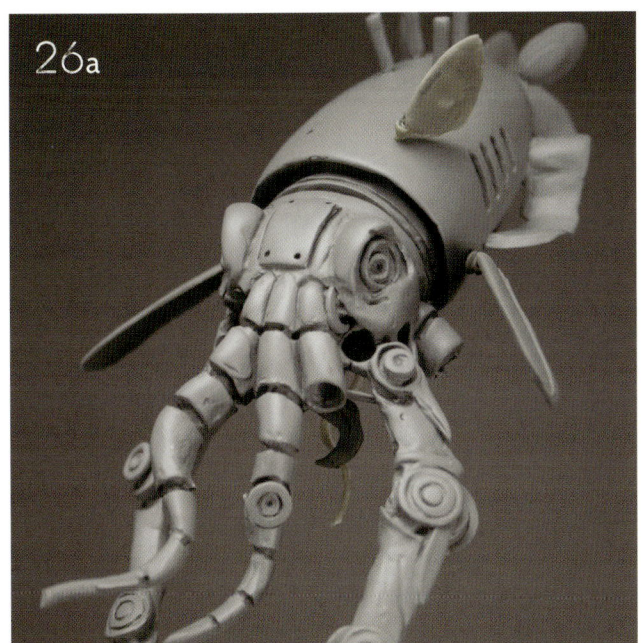

26a

STEP 26

Further detail happens atop the mechanical squid. We cover the wire mesh fins around the side of the head in clay (26a) and add new floral wire structures to hold even more robot details protruding from the creature (26b).

STEP 27

Lifting the professor off the base, we sand down parts of his clothing to create a cleaner, more finished look. This adds a sense of smoothness to the open areas of clay, such as the apron.

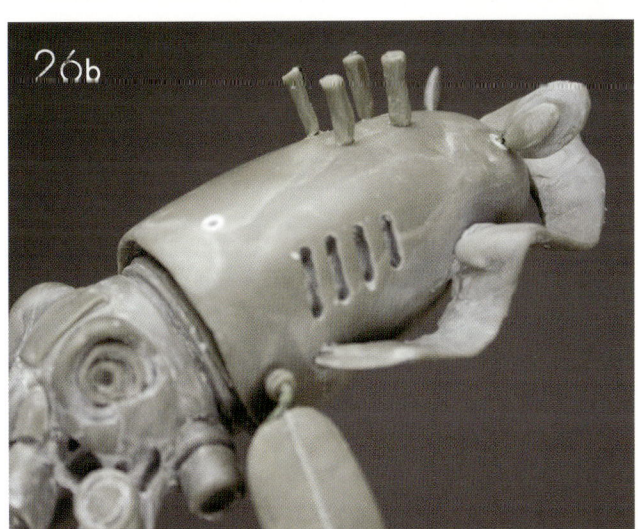

26b

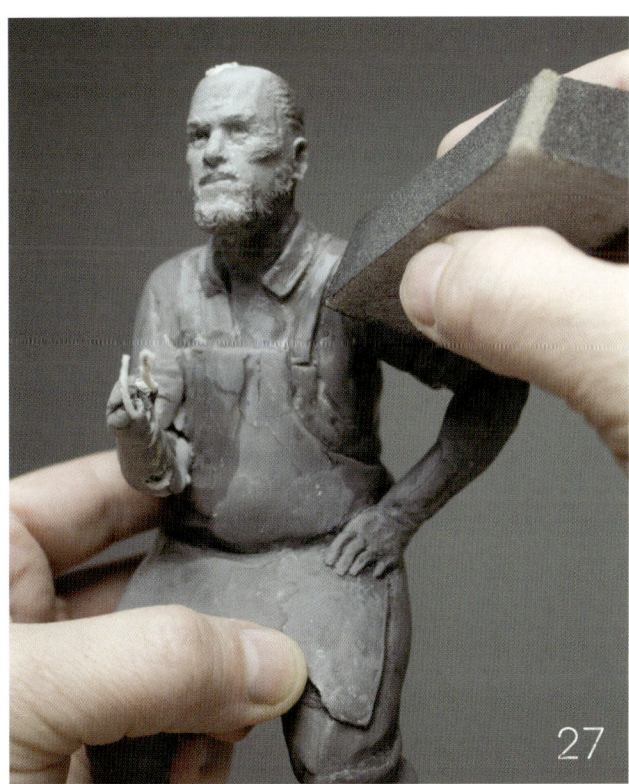

27

SETTING THE SCENE

Where we use Super Sculpey, which needs to be baked at around 200°C to harden, we use a heat gun to strategically cure those soft areas. At this relatively low temperature the heat does not affect the already hardened epoxy clay.

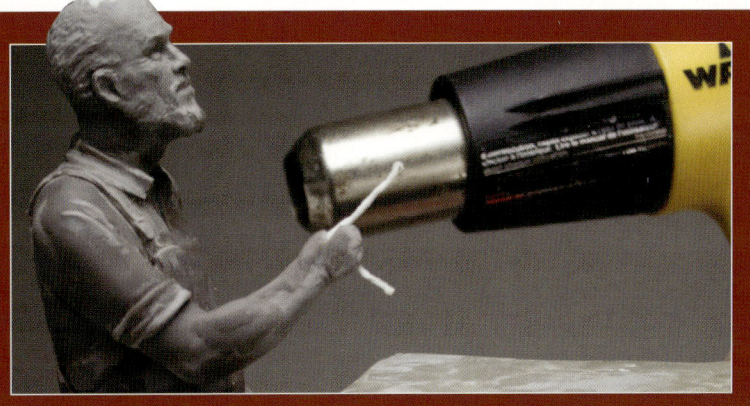

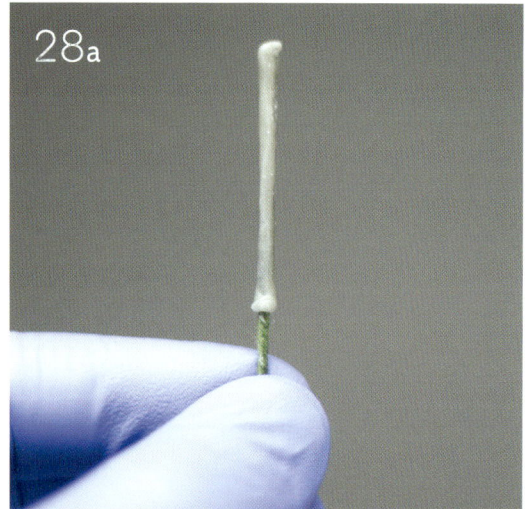

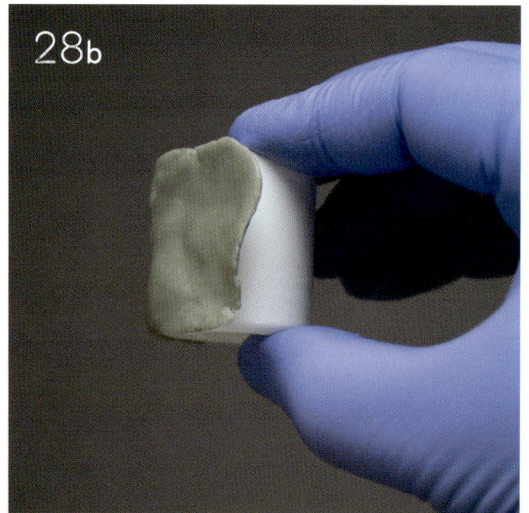

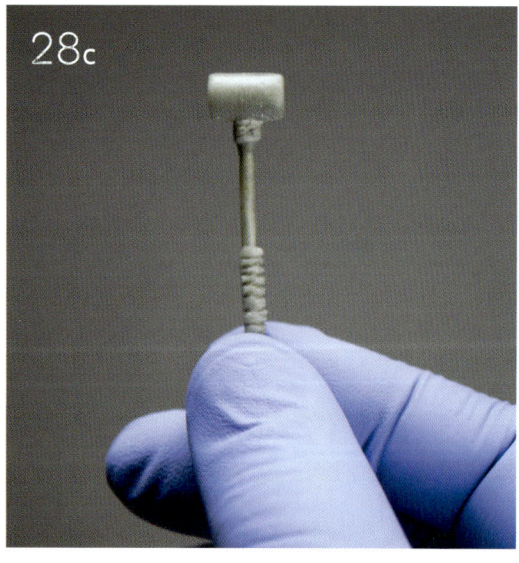

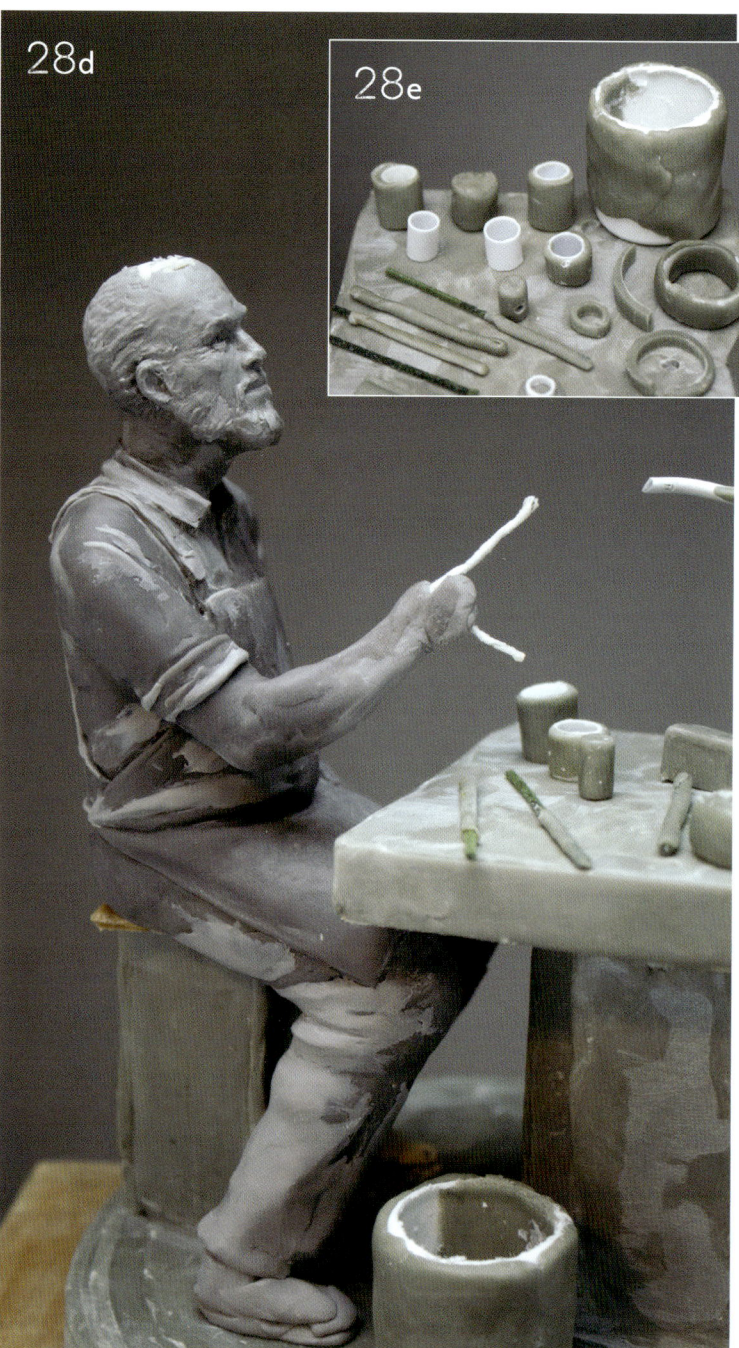

STEP 28

Next, we craft tiny tools, files, and other miscellaneous detritus to place on the professor's desk and on the ground by his feet. To form files, we simply wrap clay around a short length of floral wire (28a). Buckets and receptacles are made by wrapping clay around tubing (28b). We also make a mallet, making lines and adding tiny bumps of three-dimensional texture with our metal burnisher (28c). These tools add to the busy-ness of the overall piece and create a sense that our character has been at work for quite a while.

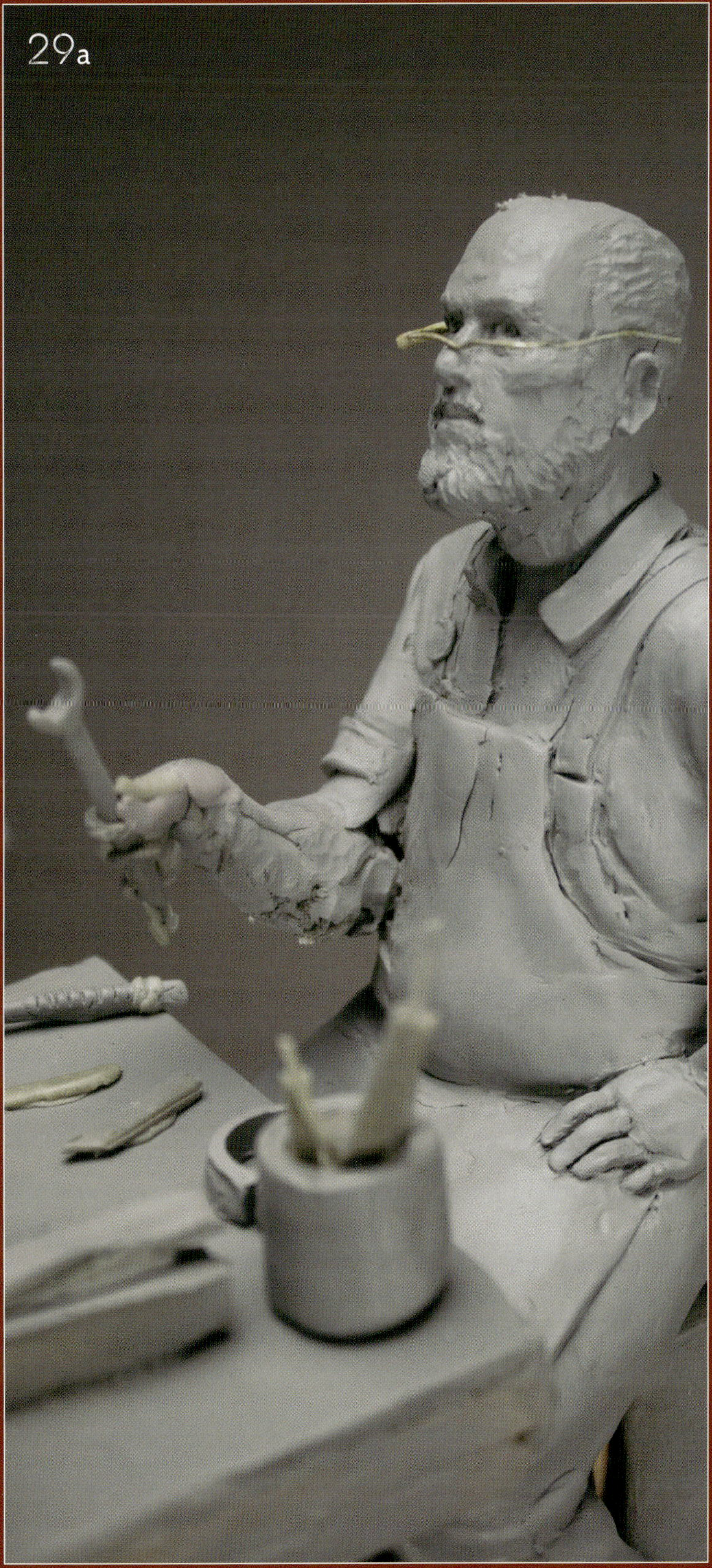

29a

STEP 29

To complete the piece, we add a couple of crucial details. We imagine the professor wearing glasses, so we start to build them by first stripping the outer cloth off a piece of small-gauge floral wire to create the frames (29a). We also build a spanner in the professor's hand from clay around the exposed wire (29b).

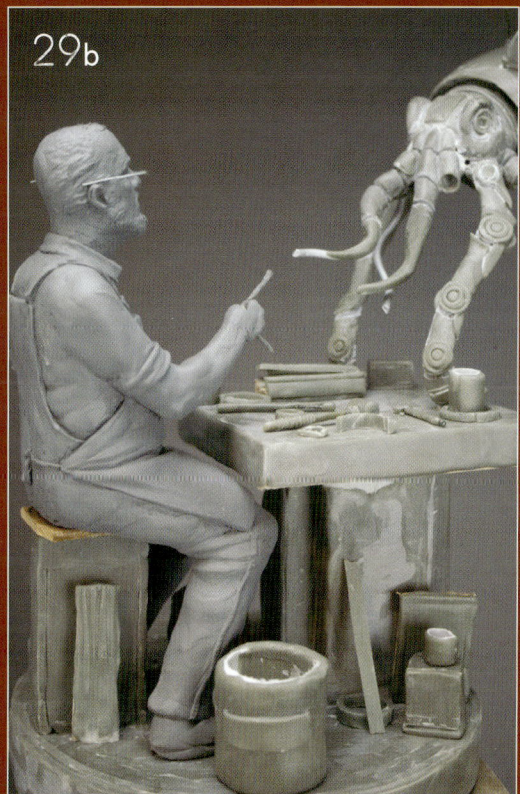

29b

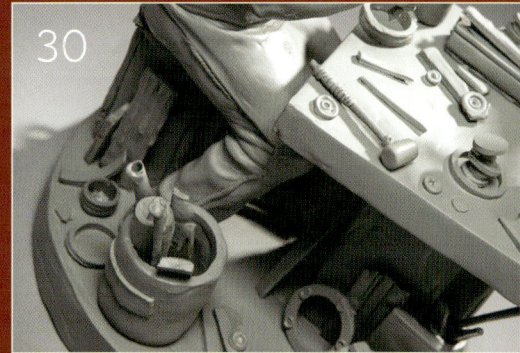

30

STEP 30

Finally, we tidy up any loose ends, perfect surfaces and details, and artfully arrange the many extra elements in the scene to make the entire sculpture feel like a moment captured in time.

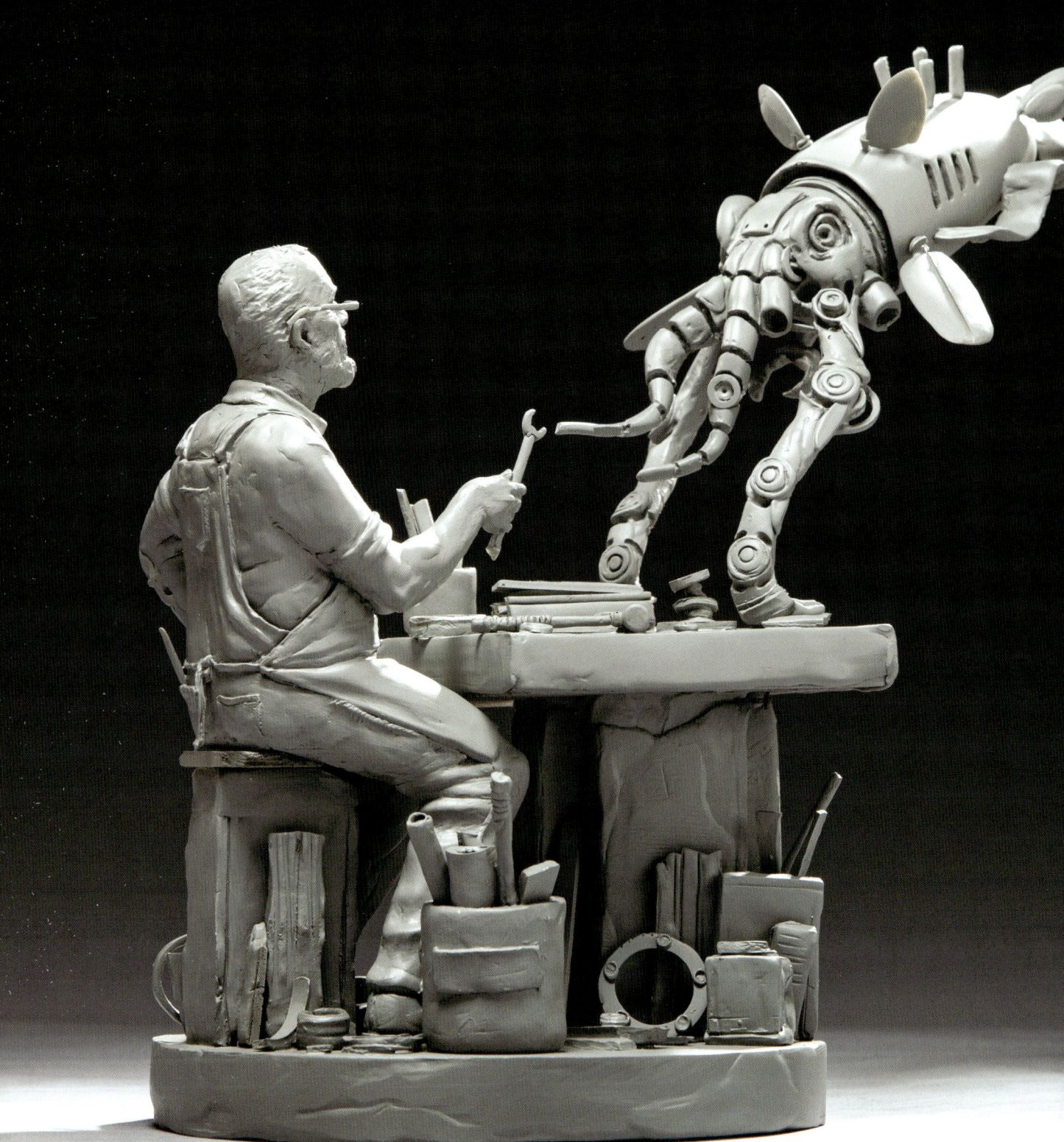

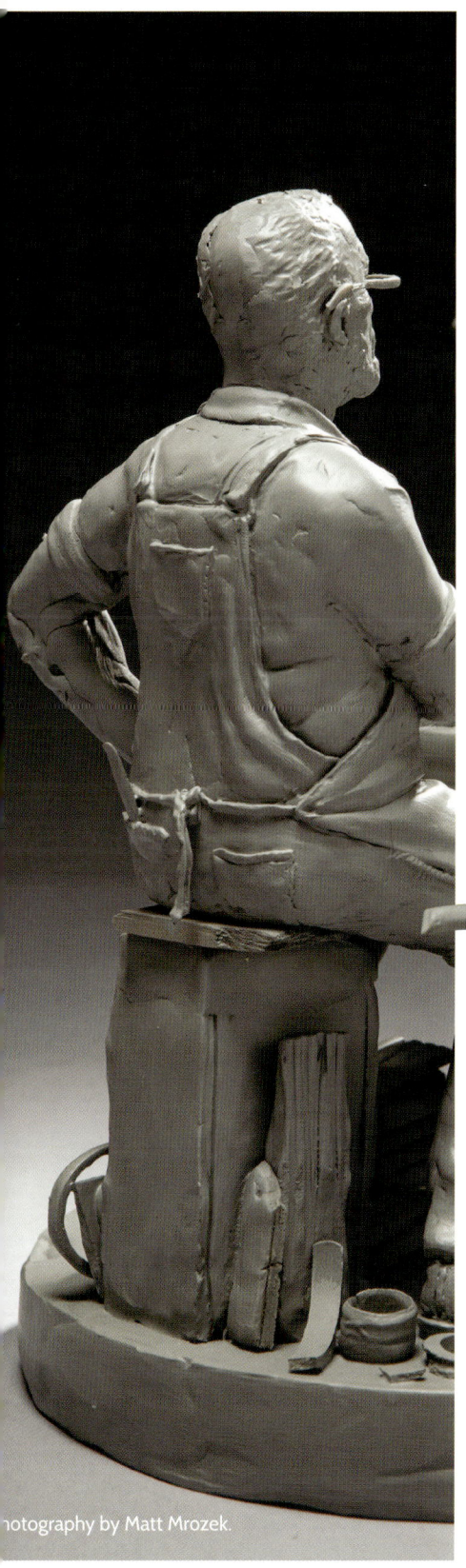

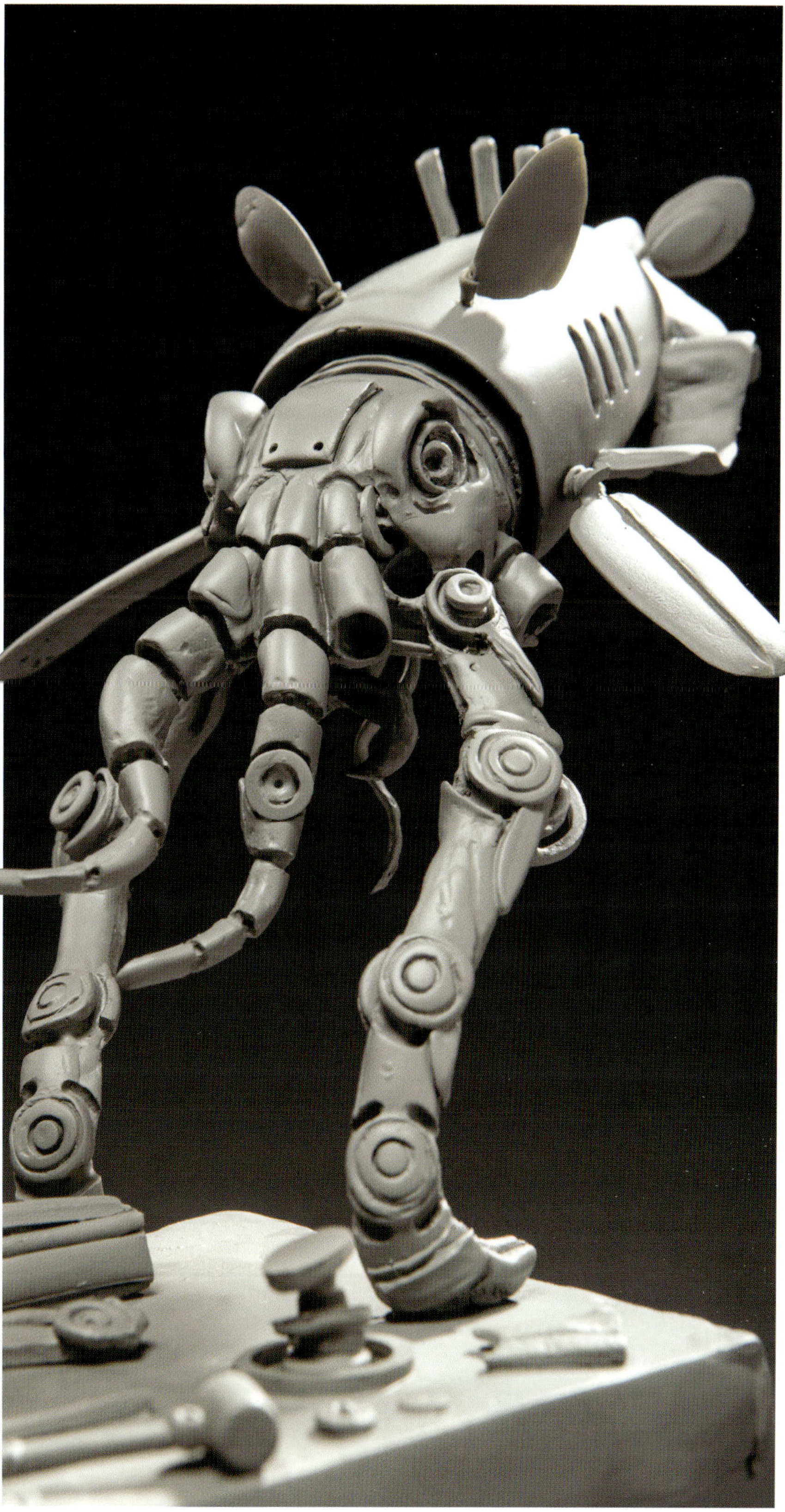

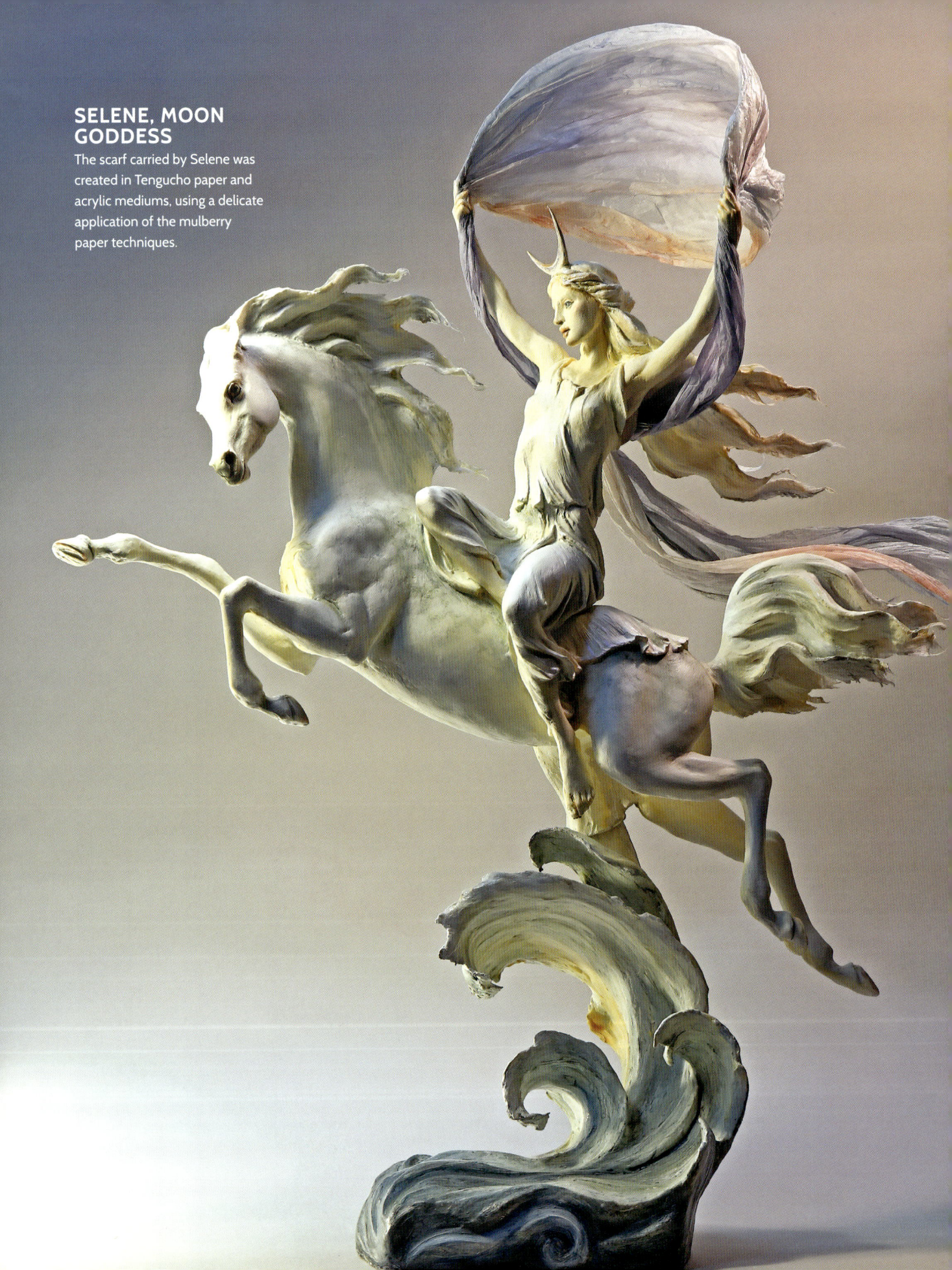

SELENE, MOON GODDESS

The scarf carried by Selene was created in Tengucho paper and acrylic mediums, using a delicate application of the mulberry paper techniques.

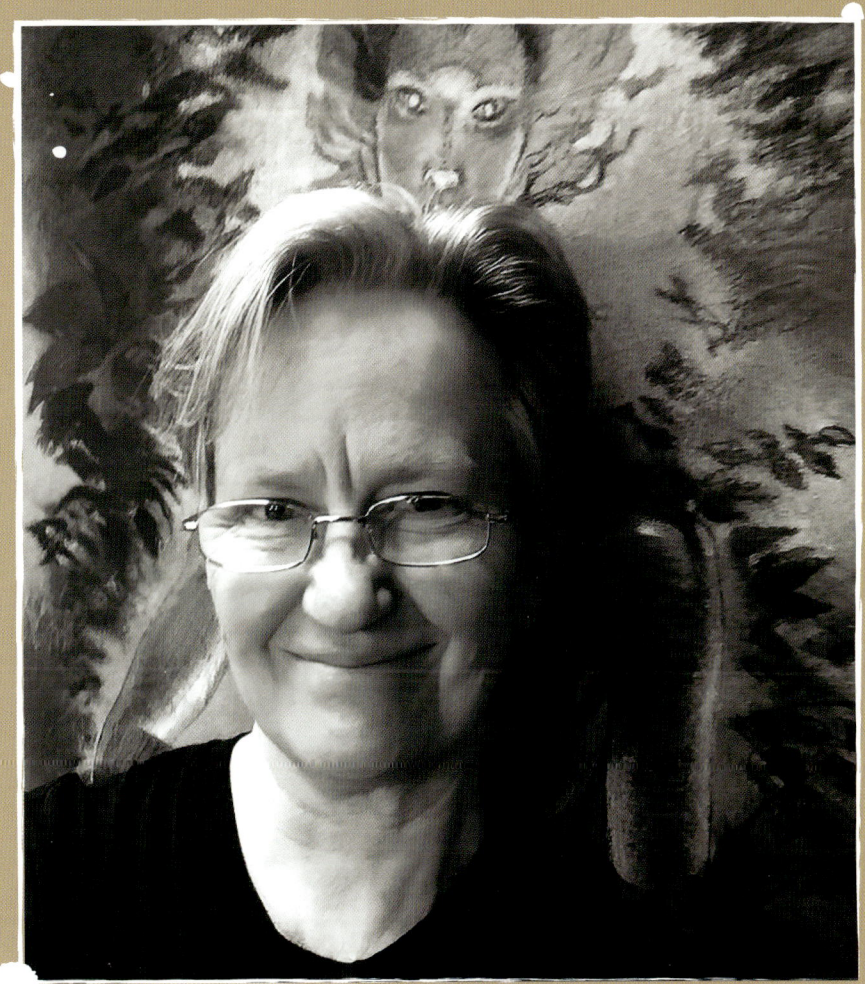

ARTIST SPOTLIGHT

FOREST ROGERS
Mixed-media sculptor
forestrogers.com

Forest Rogers, child of two painters, received a BFA in Stage Design and an MFA in Costume Design from Carnegie-Mellon University in Pittsburgh. Throughout her career, Forest has worked in a plethora of media and styles. She has painted liturgical murals, designed giftware, and produced dinosaur model prototypes alongside paleontologists. For the last fifteen years, she has focused on her own art. Her works reside in private collections and appear in numerous books and magazines, including volumes of *Spectrum Fantastic Art*, *Infected by Art*, and *Beautiful Bizarre Magazine*.

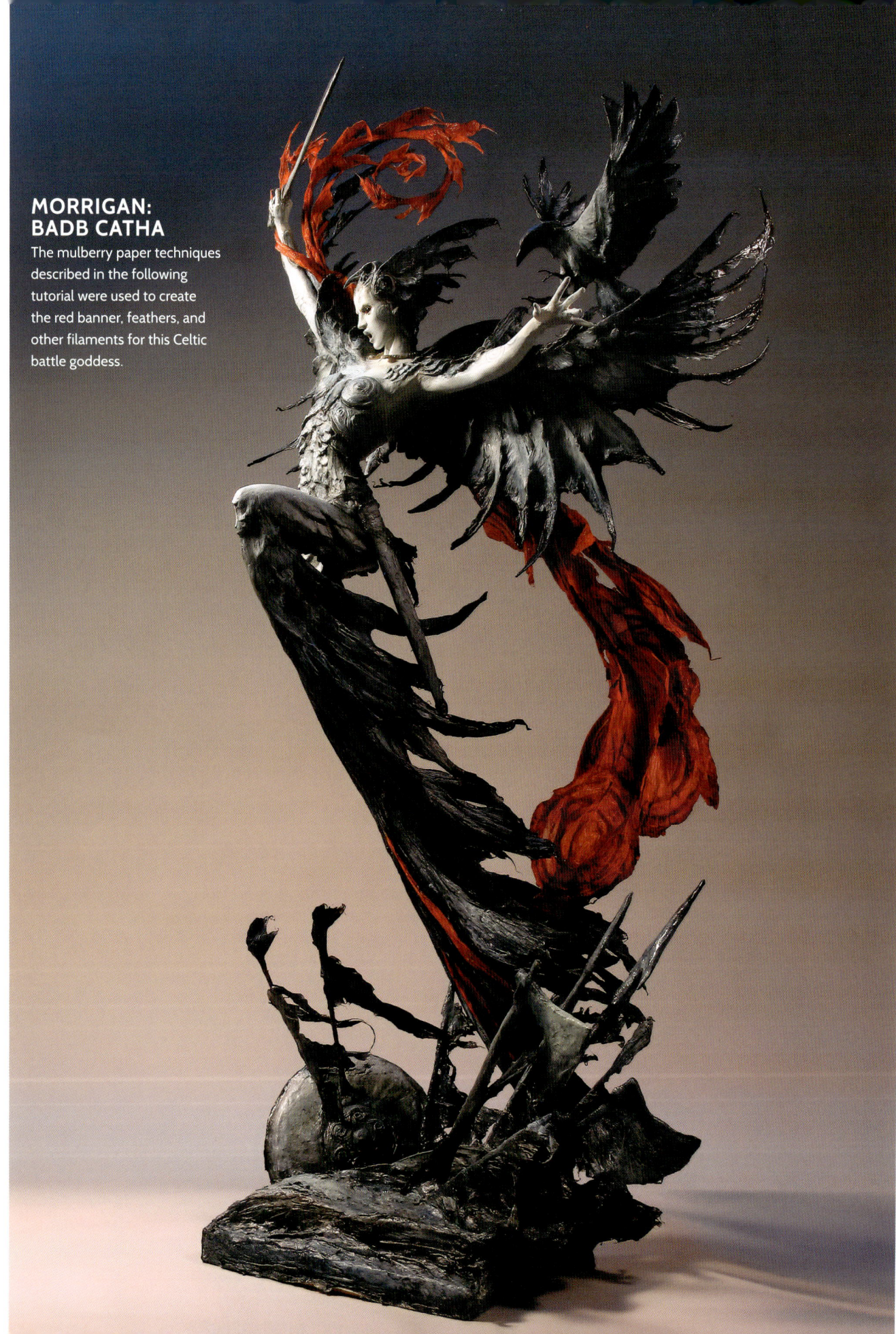

MORRIGAN: BADB CATHA

The mulberry paper techniques described in the following tutorial were used to create the red banner, feathers, and other filaments for this Celtic battle goddess.

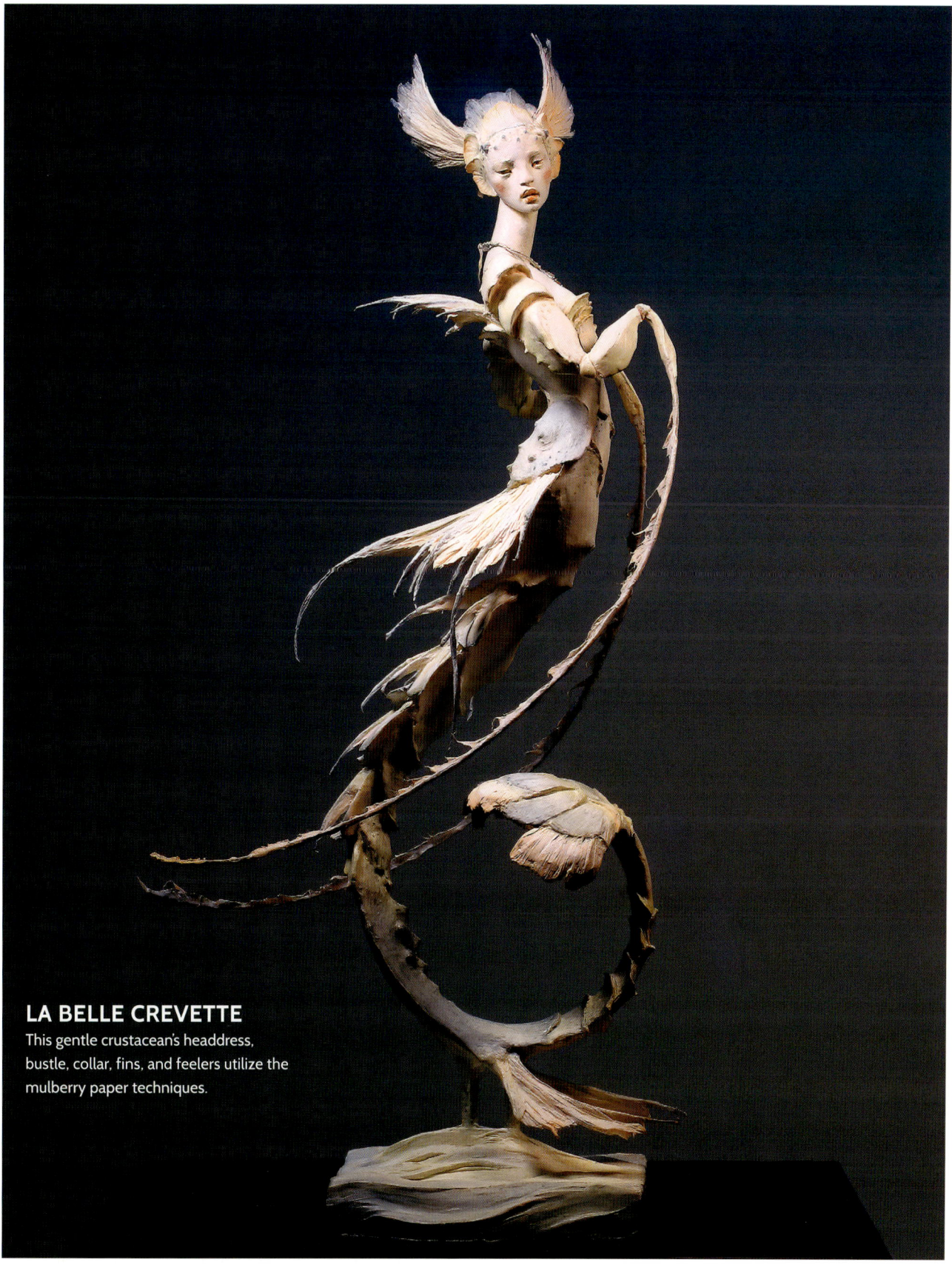

LA BELLE CREVETTE
This gentle crustacean's headdress,
bustle, collar, fins, and feelers utilize the
mulberry paper techniques.

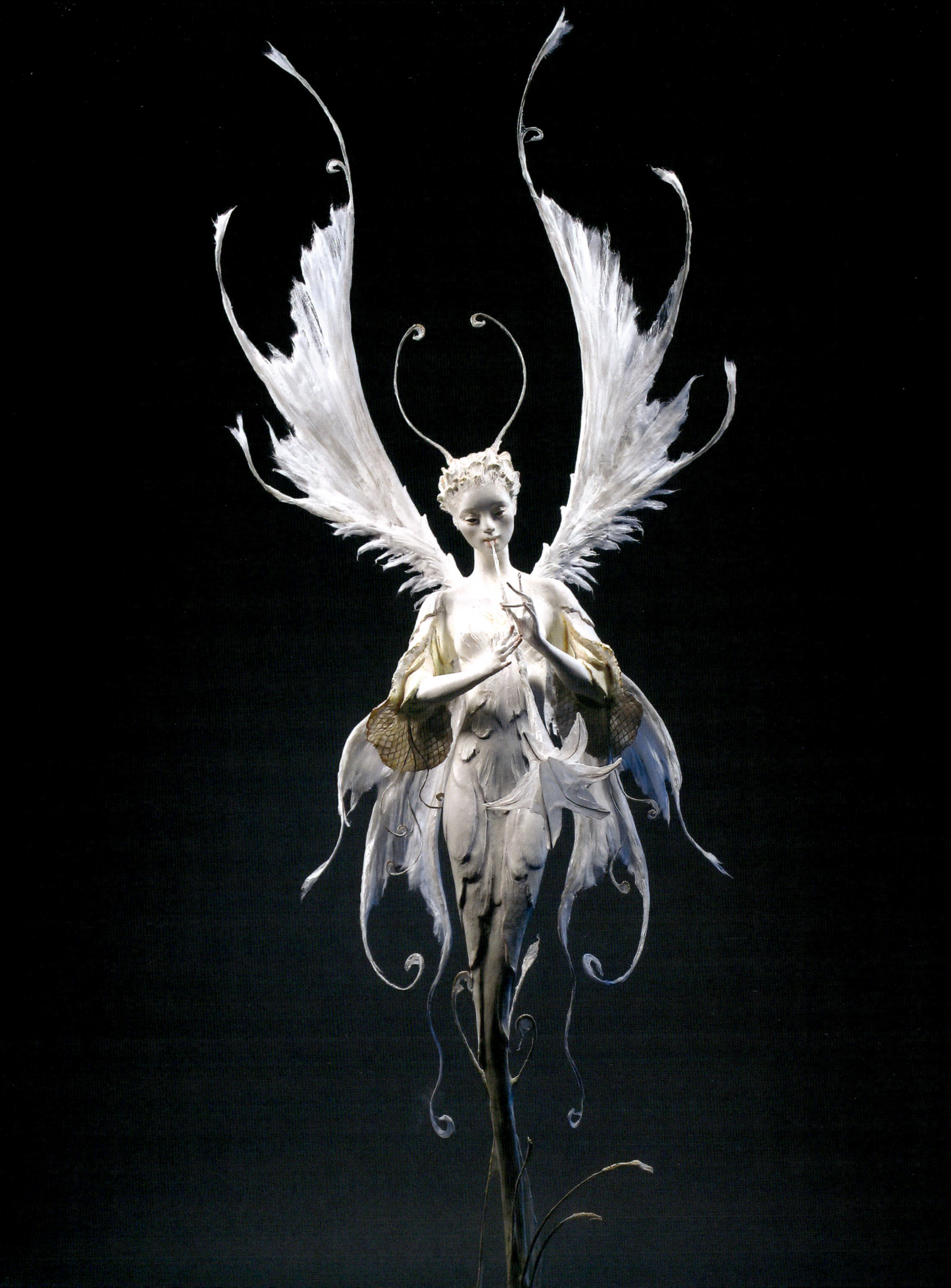

CRAFTING DELICATE TRANSLUCENT WINGS

In this tutorial I demonstrate how I create a pair of translucent fairy wings using mulberry paper and acrylic gel. The method I describe can be adapted to fins, billowing garments, octopus tentacle webbing, or any other thin, lightweight element portraying delicacy and suggesting motion. The body of the fairy was created in air-dry clay over an aluminum and stainless-steel wire armature, with aluminum mesh, reinforced with brass rods and Aves Apoxy Sculpt. The process was similar to that demonstrated for the wing armature, just more robust. The look of these air-dry pieces tends to be more impressionistic than the precision of detail that can be achieved in polymer clay: air-dry clay offers different virtues, and different freedoms. I choose the material depending on the project, and sometimes I use both polymer and air-dry techniques in one piece. Experimentation is key!

BY FOREST ROGERS

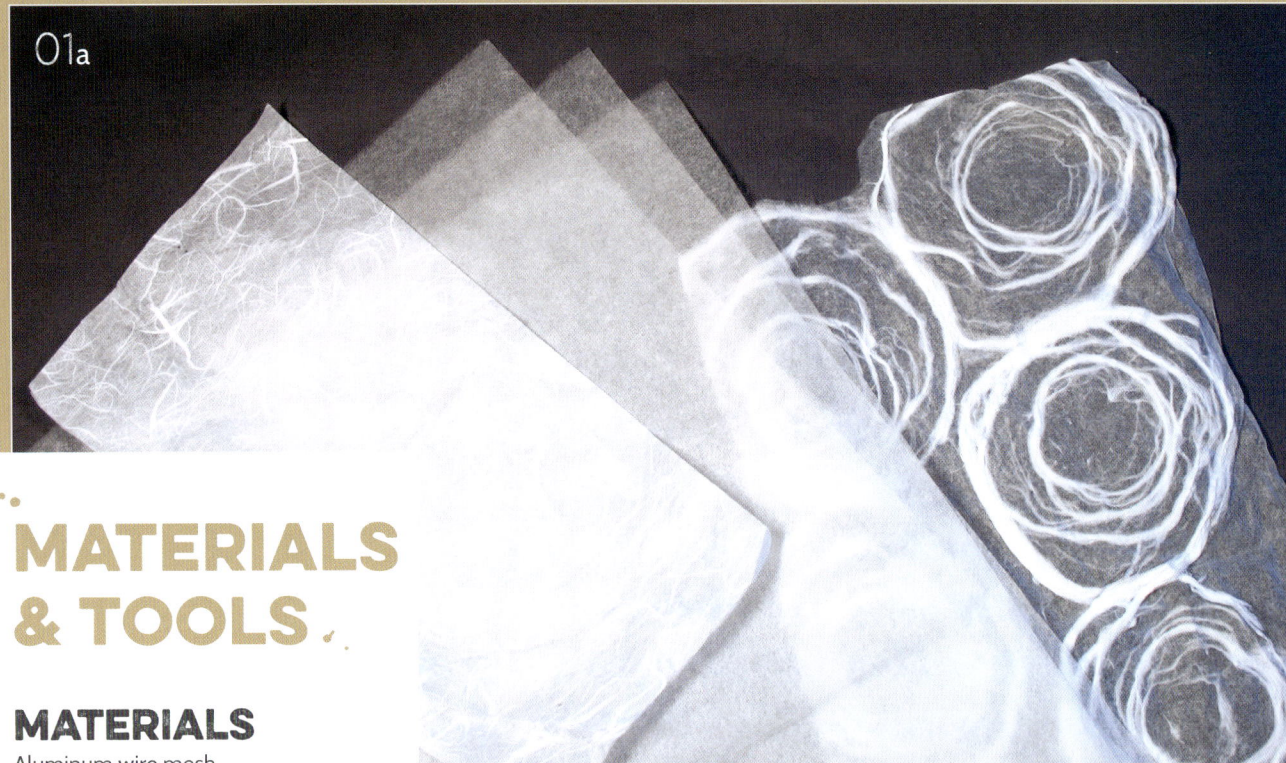

01a

MATERIALS & TOOLS

MATERIALS

Aluminum wire mesh
Stainless steel wire (19-gauge)
Fine stainless steel wire (24, 28, or 32-gauge)
Square brass tube
Padico Premier air-dry clay
Aves Fixit Sculpt
Tengucho mulberry paper
Unryu mulberry paper
Wooden dowel (¼ in diameter)
Golden Acrylics Soft Gel Medium Gloss
Acrylic paints and inks
Beacon Gem-Tac glue
Matte acrylic medium
Matte or satin acrylic varnish

TOOLS

Wire cutters
Jeweler's saw
Paintbrushes
Silicone shaper
Small round-nosed pliers
Princeton Select Filbert Grainer brush

STEP 01

I use a variety of mulberry papers. The first (shown on the top of the pile) is Unryu ("cloud dragon") paper, a somewhat opaque paper with random fibers. I often use it with acrylic gel as a base layer over which more delicate papers can be applied. The second, Tengucho, a sheer paper, is pH neutral and is often used for conservation. This is the main paper I use for this project. The third paper is a pH neutral tissue embedded with short pulp fibers. Such papers are useful both as sheets and torn into fiber pieces.

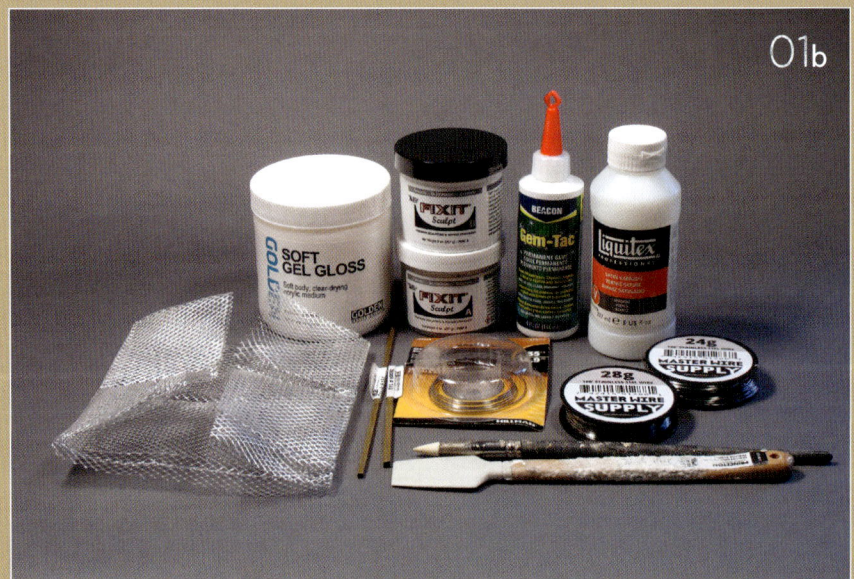

01b

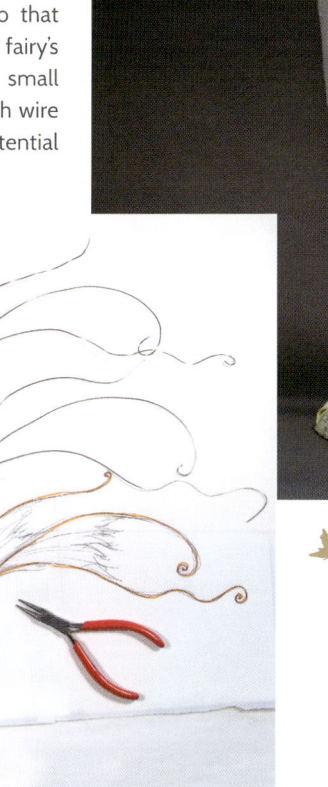

02

STEP 02

I usually start a piece with a simple scribble, often on a napkin in a café. Here is my wing sketch, held up behind the rest of the sculpture. The sketch gives me a basic flat pattern for my armature. The actual wings will exist sculpturally, in three dimensions, but this is a very useful starting point. I sometimes mock-up an entire piece in this "paper-doll" style, with the figures and parts set up as paper cut-outs, loosely supported by armature wire. This means I can study the size, proportion, and composition before working with three-dimensional materials.

STEP 03

I highlight the main veins of my wing sketch and then recreate my drawing with pieces of 19-gauge stainless steel wire. These armature wires will eventually support the finished wing. They need to be firmly twisted together where the lines converge so that at a later stage they can be attached to the fairy's body. I use wire cutters, flat-jawed pliers, and small round-nosed jeweler's pliers for creating smooth wire curlicues. I allow a little extra length for potential three-dimensional curves.

03

✦ STAINLESS STEEL

I use a 19-gauge stainless steel wire for the wing armature because, unlike other metals, such as copper, it won't oxidize and change color when used with water-based materials, and therefore will keep the translucent wings looking clean.

STEP 04

Now, I create the attachments that will secure the wings to the body. I use two brass tubes of graduated size (04a). As I construct the figure, I embed two 1 inch long sections of the larger tube into its back, held firm inside the body with two-part epoxy clay. I angle these sections about 45 degrees upward toward the surface of the body. The smaller tube slides inside the larger embedded tube. I mark the smaller tube where ¼ inch protrudes from the embedded tube (04b), then I remove the smaller tube and cut two sections of it to that length, using a jeweler's saw or a Dremel multi-tool.

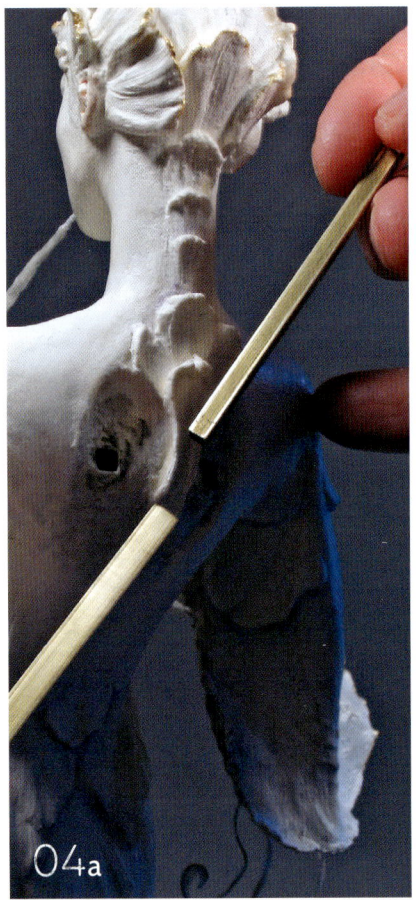

04a

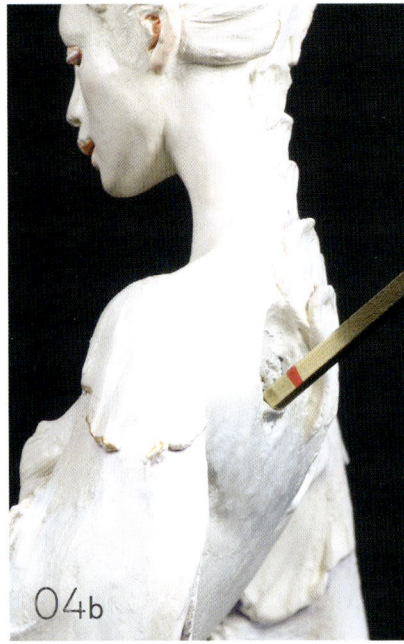

04b

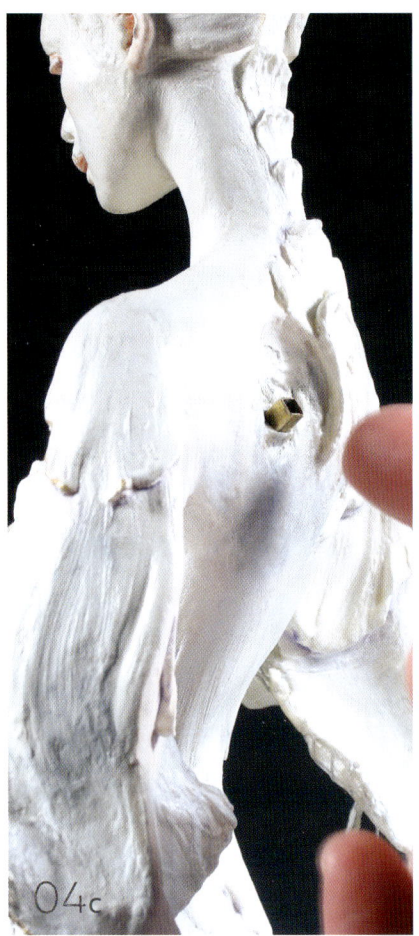

04c

✦ SQUARE TUBE

Square brass tubes provide a neat, non-swiveling attachment for parts that can remain removable, if desired, offering flexibility while working. If the outside of a brass tube becomes coated in material residue and is difficult to slide into its slot, then simply sand the tube. But avoid residue getting inside the receiving tubes, which is harder to fix!

STEP 05

Next, I create a twisted wire extension for the wings to fit inside the square brass tube inserted into the fairy's back. For a good, firm wire twist connection, it helps to spread two or more of the wires evenly off the central axis of the twist, grip them with two pairs of pliers, or a vise and pliers, and twist them so they wind evenly around each other. This is especially helpful when you want the twist to remain slim, as I do in this case.

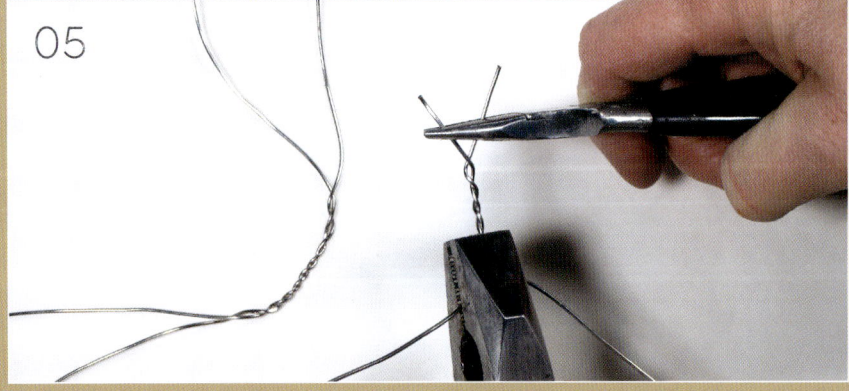

05

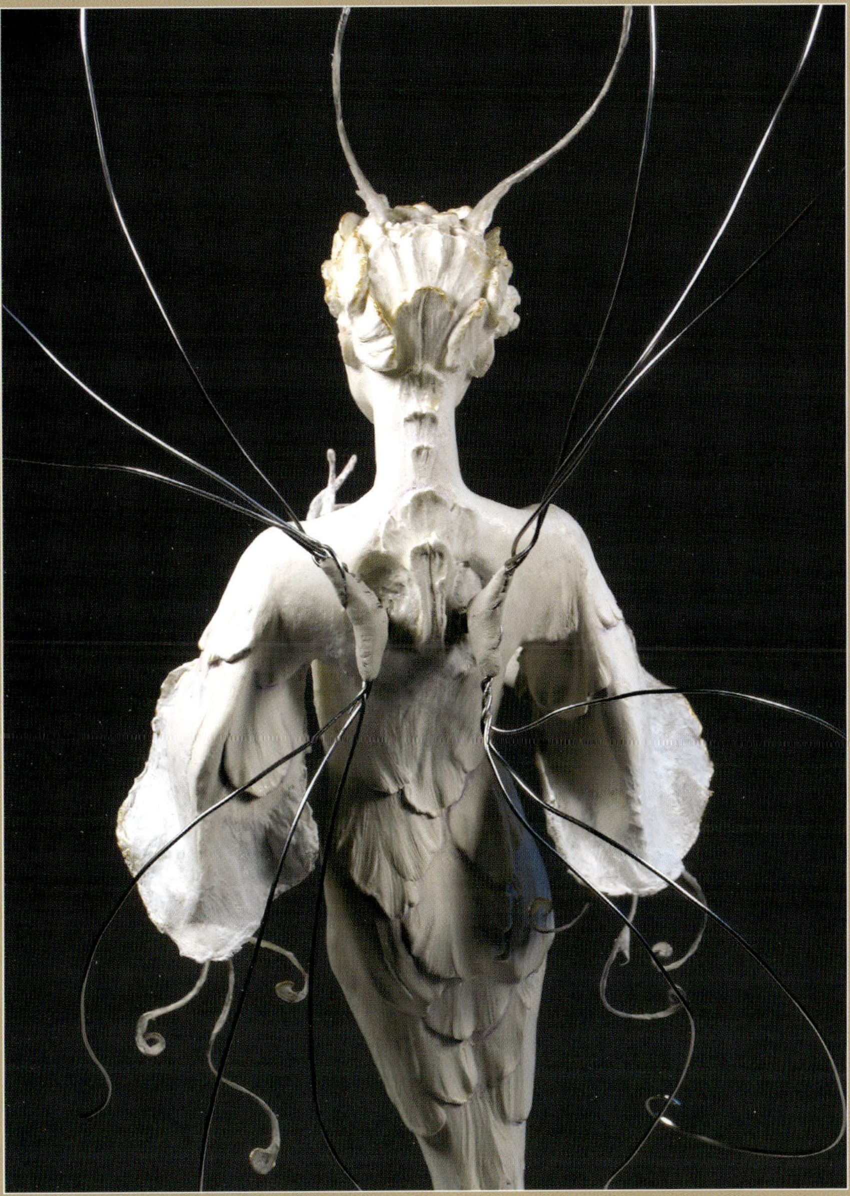

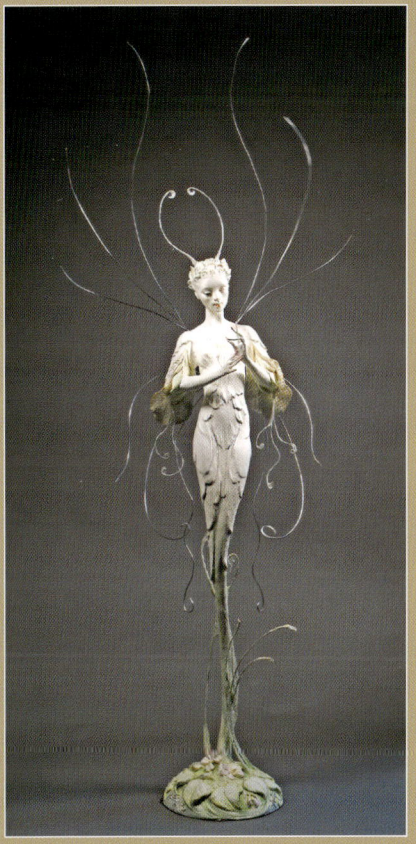

✦ NEW PERSPECTIVE

While I work, I view the piece from every angle and make adjustments. I also examine the piece in a mirror to get a fresh, backward view, or take photographs and study them. At this stage, all of these different ways of looking at the piece help me understand where to go next.

STEP 06

I attach cut sections of the smaller brass tube to the wire wing armatures. First, I hold the armature up to the figure, making sure the attachment wires are at the desired angle. Then, I smear two-part epoxy clay onto the twisted wire attachment (06a). Finally, I slide the brass tube over the clay and wire (06b). I press clay into the open end of the tube to neaten and secure the joint between the tube and wing wires with more clay (06c). I repeat this process for both wings, set them aside, and let the clay harden.

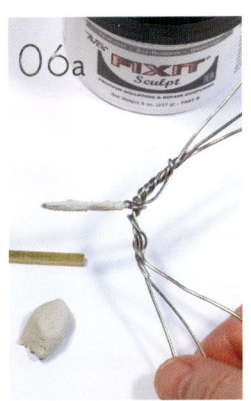

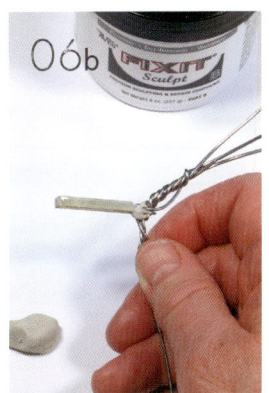

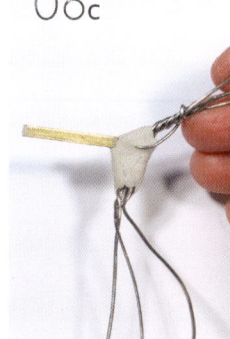

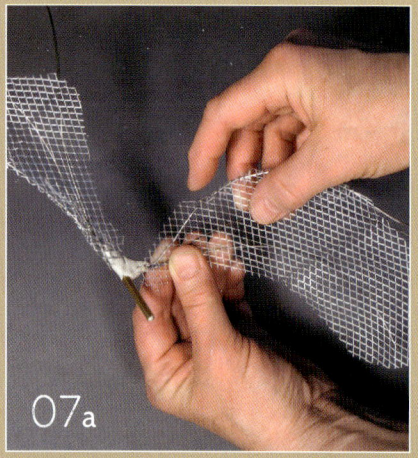

07a

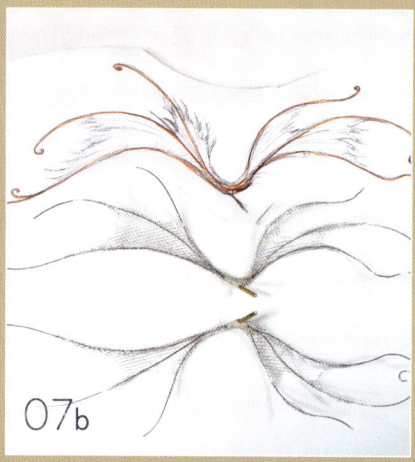

07b

STEP 07

I reinforce the structure with aluminum mesh. I cut the mesh ¼ in to ½ in larger than the area I want to cover and fold it over the edges (07a). If I want to secure a wire to the center of the mesh, I weave through the mesh and around the wire with a small gauge (28 or 32) stainless steel wire. I don't want the mesh to run to the edges of what will be the mulberry paper portion of the wings, because those will be translucent, and the mesh would show through, so, using scissors, I trim the mesh (07b). I also use my fingers to stretch and shape it.

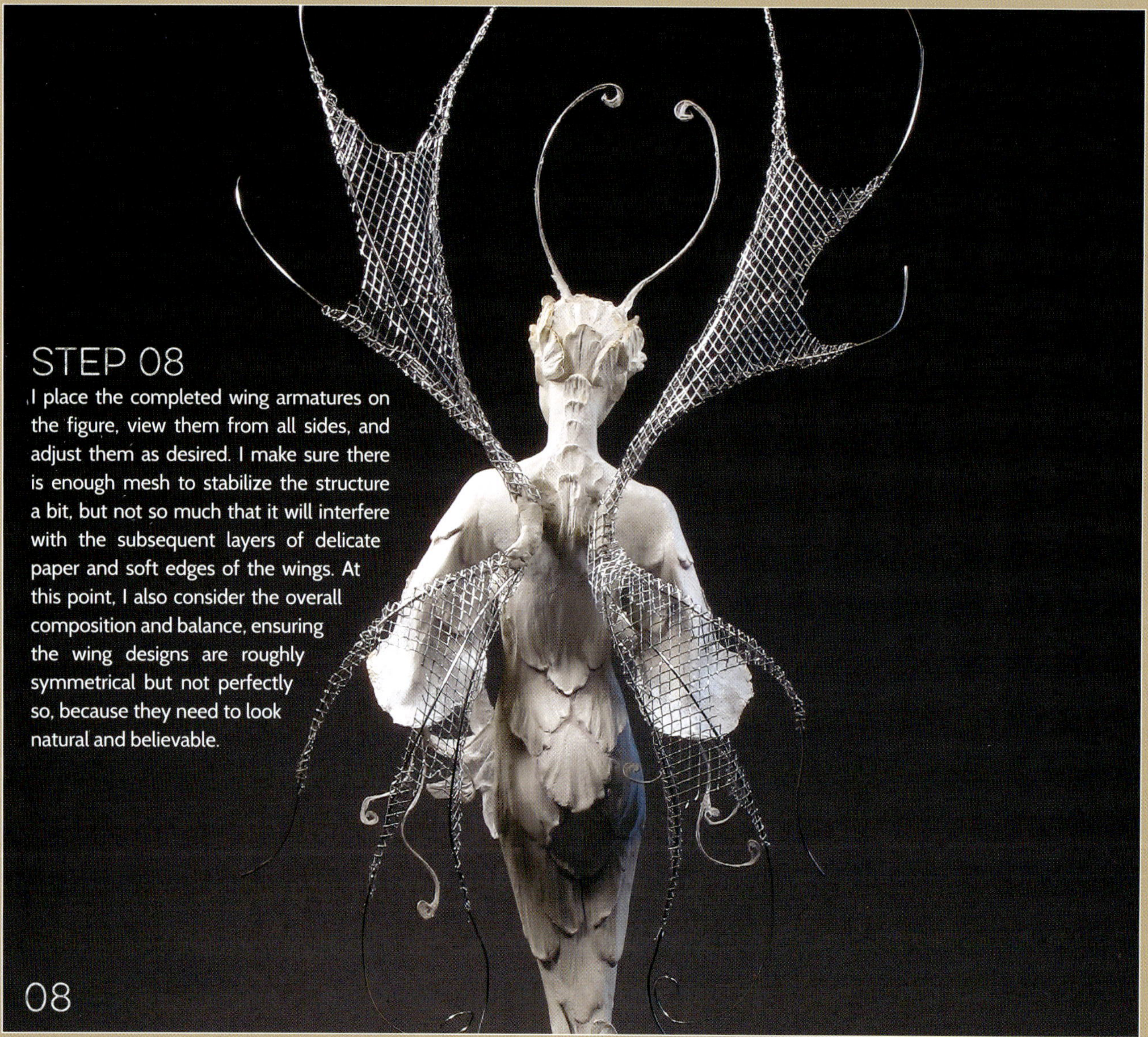

STEP 08

I place the completed wing armatures on the figure, view them from all sides, and adjust them as desired. I make sure there is enough mesh to stabilize the structure a bit, but not so much that it will interfere with the subsequent layers of delicate paper and soft edges of the wings. At this point, I also consider the overall composition and balance, ensuring the wing designs are roughly symmetrical but not perfectly so, because they need to look natural and believable.

08

STEP 09

My next step is to reinforce the wing armatures with two-part epoxy clay. I work the clay into the mesh of the more solid, central parts of the wing, and out along the main wires (09a). I leave the tips of the wings as I want them to remain extremely delicate, and I will wrap them only with paper, glue, and acrylic gel. I check the fit and look of the wing armatures on the figure (09b). I adjust the veins of epoxy clay before they are entirely set. The wings are quite three-dimensional now, with many compound curves.

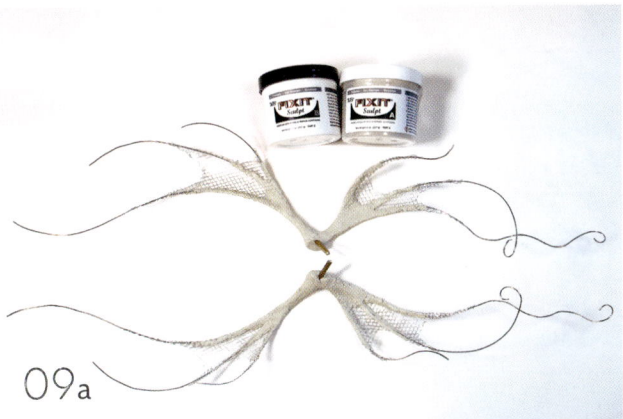

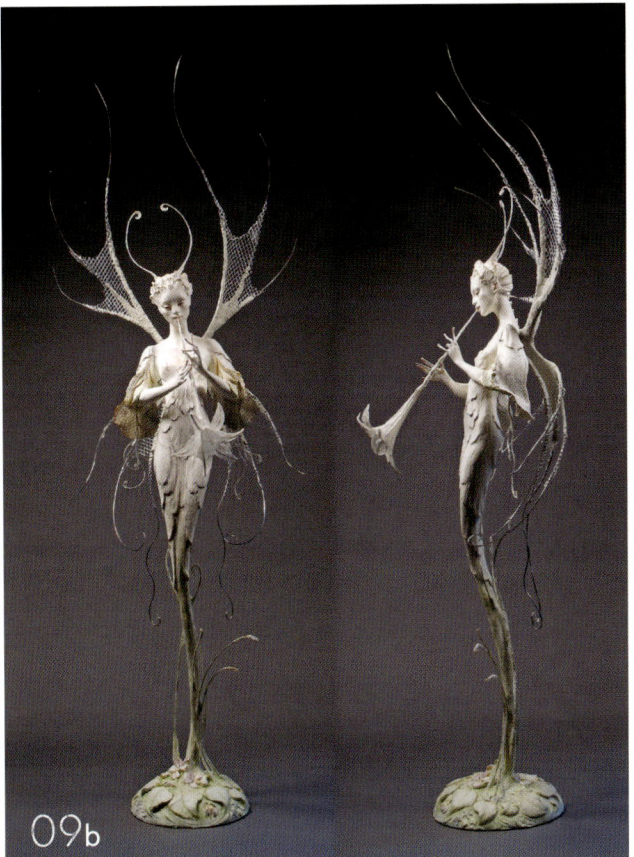

STEP 10

I wrap the wires of the armature with at least one layer of Tengucho mulberry tissue, which provides better adherence for other paper elements. I use acrylic Soft Gel Gloss medium by Golden, and allow the paper to stick to itself. I choose this medium because I am confident that it will not yellow over time, which is important for translucent white wings. I apply the gel with a silicone-tipped shaper tool.

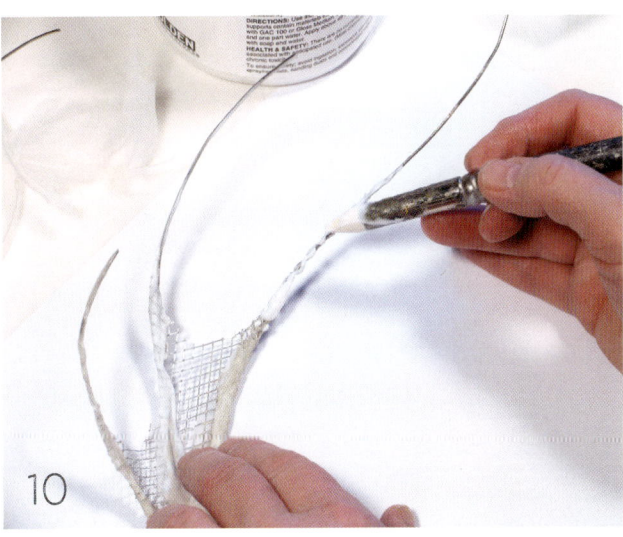

STEP 11

I apply fibrous Unryu paper over the epoxy clay portions of the armature, using Gem-Tac glue. I use glue as I am not worried about it yellowing in that area, because it will be covered with a layer of clay, or thicker paper layers. The Gem-Tac plus slightly textured Unryu will provide a good substrate for air-dry clay.

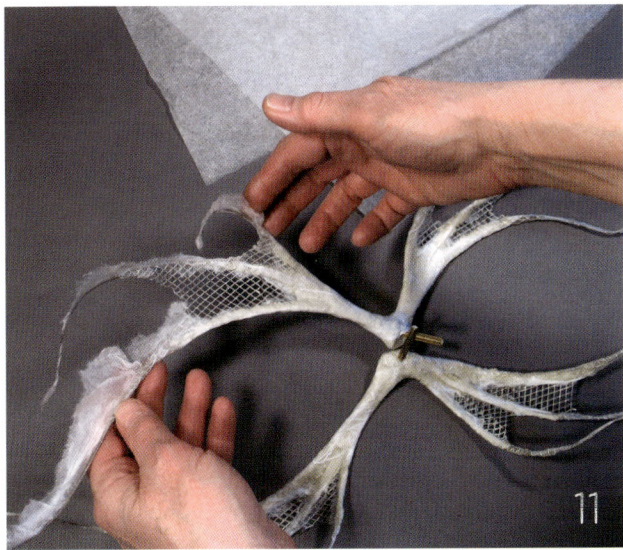

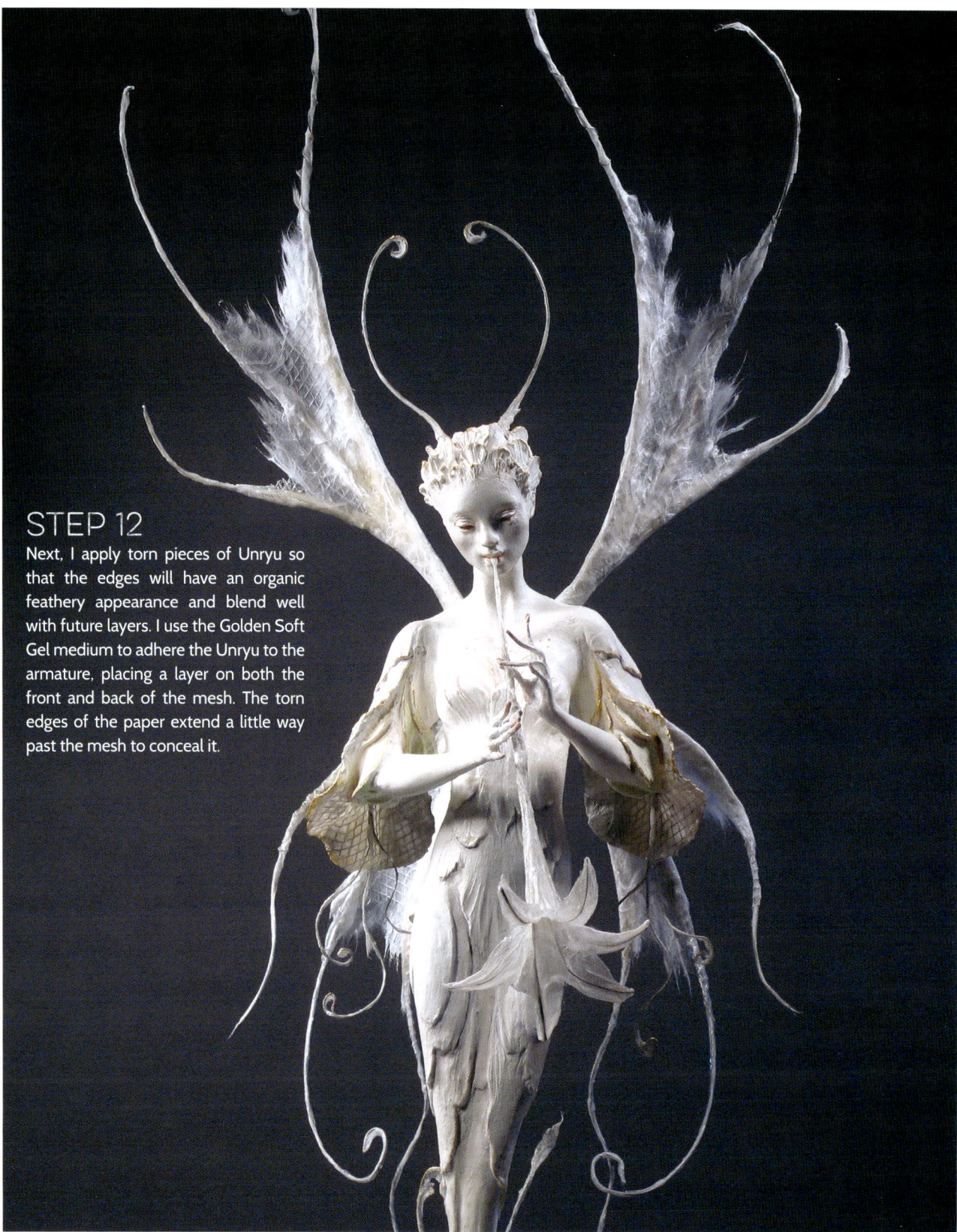

STEP 12

Next, I apply torn pieces of Unryu so that the edges will have an organic feathery appearance and blend well with future layers. I use the Golden Soft Gel medium to adhere the Unryu to the armature, placing a layer on both the front and back of the mesh. The torn edges of the paper extend a little way past the mesh to conceal it.

STEP 13

To create a sense of movement and a soft feathery effect, I "primitive pleat" Tengucho paper. Depending on the size of the project, I cut a piece perhaps 6 x 10 in, and firmly but gently twist it tightly, as shown. This can be performed more than once, if needed, or you can run the pleated paper through your hands to increase the directional crinkling and texture.

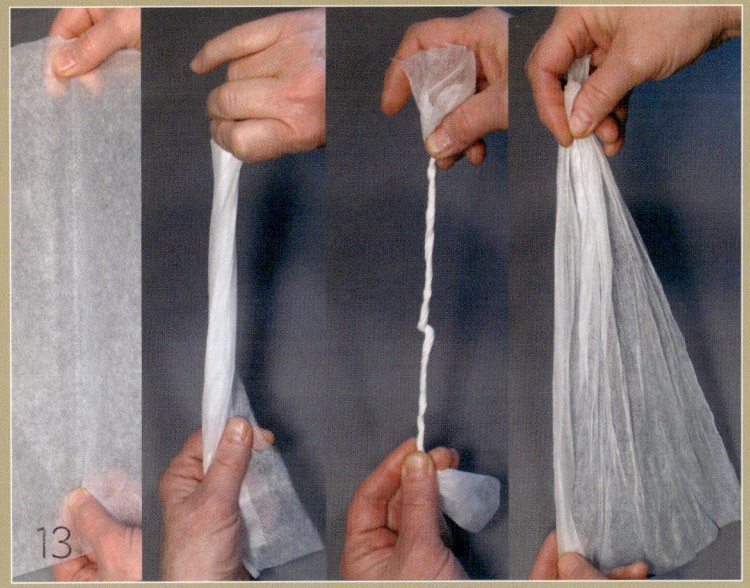

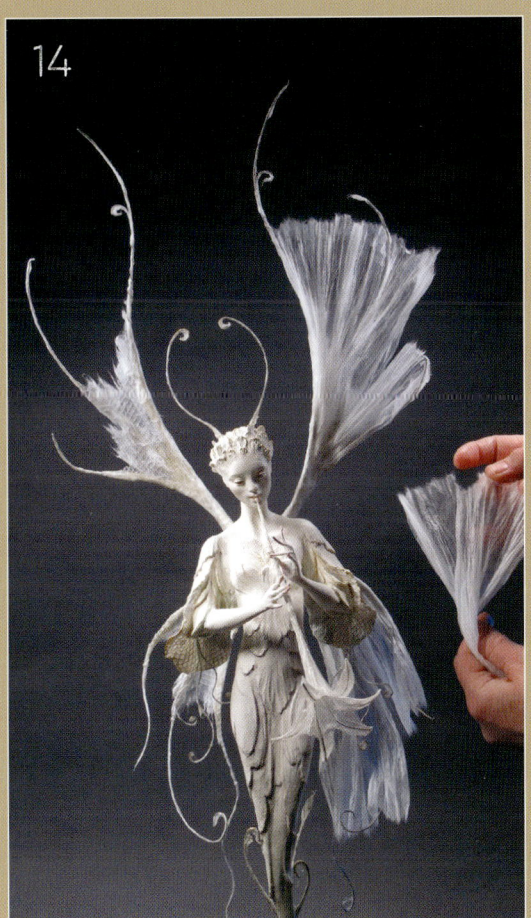

STEP 14

Pleated Tengucho paper fills out the wing. I am careful to place the pleated paper with the crinkles going in the desired direction. Before laying the paper on the wing, I cut the sides of the paper sections with scissors, but leave the edges torn where they may help form the feathery edge of the wing. I add a little curlicue along the top wire of each wing by simply twisting a fine 24-gauge stainless steel wire around the original armature and covering it with paper and acrylic gel.

STEP 15

I adjust the shape of the wings by tearing away paper edges. Then, using a small brush, I reinforce the wings with acrylic gel medium. I brush the gel into the creases, taking care not to flatten the pleating. I don't coat the entire wing in heavy gel: delicate edges can be sealed with matte acrylic varnish.

✦ TENGUCHO PAPER

Available in several different weights, (I use 9 g or 10 g), Tengucho paper is always exceptionally delicate but becomes surprisingly strong for my unconventional purposes when impregnated with an acrylic gel like Golden Soft Gel medium. In a single layer, saturated with gel medium, Tengucho can become almost transparent and good for interesting effects such as sea creature membranes or insectile wings.

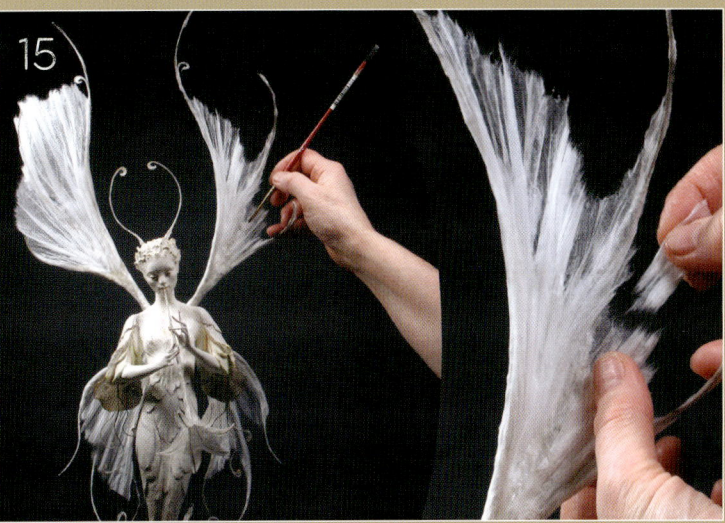

STEP 16

Fibers harvested from other interesting papers often come in handy. I tear pieces of fiber from sheer mulberry papers, picking appropriately curved pieces, and glue them down with acrylic gel medium (16a). I add feathery details along the edge of the wings near the fairy's body, for a softer look (16b). After placing the wings on the figure, I fill them out with more fibers, adding them to the front and back.

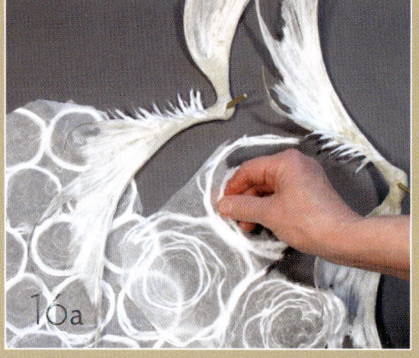

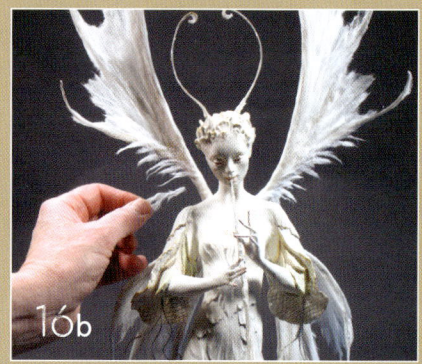

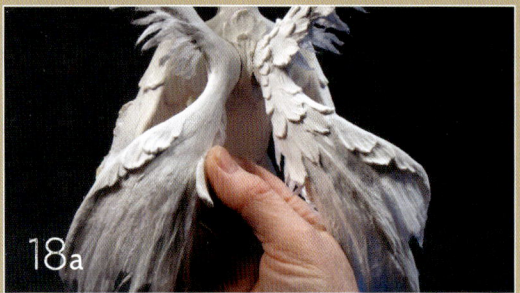

STEP 17

After most of the paper and fiber is attached and reinforced with acrylic gel, it is time to cover and detail the more solid areas of the wing. I spread Soft Gel Gloss medium as a glue for a fairly thin layer of Premier air-dry clay over the working surface. I smear the clay firmly down, and, using the acrylic gel, blend the clay into the edge of the paper portion of the wing. I let that dry.

STEP 18

I dampen the surface of the dry clay with a brush and add a layer of feather-petal forms to match those seen on the body of the fairy. I add them one by one, working from the edge of the desired area in toward the center in rows (18a). I allow the outer edges to remain dimensional, while firmly smoothing the inner edge into the base layer of clay. I shape them with a flat, stiff paintbrush and small burnishing tool (18b). I wet the brush occasionally to keep the clay surface malleable. I like the directional texture brushing imparts, and I accentuate it with my other sculpting tools.

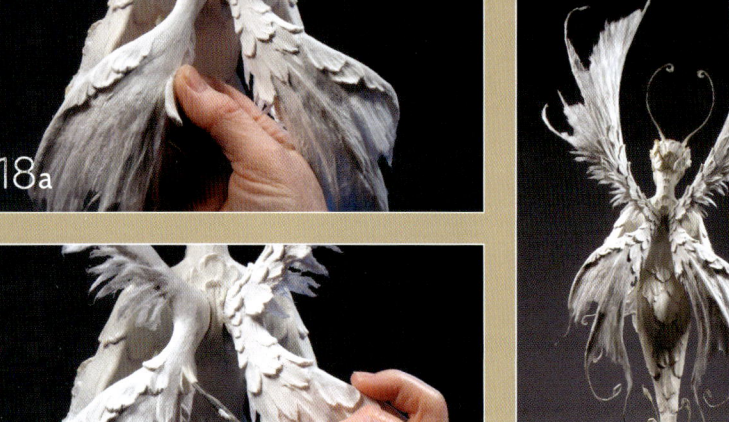

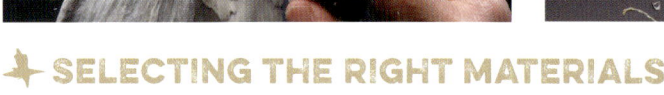

🦋 SELECTING THE RIGHT MATERIALS

Padico's Premier is my favorite air-dry clay, because it's smooth, lightweight and, if used over a properly constructed armature, strong. It feels to me like a material on its own terms, and not like a would-be ceramic. It combines well with paper techniques. I work in polymer and air-dry, and have created pieces that include both. I believe the difference between polymer clay and air-dry clay is rather like oil paint versus fresco or watercolor. Techniques vary due to the way the material handles, dries, or cures. Keep in mind there is a some shrinkage with air-dry clays, though I find the Premier shrinks minimally, probably because it's not a very wet clay.

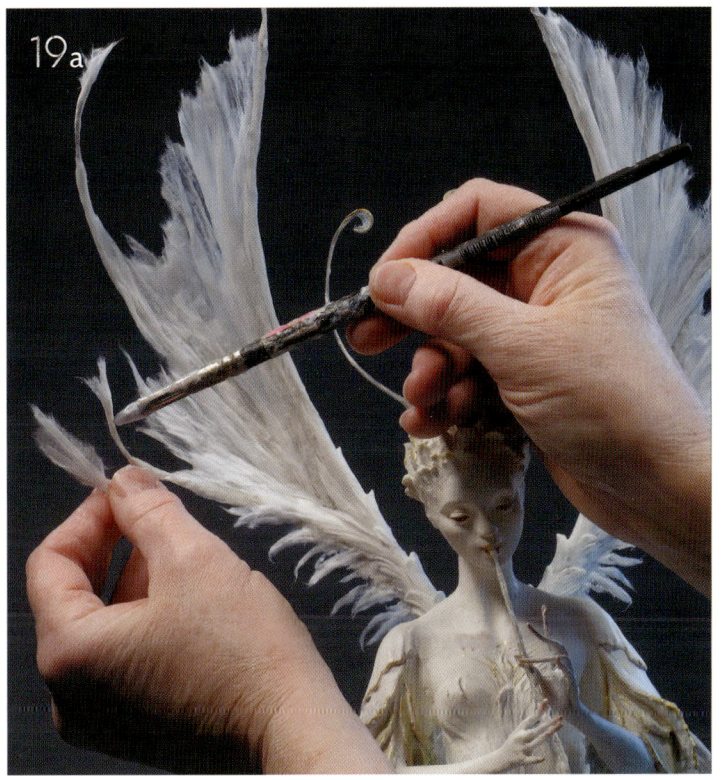

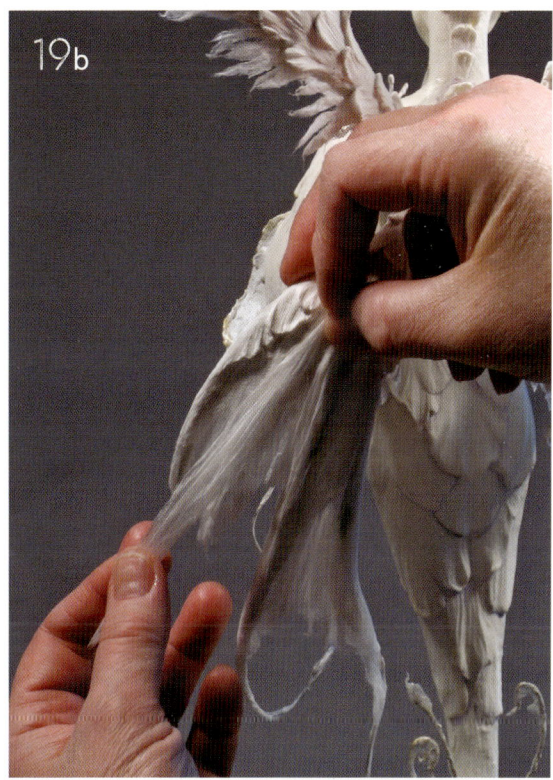

STEP 19

This mixed-media process is quite forgiving. Even at this late stage in the production, I can change or mend things to add and subtract. I add tufts of wispy pleated Tengucho paper to the ends of wing wires (19a) and apply more pleated tissue where there are spots that were flattened when I brushed on my reinforcing acrylic gel medium (19b). I also re-wet the surface of the Premier clay and use a rake tool to refine its shape and texture.

STEP 20

Lastly, I apply a mix of two parts Golden Soft Gel Gloss to one part water to the surface of the clay (20a). I use matte acrylic varnish to seal the paper portion of the wings, being careful not to flatten the texture. After the surface is sealed and completely dry, I tint the piece with translucent acrylic paints or inks. Fan brushes and soft, small "graining" brushes with a feathered edge are useful for gentle blending (20b). For a final seal, I often apply a mix of matte and satin acrylic varnish to get a soft sheen. I sometimes use varied sheen varnishes on the same piece, to get a particular effect.

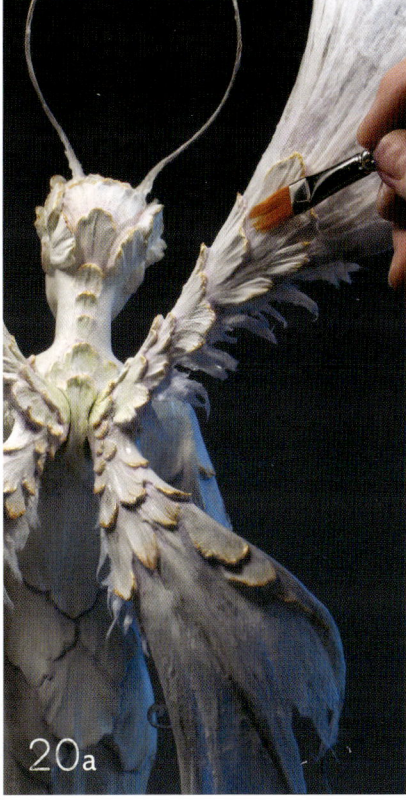

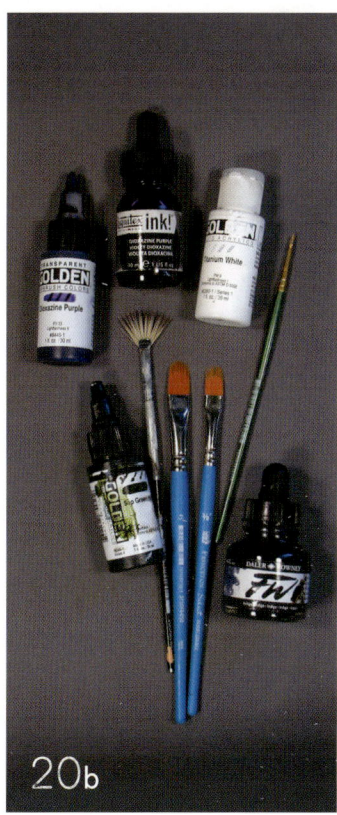

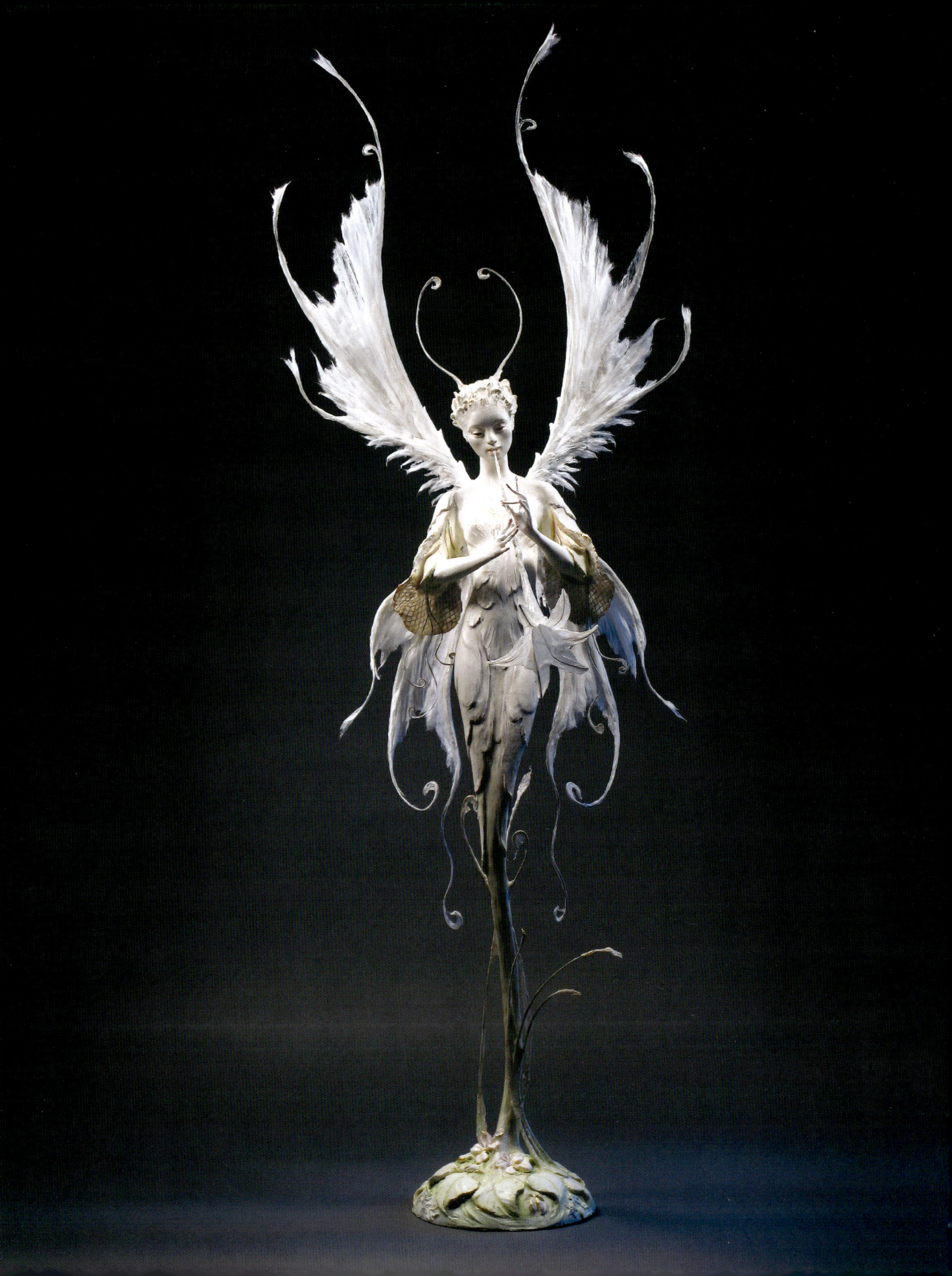

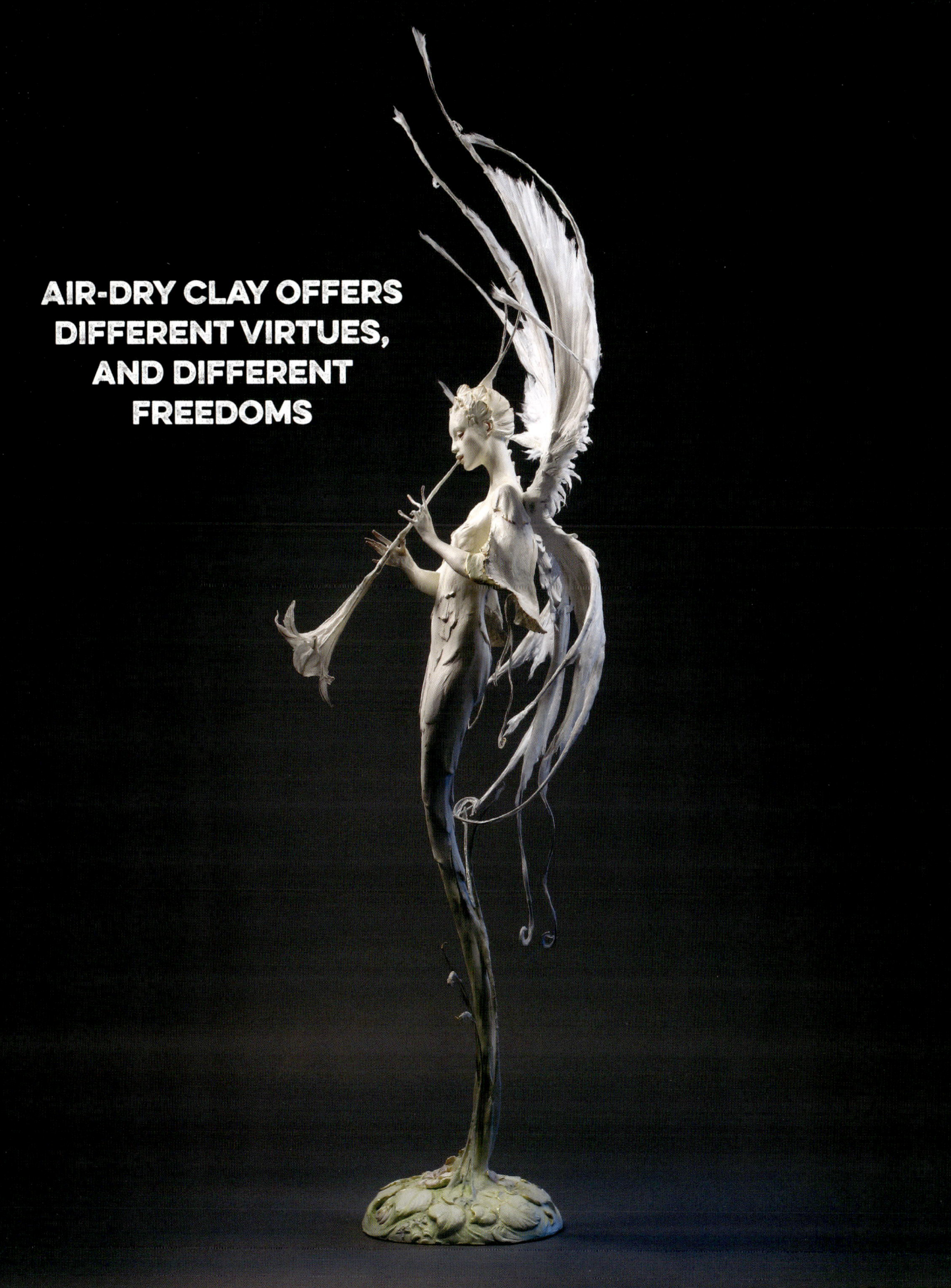

AIR-DRY CLAY OFFERS
DIFFERENT VIRTUES,
AND DIFFERENT
FREEDOMS

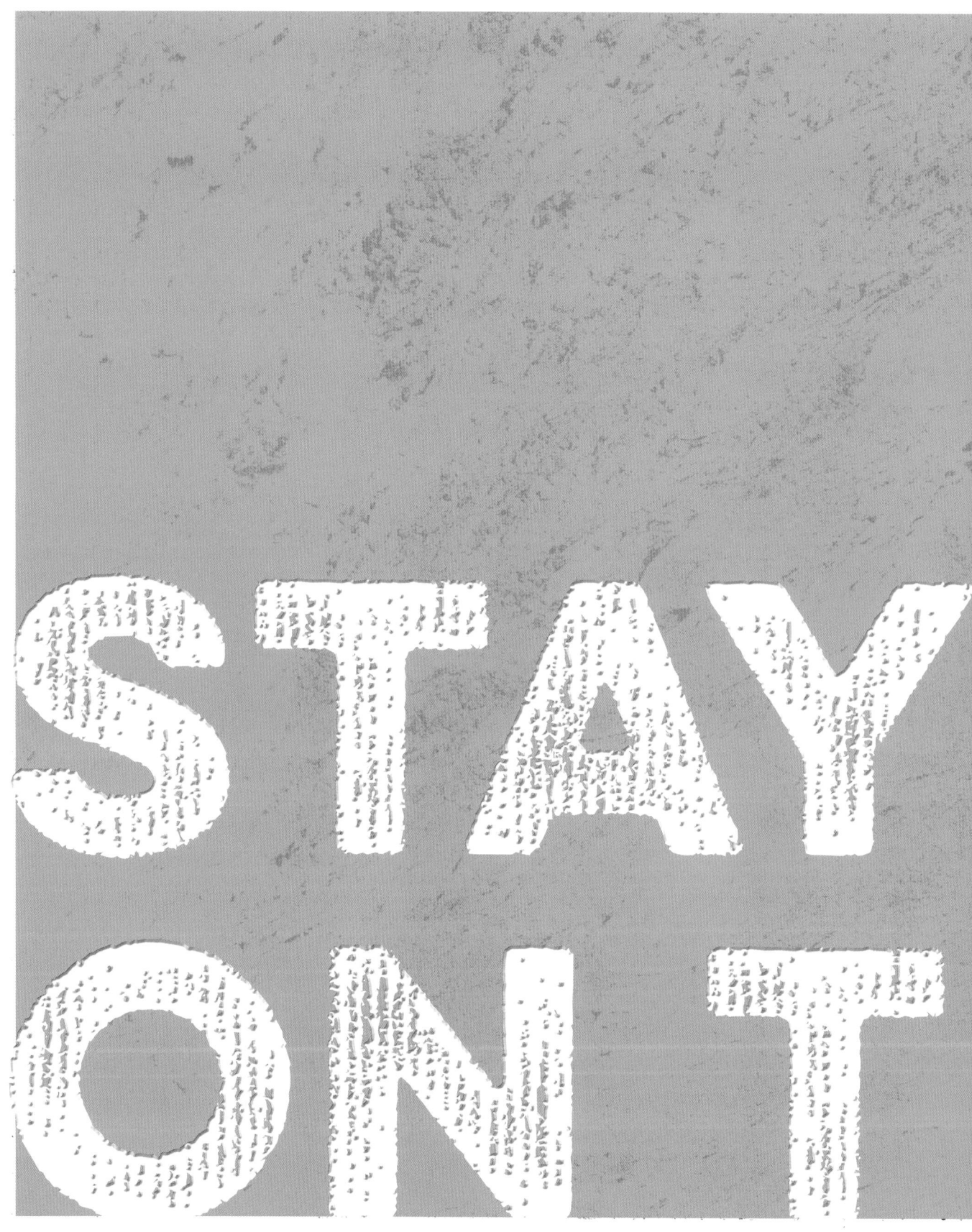

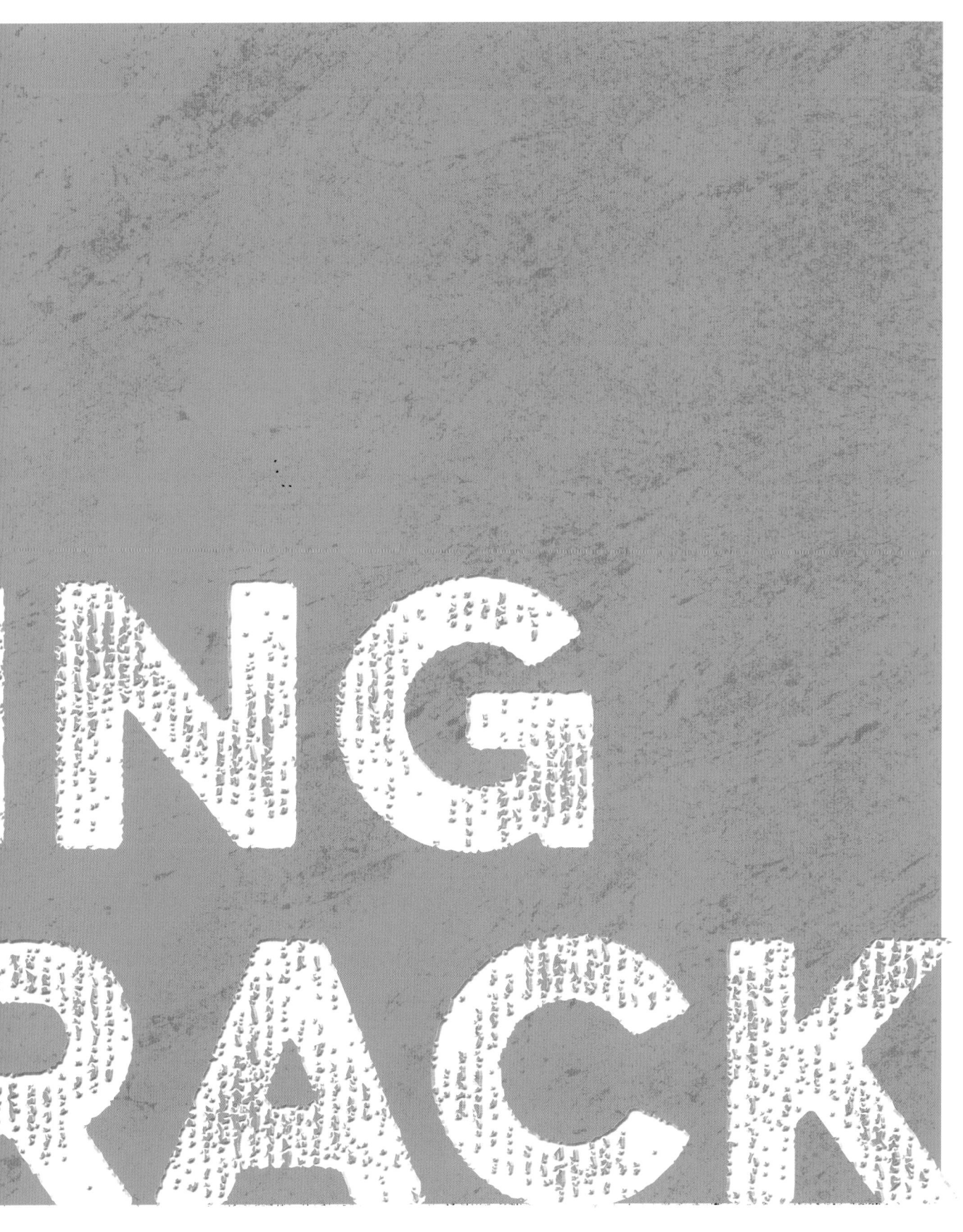

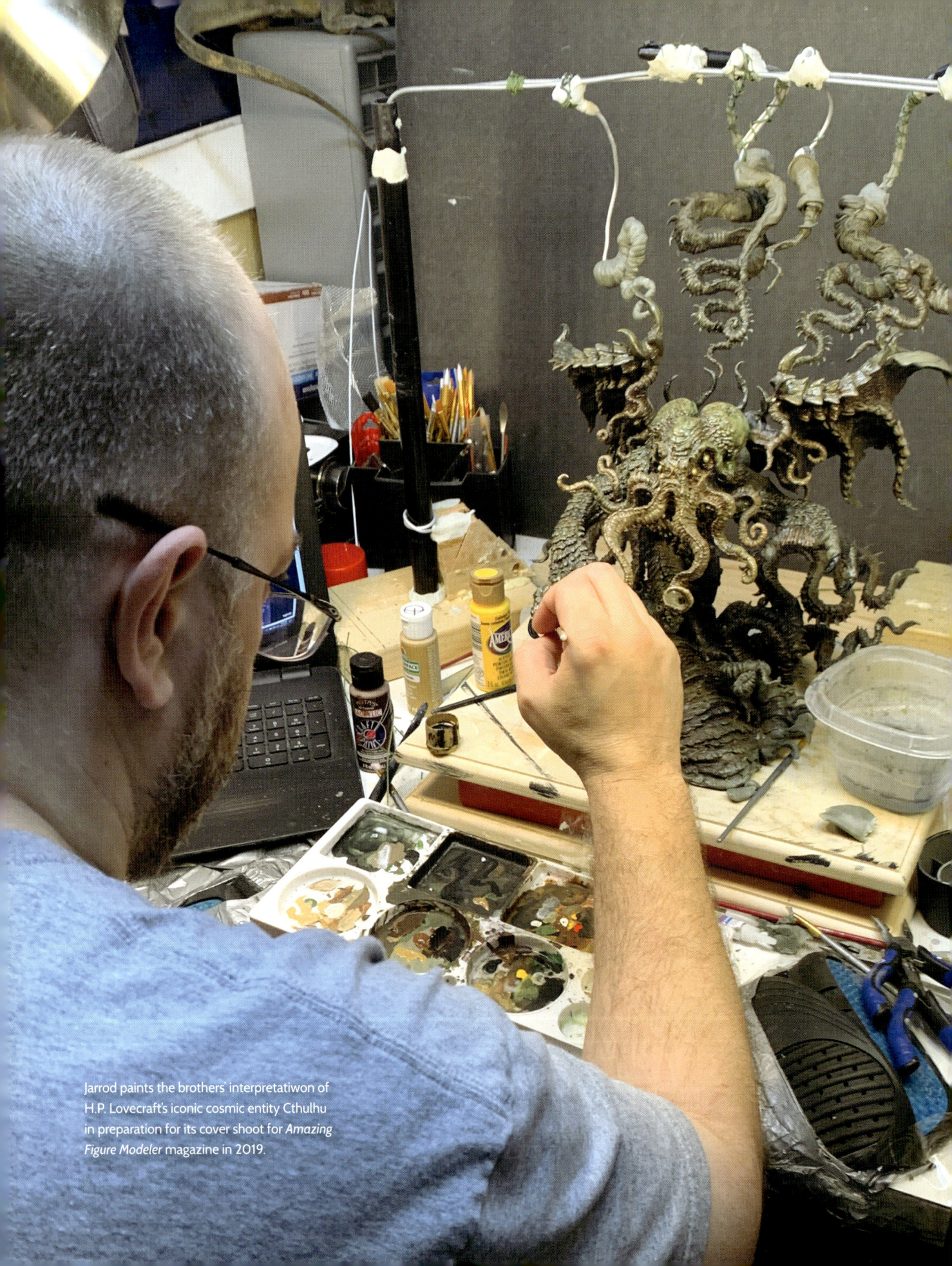

Jarrod paints the brothers' interpretatiwon of
H.P. Lovecraft's iconic cosmic entity Cthulhu
in preparation for its cover shoot for *Amazing
Figure Modeler* magazine in 2019.

TROUBLESHOOTING

One thing we always keep in mind while working is the idea that "if we made it, we can fix it." Often, when a piece develops a problem, whether an armature wire in an inconvenient place, or a crack developing in the clay, novice sculptors tend to throw their hands up in a state of despair.

Just remember: it can be repaired; all is not lost!

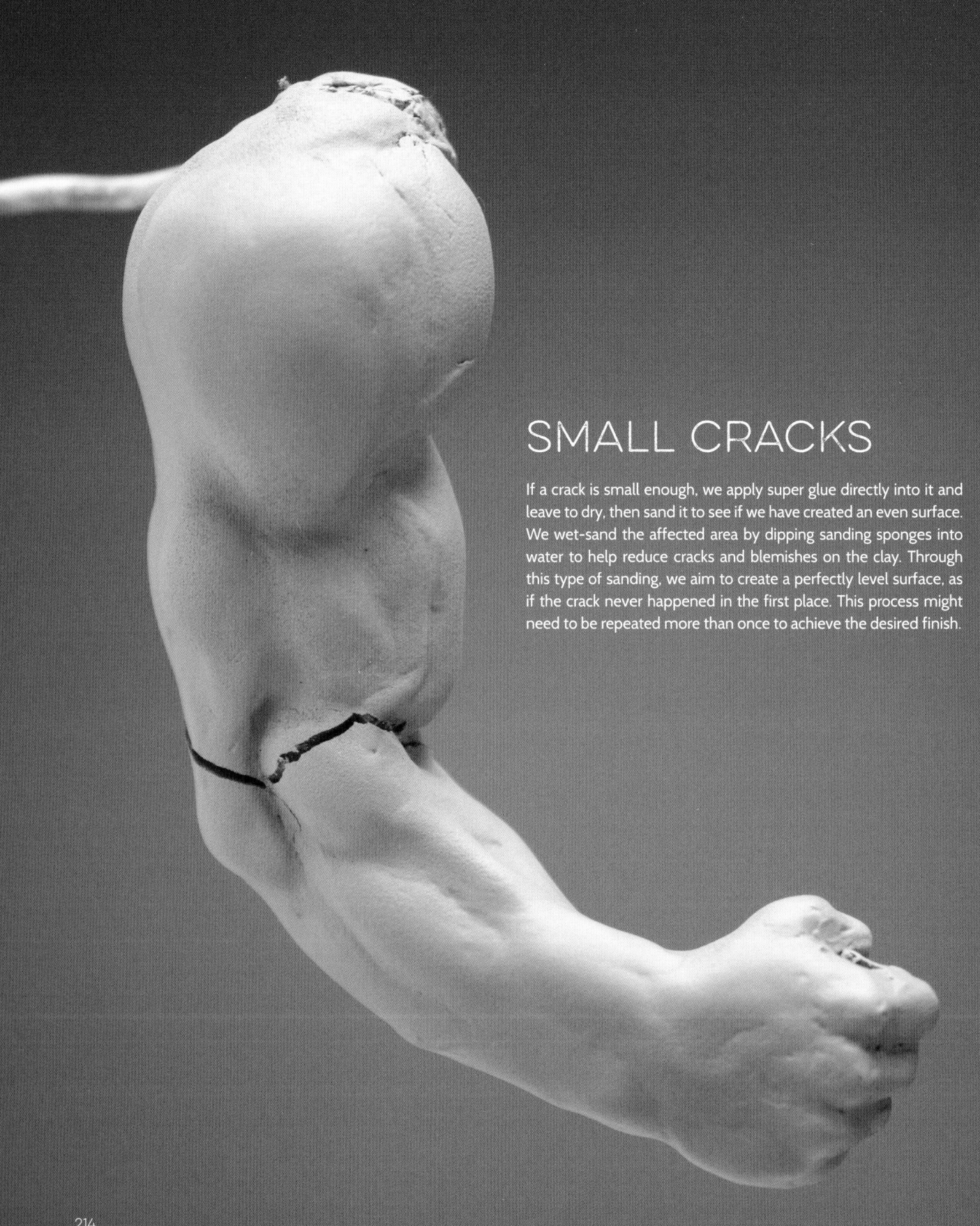

SMALL CRACKS

If a crack is small enough, we apply super glue directly into it and leave to dry, then sand it to see if we have created an even surface. We wet-sand the affected area by dipping sanding sponges into water to help reduce cracks and blemishes on the clay. Through this type of sanding, we aim to create a perfectly level surface, as if the crack never happened in the first place. This process might need to be repeated more than once to achieve the desired finish.

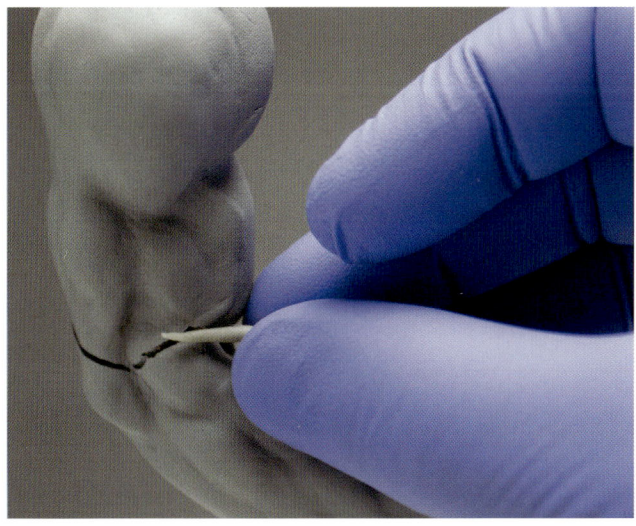

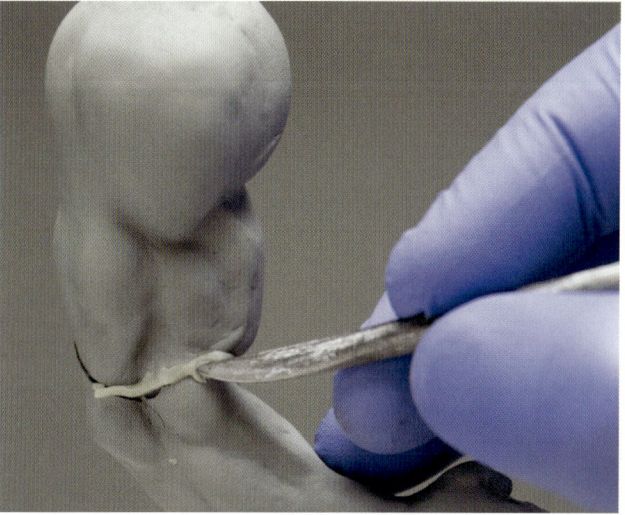

LARGE CRACKS

For larger crevices, we employ plumber's putty, a two-part epoxy mentioned in our tools breakdown on page 52. Once mixed together, the resulting material will become hard and durable, and therefore unworkable, in only a few minutes. Moving quickly and planning where and how you want to use it before you begin mixing it is mandatory.

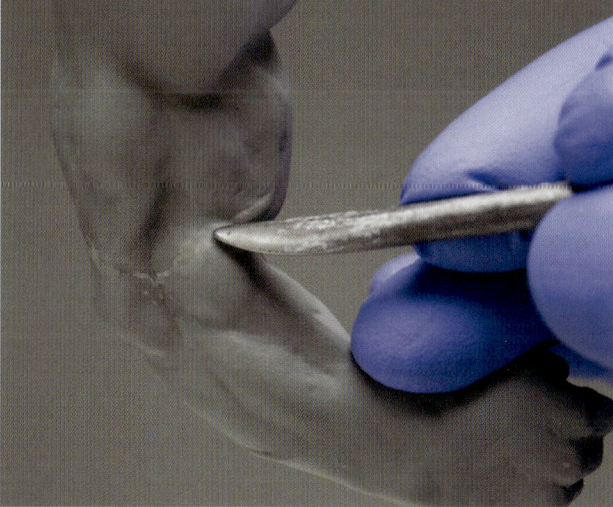

We aim to create a relatively level surface on the piece by filling the plumber's putty to the same height as the two sides of the crack. Then, as with the super glue process, after the putty is hardened, we wet-sand the area to redefine the smooth surface.

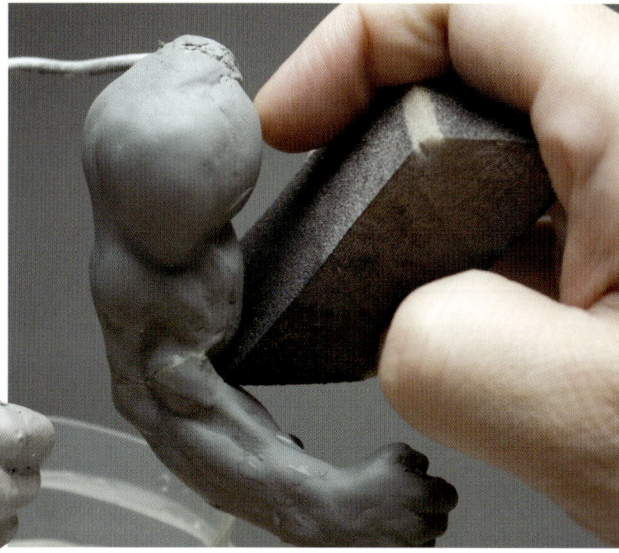

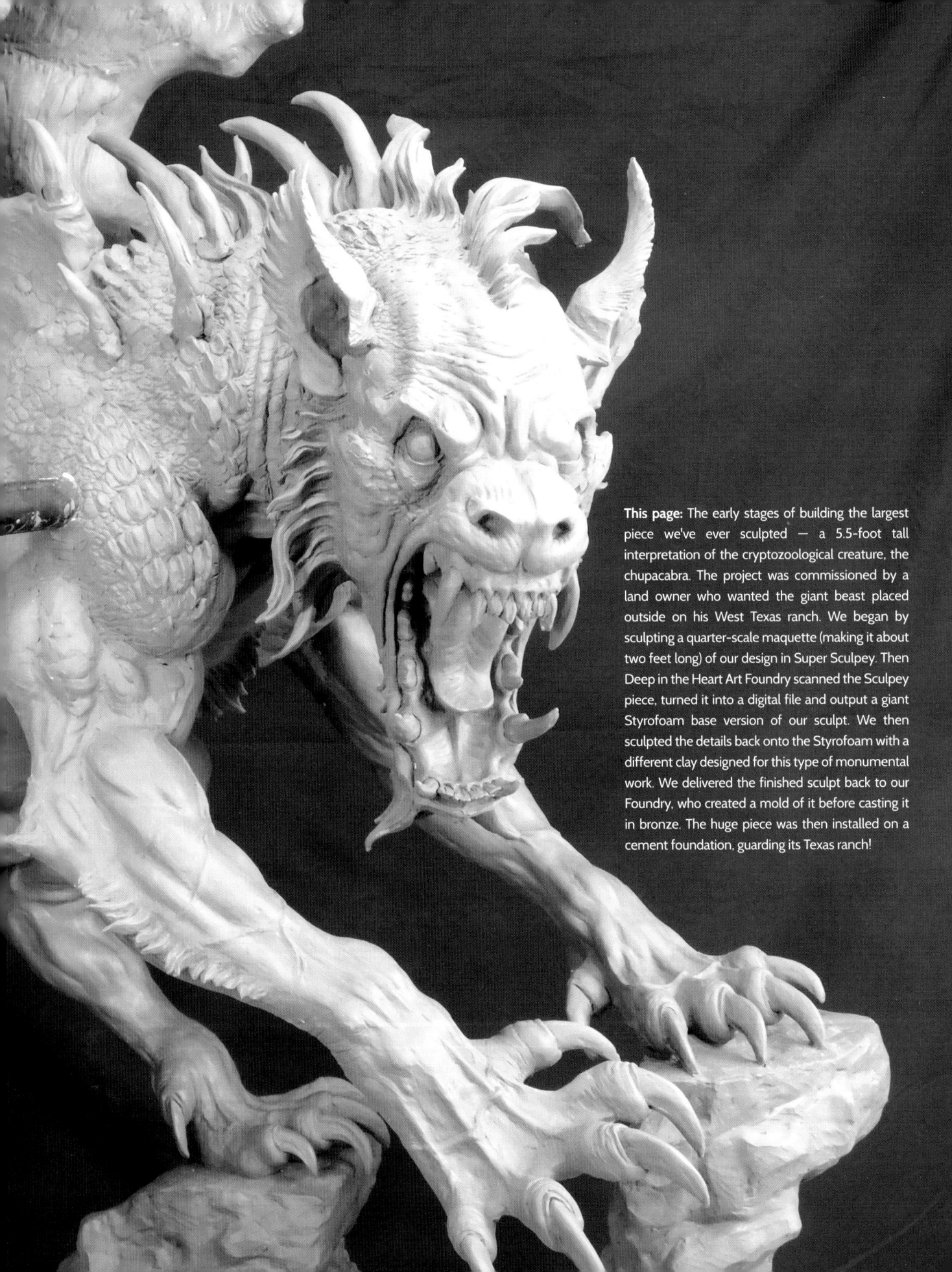

This page: The early stages of building the largest piece we've ever sculpted — a 5.5-foot tall interpretation of the cryptozoological creature, the chupacabra. The project was commissioned by a land owner who wanted the giant beast placed outside on his West Texas ranch. We began by sculpting a quarter-scale maquette (making it about two feet long) of our design in Super Sculpey. Then Deep in the Heart Art Foundry scanned the Sculpey piece, turned it into a digital file and output a giant Styrofoam base version of our sculpt. We then sculpted the details back onto the Styrofoam with a different clay designed for this type of monumental work. We delivered the finished sculpt back to our Foundry, who created a mold of it before casting it in bronze. The huge piece was then installed on a cement foundation, guarding its Texas ranch!

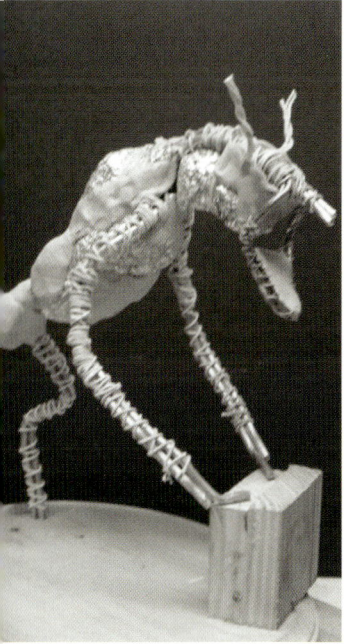
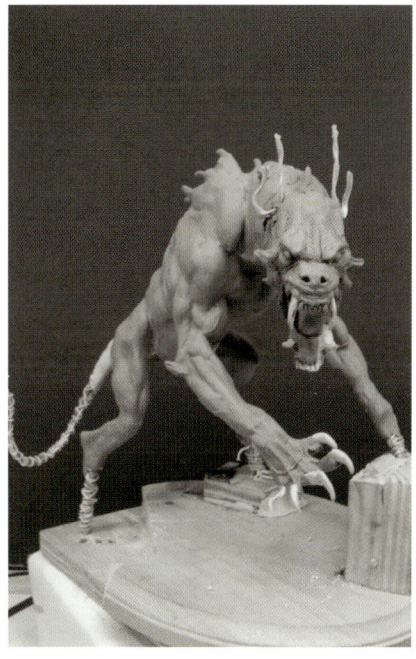

KEEP IT IN PROPORTION

Sometimes our proportions might appear to be inaccurate, for instance when the lengths of the limbs on a human sculpture are anatomically incorrect. We always advise leaving a little extra length when creating the arms, legs, and fingers during the armature process for a human figure. The armature might look a little strange with overly long arms at one stage and overly long fingers at another stage, but cutting off extra length is much, much easier than adding length later on in the making process. The extra length allows room for precise adjustments.

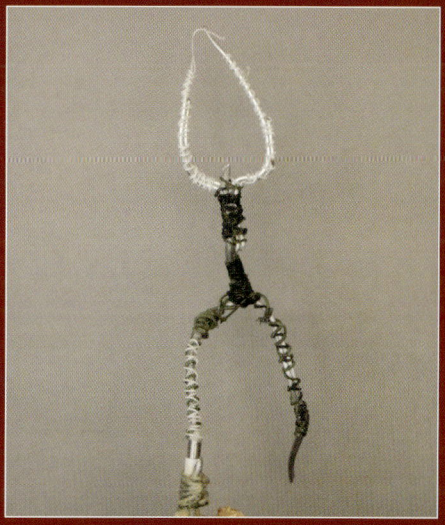

STRONG BASE LINE

We prefer the armature for our sculptures to feel sturdy, stable, and secure. We see so many amateurs (and even some good professionals!) create bendy, flimsy armatures, and we have no idea how they work comfortably on a piece when a tool pressing against it moves a whole limb or section of the sculpture. We need a solid base on which to work, so immediately take action if we feel an armature or section of an armature bending or moving under the sculpture. Even if it means we need to remove clay, we will revisit the framework and add plumber's putty to the joints in the weak areas.

No part of any sculpture ever has so much clay work done on it that we won't perform surgery to fortify an armature! And of course, this will help later on in the making process when baking the piece – a stronger armature holding the weight of the clay greatly reduces the chances of cracks and breaks.

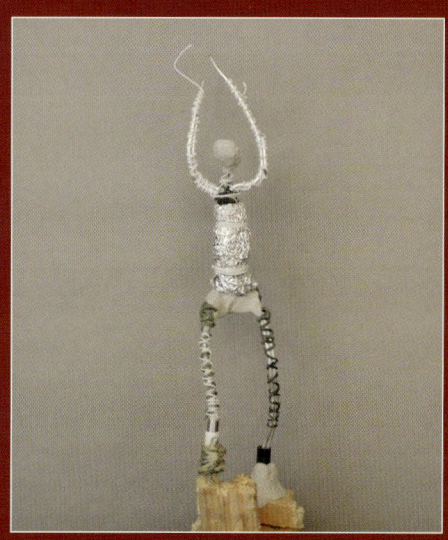

Above and right: The chupacabra at different stages of the production process. A strong base armature was important to the integrity of the piece.

PRESERVING IMPORTANT DETAILS

Another problem many sculptors encounter is sculpting and refining a key detail, such as a face, then finding it has been inadvertently altered. This can happen due to accidental touches or even small pieces of intentional work that change the look of the face more than the sculptor wanted — we sometimes hear the cries of "it was great ten minutes ago, but now it's gone!" In digital sculpting, the "undo" function will ensure the piece reverts to a previous form of the sculpture, but it's not as easy with clay.

One tool we do have in our arsenal is this piece of process trickery: when we feel that we have finished a face and we worry about losing it, we mask the rest of the sculpture with aluminum foil and use a heat gun to bake and harden the face, leaving the rest of the sculpture soft and malleable. Remember to use heat guns very conservatively around your sculptures! It's better in the long run to underbake than overbake. This method can be used on any part of the sculpture that needs to be preserved and "locked in."

REMEMBER TO USE HEAT GUNS VERY CONSERVATIVELY

WAYWARD WIRES

Sometimes we discover armature or pieces of wire are visible where they shouldn't be. This was a much bigger problem when we were young sculptors; the experience would trouble us greatly. Over time our mindset has changed and we've learned to be less bothered about having to delve into the core structure of the sculpture to fix fundamental skeletal form problems, even if it seems to be taking us one or two steps backward at the time.

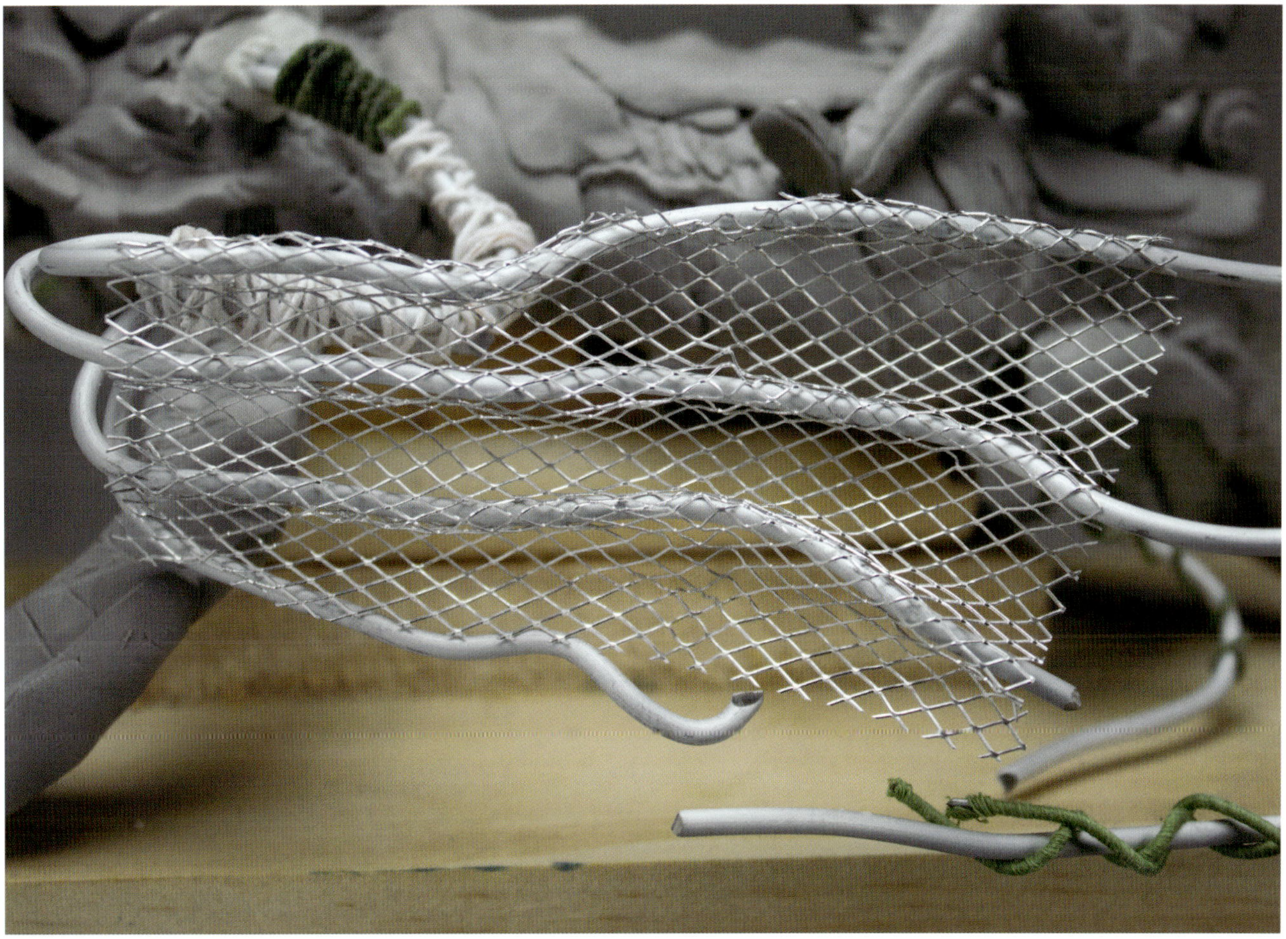

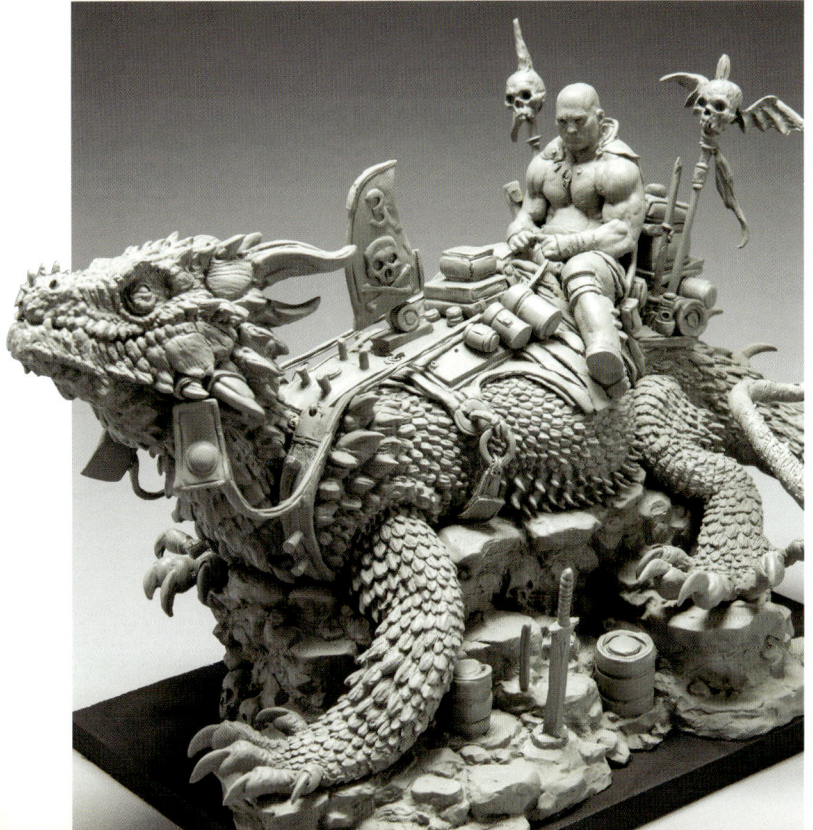

TRIAL AND ERROR

Our process is always one of trial and error, and here's a great example. The above photo was taken of the work-in-progress *The Pirate King* sculpture featured left and on pages 132-153. We had an idea to add wings to this huge dragon, and began building them out of armature wire, floral wire, and wire mesh. Like other parts of the sculpture, they were removable. However, we quickly realized that the wings, in the only good position to put them, blocked too much of the main body of our piece. They just didn't work out compositionally, and so we had to remove them completely. It's always worth being open-minded about your design and not being too set on a specific concept in order to get the most from your sculpture.

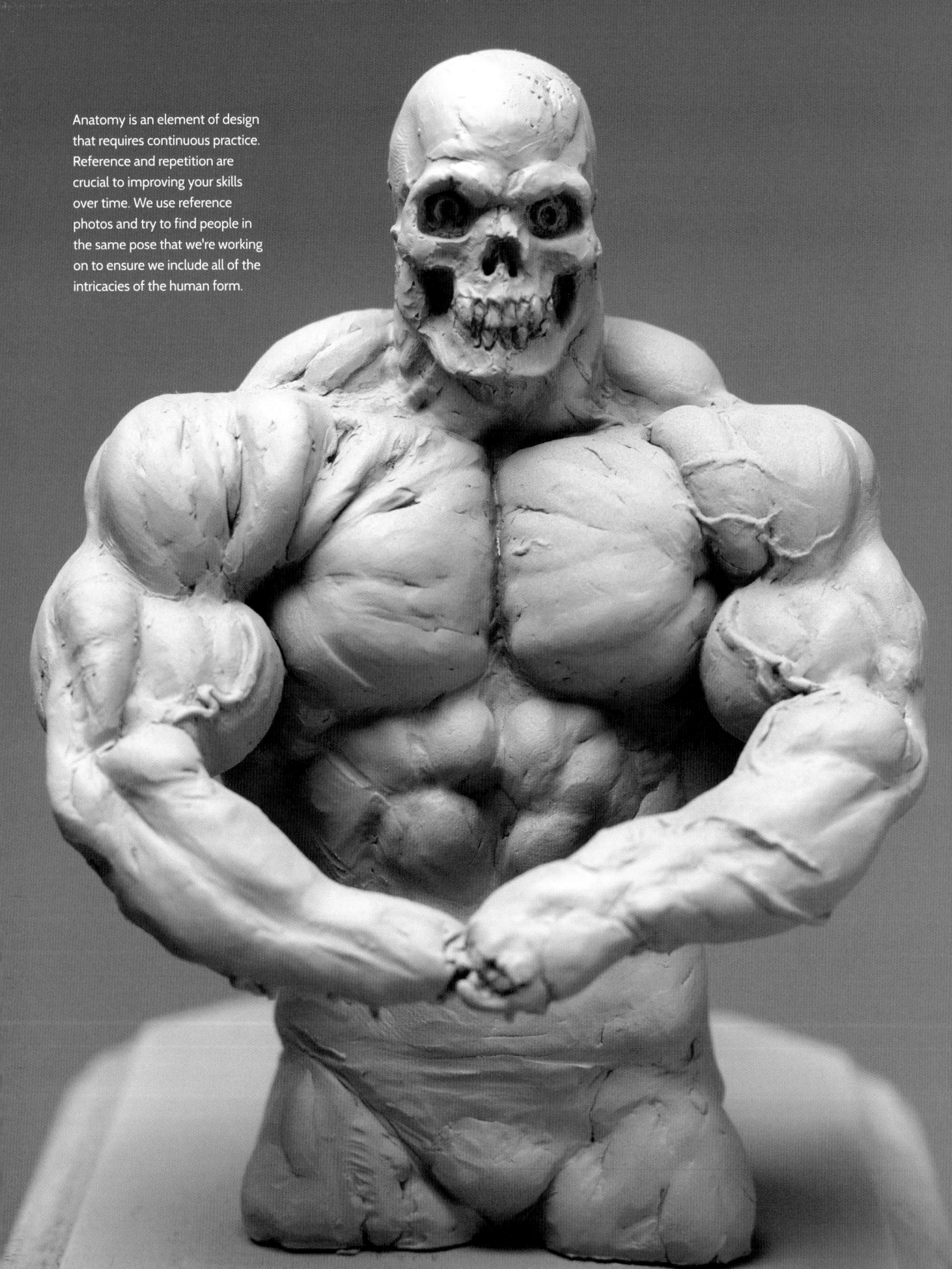

Anatomy is an element of design that requires continuous practice. Reference and repetition are crucial to improving your skills over time. We use reference photos and try to find people in the same pose that we're working on to ensure we include all of the intricacies of the human form.

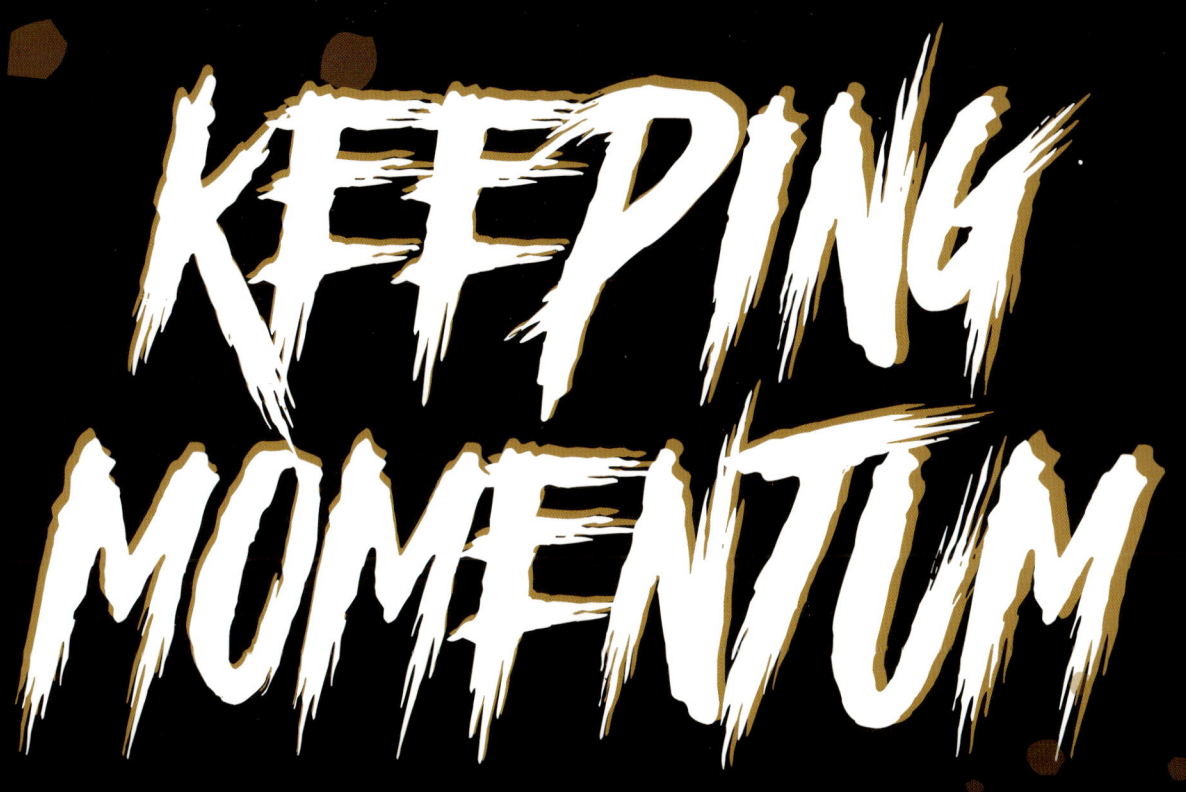

KEEPING MOMENTUM

Motivation and inspiration can be integral to success when sculpting or creating any kind of art, but the truth is, we don't sculpt *only* when we feel motivated. That might mean that we would go weeks or months without sculpting. And that wouldn't do at all!

Instead, we sit and work even when motivation and inspiration are lacking. Sculpting is a job like any other, where you need to put in the time and try to work to the best of your ability. We spend anywhere from 150–225 hours on most of our individual pieces. We know that sounds like a lot. In fact, many beginners come up to us at conventions to show us their work and ask, "Why doesn't my sculpture look like yours?" When we ask how long they've worked on the piece they'll tell us six hours or twelve hours. And we get it! Not everybody can put 100 hours into a piece, not everybody has that kind of time. But we *do* have that time and we're just neurotic enough to sit at the table that long!

We believe the longer you sit with your hands and tools touching the piece, the more chance you have of success. Often, we will work on a piece for five or six hours and not see any positive progress until hour seven or eight. Progress isn't always as predictable in art as we would wish it to be; it can sometimes come at any time, hence the need to be ready, sitting in our chairs with our hands on the piece as much as possible. Sometimes we tell ourselves, "Less thinking, more sculpting." This means that sitting around and thinking about the sculpture (something we do more than we'd like to admit) won't make it better. Only hands in action can change and improve the piece.

When inspiration hits extremely low points for us, we always look at art that inspires us. This practice can get us excited about the medium again and jumpstart our creative thoughts. Often, we dig

WE COULDN'T QUIT SCULPTING IF WE WANTED TO — A DRIVE TO DO WHAT WE DO EXISTS INSIDE US

into fantasy-art compilation books and find the entire run of *Spectrum: The Best in Contemporary Fantasy Art* edited by Arnie and Cathy Fenner and John Fleskes to be an invaluable resource for our industry and chosen genre. We also study work from the old masters such as Bernini and Michelangelo, and check out the work of our peers in the industry. We don't only focus on sculptural work — we devour paintings and drawings too, especially those in our genre. But we always seem to return to the work of the genre masters who inspired us originally, including Frazetta, Moebius, Jeffrey Catherine Jones, and dozens of other comic book and fantasy illustrators.

Another huge boost of creative energy and enthusiasm for sculpting comes from attending shows and conventions, and meeting people who appreciate our work, whether they were

familiar with us before discovering our booth or not. Because so much of the work we do is created alone in a room with little-to-no feedback (except between the two of us), events where we are able to get our work out into the world and then see, hear, and feel responses to it can be very exciting. It is a positive experience that we use to fuel our momentum for many months after. Even just attending one of these shows where we are around like-minded people can have a huge positive impact on our workflow.

In recent years, networking with our friends, peers, and fellow sculptors has been made all the easier by the internet. On Facebook, we host the Shiflett Brothers' Sculpting Forum, which boasts over 40,000 members, professionals, and amateurs alike, all trading tips and tricks, and showing their work. The group-mind aspect of places like this is wonderful, as there is essentially no question about the process — the nuts and bolts of sculpting — that goes unanswered. There's always somebody who knows the answer! And when you need instant feedback, you can post an image of the problem area of your piece and receive caring and honest advice on how you might make it better. We have similar networks of like-minded artists on Twitter, Instagram, and other platforms as well. We find Instagram to be particularly valuable because it is a photo-based app and, after all, we are in a very visual field. We have lots of fun engaging with people who enjoy our stuff, but also love just seeing the work of so many other incredible artists.

Lastly, for us, is the motivation of earning a living. It is an unwelcome reality in our world that we have to make money just to keep the studio lights on and food on our tables, but this has never been our governing reason for choosing to do the jobs we do or sculpting the sculptures that we sculpt. If we had an office job that made us lots of money, we would still be coming home at night and sculpting in our free time. We couldn't quit sculpting if we wanted to — a drive to do what we do exists inside us. However, we do have to keep in mind that we need to keep making money at this endeavor to survive. So, when all else fails, we think to ourselves, "this piece could make us some money so, motivated or not, let's sit our butts down in the chairs and get to work!"

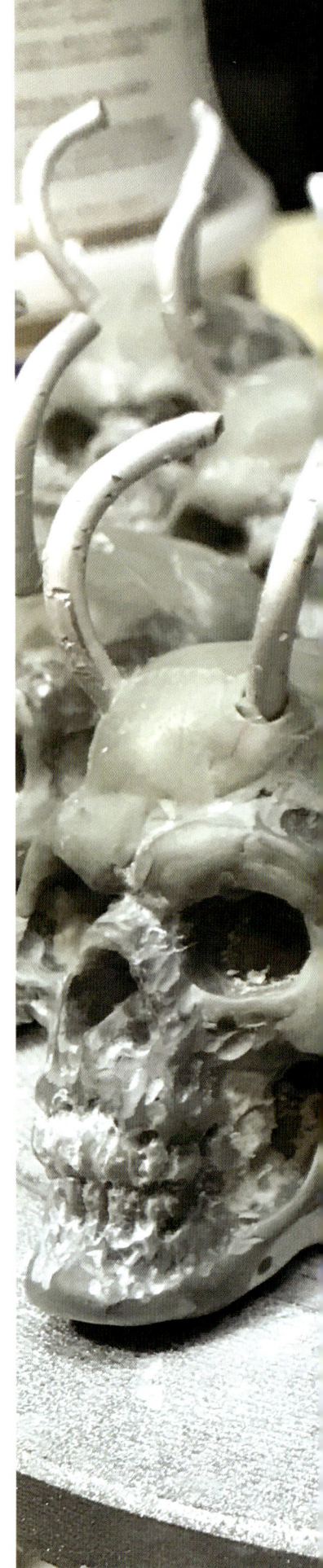

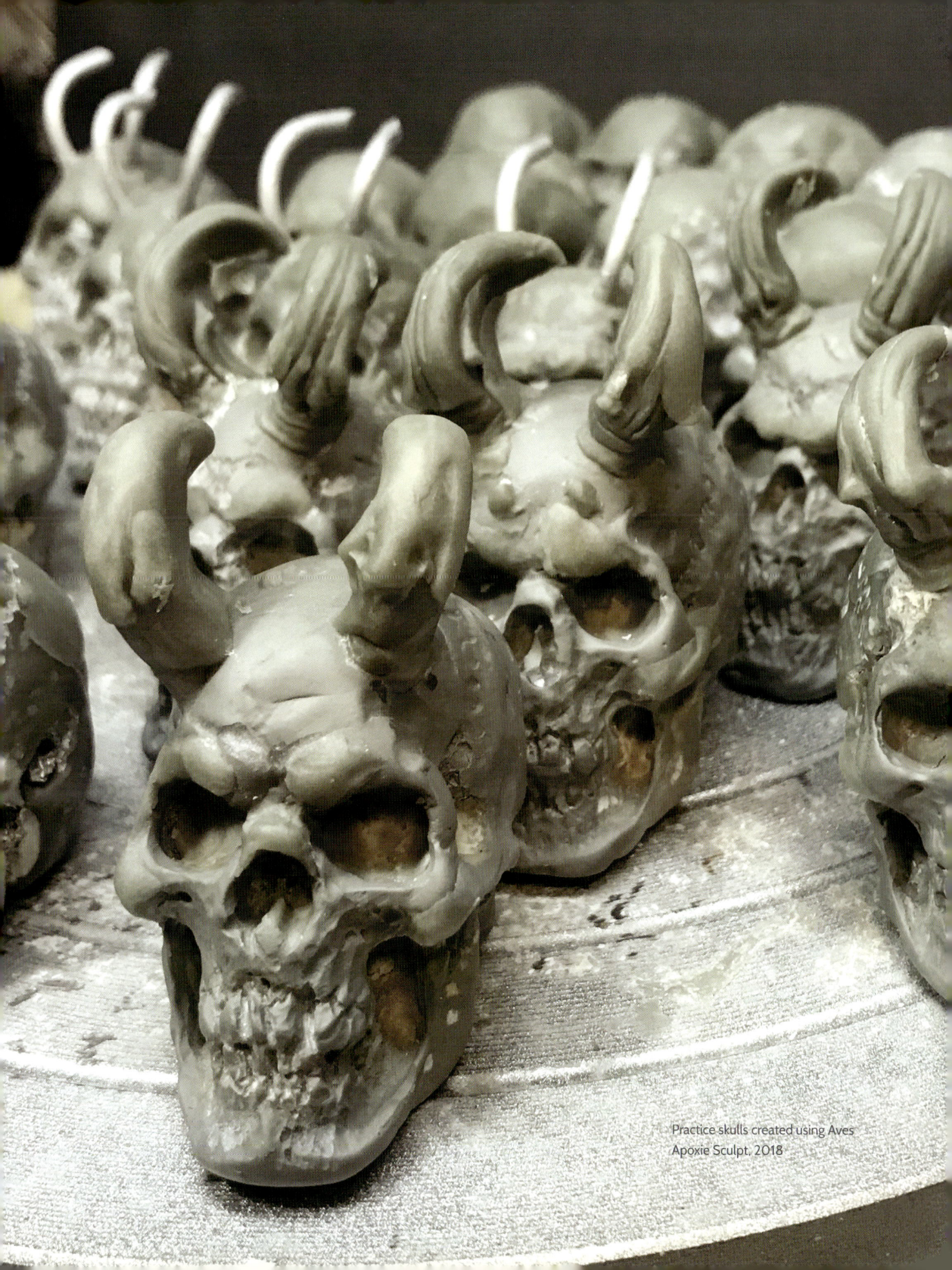

Practice skulls created using Aves
Apoxie Sculpt, 2018

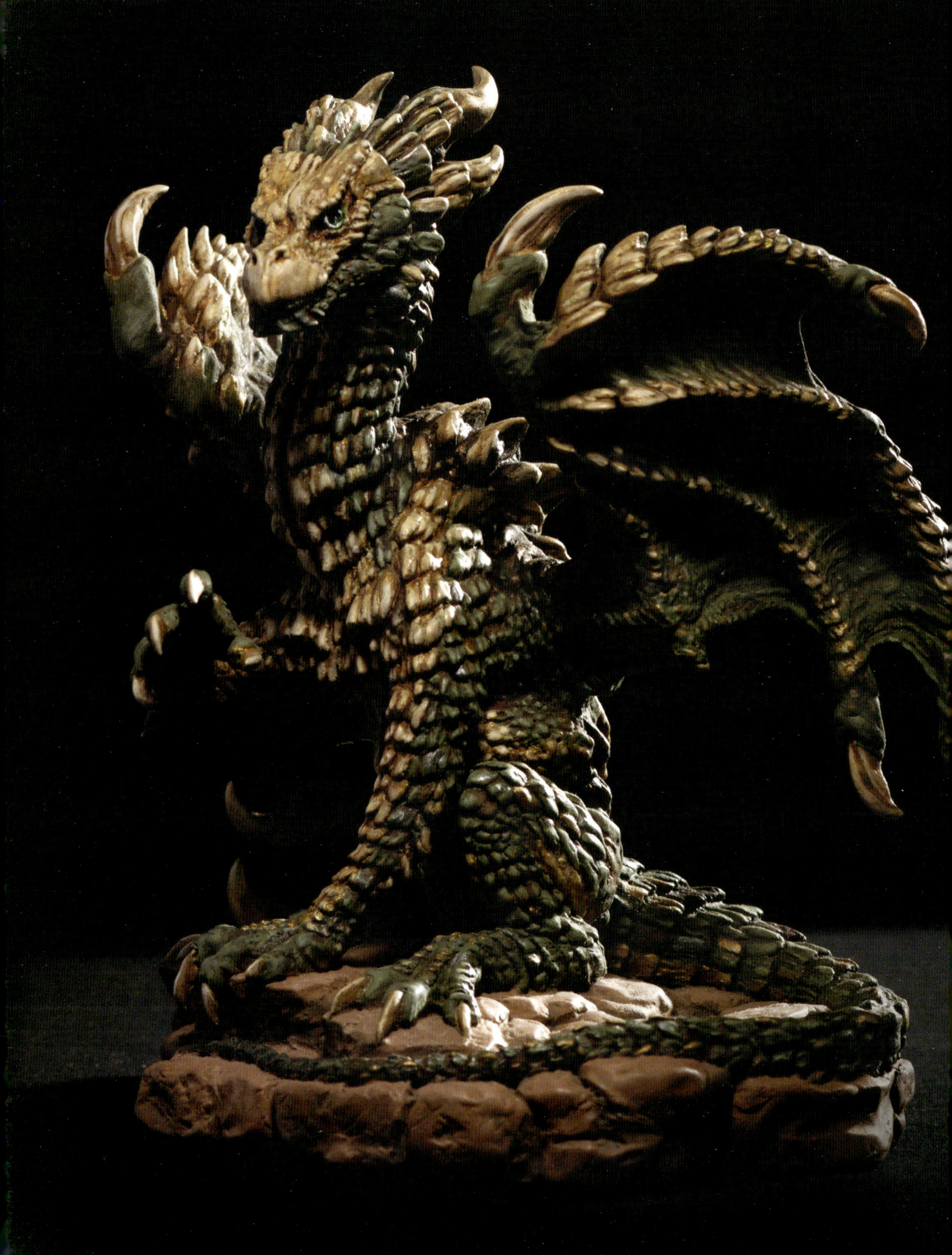

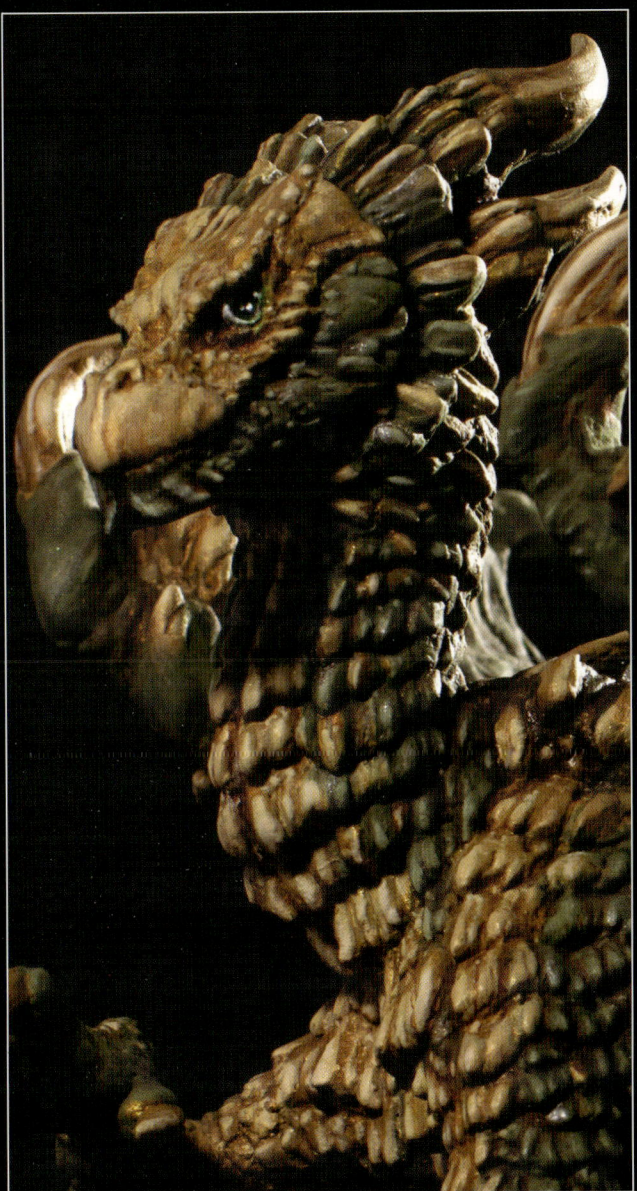

THE FUTURE

We've been attempting to sculpt more and more of our personal, original concept work, which admittedly we've done all along the way, but we do still take on a lot of client jobs to make everything work. In our minds, with our original designs we create little universes in our heads where our characters live, and some of them meet and interact. Maybe some of our characters already know each other! So, we'd just like to continue exploring these worlds, people, and creatures. And we would love to lean into more bronze work in the future. Something about the permanence of metal sculptures really appeals to us.

ADVICE FOR BREAKING THROUGH

The number one piece of advice for finding success and breaking into the industry is practice, practice, practice! Making time to practice regularly is the only way to get better and compete with the big names in the industry. They are always practicing, learning, and improving, and so should you be.

When we were starting out, in the early 1990s, it seemed the only way to break into the industry was to attend the San Diego Comic-Con, where everyone who could hire you was under one roof. All of the art directors and executives of statue companies, toy companies, etc. were open to looking at your sculpture work. People called it "the business convention"! But since then, the internet has developed and it has now become much easier for sculptors to be discovered online, without ever meeting important people in person. But, online or not, you still have to impress those important people, which has become so much more difficult to do because of the proliferation of sculptors of all kinds, both traditional and digital.

We highly recommend posting artwork on social media and art sites. All of us have to get our stuff out there for people to see. Random strangers don't walk up to doors, knock, and ask "Hello, do you have any sculptures for me to look at today?" Just like most sculptors, we don't use an agent, so we have to be our own agent. It's crucial to share your work for fans and industry movers, shakers, and decision makers to admire.

We do, however, advise that sculptors try to keep their portfolios to a smaller number of pieces rather than a large number. Everything you have ever created dating back to high school doesn't need to be included. Be discerning and a little bit brutal with yourself and cut out your weakest pieces. If you know artists whose work you respect, ask for advice in this department. We can all fall in love with older pieces that hold a sentimental value to us, but might not match up to the quality of more current work. A chain is only as strong as its weakest link and art directors are looking for weakness.

Lastly, work with joy in your heart! Because as everyone knows, if you are joyful and loving what you do then it isn't even really work. We haven't worked a day in our lives; we've only ever sculpted!

These pages: *The Hickory Horned Dragon* originally sculpted by the brothers in Super Sculpey and produced in resin kit form. Photography by Chad Michael Ward.

GLOSSARY

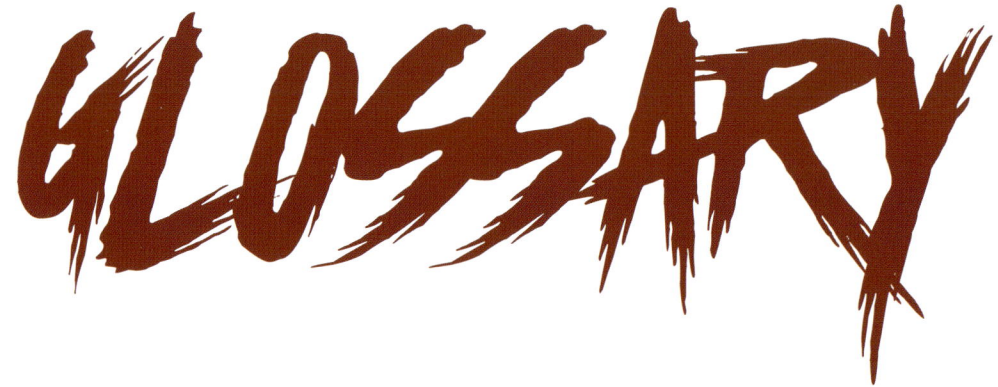

ARMATURE

A basic, skeleton-like support structure for a sculpture. Clay is added to the armature in the preliminary stages of the sculpting process.

BASE/MOUNT

The structure on which a sculpture stands. The sculpture's armature will often be secured to the mount or base to make the sculpture stable and to ensure that it will balance on a flat surface.

BLENDING

The act of merging separate volumes of material together to create a smooth, unified surface.

BLOCKING

Using rough, generalized forms to quickly create the basic shape of an object before the forms are refined or detailed.

BURNISHING

A process of making a material surface smooth or shiny, usually by rubbing the surface to compact the material.

BUST

A sculpture that focuses only on the head and upper body of a character. Busts usually incorporate the character's head, shoulders, and chest.

CARVING

Digging into a material with a tool or finger to reshape the forms or make distinct marks.

CLEANING

The process of removing excess material from the surface of a sculpture using a combination of tools and solvents. Cleaning creates a clear surface on which to continue sculpting.

CONCEPT ART

A painting, drawing, or sketch of the character or object to be sculpted. The concept art should be referenced throughout the sculpting process.

CONTRAPPOSTO

An Italian term meaning "counterpoise". It refers to a pose where the figure's weight rests on one leg, causing the shoulders and arms to twist off-axis from the hips and legs. The hip and shoulders automatically tilt away from each other in this pose.

CURING

Allowing soft or liquid material to harden. Curing usually occurs by air-drying and can take time. Some clays will not cure as they are designed to stay soft.

FORMS

Shapes that are indicative of the structure they are supposed to represent. For complex structures, such as the human head, multiple different sizes and shapes are needed. Forms are often rough at first, then gradually refined.

KILN

A specialist oven or furnace used to fire sculptures. Kilns can reach considerably higher temperatures than conventional ovens.

LANDMARKS

Marks used to signify key anatomical points on the body, sometimes called "bony landmarks." These marks act as useful guides to ensure your sculpture is anatomically correct.

LINE OF ACTION

The intangible flow of force through a moving body or object. Identifying a line of action in a character's pose can improve the dynamism of the sculpture.

MAQUETTE

A preliminary model of the intended sculpture. It is often much smaller than the final iteration.

POSE

The stance of the character or the positioning of the character's limbs. The pose can be used to imply the character's personality or an activity the character is engaged in.

RAKING

The act of driving an indented tool across the surface of a material to create lines or small troughs in the surface. Raking is often used as part of the surface cleaning process where excess material is removed by the teeth of the rake tool.

REFERENCES

A collection of images or objects that can be used as technical guides when sculpting. References can be used for anything from character design and anatomy to textures and accurate lighting.

ROUGHING OUT

The act of making rough forms or marks to be used as a guide or practice for more refined details later in the sculpting process.

SMOOTHING

The process of making the surface of a material flat and even. Depending on the intricacy required this can be done with tools such as kidney shapes, rakes, and sometimes with the use of solvents.

TEXTURING

The act of displacing material, either with tools or fingers, to create an uneven surface. Texturing is used to differentiate between different surfaces on a sculpture and add realism.

THREE-QUARTER VIEW

Observing an image or object from an angle where one-quarter of the object is turned away. Generally, this view is mid-way between the front and side view.

VOLUMES

A mass of material, or a collection of smaller forms.

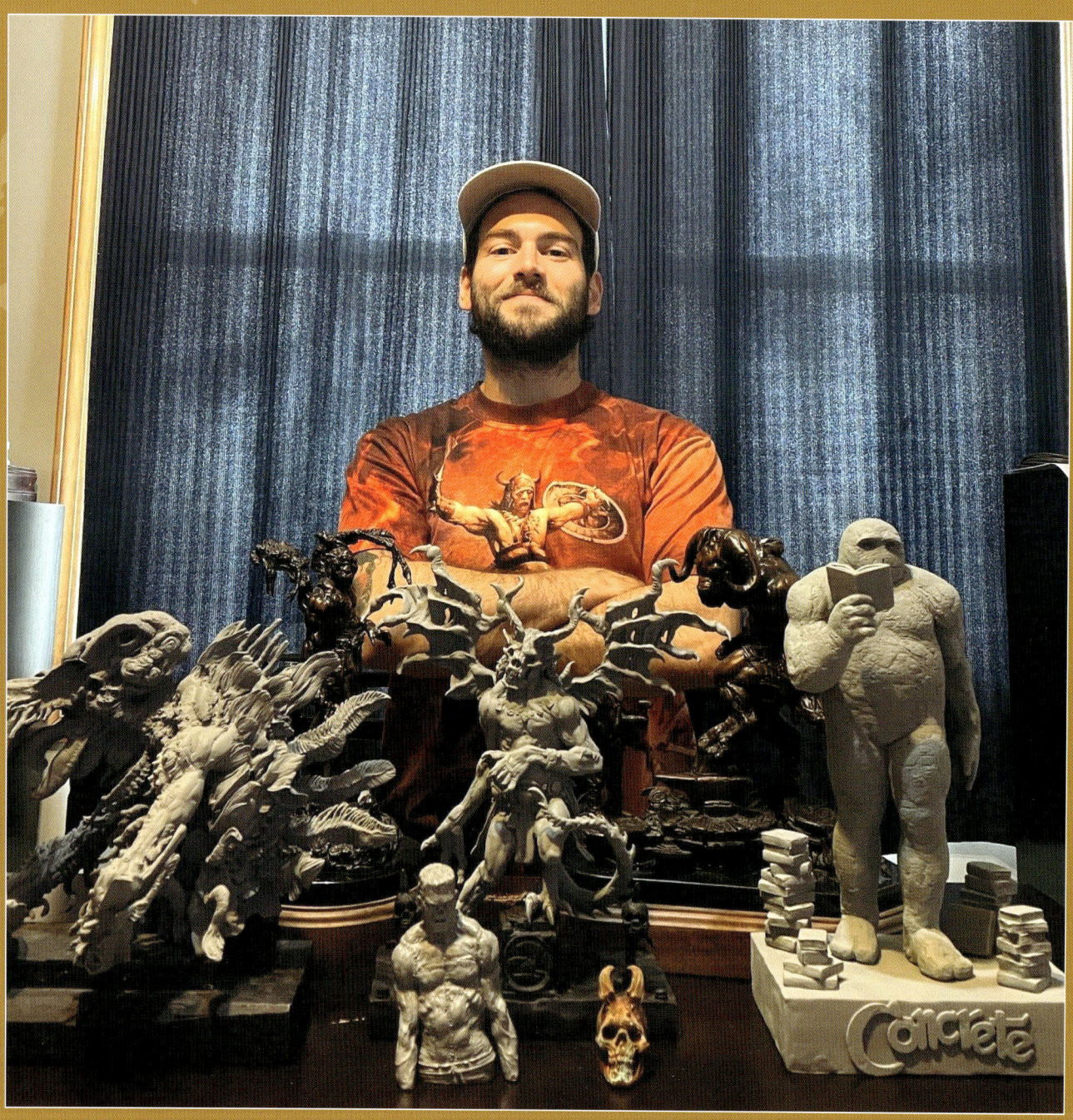

The Shiflett Brothers' friend and collector Joshua Hall standing with his many original clay sculptures and two bronzes. Collectors like Josh help make these kinds of art careers possible.

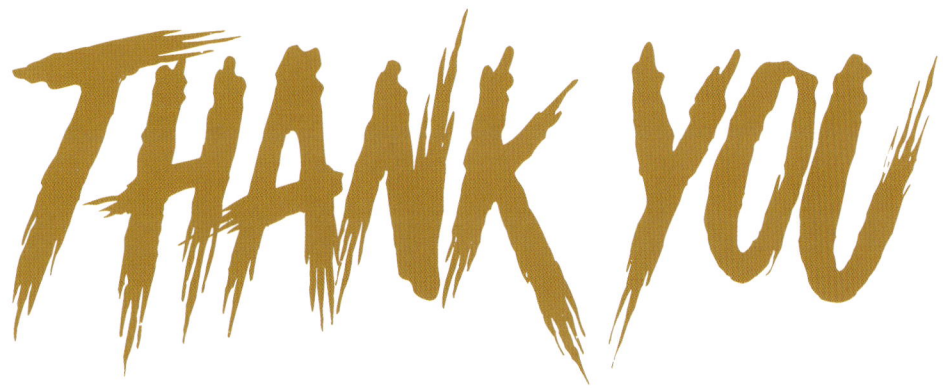

THANK YOU

The Shiflett Brothers would like to thank the following people for their support and/or inspiration during their creative journey:

Comics Kingdom (Beaumont, TX) owner Scott Smithhart, Moore Creations' Clayburn Moore, Bowen Designs' Randy Bowen, San Diego Comic-Con's Clydene Nee, photographer and designer Chad Michael Ward, photographer Matt Mrozek, French sculpting witch Virginie Ropars, the great life-size sculptor Tom Kuebler, art hero Paul Komoda, the extraordinary sculptor Forest Rogers, the Greek Freak Aris Kolokontes, our friend Melita "Missmonster" Curphy, The Weta Workshop's Sir Richard Taylor and Ri Streeter, Cellar Cast's Steve West and Melinda, *Spectrum: The Best in Contemporary Fantastic Art* publishers Cathy and Arnie Fenner, David Fisher and Terry Webb of *Amazing Figure Modeler* magazine, ToyBiz/Marvel/Disney's Jesse Falcon, designer Guido Olave, dinosaur sculptor John Fischner, Oddworld visionary Lorne Lanning, Verotik's Glenn Danzig, sculpting hero and friend Simon "Spiderzero" Lee, Clint Howard and everyone at Deep in the Heart Art Foundry in Bastrop, Texas, Sideshow's Anthony Mestas, Sideshow/Tweeterhead's Dave Igo, legendary concept designer Wayne Barlowe, comic-book painter extraordinaire Alex Ross, iconic *Lord of the Rings* artist John Howe, The Frazetta Girls: Holly and Sara Frazetta, designer Leo Rogers, actor/director Andy Serkis, Brandon's partner Amanda Fledermäuse, friends and artists Richard and Lauren Luong, Monsterpalooza's Eliot Brodsky, Alex Alvarez and the Gnomon Workshop, *ImagineFX* magazine, all 40K+ members of the Shiflett Brothers' Sculpting Forum, the brothers' patrons on the Shiflett Brothers Patreon page, their early-years comic convention chaperoning uncle Dr. Keith Cockrell, Shiflett Brothers collectors Joshua Hall, Don Bohm, and Julio Mendoza Rodriguez, their continuously art-supporting mom and dad: Marilyn and Tommy Shiflett, their late birth father, Charlie Hughes, who bequeathed them the art gene, and their siblings Tammy, Kelly, Tommy Lee, and Nils.

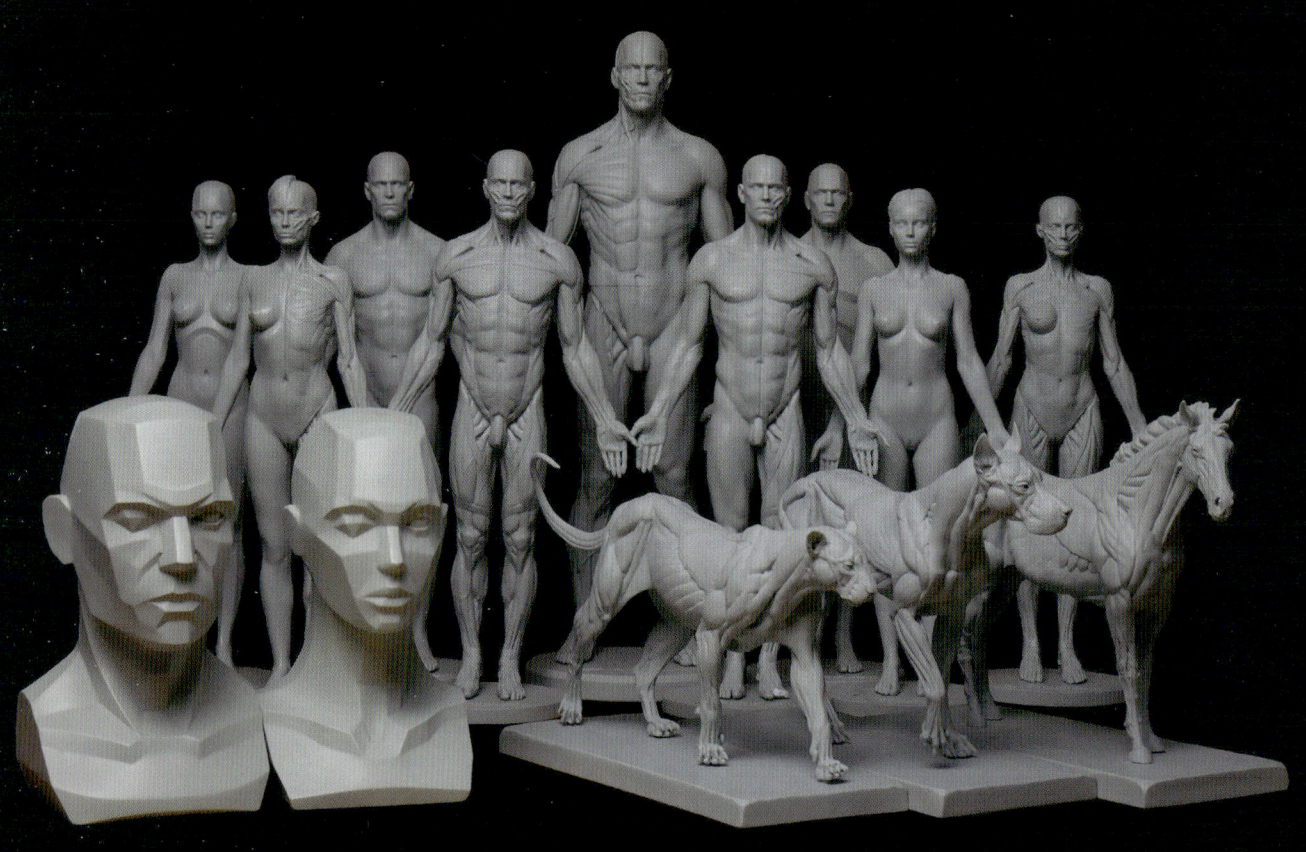

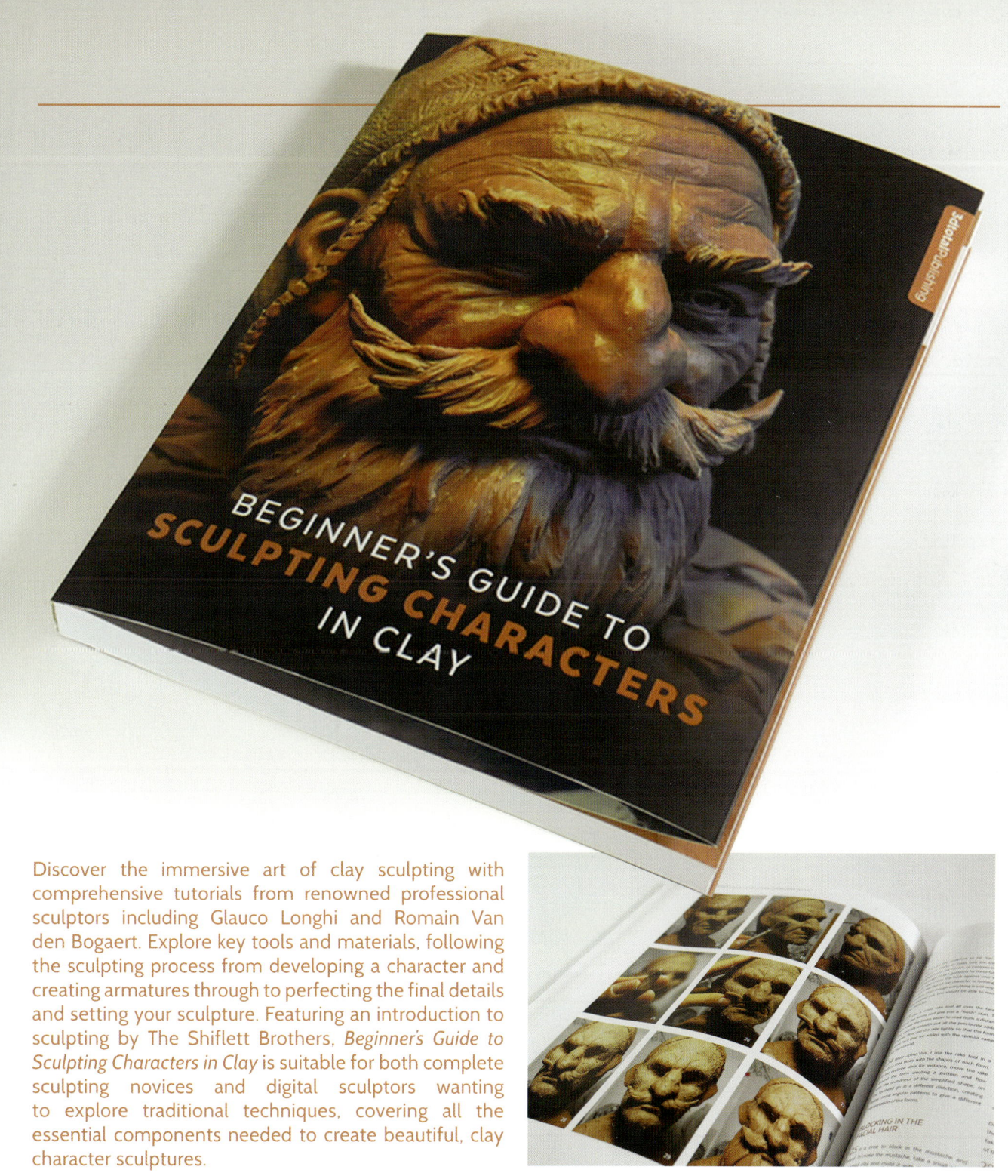

Discover the immersive art of clay sculpting with comprehensive tutorials from renowned professional sculptors including Glauco Longhi and Romain Van den Bogaert. Explore key tools and materials, following the sculpting process from developing a character and creating armatures through to perfecting the final details and setting your sculpture. Featuring an introduction to sculpting by The Shiflett Brothers, *Beginner's Guide to Sculpting Characters in Clay* is suitable for both complete sculpting novices and digital sculptors wanting to explore traditional techniques, covering all the essential components needed to create beautiful, clay character sculptures.

Available now at
store.3dtotal.com

3dtotalPublishing

3dtotal Publishing is a trailblazing, creative publisher specializing in inspirational and educational resources for artists.

Our titles feature top industry professionals from around the globe who share their experience in skillfully written step-by-step tutorials and fascinating, detailed guides. Illustrated throughout with stunning artwork, these best-selling publications offer creative insight, expert advice, and essential motivation. Fans of digital art will enjoy our comprehensive volumes covering Adobe Photoshop, Procreate, and Blender, as well as our superb titles based around character design, including *Fundamentals of Character Design* and *Creating Characters for the Entertainment Industry*. The dedicated, high-quality blend of instruction and inspiration also extends to traditional art. Titles covering a range of techniques, genres, and abilities allow your creativity to flourish while building essential skills.

Well-established within the industry, we now offer over 100 titles and counting, many of which have been translated into multiple languages around the world. With something for every artist, we are proud to say that our books offer the 3dtotal package:

LEARN · CREATE · SHARE

Visit us at 3dtotalpublishing.com

3dtotal Publishing is part of 3dtotal.com, a leading website for CG artists founded by Tom Greenway in 1999.